I0127083

Memories of Schizophrenia

Oritsesemisan Megbele

chipmunkapublishing
the mental health publisher

Published by
Chipmunkapublishing
United Kingdom

http://www.chipmunkapublishing.com

Copyright © 2015 Oritsesemisan Megbele

ISBN   978-1-78382-230-0

Book Description

This is part two of his books. The first one is titled trials of life the effects of the first book tilted trial of life, is merges with his memories of his schizophrenia. People with mental health issues all experience the illness in different ways. The content of this book, and the one published before this book seeks to open a forum from various sources related to mental health illnesses to openly quest for the reason or cause of the illness schizophrenia. As the author of his books he hopes to find out from reliable source if he is actually schizophrenic. At this stage, his readers have knowledge of his background, what he is going through as a mental health sufferer and his feelings about his life experiences.

The author has an opinion he has been resilient trying to outliving his illness through adoptive memories which are fitness related since human memory systems are 'tuned' to information relevant to survival; From the content of the first book it is evident based on his present reincarnation he is living three lives even four to be precise. In this present life with a notion he is Orunmila an African deity, he could be Superman thirdly he is presently living a life just like any other individual. It is left for his readers to identify the precise conditions under which the survival advantage are in effect and those under which it is not. They are left to determine specific functional mechanism or mechanisms responsible for the effects of his memory or adaptive values involved. At this stage, his readers may start ascertaining the effects of his schizophrenia taking details, making deduction after reading his third book tilted paradigm of his schizophrenia of what the psychological effect of schizophrenia has on him.

If one has mental health issues all is not lost make the most of your potential cope with life and play a full part in your family, workplace, and community and among friends. Some people call mental health 'emotional health' or 'well-being' it's just as important as good physical health. Mental health is everyone's business. We all have times when we feel down or stressed or frightened. Most of the time those feelings pass. But sometimes they develop into a more serious problem this could happen to any one of us. Everyone is different. You may bounce back from a setback while someone else may feel weighed down by it for a long time.

The author is a freemason his late father, is an Apeno of the reformed Ogboni fraternity cult from book one his books accounts rituals and beliefs, possession the influence of juju, moral values and reaching out to God the architect of the universe.

About The Author

Oritsesemisan Bamidele Megbele was born in Islington in the district of Tollington to late Chief Dr. Frank Anirejuoritse Megbele and late Mrs. Joy Abeni Faneye Megbele on the 27th of July 1966. This was during the Nigerian Biafra war. His parents were separated just after; he was born without being divorced for the rest of their life. He grew up at Warri Delta state, Lagos, Port Harcourt and at Oyo state Nigeria.

Oritsesemisan's father originated from Delta state of Nigeria which was once part of Bendel State in Mid-Western Nigeria. While his mother originated from Abeokuta Ogun State of Western Nigeria. These books are series of books he hopes to publish, which he believes contain his life final trials and the need for third world countries to change.

Has it ever been accounted how Adam reacted when is wife involved him with the forbidden fruit?   As with many marriages of today I think Adam would had murdered Eve for making him eat from the forbidden fruit with her as well.

But the event made them more like God, humans created in God's image accustomed to knowing the difference of right and wrong. As recorded Adam and Eve had two sons, Cain killed Abel because he was jealous of his brother. What was done to have resolved this conflict, Cain was coursed to till the soil, with a mark upon his face.

This sort of incoherent happenings is a common phenomenon in our live on planet earth. Each time humans try to reach out to God, could it be said we make ends meet or the more we fall apart. At one time in the Book of Genesis in the Holy Bible,, the whole world converged to have built the tower of Babel to reach God, did not meets God's favour?

There are many ways and believes to reach out and speak to God the creator of the universe. The event of the building of the Tower of Babel was an attempt, to speak and reach out to God.   It was an accomplishment; at least they quest to know God.

It gives insight as of today in the 21st century why we have Pakistan, India, Chinese, Japanese Africans, Caribbean Jamaican, Trinidad, Barbados, Asia, America and the European Union and much more. We are more compelled to seek even further knowing who God is, with different religion, creed, race, colour and beliefs. Religion is a practice if your attitude and characteristics implies using it to harm yourself or your friends and relatives it does not means you are adjudicating for God but for yourself this is one reason why we go into conflict regardless if conflict is inevitable your religion and practise makes you, who you are amidst race and culture why tell anyone, you do not know who you are, no body dose that the world is a forum.

Though it is a sublime nature or characteristics such as being humble to yourself what could make one feel he or she is lost for words at times in a given situation could this be related to illnesses or wellbeing considering when heritage, culture differs through birth, marriage moves from generation to generation while in retrospect man and all creature change their habitat not only by moving around but also, interacting this shows indication to the works of engineering the use of cars, trains and airplanes man has taken huge steps in changing the world we do not seems to realise it we should be happy within ourselves but we are still in conflict. Let's say, it's because the war within God and Lucifer is still taking place here on planet earth the most distinct of all planets and life forms. Entering the 21st century we have been making huge steps exploring other planets, galaxies and exploring the stars let's take a look back and grapes how in our primitive past we have come to be, what we are today. Its mind and body problems we are faced with on earth now but it's not what our focus is based on.

Why do we speak out to reach out to each other in many different languages? To get to know ourselves better and our destiny then we can reach out to the architect of the universe it seems the right option. This was Gods doing, so we could seek him when we get to know how selves better and have, search for our reality. If we try to seek God, we are more likely to have understanding of our purpose on earth in other to justify our pilgrimage on earth. Before God and man, if we seek, we shall find, we shall not have any other God but only God the architect and creator of the universe.

Everything we want, have already been given to us, God have made man very sufficient are there reasons why we should be found ungrateful. It is through getting to know who we are, and who God is, that brought about positive interface of synergy among humans.

Synergy now currently holds a great significance on each life on earth. Rather than the situation being similar to the time and era, of the Tower of Babble was built as recorded in the Holy Bible in Genesis, The situation after several centuries is now fulfilling, humans have become creative and more conscious of themselves. What overrides this is if God is

with us and had made us very sufficient and fulfilling why, do we continue to live in one sorts of conflict or another?
There is not yet an anthological proof that God exist, nevertheless with our difference in race and creed and religion, man will always believe in a creator there is no question if God really exist or not most people without having seen God believe in his existence. Probably because of his creativity yes, his creativity while he still remains a mystery to all of us. It's a right perspective in terms of creator, and the created. Infarct we have eaten the forbidden fruit if we look at ourselves it is a reflection of God. Knowing right from wrong has become part of our existence this, has been one of our aspect that distinguished us from God until man ate the forbidden fruit.

Are wrong doing defeating the world are we striving to know God? Lots of people say we are moving away from God do we know ourselves enough to think so. We do not exist to find God we need not, he dwells in us and in all things and he is the creator I cannot differentiate God from anything only right and wrong which is not tangible. It is right for us to seek God seeking God is not for us to pray our enemies to be destroyed by his wroth or to go to hell we are all living in our trials of life we should rejoice in our accomplishments. With some individual as long as they seek out whom God is? They are easily faced with their own reality, potentials and what they are suppose to do on earth, with the realisation that Gods power, myth, greatness, and wisdom over rides the whole universe.

There was conflict in Heaven before earth was created, we all on earth, a tiny myth of Gods own making and had given us dominion over the universe. It would take further myth of our own grasping the relationship we have with God and the Heaven, before we were created, and an understanding of Heaven that is to come. Our purpose on earth is to achieve a specific realisation of ourselves and the entire universe, knowing who we were, before we were created, or took form as humans when we reach such spectra we become like the Celestials.

So that before the rebirth of another existence, we would have grasp's knowledge, knowing more significance, of what it would take to be in Heaven with God. Within all who had made it through into the Heaven, no one would dear contemplate in any circumstances to rise up against God or be in conflicts of any kind this is why there is suffering on earth. Each one of us must have experiences suffering on earth, to some certain degree to deter us from going into conflicts of any kind yet we are still troubled by conflict.

We would all stand as an entity with identities based on whatever we had been or done whilst on earth, before the rebirth of Heaven is restored. It was for this reason why earth was created. We all including the angel's in Heaven and God divested ourselves. At the same time earth was created throughout our existence using our dive-station in creating a new life and purpose on earth.

Our forms now engulfed on earth synergy and our creativity, we put up immersed efforts, we suckle, we crave, for those who care, they search, while God the architect of the universe, having made man sufficient (for only in Heaven would all living things know what freedom really is, when that blessed day arrives. The evil each day is continuously subsuming). It would be foolish for any one saying he or she has no thoughts of the presence or existence of Gods is it not a reality in this whole great universe or are you a ghost.

If for instance, you where the first woman God created Eve, just after you had eaten the forbidden fruit e.g. how did you know about sex, child birth, plants, crops, farming they had to toil I supposed because, they had to flourish, starting from the scratch with little knowledge or understanding from where to begin but look at we humans of today. A good question to ask is, how did she feel after all these, Eve had to Rockne and face Adam her husband, and moreover even further, when Cain killed Abel.

Come on let's take a long short we are all educated in this world of today into the 21st century, no body is a fool or a freak. The village women of Africa know their ways and the burdens before them.

The political environment of Africa is a concern to women and their livelihood. To them in Africa, it's a matter of you are rich, I am poor, I am not educated, you are educated, within the poor it is always a question of why should there be any difficulties with my children getting educated if you feel, it is a good thing to be educated. Extending towards villages in Africa there is a craze of not being foolish and there is now a craze for wisdom and understanding people know their rights and entitlement on which, they are being short-changed by their political leaders

There is too much conflict in all parts of Africa; it overrides every peaceful means of survival in all corners of African community and livelihood. For some women in the villages of Africa and their children, they have little or no hope, or no hope of facing the next day of their lives. Women of today wants equal rights with men at home, with jobs, military and if you don't like it turf go and be gay or be a sperm donor nobody cares.

The earthiest do not always respond that science can co-exist with religion infarct, they do, whether religious or not everyone around the world are embracing science. What religious people say is we are not giving much time or consideration to God we are rather becoming science initiated response as with other aspect of human existence.

Each day in and out, we forget and do not give more inclination to difference within right and wrong with inadequacies of moral values and instincts.

Most scholars and scientist are earthiest they do not believe that God exist. Planet earth as science depict have been for more than a billion years. Yes humans have taken a huge step we have hospitals high tech, digital services, yes

But there is so much wrong taking place on earth people would rather want to be at Church or in Heaven? For instance I would rather want to be at Church than be in a hospital. Each day at least a hundred people would be in a hospital unwell when, they come out of hospital 50% of them saying thanks to God is a good response. They might go to Church for thanks giving who says, science and religion dose not co-exist? They do co-exist.

Science and technology has a lot to offer though, they do have certain levels of inconsistency and inherencies. A car, airplanes, sea liners, train transportation are all good form of transportation if science and technology is that good? Why do they crash or have accidents with people dying it is an inconsistency but what more would people prefer?

Whoops! There is insurance; are insurances policies from God for having made man sufficient? Would robots' have the same defined qualities as humans? If so, let them eat, spill blood, have their bath or wash its teeth. Let them make love and bear offspring's.

God's creation we humans are his greatest of all creativity; he knows all we would ever want or need as earthlings the rest, we would quest and do for ourselves in it, we find pleasure of all our hearts desires.

In it we would feel pain, loss, for our retribution or for the sake that we should seek insight into whatever most have created we humans and all things, question our conscience, mind, thoughts, actions, virtues he gave us charge of everything on planet earth the land, the sea, the plants even flowers so that, we can discern beauty, truth and love. For this reason, religious' leaders and their congregation would say Hallelujah.

We have achieved great things as human God before time had defined us and place us wherever we are in difference of race, colour, creed or religion and for all that we have achieved and would ever be we should be grateful because God is in all things and he made all things. In reference to this we are seeing God face to face through our physics, our heart and soul and the things we do. This is what makes humans unique. We flourish with what has been granted to us.

At the same time in everything we do or accomplish on earth or in the entire Universe, we are putting more definition into God and his creativity.

It is good for everyone to be happy; in fact it's probably one of the few ambitions which are universal to our world. We are made to believe we have to achieve, acquire or consume to be happy. Living happily depends mainly on your inner life, the conscious world of your thoughts, emotions, and beliefs desires.

It should be a matter of inner peace of mind and at heart. Our inner lives are largely based on patterns or habits, the ways we react to what goes on around us.

We cannot always control what happens in the world around us, our inner habits dictate our reaction to life inherencies, consistencies and inconsistencies but we are not always powerless. If you learn to pay attention to your inner life you can over time shape the way our social and spiritual life works.
Happiness depends on cultivating inner peace if we seek inner peace we would not only seek happiness, it will find us. Some inner peace depends on skills which can be strengthened by practice. It's an ancient idea, but somehow it repeatedly gets lost through generations.

Spirituality can refer to an ultimate or an alleged immaterial reality; an inner path enabling a person to discover the essence of his or her being; or the 'deepest values and meanings by which people live.' Spiritual practices, including meditation, prayer and contemplation, are intended to develop an individual's inner life; spiritual experience includes that of connectedness with a larger reality, yielding a more comprehensive self; with other individuals or the human community; with nature or the cosmos; or with the divine realm. Spirituality is often experienced as a source of inspiration or orientation in life.

It can encompass belief in immaterial realities or experiences of the immanent or transcendent nature of the world.

Spirituality exists wherever we struggle with the issues of how our lives fit into the greater scheme of things. This is true when our questions never give way to specific answers or give rise to specific practices such as prayer or meditation. We encounter spiritual issues every time we wonder where the universe comes from, why we are here, or what happens when we die. We also become spiritual when we become moved by values such as beauty, love, creativity or unhappiness that seem to reveal a meaning or power beyond our visible world. An idea or practice is 'spiritual' when it reveals our personal desire to establish a felt-relationship with the deepest meanings or powers governing life.

Where in this entire Universe in which God is never present? None he created all things, he his contained in all things we do we do not know what he knows or feels about us or in relation to what we are doing to ourselves. Rather, we create in our hearts what supposedly God feels about what we are which is part of freewill. We have his commandments short straight to the point his teachings and testimonies are to inspire us not make us slaves.

It is said for blood to be capable of serving the quest of juju purposes, there is something philosophical about the victim, and philosophical enough to be used for jujus and witchcrafts so should the souls and minds of those who believe in God be in worshiping God. In my own terms it entails the victims have something unique with nature which makes them a mine of nature for evil. It's either they seek the blood or the souls of their victim.

It is well known among Cherubim and Seraphim, Celestial and Evangelical Church's some children and adults confess that they are a witch, they have their own meetings and at certain times, they feast and they have their own cods of conducts. Some in Celestial and Aladura Church's tell of visions, dreams and revelation they have had that not only forth tell but give insight into their lives but also environment they dwell in and their belief in God and Christ.

They are ordained with their lives devoted to the Church. A juju priest tie jujus around a child's neck, or profess he or she is sucking evil spirit tormenting people out of their lives while a spiritual priest from celestials or Aladura Churches uses olive oil and water prayed on to ward off evil spirit it's an interrelationship within culture and religion. Africa is a spirited place, rich in culture and vastly arrayed in believes, superstitions, rituals considered primitive it serves them purpose to authenticate their race and ethnicity. The Europeans belief in philosophy one cannot say there is no reason in anything or for anything. It could be argued or stigmatised they are not philosophically authenticated it might have been because of history, eras and predicaments of human race which are divers all over the world for different reasons acknowledged before creation by the architect of the Universe slave do not serve their masters without reason because life is based on trials I do not, understand or be at peace with myself and background each day wondering why we do not perceive each other with reason without judging each other with prejudice predicaments in life are in vast arrays that we might know better who we are and for what we are in relation to our predicaments history spells a lot about our existence only those who are not masters, making slaves out of predicaments are the once causing the problems of human predicaments not human downfall if you are a slave there are many masters to serve and if, there is God, you are not in reality a slave. You are a master to your trials of life. Africa was met with drastic protocol slavery, industrial age and technological age it took them all of a sudden yet they are relentless in several ways related to their background and heritage. Backgrounds all over the world, interrelates when we starts realising this then the works of notable philosophers, psychologist and sociologies' would have beautiful meanings in our lives in relation to this effect, the philosophers' are also leaning from us if, they are not prejudice against us. So those a prudent master learns from his slave it makes their children masters of themselves doesn't this give a clear indication that God exist? A patient in a hospital gives a doctor reason for being a doctor.

Slavery took its toils all the way from Africa in ships through long see voyages to Europe till today 21st century we Africans still carry the wreckage on our head as Rastafarians' in different colours and shapes that describes Jamaicans as different from a Caribbean. I have this paranoia I was born in the UK in relation to my background, parental upbringing, part of the world and culture in which, I was born in after living 22 years of my life in Africa, another 22 years of my life in the UK to emphasis someone who was taken as a slave from Africa decades ago living in Europe, is also a master to me as an African living in the UK and in general within the European Union. Jamaican, Caribbean, Barbados have different opinions about Africans living in the UK what about the opinions of Asians about all of us from a black community? Human existence is not about colour it is about who, we are while there is no reason for not being who we are. Understanding really makes you and me humans a prejudice is a prejudice because they have a general weakness.

Africa is a grail a vast region of trees, forest, woodland, swamp its landscapes and climates are special and typical. Christ was hanged on a wooden cross with nails on his hands and feet with his blood dripping downward. The region is covered with trees and plantation with the blood draining down from the cross below the earth of Africa, there is riches in minerals such as petroleum from which we prepare our meals, diamond, gold, copper, silver etc are found below the earth crust.

If they are witch, what do they feast on? They feast on victim's blood through accidents they had caused. This has two phases they cause the accident by day and feast on the blood by night, or they cause the accident by night and feast on it in daylight. There are the once that goes out at night while some go out by day and there are degree to their hierarchy. Such are based on phenomena the phenomena are based in the spirit world or cosmos.

They are known as groups within their community with close ties, ties not every individual in the community understands, they only acknowledge themselves alone within their community.

Witchcraft is the art of bringing magical powers into effect to meet your needs, it is used to benefit or to harm, everyone has a thought or image of what they deem a Witch to be. Meaning of what it is to be a Witch or Witchcraft changes from society to society, Witches were seen as male or female who are considered old crones. It is thought some Witch could turn people into other beings, or put a course on them and they could fly at night and go to meetings.

While a Witch is sleeping she is capable of appearing in other places, while her body rests. The Yoruba in Nigeria believe Witches are female and they meet in secret places and fly about in the dark of night. They are thought to have the ability to alter the lives of humans; Witches have supernatural power, and have an innate knowledge of plants and herbs. Witches are human with non-human powers. During the height of the Witch hunts people thought that Witches derived their powers from the Devil, it was said that they could be recognized with a Devil's mark.

Witchcraft was a central part of the culture of the Roman society, and was practiced by doctors, and priests, the state employed diviners to foretell the future, and many military decisions were made dependent on prophesies. It was a punishable offence for anyone to use magic with malicious intent, magic was considered as an acceptable part of everyday life and it's quite different from Witchcraft because it has its own domain of sorcery. The Greeks and the Romans applied the same physical and spiritual laws to the gods as the humans.

The early Greek philosophy was based on the power of nature and it was believed that people's lives were subject to external powers, many gods and goddesses were worshipped, the gods dwelt in certain aspects of all things, the fields, rivers, woods and the sea. Each deity had its particular duty, spirits inhabited the countryside, centaurs had heads and torsos of men and bodies of horses and were usually associated with the lands, and the mountains.

Nymphs took the form of young women; magic was practiced night and day those who wished to practice magic had to be particularly careful when using flying ointments. Witches used flying ointment in order to change themselves into another form before they took to the air.

Witches are deeply embedded in most things it is seen in terms of spirits and those who have the ability to manipulate.

They use their powers in such ways that allows them communicate with the spirit world. They have ability to predict the future, communicate with the spirits of the dead, and can find lost objects. They are able to enter into a trance their soul then leaves their body and changes into a spirit form.

Within countries of the Commonwealth nations Witchcraft powers are hereditary, passing through the mothers or the father's line. people go to meetings while others seek for protection against Witchcraft, talisman are common in Western Africa Celestial and Aladura worshiping as Christians faith are against rituals of Witchcraft. If someone is possessed they are taken to a priest in the Celestial or Aladura Church where the name of the possessing spirit is revealed shaming, singing and clapping of hands follows.

These days Witches for some reason are not taken more seriously, and they used their magic to bewitch people, although they did not form groups as the night Witches did. The Witch sometimes buried roots in the stomach or brain of a victim or they could let them get hut, even walking in the street of Nigeria and getting knocked down by a car or a nail get cut in your shoes resulting to injury is considered as Witchcraft.

Witchcraft play a part in their everyday life, it is inherent in all aspects of their culture. If their crops were spoiled by weather, it was Witchcraft, if there was a lack of fish in the water, it was Witchcraft and if hunting was unsuccessful, it was Witchcraft. Difficulties between a husband and wife were blamed on Witchcraft, if a magical ritual fails, a member of a cult such as the reformed Ogboni cult dies it is considered due to diversionary between them and Celestial worshipers.

Witches sends their souls out to perform tasks at night when victims are at sleep, they flew through the air emanating dark lights, if a person sees it at night they threw a piece of charcoal under their bed so that misfortune would not befall them this beliefs varies in most part of West Africa if they are Christians for example it is important the person who saw the Witch fly past at night must see the (Alagba) of an Aladura Church the next day before, the soul of the Witch properly returns to its body the direction it was heading clearly defined. The Alagba known as the head pastor of the Church and the whole congregation commune with the spirit world, say prayers to God to word off Witchcraft of planting objects in peoples stomach, leg or head. If they are not Christens, they go and see a native doctor who; most people believe have dealings with the Witch cult as well who could remove the objects. In some case, it is considered that native doctor's liaises with the Witchcraft group to do harm to people or certain people in other to extract money or offerings for rituals such as goats, fowls, bag of rice, native duck and Guinea Fowl.

In Delta state Nigeria within the Itsekiris the act of practicing Witchcraft is known as 'sesho' and it has nothing to do with magic but natural Witchcraft with powers and abilities to 'winge' a male Witch is known as 'Olosho' In Yoruba a man or woman who practice witchcraft is known as 'Aje'. In most parts of the world winging in a sense is craving for personal self identity.

Groups of Witches often worked together are overseen by Witch leaders who in West Africa today are known as Madam of the house or big Madam as often found in polygamous homes that are older and much more experience in Witchcraft. They pass on knowledge to the younger less experienced Witches, they also believed when a Witch dies they became an evil ghost, who confuse travellers and make them lose their way. The power of a Witch really has nothing to do with the age. They could be young having more power which has been handed down through generation of their much for example experience grandmother, father or aunt in Witchcraft some Madam or 'Oga' known as master take them from their family home to work for them in their own homes as house girl or houseboy. These days they are more refined looking tin, languid or slender in physics' and has nothing to do with consulting oracles or they are the oracles themselves. Carved objects in relation to masquerades and the way it depicts itself in various culture, drums, and dialects are the sits of Witchcrafts and where, they take some of their forms or making one of such marking is being born with an open middle teeth or to cross once leg when standing up or whilst sitting down.

If you are religious or they want you to join them and you do not keep up with what they expect they are known to distant themselves from you and they are always, on each other's side during conflicts. It is customary for them to use sign language in communicating with each other.

They tend to avoid physical contact should there be a conflict so they do not get injured so that their witchcraft is not detected in their blood. They would rather confront their opponent with witchcraft such as inducing them to sustain injuries or give them blackout during examination at school.

Are you a student who have prepared for your exams the rest of the student know you in your class as very intelligent they expect, you will always come out with top grades, you know all, you need to know, you were very confident you are going to pass your exams, the examination starts and all of a sudden, your mind and head goes blanket blank.

Each individual likes could be other peoples likings, we are all different as humans in many ways, ways, in which in time, we would understand it is one reason, why we are who, we are.

For the centuries Rastafarianism had evolved its now common in Europe to build houses with 70% of its infrastructure built with metal, all homes in the UK have class windows most of use site indoors sometimes having tea and milk then we began using cream most of us now suffer from diabetics, 30% of foodstuffs we have in our supermarkets are tin food I don't eat tin food or, I suffer from itching. The way we live depicts what we go through in how homes and the environment we dwell in. The things we do or make part of our livelihood with each culture and race all around the world entwine. If one moves from the land of his or her origin to a land of another culture, one would have to harder in some ways to cultures of that region one might be happy, if the culture relates or entwine.

As a young lad living at Lagos in my neighbourhood are all sorts of birds the Swallow in Africa called the Swift or Keneri bird in Nigeria, Odere Kokoo, Pigeons birds wide variety of birds I told my friend Mr. Obi whose father was a police officer from Bendel state living in Lagos to get me an Odere Kokoo bird I was eight years at the time. Mr. Obi was very outgoing as a young lad; he could catch birds with traps, crabs from Logos Lagoon at Yaba. Obi brought me an Odere bird which he had caught and a bird cage he had made which I had to pay him for. Odere is a bird coloured red and gray it crows with the sound Odere Kokoo that's why it's called Odere bird.

I was very happy in all innocent I have got a bird of my own and a cage which I placed hanging by the side of an empty closet in the front view of our boys scoters this was after one afternoon I came back from school one of my relatives said to me in sarcasms why do I always bring my head back from school as if, I had been looking at my teachers panties. This family member of mine was a female I never knew what she meant at the time all I did was made a face as if, what's was she talking about. Or was it because my hair was always coyly it was something I had to understand when I grow up.

Meanwhile, I had been seeing my friend Mr. Obi who once in a while, had been giving me advice on how to look after my Odere bird. And then it came a time when he told me, my bird was well trained I could let it out of its cage it would fly and come back in the evenings it was an anticipated moment I waited for but something took my mind of it, it has to be the next day to experience what it was like, to let my Odere bird fly out of its cage and come back in the evening for its meal. By the time the moment came stretching my hands to hold the cage my Odere bird I found out was dead inside my bird cage.

My first reaction was how did this happen; then I looked at the head of my Odere it was as if, two fingers had pressed the head of my Odere it was bleeding from the head was this, the work of a human or another bird came to fight with my bird while in its cage, why treat my bird this way I was young and innocent I could not over react at the same time, over looked whatever had happened but I was deeply touched by the event with no one to console me in case we African children take such chances of keeping such play mates it has to be out of the knowledge of our parents which they are often aware of because a younger or elder family member would make small talk out of it so that in detour they would get more attention. Such issues as this experience of mine are dealt with as witchcraft in Africa and the omen would follow a person for life. Later within months, the empty closet by which I had hang my Odere bird was packed full of a relatives clothing.

An experience I had before my uncle Temitayo moved in with us at Yaba Lagos was with Cordelia Megbele I woke up one morning Cordelia asked me to accompany her to the market to buy some household goods at Oyingbo market we got there trough public transport did our shopping with me holding two bags, one with a live fowl in it as we were crossing a pavement I slipped and fell I was wet all over it was raining on that day we were almost about to get home she told me she had forgotten to buy something I should wait for her to go and get it I waited for Cordelia she never turned up. I waited and waited she never turned up I decided to make my way back home with the two bags of shopping in my hands but how? Then it stroked me that I was lost. It was not the first time I had been at Oyingbo market I had on occasions accompanied Cordelia and Aya Megbele to the Market but they had always been my guide it still stroked me that I was lost and could not find my way home. Then I recalled how I had put some money in my pocket. How did I get hold of the money? Just exactly enough to get me back home through a bus journey and I was not sure if the money on me was enough for my journey I visit my mother once in a while at FESTAC town when we moved from Port Harcourt to Lagos that was how I got hold of the money all I had to do was ask a passersby where would I get a bus going to Yaba. I moved closer to the direction then I heard a bus conductor calling Yaba I was uneasy all the way until we got to Yaba and become sure I was heading home the whole incident on my way home look or depicted itself with a strange feeling coming over me as if, I was a Spanish spear racing to a destination it come to me later in life while, I was in the UK the experience relates that from that day onward I would be alive no matter what I go through in Nigeria to arrive back into the UK alive. I just had to walk home a few distance from where the bus stopped me and I saw Cordelia at home waiting a little bit of hysteria from her and that was it. In my mind I heard a voice saying the swift, has taken him home safely. The swift is associated with the Celestial churches it's also a bird trough which they attained spiritual awareness. It was during this period I moved in with my mother at FESTAC town Lagos.

The swift is a medium-sized aerial bird, which is a superb flier. It evens sleeps on the wing! It is plain sooty brown, but in flight against the sky it appears black. It has long, scythe-like wings and a short, forked tail. It is a summer visitor, breeding across the UK, but most numerously in the south and east. Look up in the sky in summer, often very high. They never perch on wires like swallows. You might see excited screaming parties of them careering madly at high speed around rooftops and houses, often low, especially towards dusk.

There is hardly anything that moves, flies or crawls that has not at one time served as a sign of a good or bad omen. And human activity throughout time has often had a superstition stamped on it. For example people often place their beds at a certain angle to attract good luck.

For riches to come to the family, the bed should be placed facing east. For a long life south and so on even stranger, money was supposed to be coming your way if you sneezed to the right!

If you picked up a pin then good luck would come to you. And if you met the same person twice in one day on your travels then you would get the same good luck. How that one works I have no idea, but you get the point.

So why are we so superstitious? There are many footballers who will only wear the same shirt, even if it's dirty, to make sure that they win their game. Others touch the mantel above the tunnel entrance and then kiss a Cross that they are wearing. Of course there are many people who will just laugh at such silly superstitions. But I bet they still won't walk underneath a ladder!

Whether you call it superstition, fate, God's will or just habit, there are many Omens and Signs out there that people around the world still believe in.

Fate, Omens and superstition are very closely related. Back in history we didn't have the knowledge that we have today. Science was a thing of the future. Medical health literally was a case of trial and error.

Not knowing or understanding the concept of germs, virus or diseases caused by bacteria caused the population to be completely bewildered at why they were suddenly struck down with these unknown illnesses.

Human nature being what it is, they realized that there must be a reason for their bad luck but couldn't find a way to express it. So religion and fate took the brunt of the blame.

To counteract the bad we had to find a way to make good luck happen. Hence Omens, Oracles and Signs were born.

The strange thing was that even though it was through pure instinct many people did actually 'hit the nail on the head' so to speak. Certain plants were prayed over and picked under a full moon for example.

These days we know that the Wise Women back then were right. If we pick the plants leaves late at night the chemicals in the plants actually are much more potent. Instinct seems to have won out.

When I and my mother lived at Ibadan, when we moved to Mr. Osibowale a school principle at Igebu house this was after I came back from school for obvious reasons we had to move from our former landlord who makes and sells bread. On my arrival from school to our new home my mother fondly asked me out of the four bedroom flat which room would I prefer probably if I was afraid to live with her in such a large house I would move closer to her bedroom if am not afraid I would move further away which I did. My mother said you have made your choice settling down in my new accommodation I realised later since my bedroom was situated close to the back entrance of the house just outside; there were cages in which they were several live fowls kept by the Osibolwe family. I grow up later in life realising this precondition had something to do with what happened within me and Mrs. Cordelia Megbele my step mother at Lagos during our shopping at Oyingbo market.

This was not all when I moved back to live with my father and the rest of the family at Warri Delta state before my father became chief 9PM each night Cordelia was out of the house with groups of relatives and friend to catch live pigs to be slaughtered and sold in the market. When my father was to be made chief according to Cordelia our father was advised he should slaughter fowls for the celebration Haa! I knew my father very well his own wish against that of any of his wives his own wish comes first. That's how everybody in the family knows my father he chose to slaughter a cow doesn't all this ring a bell of omens, oracles and superstations'. In my next life if I have the choice Greece would be the next place of my reincarnation that's if, it's a must I reincarnate once more.

We hear of witch doctors sucking evil spirit out of children's head possessed they say of evil spirit evil witches had planted stick or objects inside them in Serra Leon, since I have notions humans reincarnate, my mother had reincarnated to a white young girl who, would be a lady very soon in the UK. All my life in Nigeria I had been washing my cloths since I was young with my hands in a bucket half full with water and soap.

If my notion about my mother is true how could it be right for me getting my cloths washed in the UK? On the day the news came out on television on the end of the second month of 2012 about witch doctors in Serra Loan in a frenzy I went out to buy myself a washing machine so that wherever my reincarnated mother is, she could have her tea and I could have mine and keep our hair without stick on our head but our heads raised high into the sky I had to do my own juju in the modern day Orunmila style I save money and bought myself a washing machine. If you are a mental health patient in the same position as mine you might be on (Igbo)-marijuana or hard drugs such priorities come first by the time you benefit comes in, you have bought what you have to buy, it's a meagre sum left, to buy just food. Before coming to the UK, I have observe how my mother prepares rice and 'Efo' soup with certain touch of essence before, the rice is almost well cooked I add groundnut or vegetable oil on the rice. Doing so whilst living in England strikes me as part of recuperating myself out of my illness because it's something which makes feel better.

Adding to the effect of my illness, I could barely iron my cloths I had to buy an iron and ironing board to iron my clothing's. As young as my mother could be in her new reincarnation, she acknowledges it in her life the joy and comfort it would bring to her present life through the things I bought for my own use in the UK through the voices I hear from her in her voices which could go on for one or two days she talks about me coming from the direction I met her she knows about the things I do.

In the United States, behaviourism became the dominant school of thought during the 1950s. Behaviourism is a discipline that was established in the early 20th century by John B. Watson, and embraced and extended by Edward Thorndike, Clark L. Hull, Edward C. Tolman, and later B.F. Skinner. Theories of learning emphasized the ways in which people might be predisposed, or conditioned, by their environments to behave in certain ways.

Classical conditioning was an early behaviourist model which posited that behavioural tendencies are determined by immediate associations between various environmental stimuli and the degree of pleasure or pain that follows. Behavioural patterns, then, was understood to consist of organisms' conditioned responses to the stimuli in their environment. The stimuli were held to exert influence in proportion to their prior repetition or to the previous intensity of their associated pain or pleasure.

Skinner's behaviourism shared with its predecessors a philosophical inclination toward positivism and determinism. He believed that the contents of the mind were not open to scientific scrutiny and that scientific psychology should emphasize the study of observable behaviour. He focused on behaviour environment relations and analyzed overt and covert behaviour as a function of an organism interacting with its environment behaviourists usually rejected or deemphasized dualistic explanations such as 'mind' or 'consciousness'; and, in lieu of probing an 'unconscious mind' that underlies unawareness, they spoke of the contingency-shaped behaviours' in which unawareness becomes outwardly manifest.

Among the behaviourists' most famous creations applied classical conditioning to a developing human child, such as operant conditioning, which acknowledged that human agency could affect patterns and cycles of environmental stimuli and behavioural responses.

Based upon ideas individuals experience things as unified wholes in response to molecular approach of structuralism rather than breaking down thoughts and behaviour to their smallest element rather, maintain the whole of the experience is important, and the whole is different than the sum of its parts.

Branch of psychology, which included existential psychotherapy, a method of therapy that operates on the belief that inner conflict within a person is due to that individual's confrontation with the givens of existence.

Existential psychologists differed from others often classified as humanistic in their comparatively neutral view of human nature and in their relatively negative or positive assessment of anxiety. Existential psychologists emphasized the humanistic themes of death, free will, and meaning, suggesting that meaning can be shaped by myths, or narrative patterns, and that it can be encouraged by an acceptance of the free will requisite to an authentic, albeit often anxious, regard for death and other future prospects.

Cognitive psychology that branch of psychology that studies mental processes including how people think, perceive, remember, and learn. As part of the larger field of cognitive science, this branch of psychology is related to other disciplines including neuroscience, philosophy, and linguistics.

Noam Chomsky helped to ignite a 'cognitive revolution' in psychology when he criticized the behaviourists' notions of 'stimulus', 'response', and 'reinforcement', could be applied to complex human behaviour, most notably language acquisition, in only a superficial and vague manner. These postulates humans are born with the instinct or 'innate facility' for acquiring language posed a challenge to the behaviourist position that all behaviour, including language, is contingent upon learning and reinforcement. Social learning theorists, such as Albert Bandura, argued that the child's environment could make contributions of its own to the behaviours of an observant subject.

Critical psychology is aimed at evaluating mainstream psychology and attempts to apply psychology in more progressive ways, often looking towards social change as a means of preventing and treating psychopathology. One of critical psychology's main criticisms of conventional psychology is how it ignores the way power differences between social classes and groups can affect the mental and physical well-being of individuals or groups of people. Contributors to the field include Klaus Holzkamp and Ian Parker. Key elements within critical psychology include the study of power relations, situated knowledge, and the dualisms of the self and the agency, and the individual and the social. A discursive strain of critical psychology was developed in the 1990s by Jonathan Potter and Derek Edwards. Discursive psychology examines how psychological phenomena are created, made relevant and put to use in discourse, verbal interaction and everyday talk. It is opposed to cognitive approaches.

It is another way of saying culture across regions entwines wherever we are all around the world. Let Africans show you who, they are not one day when they conglomerate into multi-collateral business and environment the impact of doing so, would at one end mean they are divesting themselves and subsuming less. These issues of witch doctors sucking evil spirit out of children's head or tying jujus around children's neck such as in the case in Serra Loan it is about time it is something that is done by a clown in an African children's party or cultural celebration to remind us, of our past in relation to the works of juju practice. Africa should perform jujus more advance in ways it would be tolerated and appreciated by those who feel juju have meaning in their lives. We should find reason in everything we do to be piecemeal to the rest of the world.

Even if it might be a crusade, I might view it in reasons of perspectives because they might be saying something else it's something one would always find as part of Africa's culture and our origin among the rich and notable Africans such as Oba's chief, politician and African business men and women who allow such things to gain more control who for example some of them are members of the reformed Ogboni Fraternity they are more advanced because they are involved with European ways of doing thing backed by money, sophistication, education and wealth. The world has changed we should change with it before our culture is viewed with mischief. Gone are the days when we make children believe in such things in such ways it's a case of psychiatrist witch doctor's illusion in effect it is the witch doctor who, is suffering from the effect of sucking blood while the children are being used.

As a general and fundamental problems through studies of philosophy connected with existence, knowledge, values, reason, mind, and language distinguished by addressing the problems by critical, generally systematic approach based on reliance of rational argument in a world of beauty, ugliness and death much need rely on wisdom not solely on religion or we would hardly appreciate our existence.

These relate to nature of reality, including the relationship between mind and body, substance and accident, events and causation depending on knowledge, and if knowledge would be forever possible beyond human imagination which has already taken place entering the 21st century but yet, to be very much appreciated. With so much conflicts, caters trophies, misshapes can the relationships between truth, belief, wisdom, faith, moral values, the origin of good and bad, what are the concepts of absolute ethical truths infarct what is ethical and what is not, how much truth can be known how can they all, be justified.

Would the conflicts of how is the best way we should live go on forever what are the valid augment behind our existence, are we here to carve ourselves within good and bad logic would be the basis for such augment we are yet to live our lives with concepts that explores and explain the nature and the interpretations of the law in society relationship of individuals, families, clans, ethnic origin and cleansing, the communities in general as a whole including the states with questions about justice, law, property, and the rights and obligations of the citizen based on what is good or bad and how people should live their lives or how the community as a whole should function without such functions, the community does not exist really.. Or what would be the enjoyment of its beauty, art or emotional values, perception, and matters of taste and sentiment. Culture, religion, moral values, ugliness and death are supposed to bring the best out of us.

Philosophy through several eras pronounced wisdom which embodied philosophies of life which currently we hardly take up to in this era we lack motors that establishes why we are here, particularly ethics, in the forms of dialectic, dialogues, epic poetry, folklore, hymns, lyrics, prose, and proverbs, reasoning and rationality. We are now driven by science and technology religion has done much for some few for their own good in other for them to shy away from sin in this troubled world of ours.

That the effect of science and technology might not wipe out our conception of philosophical moral values which gradually goes down the drain. Our lives are empty yet we seems to be in our peak yes, we are in our peak because this planet of ours has been ours for more than centuries it is left for each individual if they choose to be wise or ignorant. No matter what we are, have done or the road we have taken in this world of beauty, ugliness and death, we have made our choices it's inevitable.

Philosophy has had a tremendous effect on East Asia and Chinese civilization The majority of Chinese philosophy originates through hundred schools of thought characterized by intellectual and cultural developments such as the upholding of righteousness, moral disposition to be good and to do good, create harmony now it has all changed.

The main subjects of ancient philosophy was understanding the fundamental causes and principles of the universe currently we are exploring on it through economical ways by going on space mission. What I want to see put into effect are; the epistemological problem of reconciling the diversity and change of our natural universe obtaining fixed and certain knowledge such as things that cannot be perceived by our senses it would make us pursue knowledge and its order.

The effect would make tremendous impacts on our lives. In the mean time all third world nation should pursue philosophy it is a basis to create order and tranquillity it is difficult to live in a place without understanding the place while the rest of the world is moving on as for Asia and China they have lost their values and respect for philosophy economics is now more important than values.

Third world nation especially places such as Africa needs philosophical method in other to establish critical approach to received or established views, and the appeal to reason when there are arguments. The days of cultural mysticism are over they need enquires into political, and ethnic moral values. I do not see reason why you should live while I suffer in poverty and illness we are bound by ethnicity. On a basis of too much augments there should be cause for reason for every problem there is always a part for transformation our existence is based on trials of life while our planet is a unique place for such disposition.

The movements in philosophy developed contemporaneously with larger religious and political transformations in Africa by the Reformed Ogboni Fraternity cult theologians of the Protestant Reformation showed little direct interest in philosophy but with culture to empower themselves. A traditional foundations of theological and intellectual authority harmonized with a revival to control businesses, heredity with backings from native juju priests based on concepts into religious or philosophical system claiming to be based on initiatives insight into their own individual concepts some of which they consider divine of themselves meanwhile with gradual centralization of political power in nation-states was echoed by more emergence of secular political philosophies based on cultural titles which are held by people of the same groups they have members all over the world especially within the UK and America.

I know people from Africa who are caring for me as a mental health patients they use inferences from members of such cults. There is not only one of such cult as the Ogboni's in Africa there are several of them. I could recount inference from things I have gone through while in Africa scenarios of the occurrences, how they are involved directly or indirectly. I could recount details of people involve and what inference some of my cares use that associates them with such cults could it be said that they are philosophical? The Ogboni's have their own disciplines, ideologies rituals, giving's and misgivings they could impact on people who, they are not in favour with or on people who are not in favour with them.

Imo poly warns lecturers against extortion I have never been disobedient to any member of my parent whilst in Africa, I came into the UK and complained about my father to his face what do I get. Victimization from my friends and relatives from my Africa background, until children from African background confront their parents things might hardly change. Years Africa has been trying to develop more has been put into it by foreign aid, advancement and technology, The young once who have further their education are facing a new world most of them in Africa are still just trying to become elite not developers. Would be for selfish political, economic and social misshapes because they are only going to school to become wealthy and not confronting the countries development growing stronger.

Come into the UK my father had become a chief I want to marry an English girl friend I had, some of my friends would say they want to do the same, I am on benefit my flat is well furnished my friends will also want to do the same and we quarrel among ourselves about it. We even steal each other's things.

Since the early 1970s Europe had been exporting goods not only food stuffs but also luxury and technological goods into West Africa such occurrence or interaction with them takes place within my parents and relatives in Africa.

The Asian sell most of Africa's food stuffs in the UK, and for years the interaction of Jamaicans', Caribbean's, Barbados and Trinidad's with Europe have made them unable to consume African diets have they become white people no, they are more still Africans in different dimensions how is it bringing peace among the black communities in relation to East, South and West Africa within the EU?

The least my father could say was that he had brought food of African diet to me in the UK is probably to ask Jamaicans, Caribbean's, Barbados and Trinidad's why should they have left African foodstuffs to be sold in the hands of Asians in the UK that is, if he had been sent by the Delta state government in Nigeria on the other hand, they or other ace could use the foodstuff he brought to me from Nigeria to put me in a voodoo nest. Slavery or the way Europeans are developed especially Britain the way they live their lives would not have allowed this to occur the effect of slavery and the effect of their industrial developments and architecture.

If you say alright to this, please consider my father's background and his upbringing when the Europeans' in the 21st century are telling we Nigerian, Asian, Jamaicans', Caribbean's, Barbados and Trinidad's who have spent our lives within Europe coming from across Britain and America to start as from now from as young as our little children not only to know what it is to be British but also a conglomerate to understand what it is, to be EU.

It's like sending you back to school and free schools is being introduces in the UK. They are countless restaurants within the UK even burger-king, wimpy and McDonald I have never heard of an African not to talk of Jamaicans', Caribbean's, Barbados and Trinidad's restaurant in Asia not even in India. So my father was just showing his entire grievances which are different from mind I should be complaining not him. Considering my father dose his business in shipping it means more money and responsibility among his comrades when he gets back to Nigeria which is quite divers among them when considering such issues within Nigeria alone through importation of African foodstuffs into Europe.

Owerri Management of Imo State Polytechnic, Umuagwo, warned that it will not hesitate to administer appropriate and commensurate punishment on any lecturer found to be extorting money from students.

The institution's Rector, Rev. Fr. Dr. Wence Madu, who read the riot act while interacting with students, also warned that the Polytechnic had zero tolerance for cultism, examination malpractice and other anti-social activities. What have we used in achieving what Nigeria is today in technology, housing, and international affairs? West Africa is yet to manufacture soap for house hold use to go round for house hold use in Nigeria.

The school will not tolerate truancy from any lecturer as well as extortion of money from students by lecturers. Any lecturer that goes contrary to the rules of the institution would have himself or herself to blame, the rector warned.

Don't mix politics with academics, vice-chancellor advises lecturers it is too complex an ideology now at this stage give them a chance to express themselves in positive perspectives how did Britain came to be in their ideology should be in question by African scholars how they reached their stage of development it took years, confrontation and hard work before Britain to developed. Rather, they should use theories based on fundamental African background and parentage of children growing up under cultural principles. If it is in view of students are deliberately going to universities in other to enter politics and work places to make money by embezzling the country's wealth then, they Universities should look into it and say it.

AWKA – Vice Chancellor, Anambra State University, ANSU, Prof Fidelis Okafor, urged lecturers in the nation's universities not to mix politics with academics, saying there existed in the universities those he described as political lecturers who did not believe only hard work could make them excel.

Prof Okafor, who spoke at the 12th matriculation of the university at the Igbariam campus of the institution, reminded lecturers universities were places where lecturers must conduct research and publish verifiable works, adding those who preferred to do otherwise were most likely to tarnish the countries educational system academically and socially in view West African countries are striving towards development they should behave in proper manners.

According to him, those who believe that godfathers can help them achieve greatness in academics are making a mistake because the two do not go together. This has cultural implication in view of his words. Young people from any cultural African background do have strong men within the country who, have stronghold in business and politics who, they look upon for backing in their lives endeavors. Some of whom, are cult member oriented and their parents are also involved on a basis of doing me a favor and I do you a favor we are talking of development of the nation it in no ways leads to enhancing the nations growth towards modernization.

He said they should therefore face what they have come to the university to do which was to pursue academic work and not to engage in politics and frivolities,' he said.

The vice chancellors address to the matriculating students, which centered mainly on the need for them to shun cultism and examination malpractices, stressed the institution has zero tolerance for such vice.

His words were 'You must particularly guard against cult groups and cultism. Cultism is proscribed by the law of the Federal Republic of Nigeria and membership of any cult group is therefore an offense punishable by law'.

This vice chancellor put his intention through using his words with some terms. He should boldly advocate that the corruption of the youth, which is very prevalent in Nigeria, should not be confused with what Politics is, in the right and scholarly sense of the definition of the word and term. They should be able to differentiate between amorality, corruption and the true meaning of Politics, social life and striving towards life endeavors'.

Good Politics affects all areas of human life and spirit for the good, and it has nothing to do with what is practiced in Nigeria, which is evil such as godfather games, culticism, the looting of the treasury departments, kidnapping, ethnic divide and the Northern Boko Haram killings which had religious political implementation. They are very bad politics which was not good for the country. Good politics changes the human life cultivating its environment and society for the human goodwill, recreation and productivity.

At Abuja the Chief Judge of the Federal Capital Territory, Justice Lawal Gunmi, blamed pervasive 'get rich syndrome' among contemporary legal practitioners on the deteriorating standard of the justice system in the country.

The Chief Judge maintained that the standard of legal education had fallen with an alarming rate, observed: 'The decorum in the court room is fading and the mode of dressing is no longer in line with the professional calling.'

Speaking at Young Lawyers Forum Annual Summit, at the headquarters of the FCT High Court, Abuja, Justice Gummi said: 'Permit me to join others in observing that the standard is falling; it is not only falling but it is falling at an alarming rate.

We have observed overtime that the young ones are not prepared to learn, no stuff to dish out. They no longer respect their seniors, talk more of the court.

The decorum in the court room is fading away and the mode of dressing is no longer in line with the professional calling. Honesty and prudence are no longer in our ways of life, the young ones are eager to get rich quick; they no longer have value, honor, integrity, perseverance and scholarship.

Gummi, stressed that a number of things could be done to restore the capacity of the lawyers in the country, insisted post-court tutelage of not less than two years would be an antidote.

He further recommended an appreciable extension of the academic year of the Nigerian Law School with compulsory course study on professional ethics in the universities.

Similarly, President of Nigerian Bar Association, NBA, Mr. Joseph Daudu (SAN), said the future of the profession was in the hands of the young lawyers, stressing young lawyers desirous of making a name in the profession must abhor corruption and get rich quick syndrome.

He said: 'The profession requires integrity, value and honor which he finds lacking in most of the young lawyers; those that are fresh in the profession must be susceptible to learning.'

Chairman of the Young Lawyers' Forum, Mr. Ifuan Igbuan, expressed satisfaction on the quality of speeches delivered by the chief judge and NBA President, adding members needed platforms to enhance their capacity.

I want a polytechnic in Nigeria where they could make household furniture's such as sleeping bed, chair and tables I mean things we need for survival, brick making, house building and road work. Britain in its development started from a grass root we should invest on what we can do and need simple things to make life more comfortable in regards to our needs. Such as through the science of medicine manufacture some medicines and ointments to keep our skin smooth from sever heat or treat mosquito bites, to heal injuries small minor things we need to live healthy lives. We need to understand God uses us all and we have need of ourselves. If the nation had been making such efforts it might had induce native witch doctors to stop using crude methods as a means of healing and rather consider advancing or developing their methods .

To be educated for a simple reason of education just going out to make money is not right education has values which are to evaluate and improve the recourse we have in other to enhance our quality of life which means work, work for our wages and salaries and make development and access risk.

To prune the nation for our children to look up to and appreciate a basis of wellbeing then, they would be grateful to their parents, heritage and capabilities.

It would not only enhance our quality of life it would enhance our recognition based on moral values and intention to do just and be grateful to the architect of the universe the more reason we would be bound to live dedicated lives The more we learn and are educated, the more we become empowered education is human creativity. People would love you; if you are creative we can see from all corners of the world that God is very creative his creation is awesome and magnificent. We cannot be creative if we cheat during life's trials it is about time we start authenticating our culture, tradition, our ways of life and standard of living in so doing we are authenticating our existence.

Nigeria's steady development should be brought into focus depart from erratic and unsteady government there should be willingness to develop Nigeria and find chances to develop further.

The public sector under independent and sovereign Nigeria should at least undergo few stages of administrative reforms if proper development of the Nigerian people is to be achieved. I believe that public sector reform would pave a great way to development. Progress that does not only mean modification of roads, water facilities and renovation of government offices, it goes ahead to promoting standard and quality of work delivered. In most occasions, strong public sector facilitates better education, speedy hi- tech and simplifying complex cultural stereotype.

Though drawbacks are best explained by long periods of political instabilities stagnancy in development that we should be successfully emerged from better still, more need to be done to cement the envisaged stage of development and progress through hard work, some remarkable achievements will at least be registered and mark total improvement on other fields of development.

Public sector development simultaneously grows together with public enterprises of the nation; all public enterprises should not only include government institutions, it as well covers areas like commercial and agricultural activities in order to overcome its economic stagnation and the poor rate of growth we need to enter the field of industrial and commercial enterprise to ensure better utilization of available resources and build the essential infrastructure we need for national development.

A large public sector in state and central government will significantly mean progress of individuals, communities and the whole society for Nigeria including West Africa in general with wide economic and social activities. Any move in solicit of growth of public sector brightens national mission and vision in enhancing objectives to be achieved where citizens enjoy equal rights to development and fair play which could be achieved in reality when functions and activities are allocated categorically within individual, organizations and public organizations concerned.

Reading culture as an aspect of the educational system in the development of a nation with Nigeria as the nation in focus, it laments the neglect of its education sector including libraries over the years in terms of funding and inadequate infrastructures for human resource development; and emphasizes facts that are qualitative and functional to education remains the focal point for development. Improvement in reading culture would encourage young West Africans putting more effort into strategies for development as they see the rest of the world in what the aspect relates to in their motherland.

The above assertion indicates the place of reading in the general development of man and his society. A situation in which a large number of people rarely read, either because they lack the skill or simply because they do not care enough to take time to concentrate will pose serious problems in the future. Reading is essential for full participation in modern society. It adds quality to life, provides access to culture and cultural heritage, empowers and emancipates citizen as well as brings people together.

Reading is one of the fundamental building blocks of learning. Becoming a skilled and adaptable reader enhances the chances of success at school and beyond. Reading is not just for school, it is for life. Reading in all its variety is vital to being better informed, have a better understanding of who we are as well as others. It makes man to be a thoughtful and constructive contributor to a democratic and cohesive society.

Development generally means improvement of people's lifestyle through improved, qualitative and functional education; incomes, skills and employment development and life fulfilment. Development also means that people should be able to read and write. In Africa, this is a problem as most people are still illiterates,

The Council for the Development of Social Science Research in Africa (CODESRIA) celebrated its 30th anniversary it is recalled the Council was established in 1973 out of collective will of African social researchers to create viable forum in Africa through which they could strive to transcend all barriers to knowledge production and, in so doing, play critical role in the democratic development of the continent.

As part of the series of events planned to mark the anniversary, five sub-regional conferences were organised in Central, East, North, Southern and West Africa. These sub-regional conferences were to be held followed by a grand finale conference to be held at the Council's headquarters in Dakar, Senegal. The West Africa sub-regional has another conference scheduled in Cotonou, Benin Republic. Its theme will be West Africa and the Quest for Democratic Nationhood mature to development.

Regardless of your background, regardless of your beliefs, the ancient art of Voodoo embraces you. Once you open your heart and mind to its awesome power, miraculous changes in your life could bring you instant money, instant love, instant happiness!

Voodoo could reverse current, turn the tide, and alter the shape of a mountain. If it could do all this, imagine what it may do for you only if you believe we are told.

Make your relationship stronger, closer, and more secure. Enhance compatibility, making your companion softer, nicer, and sexier. In this respect, it is becoming more advance.

- Enrich your life with money and wealth, plentiful gifts, fabulous material possessions.
- Provide instant luck in love, companionship, and career. Not last week or yesterday. Now!

- Return a lost love. Awaken them to your irresistible charms that will make it impossible to stay away. Soon they'll rush into your waiting arms!
- Wreck vengeance on the person who has wronged you, allowing them little sleep, implanting fear of you in their mind, bringing peace and respect back into your life.
- Change other people's opinion of you.
- Knock out barriers, smoothing the path to your future.

Once you accept Voodoo, spectacular opportunities could present themselves to you, allowing you to fulfil your true destiny you could choose the right spell for you:

A very powerful spell that should be cast only if a person has truly done you wrong once psychic contact is made, they may feel the wrath of your anger and be sorry they ever messed with you. Think carefully before requesting the spell! All you've ever dreamed of could happen when awesome spell is cast. Prepare yourself to be blessed with material wealth and a lifestyle of ease, respect, excitement and pleasure. Are you ready for a great sex life? Are you ready to experience the sensual pleasures very few even dream of?

Juju Hot Lust spell calls upon powerful spirits to make you irresistible to the special person you wish to attract. If you are a sensual person and you want to be loved and make love, get ready for the time of your life. Potent spell calls upon powerful spirit to bring you prizes. Whether you yearn for love or riches or contentment juju spell could be designed to fulfil your wildest wish. If you despair over a lover who has gone astray, or perhaps you crave to be touched and cared for by a new love it could call upon powerful spirits to do your bidding. If it is everlasting love you seek, look no further. If it is wealth and a life of ease you seek juju spell are what some people want for you can show others your strengths, your beauty, your uniqueness in both ways natural goodness or by means. The power of juju flies higher than most creatures hovering in the wind as it looks down upon our planet its keen eyes look knowingly at the earth below. It is as if it is the lord of the universe and all other things are its servant.

Voodoo is an indigenous organised religion of coastal West Africa from Nigeria to Ghana practiced by the Ewe, Kabye, Mina and Fon peoples of south-eastern Ghana, southern and central Togo, southern and central Benin and the Yoruba of south-western Nigeria.

It is distinct from the various traditional animistic religions in the interiors of these same countries and is the main origin for religions of similar name found among the African Diaspora in the New World

Voodoo centres around the spirits and other elements of divine essence that govern the Earth, a hierarchy ranging in power from major deities governing the force of nature and human society to the spirits of individual streams, trees, and rocks, as well as dozens of ethnic voodoo, defenders of a certain clan, tribe, or nation. they are centre of religious life, similarly in many ways to the cult of intercession of saints and angels that made Voodoo compatible with Christianity, especially Catholicism, and produced syncretism religions such ancestor worship and hold that the spirits of the dead live side by side with the world of the living, each family of spirits having its own female priesthood, sometimes hereditary when for example it is from mother to blood daughter.

Patterns of worship follow various dialects, gods, practices, songs and rituals. Juju recognizes one God with many helpers called Orisha who in tradition bore seven children and gave each rule over a realm of nature - animals, earth, and sea - or else these children are inter-ethnic and related to natural phenomena or to historical or mythical individuals.

There is messenger deity who relays messages between the human world and the world of the Orisha, and then we have Esu depicted as a dark, short man with a large staff and often a pipe, candy or his fingers in his mouth. They are mediators between the gods and the living in order to maintain balance, order, peace and communication.

All creation is considered divine and therefore contains the power of the divine while evil is an initiated concept. This is how medicines such as herbal remedies are understood, and explains the ubiquitous use of mundane objects in religious ritual. Voodoo talismans, called 'fetishes' are objects such as statues or dried animal parts that are sold for their healing and spiritually rejuvenating properties. Sorcerers and sorceresses are believed to cast spells on enemies on behalf of supplicants, calling upon spirits to bring misfortune or harm to a person or group. Animal sacrifice is a common way to show respect and thankfulness to the gods.

Women are given the name of one of their highly respected female ancestors. The woman who is chosen is usually the oldest women in her clan, but this tradition may be overruled due to factors such as health, education, and national influence accustomed now to the Ogboni cult. The responsibilities geared towards activities among men and women. They take part in the organization and the running of markets and are also responsible for their upkeep, which is vitally important because marketplaces are the focal points for gatherings and social centres in their communities. When there are problems the deities would be consulted rituals are made which would lead to prayers and ceremonies.

About 51.5% of the populations referring to themselves as Christian are cult members attached to religion groups about half the population practices indigenous religions, of which juju practice are part of.

As a reaction to being torn violently from their roots through slavery, the slaves tried to resume their cultural and religious traditions. Ancestral spirits, forces called supernatural, were invoked and celebrated in secret now in the shadow of the Church, as the worship of saints and the Catholic sacraments served as a screen and a support for African beliefs. The creation of a coherent belief system was extremely important in the development of a feeling of cohesion among themselves today through activities of cult which provides them with a sense of self and community.

The process of syncretisation among the African religions helps to explain why those cults found it relatively easy to accept and integrate parts of Christian religious belief and practice into the local cult activity. Initially this integration was purely functional, providing a cover of legitimacy for religions that were severely proscribed after a few generations a real syncretism became part of the duality of beliefs of Africans who soon found it possible to accommodate both religious systems.

The strong belief of the community in juju ritual helps to aid the desired result in its secrecy and mysteriousness of its sources of power, in connections to ancient African sources believes in Christianity and its scriptures, and in the masterful improvisational skills of European medical scientific medical progress had changed things a lot and the way juju practice are viewed. Spiritual healing, Cleansing, guidance, spiritual growth and spell casting are still part of our African ways of life in Africa and abroad. Juju spells can be spell casted for all purposes love spells, money spells protection spells and juju healing spells.

As a born premature baby at birth in the UK at one year old, I was in Africa there I grow up until, I was 21 years of age. Many would say Hoo! Such a poor child why should this happen to him; he should have been left, to live in the UK where, he would be well looked after! How thoughtful?

For my 21 years in Africa and back in the UK I began to examine myself in my new surrounding it was nature taking its toil in my past now, am in the UK. It was left, for me to access myself and the situation around me and what lies before me.

In truth and in honesty, if I had been left in the UK with my condition of birth, I wouldn't have survived I would have gone into extinction before; I was 21 years of age. I wouldn't; have been able to come this far. And the experience I have had over the years probably, I would never have been able to use a computer, work or feel healthier. Children born premature are more likely to suffer from pneumonia living all their lives in the UK but the same thing would had occurred if I had remained in West Africa the change in environment is good for me.

We all have our purpose in life as far as you and I take the part God had ordained for each of us. Sometimes it's because of nature, our own doing, conditions that makes such things happen and we just have to take it as it comes. My mother at the start would never have believed I would have come this far.

This is one reason for us taking the part that God and our existent have lied down before us and you or I would never know until almost at its end. Yours or my achievement and experience at such stage in our lives are like being at a specified number of points or goals in front of an opponent.

Christ had died; Christ is resin and Christ would come again with the bread we eat, we feed on his body and the cup from which we drink, we drink his blood.

I know about the climate of West Africa many of us know about it some even better than I do but what does it mean to you?

I would tell you, what it means to me basically about West Africa Nigeria in particular which is not as humid, as the Sahara desert or the far north of West Africa.

I have experience not once but more than a hundred times in Nigeria where the sun rises before seven O'clock in the morning all day in Lagos until about five O'clock in the evening.

With the sun shining at certain times with no clouds on the sky able to wipe the smile off the sun face from morning until dawn. People going about their business such hot weather and very humid and the rain all of a sudden powering down with thunder and lightning to cast off evil spells that covers the whole nation. That is when you see them in groups gossiping because they could not go out from their body in astral travels to cast their witchcrafts.

Thunder are loud cracking or deep rumbling noise caused by the rapid expansion of atmospheric gases that are suddenly heated by lightning as if something is speaking aloud and in angry manner.

This, are during the time most witches of Africa seek bloodshed through accidents most people travel at this time of the year to visit relatives far and near when the weather is favourable for travelling.

Which is always after the Easter slaughter of caws, sheep's and live fowls for the Easter celebration, which put them at far and the harvest with fruits and vegetable to protect religious observers, which holds down their parade of witchcraft at the same time, the Celestial Church, Cherubim and Seraphim and the Evangelical holds crusades against them. So it goes on until about Christmas when another slaughter begins for the Christmas celebration.

At Christmas the sun shies away covered by African dry wind and dust with the slaughter for the Christmas sips into the sky with praises and shouts of hallelujah to call on the

Heavenly bodies to protect them at the coming year. So do they also calls on the Lords and chosen once of the Abyss to protect them from evil as they make obeisance to God each Christmas.

Sheep's, caws and live fowls or turkeys are slaughtered all over the world, camper this sort of ways the slaughter are carried out in the Western part of the glob on how, they do their own slaughter some children do not even know what a sheep looks like or ever dream of seeing a live sheep slaughtered. How ironic?

The sun and the moon interpret and record all natures of human existence this is from my own perspectives. One of them repels while the other attracts. Man has gone to the Mood on several space missions, to planet Mars and they plane to go even further to other planets. Man. has begun using solar energy from the sun to power electricity, cars and probably very soon aircrafts.

Science is taking huge steps into human reality that God has from the beginning made man and the entire Universe very sufficient.

And what has religion got to offer? That we would go into Heaven, that God, is creating a place for us call Heaven. We are yet to understand the planet we dwell what is this place call Heaven we Christine's especially are waiting for. If you are religious and you have had no three square meals for three days how would you feel like. God can never have made man to hope for Heaven this way. There is a delusion involved our religious leaders should preach about us all turning the world into a better place. We would know about the universe and why we are here before we get to know or understand the Heaven that is to come.

One thing is for sure no matter what faith you believe in the world we are living as of this 21st century we are existing as to what the world was when God created the Universe and all that is in it we have come a long way knowing more to what we already know it has been a blessing and we would know more.

God is all greatness of everything that is right and not wrong. This is why; we have been created with vast differences. A lot to understand, and quest for, we seems to say we appreciate God when we do not appreciate the whole beauty of it all or ourselves. Many believe ages ago, that this world would have come to end but planet earth, is still waxing strong at the same time, with inherencies' phased for more than questions, to be asked.

It is partly why most faith groups are having less to do with religion or faith because, they have problem or feel they are destined to face the real world we live in, as, it is coupled with customary change

And yet, there is suffering in our existence they, hope for Heaven to come. What more Heaven or hell, can there be? The scenario implies we are on a journey. Life is more than a journey it is a quest. In all that we do and all that is in it would define the quest. Science and religion do co-exist it is part and parcel, we have to accept.

Existence is based on bargain and fulfilment to bargain it calls for religious faith and their teaching having more insight into God, and Gods creativity. Science, technology and engineering are also, the making of God through human initiatives. Whatever we do, we do for God and in the name of God blessed we would forever remain.

Man could travel into space, into the future and the past and what more could put us into reality our existence is to explore. We have been granted initiatives and purpose, to distinguish right from wrong what more can we ask for? We go into deep sleep we later wake up from, in our sleep having dreams of realities and sleep we cannot wake up from into death.

We have inconsistencies some which we find reality to ask questions about and we could use our initiatives. Think of me as a child with such nature of slaughtering sheep's, caw, goats and live fowls in Africa. Think of the Celestial, Cherubim and Seraphim and Roman Catholic congregation with olive oil, burning of incense and candles by the time, I left Africa for Europe by the age of over 21 years, I was nothing else, but a spent force.

The wealth my father had and employment relatives of mine had at Briscoe and Pfizer pharmaceuticals was sponsored, by Roman Catholics, with the aid of Jonson and Joe pharmaceutical. At one point in my primary school days we pupils of the school were given Holy bibles I was surprised the one given to us at my school only contained the new testament of the Holy Bible some boarding schools were given complete Bible the effect in my own experience has given rise to an androgynous 'Esu' or partly human and partly plants, partly human and partly metal or partly human and half creatures the harvest is taking place. Those who are ready to spend money buying gifts for the Church e.g. Church Organ, Digital Piano or throw lavish parties inviting members of their Church should endeavour giving honest earned money to the church or any other beliefs. Juju, voodoo, religion, belief system and science dose correlate it gives us a sense of belonging and interaction it's all part of who we are and parcel to what we might become in life if we have the gifting we should use them well for more good than bad. If one says he or she recognises witchcraft in science it would be argued against to keep an open view science especially in health know a lot or experience witchcraft is still ongoing in earnest but in different dimension Great Britain deals with it in close doors leading to situation that gradually boils up before it comes out in the open you just have to live with it until they unfolds which normally take measures. One must have advance to understand its proceedings the world and its activities are changing those who understand this related to juju, voodoo or witchcraft in its new technical terms might tend to hold something back that could be personal about life to themselves I experience even furniture like chairs, tables, cutleries manufactured goods showing effect that they have life. My advice to public users of the NHS or any other organisation is I understand you can sometimes be hurt by those who care for you shout as you like but do not physically harm them.

Whatever is against the science of medicine, inconsistencies and inherencies in Europe before I arrived into the UK are my adversaries I hope Africans would develop to meet the current demands of modern day issues and awareness. In strides that would be beneficial to the whole of Africa. My life in Africa in good or bad health was that of a linesman for a child with my condition at birth, I was very active.

As I was word processing, it was Wednesday the 25th of May 2011 It began to rain in the South East of England with the sun shining at intervals, as if there was battle going on within the clouds. This was not going to be all; there was more to come the next day which did put me in an awareness of what a typical day was if one could be in Africa in the month of May, June or July.

At the back of my mind I felt as if, the weather change had been moved from Africa to Europe. But if, it where in Africa, the hot sun, the rain and the thunder and lightning would take all my pains and burden away and lighten up my spirit but here in the UK, it was as if, the world was crashing down on me at times and later changes covered by the difference of the environment and the way people here live their lives it makes me think or plunder on various issues.

The next day 26th of May I met with my GP doctor Brown with complaint of pains in the joints of my arms, back and general body weakening. I had not slept or eaten for two days and I had been parp from my mouth.

As I was coming back from my appointment early on this morning I dashed on my way back into my flat to Sainsbury's food chain store in Woolwich and bought myself a bottle of whisky.

Getting into my flat the rain started again which turned into something I had only experience in the UK for the first time in such intensity thunder, lightning with the rain coming down with ferocity. I had the feeling, some people were asking themselves is the world, about to come, to an end?

Christians might say taking the milky-way one aspect that is difficult to understand or accept is that, it is practical and not just an illusion. I would describe it as no different from using reason into human nature.

This is the modern technique in the presence of science and technology in experiencing once true faith religion does not just mean believing, it is practical considering our ways of living is moving towards a more sophisticated level. There is no reason we should feel, science and technology are exploitative to our faith or religion it makes the world more an interesting place of what we feel, want, like or dislike. Nobody likes being unwell someone or anyone would like to be looked after all purpose and initiatives have its advantage and disadvantage.

Someone over eats and become obese while, the other smokes until he or she becomes skinny like a skeleton life, it is for us having understanding of such phenomenon. Who among them, is giving up hope and who, among the two is gagging for more and there is death.

Most patients due to the amount of food they consume through their medication at certain points depending on the medication began to gain weight. Nature, is speaking to them they need to know or understand something they should know about. The body is speaking for the mind. Religious leaders have more work, to do than they bargained for.

Or members of their faith should begin to realise the current trends of religious groups relating to being gay or lesbian clergies, homosexual, surrogacy or cloning in respect to such acts coming from them we should focus more on the concepts of individuality. And the concept of good and evil, being subjected to each other and round it up with our recent science and technological development related to our ways of life. Close to when these recent development were taking place we should had somewhat moved towards an age of reason, thanks giving, more people are happy. One aspect of human nature is that it is when we go into disagreement or conflict that is when we tend to reason which are often too late and could be upsetting.

Most people say the world, is a crazy place it is not the case, we know the problems we face in this world it has been created for those who are problem solvers, tackle obstruction and confusion what more can one do?

Is it evident you come into this world, you are born with a medical condition or disability that you have something to say about that words, cannot recite? No different from reciprocal action or relation of mutual exchange in nature.

How queue, some people might say? We have heard of UFO sittings in America, It happens everywhere in the world. Depending on the nature or what part of the world, you are situated on.

You live in Africa, you are found of a particular fruit you enjoy and could eat at any time. After some months, years you are aware of a small doted colour spot on the fruit and several of them. You ask yourself what is this? Thank you star that you were embarrassed because, you have received a message and the message is stop eating that particular fruit even if it's for the meantime or take thorough care.

As time goes you will still get the same message if you do not stop eating the fruit; All of a sudden you become unwell. You are rushed into hospital diagnosed with an illness this, is what science of medicine is about their environment relates to hypothesis or theories of chemical and biological observation and testing.

Came to make reason out of it, What are all these ups and down relating to surrogacy and cloning if not through realisation earth and human endeavours at one stage of our existence, would be finite based on the circumstance, we should have lived through an age of realisation before this it is better done before it is too late.

At certain points, when doctors diagnose some patient, patients find it difficult to accept when diagnoses' are made, they find it unbelievable demanding for another doctor or examination the level of awareness and realisation in the 21st century of the problems we have are not enough.

It could occur with clothing, furnishers anything. Jamaicans', Caribbean's, Barbados have lived long with the British I would expect from years of their experience in dwelling within themselves and the British, one would put into history in perspectives how an old Jamaican women feel if she could no longer use her gas oven rather have to use a microwave? How do they fear in their homes in preparing meals for their families? Considering human processes subsume, we have to look for more adaptable ways to make end meet. It is not all about the technology, the amount one has paid in acquiring a microwave rather what has call for the use of such method.

It would be an interesting documentary. Life goes on, we change or we are forced to change through nature and our own endeavours. What does it bring, what does it tell us or mean in relation to our existence? In death, we find truce yet some people say in time God and the Angels would come and destroy this world.

I bought and used plates several of them I experienced something of a paranoia, UFO in which the plate told me, I was meant to use the plate and in Heaven, I was using this very particular plate on earth at the same time, it would be one of the plates, I would eat from while in heaven. I wanted to ask myself how could it be but my consciences responded by saying to me was there anything wrong in the holy bible which says as it is on earth so, it is in Heaven? This experience goes deeper into what synergy really means.

I awaits a military personnel who would have had the same experience or phenomenon with a gun, a rocket armoured vehicle, missiles. If, it ever happens such weapons are part of Heaven would a military personnel, experience it as real if fired in Heaven if it would be an illusion or remembrance of what went on earth that would be fine with me whilst in Heaven according to my dictionary illusion is said to be a false appearance or deceptive impression of reality? I live with three mirrors 92.6centimeter meter high in my flat science had invented a mirror would it replicate for us in Heaven?

How far could civilisation have come this far and my psychiatrist tell me I am living under an illusion I have my physics, mind, soul, and I could feel pain, sadness and happiness I bleed red, the things that goes on in this planet of ours are huge some of them unbelievable I would not wonder how man has become very creative most of human creativity started through illusions.

I do not cheer the same views that the first Sheriff who invented a gun had invented it definably to kill. It was invented to frighten the physically strong abusing the physically week within a community.

With regards to my illness I feel repressed by my trials of life it is not a strange feeling in a world like ours or I might not understand suffering.

In time, I felt mental illnesses such as schizophrenics is an inclination humans are subsuming, to be left as residual image, where sufferers can hardly do things, they normally do or enjoy doing before, they became unwell. The illness I would describe as one suffering from spells, spiritual degradation, deteriorating mental, physically and spiritually.

If theft, smoking hay marijuana, cocaine, anti social behaviour and mush more are issues of concerns about the patient's life. It is definite there are two types of schizophrenia, one good and the other bad.

The part played by doctors, social workers and NHS had not properly been looked into, to ascertain the reasons why some of them are attacked physically or patients using abusive words towards their cares. Nobody just walks out into the street and starts attacking other people for nothing even man's best friend dogs don't just do such things.

It is doctors, and cares who should at the first stage, readdress the situation of why cares are being attacked by their patient. The situation called for a compromise, were by they reached a stage of compromise within the NHS staffs and patients. Instead all off a sudden, a fine of £1000.00 is inevitable if a patient attacks or abuse staffs of the NHS consider stigmas attached to mental health and how different patients feel or react over it a care can use such an arena becoming popular at their work place. If you want to understand real attitudes you should go to Africa here under our nose an employee can do a fast one to gain more control and recognition.

Some patients who could be found to attack or use abusive words towards their cares, are mostly patients, who are distressed, While others could live for months, without capable of being able to change their clothing's, they look poverty stricken such are akin to aggression or their cares are fed up of sectioning them every now and then,

Fining an individual who cannot fend for himself, on a daily basis to pay a fine of £1000, 00, because of a conflict within a client and a customer, I regard this as being vulnerable and threatening to the customer. Something should be done about why any patient could attack his or her cares. Caring for me, I feel vulnerable to them why should I attack someone who cares me it's all part of stigmatization.

If the NHS as public services provider are doing a good job in the first place, in our communities, if there are good reasons and explanation, why their patients are not happy with the services they provide they should complain but why should the situation lead to abuse they are likely to be vulnerable to their cares, cares are there to help are they implying patients are not taking this into consideration it's not the kind of things patents or anyone would normally do.

With difficulties speak some people could find it difficult expressing themselves this could lead to frustration it is no excuse for abuse, we are likely to spend no more than thirty minutes with our cares, Talking to them more in dept about what we feel about our illness or go through the more easier they can help us through our illness and prescribe the right medication for us how do they lead to abuse.

The situation puts me in great pressure to make this communiqué either to relieve my mind. On two occasions I was hospitalised diagnosed as schizophrenia throughout my stay in hospital fells on the month of my birthday 27th July I was in hospital with mental illness in 1995. The second time I had to be hospitalised at the same hospital for an operation I had to undergo an operation for appendicitis in July 1999, also did fell on my birthday. How would most people think and feel. If I were in Africa many would say I am being bewitched or am an Ogbanje.

On the 8th of June 2006 I had an appointment with Dr Andrew Brown at the Ferryview health centre, I complained of nasal congestion, sneezing, headaches, and constipation if, I were in Africa who, would I complain all these to? I told him I had bought Boots antihistamine for allergy relief syrup. He let me out without a prescription, I should still stay on whatever medication, and I had bought from Boot the chemist.

My income from my cleaning job was not enough, for me to look after myself, not to talk about my health cost the government provides. You see, most of us who are doing all we can to stay off benefit hardly know about such things as our benefit entitlement.

Some mental health sufferers could easily become frustrated, while others could be doing a lot to vouch for themselves regardless of their illness some, with extreme disabilities.

When I was taken ill into hospital Dr. Mougoud and Dr Patel was my psychiatrist at Greenwich hospital in GD ward. Though, they are both from different race Dr. Mougoud had good resemblance to Mr. Gabriel Awe during the time I was hospitalised at the Greenwich hospital.

When I was discharged from Greenwich hospital, I went to my GP at Samuel Street a Dr Patel told me, all I was suffering from was depression probably because, I recently lost my mother. Three months later, I was summoned by Dr Pereira at the former Woolwich Arsenal for people with mental health problem at Powis street Woolwich.

The way, he brought out the file and from what he told me, the file was written and compiled by him or Mr. Akim a care. Dr Pereira was nowhere near the Greenwich hospital when I was in hospital. It was Mr. Akim two police officers left me with at GD Ward at Greenwich Hospital.

When Dr Pereira read some of the contents of my files, I felt flabbergasted, I told him it must be someone else file moreover, if any one should redress my illness, I would prefer it if Dr. Mougoud or Dr Patel whose care I was under during my stay in hospital and that I had spent a enough time in hospital to have been told whatever my illness was all about. I told Dr Pereira when I went to see my GP at Samuel Street he told me, I was suffering from depression. There was nothing more I could do to convince Dr Pereira to change the opinion of being diagnosed as a schizophrenic. I became worried about my diagnoses for a very long time and by the time the hospital was short down it came to my mind, they hospital most had been suffering from depression this was why it was short down.

Prior- to my discharged, I wondered what could be the connection within Dr. Mougoud and Mr. Gabriel Awe who was a co-worker with my mother at R.T Briscoe pharmaceutical Lagos Nigeria. I became paranoid; I was really puts off by the thought of both of them having any connection.

These memos I wrote to Dr. Fisher about my illness, the way I felt after I was out of hospital, my background in West Africa and now in the UK. I felt each day as I word process that I was making much progress, in time not with ease I could out live the illness managing each day with daily activities.

Sending another part of these memos to Ms. Sally Bryden head of strategic information of Oxleas for a simple reason it could relieved me out of tension and depression I suffer from. At least they would know the state of my mind and temperament.

Within Mr. Akim and Mr. Fidelis both my cares whilst I was hospitalised at Greenwich hospital in 1995 right from the time based on the scenarios, I felt the only thing I should not do is loose my ego. Within Mr. Fidelis from Zimbabwe, Mss. Flavia Kulibia a fellow female student of mine at Charlton Collage and at Greenwich University from Uganda and Mr. Akim a Ghanaian not far in distance from Nigeria compared to Uganda or Zimbabwe. It is a matter of using once discretion understanding the relationship within East, West and South Africa and the way they interact politics or family feud are always involved.

Just before I was hospitalised I was completing a course in emergency aid at Charlton Collage in e.g. resuscitation, treating preliminary injuries e.g. dousing burns and bruises off in 1993. This I told Dr. Mazaroli who took over my care from Dr. Pereira in one of my outpatient appointment at the Ferryview mental health centre that I was making my way into Westminster college on a course of study in computing or catering before I was taken ill into hospital. I am still yet to be told, what sort of illness, I was suffering from.

I showed my recent certificates on short course I had accomplished to make the health centre aware of my situation before I was taken ill and hospitalised. At this time I was wondering what could have made me unwell. Unfortunately, they do not always really consider such issues as briefing patient about their progress until 2008 through the post.

This calls for the condition in other to make things easy for them by passing a bill through parliament for all patient records to be surfed through the internet. Not all public users would like such this proposal conflicts with individual privacy. This I would call labelling in a democratic society just as people with mental illness are being labelled but the most important aspect of it is that all patients would be aware of their medical records which would cost the government more founds in keeping the data base very well protected.

I had to inform Dr. Mazaroli as my new psychiatrist that my cares become aware of my situation and how I felt by writing to them up until 1997. By which time I felt I did not know why I was hospitalised certain realisation draw on me but it wasn't enough. I had no information based on the illness of schizophrenia or any explanation of what schizophrenia illness is? Until Dr Robert Hughes my GP at Ferryview health centre gave me a handout on bipolar having an inclination to surf the internet there it was. But how does it correspond to me, my background, race or creed?

I became aware before I was hospitalised, I experienced recalled walking aimlessly on the streets for example walking from my flat to Bexley and Bexleyheath, Peckham, Brockley, East Dulwich and Greenwich aimlessly after my father's visit to my flat in Woolwich.

From the report made about my illness nothing was mentioned about why I was taken into hospital by the two police officers, who picked me up just by the Riverside housing office in Woolwich.

Questions such as where was I, before the night I was taken into hospital, what was my passport doing in my hands at the same time when I was in hospital I had always asked Mr. Akim several times for what reasons did the two police officers brought me into hospital that morning? Mr. Akim was the one who opened the entrance door for the two police officers who ushered me in into GD Ward at the Greenwich hospital in 1995 I wanted to run infarct I even ran a mental health ward! Being held back and ushered into GD ward a female patient inside the hospital rushed towards the entrance do thinking she was running away I ushered by nudging back into the ward.

The explanation Mr. Akim gave was that I ran into the front of a moving London bus in Greenwich. I asked Mr. Akim were in Greenwich, he replied just by a wine shop close to

Iceland and Somerfield food chain stores in Greenwich. I had not been at Greenwich for weeks. I was picked up by the police officers just by the Leisure centre by Riverside house in Woolwich after coming out of my flat.

I told Dr. Fisher and Dr. Mazaroli they should keep Mr. Akim close to my care because he could give reasons to why I was hospitalised that relates to my family the thought came to me, after several years I was hospitalised. Mr. Akim moved on from working at the Greenwich hospital to Woolwich Arsenal, then to the Ferryview mental health centre in John Wilson Street and now at Queen Elizabeth mental health home treatment team. While he was working at the Ferryview mental health centre I told Mr. Akim that the police officers picked me up not more than some few yards from where the Ferryview health centre was recently constructed just before the year 2001.

I told Dr. Fisher and Dr. Mazaroli I was working for initial cleaning service at Woolwich Gala Bingo club before my illness; the incident within me and the officers took place just behind the Woolwich Gala club. A club manager, who left the Woolwich Gala club for another club as manager while I started working at the club I reckon was an Ex-police officer he has resemblance to Mr. Gabriel Awe. He came back to the Woolwich Gala Club as manager just about the time I left my job at the Woolwich Gala Club in 2007 which was just after I renewed my British passport that was handed to me in Lagos state Nigeria because at that time the passport got expired.

On the day I got the idea I should go to the Woolwich Gala club to look for work was in a dream after several days ago I was couth-up in a rain storm on my way back from a job interview in Rotherhithe in Surrey SE16 it was not only a rainy day in the South East of England, it was also a very stormy weather with thunder strikes. Standing in front of the Gala Club to hide myself from the rain I was wet from head to toe when the rain subsided, walked home to my flat.

Few days later it rained heavily again in the night but this time, I was inside my flat, I did not know why on this night, I could not sleep the rain was accompanied with thunder storms and lightening. I opened my bedroom window and watched as the rain came down trickling down against my bed room widow. All of a sudden, I had a phenomenon as if it was raining the stars come out shining in the sky and the sky become blue in colour. I opened my eyes wide open in surprise then all of a sudden my eyes were closed as if I should fall asleep.

Words entered my ears, I should go down to the Woolwich Gala Bingo club in Woolwich and ask for a job vacancy that very morning, as I was unemployed looking for work, there I was that very next day in the morning speaking to Mrs. Joanna Tarker the cleaning supervisor at the time in 1992. I asked her about a job vacancy I got the job just afterwards I lost my mother at Ibadan Oyo state.

I got my job back for the second time as a cleaner at the club to start immediately on the very same morning after I came out of hospital in 1995 diagnosed with paranoid schizophrenia. Mrs. Joanna Tarker and Mr. Brain Asher was still the supervisor and the deputy supervisor both of them stopped working for initial at the Club in 1999. I became deputy supervisor with Ms Janet Clark as the supervisor.

This was the time Ms Joan Ashley a Jamaican lady was employed by the company at the same time, two Jamaicans Mr. Green who I came back working for the club met as a staff left, Mr. Brian Archer I took over from him in 1999 as deputy cleaning supervisor also left working for initial cleaning service I was at this time a student at the university of Greenwich on a degree course in BA Business Studies.

War was going on in Iraq; disaster is striking everywhere in the world. Work practice in the UK has gone dry, as a paranoid schizophrenia sufferer, with my condition of health; I can only contribute just two and half hour a day's job only, on housing benefit.

My father a freemason patron of Warri Island Lodge Delta state Nigeria of which, I am also a member with my initiation followed by a loud bang thou architect of the universe'.

My father was an Apena of the reformed 'Ogboni fraternity' cult; he is a chief, as well, a business company managing director, owned two houses built side by side. The land is coloured red mud.

The land is a family plot of land given to my father by his lat uncle once the Ologbosere of Warri Ayeye-Dudu the second in command in all chieftaincy and traditional titles in Delta state Nigeria. My father waited for too many years before any attempt was made to build his house on the land. Some years after our arrival into the UK my immediate elder brother Mr. Omagbemi suddenly divulged in a job as housing officer but left just after I had an experience of housing overpayment in 2007 to work for Network rail.

Quite different from my father's plans for Omagbemi his plan for my brother was in shipping. Omagbemi had been taking shipping course to qualify in shipping right from Nigeria before we both came back to the UK. If Omagbemi had made it his major interest it would have been with regards to my father's business, which he could have easily taken over from my father. It would have been even better for my brother because importation of goods into Nigeria is a very huge and profitable business.

In a given situation would you enjoy the next person having it both ways? I was the one who carried cement for the building of my father's house. Invariably it means I had been embedded below the house as a seismograph. I become interested in obtaining educational qualification in advanced diploma in housing management and law. My eldest brother from my mother Mr. Oritseweyinmi is now a barrister within Warri Delta state and Port-Harcourt he studied law at Buckingham University.

I could not at this age be called a young lad, juju culture depolarizing African children before, they are born. One has to push, push for themselves it raises conflict and family diversity in a world were individuals seek by means to be the strongest link if you do not push around, people say you are week or you do not want to join them which might make life difficult for you.

Man have achieved the greatest of achievements' for hundreds of century's infarct before time was created man have been existing not only in pain but in glory we have become very creative and advance in our ways of life and the way, we perceive things. The greatest of human achievements above all would be their achievement; of living a life without sin or wrong doings.

On two occasions I had seek admittance into the Nigerian defence academy most importantly what I wanted was to redress my country and family issues they are array with too much conflict within themselves considering Nigeria is privileged among other nations in Africa. There are conflicts all over the world they should be able to contain their conflict enhances the nation for their own good. They need to show understanding among themselves.

After my secondary school education with good grades I began working for my father at Port-Harcourt Rivers state Nigeria. I was soon admitted into university of Port-Harcourt rivers state after a JAMB examination, prior to my arrival into the UK.

What are my own opinion about illegal immigrants into the UK, rather, you should ask me, why was I not readily admitted into the Nigerian defence academy without any implications because I was British born African Such situation in Africa has not yet been faced with constructive criticisms but I would say a bit!

Prior-to FESTAC 1977 regarding all West African nations get together held in Nigeria.
Many Africans abroad e.g. UK, U.S.A Europe studying or on business never came back to Africa to stay permanently.

Why should so many had left Africa to reside in Europe as commonwealth nations as immigrants at such times it was a period of development and awareness in West Africa.
Mind you then they were not asylum seekers.

Many of them embezzled money. Immediately they come into Europe within three months, they have bought houses.

It was a joyous period for All Africans.
But why is it all erupting now.

Bearing in mind at that time some like me where in Africa who were born in the U.K no attempt was made about young boys and girls my age coming back into the UK until later.

This same people come and streak, strip; strike us from our place of birth as if, they would have better intentions.

When we were brought back, most of us did not come back with our own accord the British consulates/citizens advice bureau took action intervening on our behalf within the UK government and the Nigerian government including our parents. As for me at this time, I took myself as any other African; I never looked at myself as different from other Nigeria. I never knew I was British or what it takes to be British.

Why am I this unwell in the UK, than I was, when I was in Africa. This is the surest way I feel I can make most people understand how I feel in so divers a scenarios about my life and my illness and how it affects me, through which I believe you will easily provide for me, the optimal help for me to get well or coup with my illness, and medication that soothed the condition of my illness.
Do I have choices based on my identity, yet every choice I make determines who I am. Identities I construct yields decisions, attitudes, and actions that are pieces of my life, which fit together intricately to create a beautiful mosaic that is me. What should be my picture reveal I could be proactive or allow others to take me along for the ride? It is easy to figure out who you are: you are who you create yourself to be, who you become. Every decision you make contributes a piece to the art of your existence. Search endlessly to find who you are, and your masterpiece will be filled with longing, existential angst, wandering, and aimlessness. Decide to create a better you, to design yourself around your desires,

priorities, beliefs, and gifting and you will see the masterpiece that is meant to be and there is more to come on completing these exercise.

By choosing to act in alignment with your core self and follow what path you have chosen, you are already making changes. You may not be who you will become, but you are not who you once were. So who are you becoming today? If you find your identity in others, your self-esteem and sense of worth will be dependent on their choices and leadings. If instead you recognize that you are an original, then act like it.

To construct a masterpiece work of art, there are defining lines and shadows. Without the contrast, the beauty and starkness of the image is lost. Contrast allows for the vivid colors to stand out as beautiful as the designer intended. Dark shadows, like hard times, can color a portion of our journey. Will you allow your dark shadows to define you, or will you rise above and make the statement you were intended to contribute to the world? You have a vivid, brilliant image to create, so do not get stuck filling your canvas with shadows and miss the masterpiece waiting to emerge from them. I have decided to move beyond circumstances.

Why can't we do this in life? Get comfort, take courage, and then try again. Instead, we are often confused on how to handle life? Do you structure your identity around hurts or blows, or do you move on despite your past? You are not defined by what happens to you, but by how you respond to the happenings of life.

If my life were an open book, would people care to read it considering belief system sway with the wind? Am I manipulated by motivational speeches from fast-talkers with empty, shallow promises that do not deliver but often cost you money? Do I think my identity depends on my career or other prospects? Do my life's journey correspond to a map, or do I know where I am or where am heading? Am I confident in who I am at list, I know am not an arrogant sort of person.

We hear of archaeologist who, have gone to the remote places of Africa, to look into case of mythical demons in Africa, more of the works of the archaeologist are still yet to be revealed to the general public eye as the use landmines' to shed blood in waking up demons through liberation of the land with blood in some areas of Africa continues. In time because of clearing up within NHS and its infrastructures' careful time will come to turn the table, the other way round.

It's now a common experiences of patients under NHS care, during their care and treatment in hospital, or at home experience that the effects of some cares and staffs of the NHS result to patients feeling more unwell, e.g. general body weakening or swaying, What have the NHS got to say about such occurrences. It is evident that very soon Europe will be experiencing another era of the exorcist and spiritual archaeologists related to wellbeing, psychology, human nature and behaviour for those who have made God their refuge he is intervening on their behalf in various ways for some of us our getaway is through e.g. what is termed as civilisation, positive culture of Britain e.g. democracy and human right, termed as a developed nation of the world through which we by cut negative corners for the sake of our peace of mind because in a place like Great Britain when people withdraw it involves something serious but very delicate for example to express.

The way, people with mental health problems such as schizophrenia or manic depression are treated, some of us feel threatened, many of the NHS staffs give false impression that they care for their patients, we cannot be schizophrenia sufferers, coming close to our cares, for some or any other reasons feel we are being demonically possessed and they could help or understand the situation.

The NHS and the law have over reacted, of which some mental health sufferers view with suspicion. While some mental health patient who might feel in certain situation they have less in life to look-up to such as appreciating their worth within the community they live in probably because of stigmas attached to mental health should be fined £1000.00 because of conflicts within patient and their cares.

Instead of being fined, questions should be asked why patients should attack their cares there are lots of information in the internet about abuse of NHS staff more than any I have come across about within any working organisation. It's not a war going on there why create situation as if, there is an ongoing war within patients and their cares. I do not like it when people create situation when it's of no use and it goes on and on while most people view Great Britain is a problem solving nation.

Another era of the archaeologists has arrived once again, but this time in Europe and not in Africa for the last time. Yet prison sentence are being congested with unwarranted imprisonment, they are offered hard drugs and now they could be offered hard drugs within the NHS environment.

Since we are people suffering from mental health issues, the NHS, its staffs, and care workers, should know and understand better of how to rehabilitate people with mental health issues it should be concise, based on what we need should be real cure for mental illnesses. Rather than being offered drugs in hospitals if this happens how far would it go within her HMS Prisons services.

26th April 2010 it was on the news drug addicts should be prescribed heroin on the NHS a nursing leader says. Peter Carter general secretary of the Royal Collage of Nursing said the move would drive down crime rates while helping people off the drug. The views of other nurse at the RCN annual conference in Bournemouth were mixed Mr. Carter backing came after positive results from the NHS pilots in London, Brighton and Darlington.

This issue is one of the reason why I have written this book because it in no way leads to patient recovery it rather worsen a mental health patient life advertising heroin to them is no solution to their health problem. The police within our communities in relation to drug abuse, the Navy at sea defending the trafficking of drugs should go and seat on their back-side. All the government have been doing in restricting smoker's from lighting-up in certain environment is no good, now it should be made worse by introducing heroin openly to addicts within the NHS.

Certain issues should be made clear no smoker enjoys smoking, no drug addict enjoy taking drugs just as no alcoholic. To some drinking in real terms they are programmed through causation or they programme themselves to be addicts because of probably life inherencies bearing in mind mental health issues goes into a deeper level than just being an alcoholic, or a drug addict we look forward to positive and not negatives involvements while addressing such issues.

Treatment of patients should be based on positive involvements. It's the only way for some patients outliving the illnesses or less being scotched by mental illness. An irony is patients who do all they can to understand and manage their mental health illness are overlooked. No mental health patient in the real terms is ever doing fine since it's an illness a patient could be trying if they could to outlive.

It is said that 45% of mental health patients are unpredictable they could be predictable. One needs not really be diagnosed to be considered psychiatrist cases; all humans have something psychiatric about themselves certain crazes are psychiatric. Being gay, a lesbian, are all forms of mental illness. With some people, it could be food a particular sorts of food mine is African plantain, rice and beans prepared with fish stew or banana with cashew nuts.

Too much of anything is not good for us especially if it has a causation that could be harmful. There is awareness on how to stop smoking it causes cancers, government have been pumping money on stop smoking forums at surgeries and within the NHS environments, man have been smoking for centuries haven't we leant enough from smoking and its inherent defects should our doors be open and face worse scenarios in the future in relation to hard drugs.

There are times when I smoke a whole packet of 25g of roll-up tobacco a day. I have been to stop smoking clinics, nothing can anyone do for me to stop smoking. I had to do it myself after some time go back to it. It's something each smoker can only do by self initiatives. I know how I frequently burn my shirts and trousers when smoking, as part of my giving up smoking I now have to wear white shirts and wash my mouth frequently I feel keeping an open doors for the use of hard drugs is somehow moving out of consideration.

Over the years, the government, NHS, research and charity organisations have been going into a lot of trouble helping people on how to quit smoking they should try and look into what some addicted have gone through before giving up smoking its hell honestly and to be sincere, It s hell!

It is those who seek to drive this country deeper into anti-social behaviour that would permit it should be legal to be a drug addict in real terms this is what Mr. Carter's statement means. I have been diagnosed as a paranoid schizophrenia for years within which I had been a heavy drinker and smoker my advice is if you are on any hard drugs, do not border taking your medication because it's of no use you will never show any signs of recovery from your mental illness infarct it is a case of medication and self abuse because it relates to the more we abuse our system.

Issues of being on drugs, a smoker or an alcoholic are emotional if they refuse in resolving such issues it doesn't help in tackling its use. The more users become emotional. Emotional in what sense; feeling guilty which does not help much but after probably it amount to causation of a diagnosed illness caused by its use are enough which users are aware of yet they continue. Unable to stop make them scapegoats while at the same time thoughts of giving up doesn't escape their minds moreover they know they are to blame for whatever concurrences as users. The NHS knows users are scapegoats to drugs they should deal more on the emotional aspects infarct what makes them scapegoats to hard drugs or alcoholism?

26th of April there were NHS job cuts in the spotlight as NHS job cuts was on the top of agenda as nurses gather in Bournemouth on their annual conference.

Royal Collage of Nursing general secretary Mr. Peter Carter warned over the weekend pressure saving money in the NHS would threaten jobs. While an online RCN survey of 287 nurses ahead of its four-day meeting suggested that the pinch on the NHS budget was already being felt.

You need to be aware how open some patients with mental illness come out aloud carefree about their drug addiction. The thing that bugs me most about this is only such patients' gets full attentions of our psychiatrist, care workers and social worker.

The UK is a developed nation, who most people around the world are forced to learn and be educated within; they should not make themselves low with such occurrences. It's now a common episode in every working environment in the UK. Many countries look forward every day to learn from the British and Americans! There should be better approach and outcomes in our community around the whole of England on how people with mental illnesses are observed and treated in the hospital and at, their homes. And bringing down stigmas we should tend to be more philosophical.

It was the first time in Oxleas Exchanged issue twenty 2010 I came across the most in test agenda of Oxleas intention on mental health and depression in Greenwich which was part of the opening in Eltham by MP Clive Efford in February one of the service offers psychological therapies like cognitive behavioural therapy (CBT) and counselling for mental health conditions such as anxiety and depression.

Clinical lead for time to talk, Consultant Clinical psychologist Katy Grazebrook was master of ceremony Katy explained the new service would both help to improve mental health of local people and save money by helping those on benefits to return to work.

While Jane Schofield Chief Executive NHS Greenwich said mental health problems is one of the top three priorities in Greenwich, alongside the prevention of cancer and cardiovascular diseases because it affects so many local peoples live in Greenwich.

29th April 2010 Australia set out plans for new rules forcing tobacco companies to use plain packaging carrying graphic health warning. From July 2012 manufactures they would be required to drop all colour and branding logos from cigarette packets. The move billed as a world-first come after recommendation were made by the World Health Organisation. Australians also announced 25% increase on tax on cigarettes.

It was a great move because it would support people with mental health illness helping them, to recover and start enjoying their lives. These are based on explanation to improve patient lives at the same time comes the issue of giving drugs to patient within NHS environment on the mouth of April 2010. It's contradictory to positive care. I wait to see them deliver their priorities for people with mental health problems.

Their annual plan for 2010 to 2011 over a three year period is the trust overriding priority protecting the quality of service they offer to patient and their families with a logo they need to be bold, creative, and responsive to all opportunities focusing on quality.

They are now keen providing information for service users and cares, improve care planning but how? And, improve relationship with service users and cares and to promote clinical qualities how can this take place when you have drug addicts all over the place some are trying giving up, promote social inclusion, increase access to psychological therapies.

Strategic priorities are patient safety focusing on hygiene, privacy and dignity in acute care.

Early 2010 Oxleas trust consulted with members about its plans for the coming year at a focus group held in each of the three borough of which over 100 people attended. Members feedback received at the annual meeting made important contributions towards the formation of the trust plans some of them took my attention.

Improving relationship with social service

More time listening to families and friends

Early contact with the service users before, the situation becomes difficult

Support for the users based on self management course which would be valuable for users especially those who are recovering

Consistent monitoring of cares and their abilities to care for their patients

Continuation of cares support course

On one my outpatient appointment at the Ferryview mental health centre on the month of February 2010 one of the receptionists Barbra handed me a questioner to fill in relation to such issues I ticked negative to having a care plan and a social care worker. All I do is see my psychiatrist spend 10 or 15 minutes with.

It takes twice the effort needed to display positive mental attitudes with some patients. While the room is open for others with drug and anti-social behaviours who would shrug me off saying if I cannot be like them I should bug off if it pays them it does not pay me for being a smoker which becoming more expensive than it is to obtain hard drugs.

Having the chance to talk about medication with someone to increase or reduce it helps with the side effects I want to be listened to. Involving service users in care programme approach and stop talking in jargons and use plain English. Crisis team should give advice to clients on what is available; care plans should be adaptive to follow the needs of patients and the NHS.

I admire the Oxleas NHS trust upcoming appointment reminder with text message it means cares are keeping in touch with their patients since I live an isolated life, if they do not hear from or am not present for my appointment they would be concerned the pace at which technology is moving with positive innovation about the NHS moving towards strategic service improvements with the help of technology would one day solves the problem of tracking a patient or missing person.

Every day new immigrants come into the UK from different countries of race, creeds, culture, and backgrounds. There is competition in every environment, even within people from the same family.

The results are duplicity and conflicts at work different background and race within the UK. If well observed, you will either find out, that another person from Africa is doing another African in, in his or her working place, or within a family.

In my case, I am resilient in confronting such issues regardless of my illness and background.

In my opinion we are neighbours as we sat down together looking for some action, as we look over the past year it seem we are being besieged by players in our neighbourhoods with very little to contribute in time of crisis if it should occur. Yet each day is always just an ordinary day, it should be lively and productive.

We don't have to be knocked of our feet, rather let us do each other right, we lay our body down to do with just as lovers do, it would make us feel right to get on well, we should be happy for ourselves. We should be yarning for each other without heart ache we have been around for too long let's keep each other going.

We should be yarning for each other's friendship and love; we should be looking for each other's embrace, appreciating each other within our community. Let this goes out to all the players in the neighbourhood who are up to no good i.e. racism, anti-social behaviours, sex offenders, gay, lesbians and much more in our communities, our existence is worth more than for it, to amounts into corrupt lives. A world with no defiant aims, goals with more augments and conflicts books can recite.

It is when the cup with such occurrences has gone this full after the death of Christ, that the Engel's will come and rapture us, the down trodden once so let us take courage. It is when, there is no hope and the cup is full to the brim, that we would be ruptured. Where do dead people go, where is paradise? I am of the opinion we can achieve all these by ourselves if Christ had died for us, in the name of his father if you believe in them, we already have the grace it is hidden in us and all things created.

No matter what faiths we belong to, where else do we go apart from our religious faith? To the hospitals, to our homes and families and the works of the archaeologists in a world we live in besieged with different kinds of conflicts in our life and communities each day we find difficult to resolved, some of which are too complicated and delicate to express and resolve. When situations become intricate it, gives us aim for credibility's we can make them right our existence is a challenge. It is more than a challenge than a gift.

If I or another patient should have conflict with his or her care worker; we possibly face consequences of a police officer coming to take me away for a fine of £1000.00 or forcefully imprisonments. If such are the consequences' I would face in an hospital because of a conflict, It's about time I begin my prayers that it is about time the Engel's from the Heaven come riding on their horses to take me up or strike me down. If nothing happens, I leave the situation to the NHS for example privatise its establishments, leave it to the Priest's and archaeologists as I return to the source I came from as an entity my point is that Britain is a civilised nation. The idea of confronting patients in such way is not ideological am sceptical about it the more it could lead us further into emotional, anti social behaviour continue, on drugs and alcoholism or estranged from members of our family.

People from different race and background come into the UK to reside if they have problems within themselves, do not be one sided they know each other, from what they are like within their own origin, do not take sides the issues of racism in the UK, is confusing enough while we are meant to seek lasting peace within ourselves.

If someone invades our personal space or our rights, we want them to change their behaviour. We can assert ourselves without violating the other person's right. If our personal territory is invaded, it is our responsibility to defend our right. Being able confronting them is also in their own interest. If we have been offended it also means other people have been offended too in confronting them, we try to make them change their behaviour.

If massages often fail to influence a person to change his behaviour it tends to make the other person feel guilty, criticised, resentful, or hurt. It still offers advice the other person changes his behaviour. Most people don't like being told what to do. So instead of losing face, they resist changes. Could such a reaction ideologically come within a carer and patient relationship? Not even within a lawyer and his client.

An act of spiritual aggression is when we impose our values on another person e.g. our children is the result of an act of spiritual aggression. E.g. a married man or woman having two or five children showing attitudes within the family that one child is more loved or valued than the other; it becomes even more an act of spiritual aggression if a man has more than one wife vies-vase. Imposing our values on another person can damage relationship.

It may, however, be appropriate at times to influence our children or spouse's values, but if we expect them to live according to our values, we are invading their personal space. If one child may feel he/she is more loved while the other feels he/she is less loved would cause intra- and interpersonal conflicts which result to friction, wasted time, ill feeling, bitter divorces, bickering and back-biting in our family and working environment.

Assertion those imply a pro-active behaviour and initiation of a verbal message, it involves communication of positive and negative messages. It enables us to express our needs, views, doubts, feelings and wants directly without violating the rights of others. Like one I had about Miss Jacky Reid Ms Janet Clark' daughter she had been off work on maternity leave from the club for the past three month.

On this morning her boy friend Mr. Mark had visited us during our working hour's pro- to our hearing the good news. 18th May 2005 I was happy to hear Jacky Reid had given birth to a baby boy. Janet Clark daughters are Nucleoli, Jacky, Christine, Cathy and Miss Joan Keeble.

My mother Mrs. Tomori Abeni Megbele had five children, four with my father, then had her last child for Mr. Gabriel Awe named Mr. Sola Awe. My mother only had one female child Miss. Oritsegbubemi Megbele now Mrs. Ajagunla her husband works for a church in Nigeria they moved from Lagos state to Akure I was told in 2003 her husband was transferred from Akure to Port Harcourt their children now at university were still living at Akure where my sister runs a canteen at a university.

I called my sister resident in Nigeria I told her on the phone on this morning while at work I was happy to hear the news about Ms Janet Clark, I told my sister a change had come into my supervisor's life, because she had become a grandmother her daughter Jacky had given birth to a male child.
Later in my flat on that very day, my Mobil phone piped it was a message from Janet informing me her phone number had changed again she was giving me a call as well, to make sure if I had any problem opening up the next morning because it was my day off work, I should get some part of

her job done if she doesn't turn up. I should give her a call if I would not be available the following morning.

All humans perceive things in mind body and soul we could hear the wimps of our minds or consciousness. 15/06/2005 a Wednesday as, I was walking out of the Gala Bingo that morning having, being working there for some years an experiences I had by Saint Marys Magdalene church garden at Woolwich after several days work while walking home to my flat.

There was a squirrel, a Raven, and another bird which looked just like a crow but smaller with black and white strip by both sides of its wing it was a Magpie. In my mind it was as if, I heard the Magpie telling the squirrel as it picked the earth, at the same time it was as if the Raven I saw as it landed on a tree spread its wing blushed with me going through a phenomenon as if it landed on my head to gain my attention.

It was about time I stop working at the Woolwich Gala club for initial the place was being taken over at this time not much customers came for Bingo game as they used to before why because too much was happening that took their attention than Bingo. I could not tell if it was a male or female as words, I perceive was directed at the squirrel I had to stand still and watch the squirrel in its ceremonial dancing it had effect on my feet's as if, I was moving to its tune as I always do with the Raven bird which in its own case seems to roughen the hair on my head....

I was tiered on this Wednesday morning as I was walking home after lucking up, had a cover done as Janet requested through her phone call. I heard another voice say no! You should not stop working at the Club it was the Magpie. I do notice the squirrels must of the time each morning ever since I have been working at the club. Some times on the puffing crossing to the club, it could be coming right from saint Mary's Church or from the Farryview health centre close to the Castle Tavern Pub crossing towards saint Mary's Magdalene Church Woolwich. This morning the incident took me by surprise I could not believe myself for I stood still as I watch the scene with interest.

Then, I saw the other bird which I described as looking like a Crow but smaller with white and black strips on both wings just alighting on one side of the metal barriers surrounding the Church it was the Magpie again. I heard the bird saying, we always take delight on land and the air, look at the squirrel always scurry movements on the earth who should the land, where the Saint Mary's Church or the Woolwich Gala club belong to. All of a sudden from nowhere near my sight I was taken by a scurry movement it was the squirrel who said timidly but we climb trees. All this while, the Crow which started the conversation by roughen my hair was watching then it took off.

Then the bird which looked like a Crow with black and white stripes took off and the squirrel began as if making gestures towards me as it nibbles a nut steering at me directly. You could continue to go and work there then if you like it said. Then, I remembered many times while walking from home to work in the morning, I had in many occasions seen squirrels pass me by and when going to work in the afternoons as if, one of them are walking me home in some cases, they are more than one Squirrel.

Magpies is a bird described as seem to be jacks of all trades - scavengers, predators and pest-destroyers, their challenging, almost arrogant attitude has won them few friends. With its noisy chattering, black-and-white plumage and long tail, there is nothing else quite like the magpie in the UK. When seen close-up its black plumage takes on an altogether more colourful hue with a purplish-blue iridescent sheen to the wing feathers, and a green gloss to the tail. Non-breeding birds will gather together in flocks. Found across England, Wales and N Ireland, but more localised in Scotland, absent from the Highlands. Seen in a range of habitats from lowland farmland to upland moors.

The raven is a big black bird, a member of the crow family. It is massive - the biggest member of the crow family. It is all black with a large bill, and long wings. In flight, it shows a diamond-shape.

Ravens breed mainly in the west and north although they are currently expanding their range eastwards. Most birds are residents, though some birds - especially non-breeders and young birds - wander from their breeding areas but do not travel far best looked for, in upland areas of south-west England, Wales, the north Pennines and Lake District and much of Scotland.

Squirrels belong to a large family of small or medium-sized rodents called the Sciuridae. The family includes tree squirrels, ground squirrels, chipmunks, marmots including woodchucks, flying squirrels, and prairie dogs. Squirrels are indigenous to the Americas, Eurasia, and Africa, and have been introduced to Australia. The earliest known squirrels date from the Eocene and are most closely related to the mountain beaver and to the dormouse among living species.

As I looked out the window it was raining just as I was about to go out and do my shopping at Sainsbury's also, wished Loraine was here to share this moment with me. I had been thinking of her lately to my surprise the feeling was so strong with the hope that I see her again.

The following day 16/06/2005 was Mr. Thomas day off work. I had to do his job of rack and vacuuming. On getting the work started as I was about clearing all the rubbish off the tables and carpet Mrs. Janet Clark walked in about 7.00 am. I told Janet, Mr. Thomas Hoover had developed problems since the following week. She reapplied; there was nothing she could do about it at the moment. I should wait till Mrs. Linda Andrews our manager comes in the next week. Since, I could not use the Hoover I put a sticker on it (out of order).

I had to swap my Hoover for the circle with Mrs. Mary's Rodney, taking hers down for the hovering using it for awhile I had someone saying good morning on turning round, it was Linda I replied good morning, Mrs. Linda Andrews you are the right person we want to see today because some of our Hoovers are out of order as I left her and Janet to talk.

Janet later came over to me and told me, Linda would swap one broken hover with the one she had got in the company car parked outside. I had to go out to the company car parked outside the club to swap both Hoovers. After which, I went back to my task inside the club.

Minutes later, Linda Andrews called me while she and Janet where sitting down having a discussion on how we have been progressing with our work and asked why, I did not call Janet the week before on a last week Friday to tell her it was just me on the job in the afternoon session because Mr. Amos did not turn-up for work.

I told Linda it was not the first time it had happened and while at the job I was at the point of completing both job in the afternoons mine and Mr. Amos that's when Mr. Amos comes through the entrance of our working area. Linda says when ever such a case arises again I should give her or Janet a call. I told Mrs. Linda Andrews I had already told Janet if it occurs again I would inform her.

On Friday 17th June afternoon job, I was weary Mrs. Ann Mark; Anthony's mother was washing me whilst I was working instead of as I usually do take the cigarette can to empty the cigarette ash trays from the tables.

I first of all cleared the rubbish of the table before removing the ash from the ash trays this was done just to make Ann aware she was always washing me while on the job. We had to use the red tin cans which were recently introduced to empty ash into rather than just emptying the ash trays straight into the refuse bag. It is her job as duty staff for the Gala Club she always watch each afternoon as we cleaners work.

Lots of gossip goes on at the club. Each afternoon I always empty the ash into the red tin the rest of the cleaners know they should do the same why not do so? As duty staff I had to make her understand what we have been told to do by demonstration more focused on my co-workers of what we are supposed to do. This is not a case of because Janet was not around Ann knows what goes on around and I only now work three afternoons. If I tell Janet some members of staff are not putting their ash into the red tin Ann would bark me up and I always keep Janet informed.

The next day during the night, I had a dream in which I felt I had to increase my fish tank with more gold fish after my early morning job.

I took off to the Woolwich market after breakfast and bought two gold fish and a tub of gold fish flacks I only had £8.33p with me the whole bargain cost me £7.50p my plan was to return to my flat by bus for a pound since, I was left with just 83p, I had to walk home its just 15 munities walk.

Miss Loraine O'Connor had been very particular about my fish tank since 1998 when we became friends and also about my hair, I should no longer visit the Baber to cut my hair she said one afternoon. During our courtship after her first visit to my flat when she saw my fish tank, she very much wanted me to buy gold fish and put my fish tank to use, I promised I would, few years this was why I took to my dream.

I and Loraine became friend at Woolwich Collage were we met each other to attain our A level after I had completed my return to learning course under Mrs. Karen Hearne while she become my fellow student under Miss Margi Knight the head of department for 'A' levels.

The relationship of mixed race, inarticulate e.g. the family are always quarrelling within each other. In such homes, there ought to be lots of cooking, merry-making temperaments that, express to the outer world, there are strong insight into their relationship and not just as insignias attached to the rest of the world attached to them as missed-race. For example they want to unify the world.
I have never come within a mixed race family, with any form of cultivated English aristocrat attitudes. E.g. the father of the house could come in one evening, with suggestion that he would do the cooking. I would like to see some sort of culture attached to mixed race demonstrating, they have an identity, based on tradition, something customary, something of an impartial attributes of themselves as mixed race. I form the habit of calling them mixed blessings

I hardly see them with attitudes of preparing English meals even from a cook book. Some of them hardly know what, coriander seeds, cumin seeds, paprika, ground traumatic, garlic, lamb stock. I wrote to my father in Nigeria sending picture of me and Loraine to Warri Delta state Nigeria. I told my father on the letter; Miss Loraine O'Connor was a good cook in the kitchen. I felt it was an ideal thing to say.

Something of Jeremy Kyle show or Trisha Godard, or Hensley ready steady cook chef should introduce on their television show for mixed race parents to show us some cooking techniques. Its phenomena European women especially English women are married to men of race from all over the world.

On my arrival to the U.K Miss. Michelle Cook a young beautiful girl 2 years younger than me of English and Irish birth was the closest opposite sex I first came into contact with who took my notice. I realise some inevitable issues regarding my family I had to take a step backward.

Then I became friends with went Miss. Nathalie Anet-French from France who, was of two twin sisters, for some family pressing matters, Nathalie had to return back to France! It was during my courtship with her when I just moved in to by Gorman Road blocks of flat I lost my mother at Ibadan.

My father told me and my brother Mr. Omagbemi through a telephone call to Mrs. Comfort Iyinboh a relative living at number 1 Chelsea Deacon way at the elephant and castle S.E 1 we should not be in Nigeria for our mother's funeral. Mrs. Comfort Iyinboh sent for both me and my brother to her home in Elephant and Castel where she told us, we had lost our mother at Ibadan. My fathers had sent a message; we need not come down to Nigeria for our mother's funeral. But why I asked, it should be a natural thing for us to be by our mothers side during such a time. I felt unhappy.

It couldn't be because our fathers was unable to finance my visit to my mother's funeral at Ibadan; while in the next year, my father paid another short visit to the UK, which was his second visit after my arrival into the UK. The first visit was close to the time I was working for Iceland frozen food plc with Miss Michelle Cook while his next visit was when Miss Nathalie Anet-French moved back to France.

On my father next visit to the UK at my flat at Gorman road in 1994 after having informed my bother Mr. Omagbemi of my intention beforehand I would not let our father into my flat. On this my father's visit on his presence on my door step which was a one story blocks of flat, I came out of my flat door, locked the door went down stairs, and shouted at the top of my voice, he should step down from my block of flat and go his own way. That he did not see me when I was born in the UK in 1966.

I was brought to him in Nigeria, he was at his mother's funeral in Nigeria at the time I was born in the UK, I was the last child he had with my mother when he lost his mother and had to be in Nigeria for her mother's funeral. I took no notice of my   father's all cooked up dressing in his chieftaincy attires as if he was going for a ceremony, With another new wife, my father had just got married to, who also accompanied him on this visit to the UK.

My father left his children under the care of his wives each wives are more concerned about their own children and he was not always present at home with members of his family because he runs a business elsewhere. He had to be pushed before he becomes keen for contributing to his children's welfare, after my dramatic display of attitude towards him in front of my flat my father went back to reconsider his family affairs. Some of Mrs. Cordelia and Aya Megbele's children are now graduates this was not all I was told their mothers had to put in their own effort still towards their children's achievements.

On the 15th of May 2009 I received a phone call from my brother Mr. Omagbemi that he had been making phone calls to Nigeria my step brother Mr. Sola Awe from my mother's side, had graduated from University.

My father's other children are still struggling in life. The son my father had for his fourth wife Mr. Oneoritsebawo Megbele as far as I know would have completed secondary school. Most people who have visited or lived in Africa, with experience know how I feel! We know the situation in Nigeria including its environmental issues e.g. devalued currency, lack of government sense of direction. This applies to all African nations, religious indifferences, the fear of family members using juju to influence each other's well being, its impact on West African Nation as a cultured group when would they seeks to develop in the right perspectives? There are whole arenas for them to pull through difficulties and initiate better prospects and a need for cohesive maturity to learn from other nations around the world which are developed otherwise, they make their mother land or other nations of the world a dumping ground.

The 21st century should be the real age of reasoning to revive the world as we walk out of the twentieth century evolution of man. More needs to be considered in our scientific and technological world of today. Are marriages and family lives working, would it be kind to admit God does not exist, do jujus or voodoos really have power over man, and are there small gods.

Do we live in combination on earth within the presence of several architects of the universe, do we live in a world, where we reincarnate, or are there anything as false believes? Have matters in references to such issues been dealt with on earth, before man e.g. astronauts are racing higher into the sky to see if God or they themselves exist in another planet.

Blessed are we who are associates ourselves with Humility. It is one of the most assuring ways we get by, if we know what it means to humble oneself at all times even if we have to make some sacrifices. The going can be good or bad, being humble one could stand up straight in confrontation one could at certain times make a difference in setting an unpleasant situation right or wrong based on the predicament, at certain point rather than being too humble it is better coming out aloud, or the situation would be far worse if we had kept quite.

There could be unhealthy kind of self-enforcement which could often be confused with humility, of which; some people could take my action towards my father against me. Nevertheless, if we were doormats', always subordinating ourselves to others, we will be failing to reach out with our full God given potentials.

My father in his life time, had enough money to have purchase my council flat if not for me or any of his children, he could have bought it for himself.

Most people can understand why this had happened within me and my father or why I had behaved in such a way, with my fathers. If I had come up with such an action, it means I think well of my father in the real scenes, it's not because of hat, dislike, or I wanted to have my own way. With any African parents, a child who does such, is only beating around the bush because, its parents who rule infarct the more one would be dominated.

One physiological trait I have is being born each stages of my reincarnation to parents who I know very well, including my brothers and sister, I usually take the edge of the stick where it hurts as my camouflage in other to experience how they weigh down on me with their own respective lives.

Human personal well-being through sociology, physiology and philosophy in up-bringing has been sad but very interesting from my youth something to consider is why are we always starting from where we have stopped?

Everything we do e.g. religious, cultural, historical, sex, gender, race are a part of God's nature that we would depict on earth with our own individual choice, to either make the Heavens pleased with us. To some length realise why we were created and who we are, why are we on earth?

We hardly know who we are not to talk about knowing God what we know are from people and organisations who take certain expects of our existence into consideration we are informed and educated it should have much impact on our lives. Knowledge is strength the more majority of people know, the level at which we are made aware makes us more predictable of our existence.

Take for instant a mobile phone it's a craze everybody would like to have one how they are made takes us into history of information technology isn't it awesome we have come this far with so advance in disseminating information things like these interest all children and we are seeking out life in other planets in this great universe.

- How come people became less considerate during the era of Noah?
- Noah through Gods wish took two of a kind of every creature into the Ark
- Consider thing that are right as far as they bear reality
- I believe the whole world, man and the creatures and all that is contained in it, including the abyssal on all corners of the earth have more than purpose
- Man would reach its abyssal, all the minerals, what all medication are made up of known or unknown substances would be identified and use for more than different purposes. One day it would get rid of all illness and diseases. And probably one day man would eat from a fruit and no longer live in sin
- We all have destination to reach as part of our trials in life
- Man would suffer all kinds of illness and tribulation until all that is Lucifer, is drain out of man, all creatures and very thing of which the universe is made up of.
- All men and creatures would have chosen their own individual ways either for good, or for bad
- The universe is like an equation e.g. two plus two equals four, one side for the better and the other side for the worst, the conflict would be over and then, Heaven would be restored on earth and God would dwell in Heaven.

Do we all know what it takes for humans to have reached these conclusions that earth is finite?

It is through the crystal of the planet Krypton. Of which only medical terms, and languages could be derived from. I gave up my chemistry and physics studies at Secondary School because whenever we are at the laboratory if I do suffer from dizzy spells, my mind and head go blank, I do experience phobias that the whole laboratory is checking or there is a cloud over my head when ever am at the laboratory I only tolerate the laboratory when its biology class.

As part of my hallucinations and meditation it occurs to me about all creatures both great and small, how was it brought to conclusion which creature are feet for consumption and some are not feet for human consumption. Are we humans keeping up to what the book of Chronicles and Deuteronomy in the Holy Bible entails about such creature feet for food or not feet as food for human consumption? I am aware it was Gods command what are the reasons behind it do creatures sin why should some of them be favoured as food than others did God made it so, do some creatures contain the seal of Lucifer, Satan or the Devil. Nevertheless it is obvious we can feed on some of them, others, we cannot feed on.

Or why some creatures are better left to remain in the wild while some as domestic pets would all creatures one day invariably during the close of dawn become man's best friends they also have their purpose in life. Lots of these creatures which should be left in the wild are gradually finding their way within human environment.

They also would be in the kingdom of God as it was said the children would play with the lions and the serpents but, the creature would not harm them.

Some parts of the world feed on Monkeys, cat's dog's rates, bat's snakes, alligators and gorillas just to mention a few. While some are used for Juju's or voodoo some parts of the world feed on bats, snakes and dogs. Do consumption of such creature leads to mental illness.

At certain times in Heaven it most had been realised the reality of Heaven could not come true because of conflict which took place within God, Lucifer, the Devil and Satan, earth and all that is in it had to be created to make this reality of God creation come true, Earth would have to take the place of Heaven for a new reality of as it is in Heaven so it is on earth.

Some of the Angels who where on Gods side before creation definably dedicated themselves to God it is for this purpose we humans humble ourselves before the gods and deities also on trials standing or taking their stance before the Angels in Heaven then without form we now occupies this planet. We have been given charge of everything on earth for example to administer to all creatures, land, fruits, and well being of every things on earth, until the entire wish of God is done and fulfilled on earth and in Heaven.

The Watcher is stardust in outer space article written by Paul Sutherland on the Sun news paper dated 26th February 2009 , about astronomers taking stunning photos of what, they believe to be the Eye of God from outer space could all be part of God unveiling himself, to use or divesting himself.

If one part of human components is made up of blood as well as in all creatures, it could be distinguished as to which creatures are feet for food or not feet for food. At the beginning God created Adam and Eve who had two sons Cain and Able. Cain Killed Abel, the point am not raising is who did Cain later had sex with at that point in time? God in his own way corrected the abnormally through Abraham and his son Isaac considering circumcision, wives to be taken, Jacob and Esau and then Joseph it also portrayed trials of their wives and chronicles until women became priest.

Are there probabilities creatures of the earth holds certain seal in their blood proportionate to sustain humans which resulted to some creature feet for food, while other creatures are not feet for food. We were only aware of the fruit in the Garden of Eden how did we began killing creature for food determining which once where feet for food or not?

I have compiled the component of two simple chemical components of Boots essential shampoo and Boots basic hair gel.

Boot essential shampoo & conditioner 2 in 1 for normal hair 500mle. Chemical components:-Aqua, Sodium laureth sulphate, Cocamidopropyl betain, Sodium chloride, Glycol distearate, Glycol sterate Parfum, Polyquaternium-10, Dimethicone copolyol, Citric acid, Disodium phosphate, Benzophenone-4, Tetrasodium EDTA, Linalool, Magnesium nitrate, Sodium Acetate, Isopropyl alcohol, Methylchloroisothiazolinone, Magnesium chloride, Methylisothiazolinone.

Boot basics Hair gel shapes, style and holds your hair 250mle. Chemical components:- Aqua, PVP/VA copolymer, Carbomer, Phenoxyethanol, PEG-40 hydrogenated castor oil, Sodium benzoate, Sodium mehtylparaben, Polysorbate 20, Sodium hydroxide, Dipropylene glycol, Tetrasodium EDTA, Parfum, Hexyl cinnamon and Linalool.

God made all things and he did made them well all creatures great and small man has been moving through the earth on a gradually pace of understanding, nations great and small, the strong and the week, and that the week might learn to be strong. The poor and the wealthy in other that men would learn to give and take.

Why should a stronger creature leave a stronger pray it can kill so easily and rather go for a less weak pray. Such occurrences do take place within humans in different scenarios.

Lots of people are suffering from illness known as schizophrenia, it's a term just about everyone has heard of. However most people do not know what it really is or what causes schizophrenia or what can be done for individuals who suffer from the illness. Many social workers would see them as a set who just want to influence the social security system.

The illness is a deadly illness. It kills its victims slowly, taking over its victim soul, mind and body functions, and hearing voices that could be harmful to them.

Illness of mental health, which could be diagnosed relating to all walks of life, could lead to a life time of distress, in relation to our needs in life, wants, proprietor, our intentions, social, culture, historic events, cultural background, religion, race, creed, industrial, agricultural and technology.

Each stage going around a sufferers life on a daily basis, relating to their inability to recap, such as carrying out basic task within their environment and social contest, in which they encounter contrast based on what psychiatrist later term as psychotic diagnosis. Most of the diagnoses after a patient is diagnosed with mental health are emotional, feeling less resilient and unhappy.

For some reasons sufferers finds it difficult to recap and adjust for some reason beyond their control, could it be as a result of subjugation based on some of life inherencies, incoherencies or is it partly a control under certain laws of the universe? We encounter obstacles in our way it is part of life inherencies, we have taste, and we are faced with satisfactory and unsatisfactory issues in life. In some cases it could be just certain things to worry about, and then it becomes worse which leads to mental illness.

From such epilogues, it deepens on how an individual react and the people around such individuals confronts them. In some circumstances as a schizophrenic sufferer, it could be that you are being called by God, or the Heavens is seeking one out for a purpose, Heaven is calling you to make a change for a more advance purpose, to face a reality, search your conscience, know who you are and in the process, identifying God in you, the good and the bad in you, and more important the purpose of your life! Bearing in mind there are three aspects of everything we humans are confronted with the good, the bad and the ugly

Bearing in mind all things are created in God's image, do consider that the world has changed from evolution to several revolutionised era's, from the old age, to the development stage resulting to this present technological age and to this twenty first century to scientific, technological and digital age sort out anomalies that might have caused your mental illness.

We have come this far with illusion on our television screen of various episodes of star trek enterprise, space 1999 or the voyager of what could be in other planets in the universe. One thing that is always clear in these televised series are that other planets where in one problem or another for example, a planet had to be evacuated, or a revelation based on something that had occurred before our creation. Doesn't it all seem clear from what had been taking place since evolution on earth up to this 21st century that the universe especially planet earth if not in conflict is subsuming?

Cain killed Abel, why don't we ask through our lives and our conscience why Cain killed Abel. Some of us might read the bible and pass judgment on Cain he is wicked. This was the first family conflict human lives have encountered could it be only because of jealousy? Both Cain and Able were the only children then it is human nature for one of them coming to a conclusion this, is both of us, we are brothers we only have our father and mother, where do we go from here? In another aspect, the serpent with the backing of all other creatures tempted Eve to eat from the forbidden fruit because it was intended for Eve to eat from the forbidden fruit she began to menstruate that the tree would hold her down and Jesus Christ died on a wooden cross. Cain failed on his own thoughts and intentions think of all detectives' television series we have seen motives for murder some of them are found to be awesome.

It was all based to compromise, knowing before hand, what had happened in Heaven what man must do to become like God knowing good from evil which is based as the true image of God. Before our creation we had no form, with, flesh and blood, mind and soul, God deemed us to undergo trials to really understand good from evil and most important to achieve a Matrix of a human soul, body and life. This was after the revolt of Lucifer, Satan, and the Devil in Heaven against God.

We humans on earth hardly consider what must have taken place before God decided to create the world and the entire universe they are left for us to discover placed under and ever changing planet. Or what are the true concepts about evolution before and after it took its place, until this twenty first century, we are still yet to know as the big bang and hydro seeks understanding as to how the universe was created.

There are still more questions to be asked what are the ingrained reasons for our toils and pains? Is it for our own glory or for Gods glory or is it both a right frame of mind would say it's for ours being who we are. Planet earth is filled with all sorts of conflicts relating to suffering, pain, agony, unhappiness, there is beauty, ugliness and death, are we still going to be judged? Is the glory of God being taken away from humans each day of our existence or it is being vitalised?

With the glory of God the architect of the universe, with all the toils and pain we go through each day for hundred of decades, what is it, that is behind human existence? What would be our end result? In fact, where do dead people go? It had been intend that everything in Heaven would subsume to earth, with realities of what had happened in Heaven before evolution began on earth. .

I believe in reincarnation the dead are still with us in death if our work is not complete, we are guarded back to earth if one has been good paradise would guard them if not, they are just washed back to earth.. The breath of God which gave life made man become like God though subjugated on earth. We all should glorify God for giving us purpose, what he is doing for us, through several repeated lives and trials through our reincarnations a good soul doesn't die.

In the beginning, God created the Heavens and the earth as far as man should know

The earth was without form and was void, darkness was on the face of the deep, and the spirit of God was hovering over the face of the waters.

God made light and he was the light which he divided light from the darkness. He made the firmament in the meads of the water which he called Heavens.

He also made the sea and the land which he divided which brought out grass, herbs that yielded seeds and fruits.

He made the stars, the moon, and the sun.

He created the creatures living on land and sea and birds to fly on the air.

God saw that all was good and it did please God.

But it was written as quoted from King James version of the holy bible' God said [let Us} make man in our image, according to Our likeness let them have dominion over the sea, the birds in the air and over every living thing that move on the earth he made man out of the earth put his breathes in man to give him life, then he took from mans pound of flesh to create woman.

God made all things well is all, I would say as my reality and conscience tells me what more do I want for he had given me a privilege of being the architect of my own life praise be to God would all my prayers be to God almighty filled with songs of joy and thanks giving and this is what, I believe God wants out of me.

If you ask me why I am a schizophrenic and why had I put all these in writhing? I would answer am a schizophrenics because Jesus Christ said even if all living things stop to call my father's by his name, the stone of the earth, and the stones of the walls of the Church will call my father by his name giving him praise and thanks giving saying, there is none like the Lord God almighty.

Exodus:
God sends Quails as Manna
God gives the people water
God appointed judges
The Ten Commandments
I am thy Lord thy God who brought you out of the land and bondage you shall have no other God before me or any likeness of anything that is in haven you

shall not bow down to them or serve them for am thy Lord thy God am a [jealous] God and show mercy to those who love me and keep my commandments.

We shall not take the name of our God in vain.

Remember the Sabbath day to keep it Holy.

Honour thy mother and father that your days may be long in the land your Lord our God is giving to us.

We shall not murder.

We should not commit adultery.

We should not still.

We should not bear false wittiness against our neighbours.

We should not convert our neighbours house or things that belong to them.

And all the people witnessed the thundering, the light-ling flashes, the sounds of the trumpets, and the mounting smoking; and when the people saw it, they trembled and stood afar off.

What gives them to believe this as a reality am sure was less considered at the same times this happenings took place not only men and women of God's creation were being involved; but also Lucifer and his followers in particular and certain aspects of our lives that had before the happenings had cause to follow God or Lucifer and their own course.

For God gave life to men and all living things even if though today it has been discovered that plants breath the opposites ways as men breaths in oxygen and breath out carbon-dioxide but as to plants vice vases if, it entails our existence is finite, it is based on a cup we drink from in time the cup, will run over yet, all that is right would be fulfilled as contained in the cup.

What followed after the giving to the Ten Commandments according to the Holy Bible and also the Qumran accordingly

The treatment of servants

Responsibility for properties

The Lords Angels sent to lead Israel [but why!]

Moses and the Elders on Mount Sinai

The Ark of the testimony
The tabernacle
The Alter of the burnt offerings
Stopping at exodus how the priest where dressed.

The fourth book of Moses called NUMBERS stated with the first Census of Israel followed by the camps and leaders of the tribes, the numbers and duties of the Levite, Task assigned to the Levites the law concerning jealousy, the offering for the dedication of the Alter and on how the Passover is kept .est.

The Fiery Serpent Moses made a bronze serpent put it on a pole and so it was if a serpent had bitten anyone, when he looked at the bronze serpent he lived. In my relapse of what I recalled as a schizophrenic the serpent was not in any way to bring man and women to their down-fall it is said God created all things and had created all things well.

We humans through our existence have become very creative, in everything that has to do with our existence. I have course to believe men and women are the most God given grace ever given to human existence especially women.

What is it that has prompted me to be a celibate? A celibate is someone who had never had sex before or had had sex but do not want to have sex any more. In my life time I have witness ways we humans involve ourselves in many ways in what I would call immoral sexual acts. Why was Jesus Christ conceived by the Holy Spirit? What is it that has brought about the advent of surrogacy and cloning of humans I no longer believe in the male sperm not after, I have come this far moreover I was born premature I am a Seal.

I am not ashamed of being a paranoid schizophrenic I feel am a legion in perspectives of the good the bad and the ugly while the NHS and those who care for mental health patients are yet to understand that all legions seek one thing, deliverance or are in battle with something from the paranormal!

The inclination of this could be explained for example. In this computerize and digital age, all men and women should have identified themselves relay their genetic make-up; most have identified their moral code of conduct within themselves and with God who had created all things. If there are other gods or deities they bow down to a supreme deity who wants all that is of Lucifer and his fallen angles obliterated? This supreme deity we all know as God. Lucifer created problems in Heaven before we or our planet was created its one reason why we are here if other deities exist in order to do just and right within certain scenarios' they might have to cut corners to set things right. It's one reason why I am a celibate; I would rather prefer be a celibate than allow a creation of trillions to occur in human genetics make up mine would not comply with. I seek to identify my source and return to the source I emanate from.

I would rather prefer to be a frog shedding its skin to be replenished with a more suitable skin for survival. All scientific discoveries are first attached to our preliminary existence before it becomes developed. Who knows it might one day make me conducive if am reroute to earth once again through reincarnation to become one of the most rear-bread of humans in centuries to come. Life is choice we first of all make the choice before we become whatever, we are.

My grandfather from my father's side Mr. Gold-Pin Megbele was a devoted Christian faith of the celestial Church of Zion at Obonteghareda the name of my father's village in Delta state of Nigeria. Gold-Pin was a fisher-man, forth in the Nigerian Biafra war, later opened a chemist selling English medicines e.g. Epson salt, pain relief tablets and malaria medicine.

He had traditional tribal- mark on his face; he died in 1989 just after my arrival into the UK. He had obliterated the use of the grinding stone; he gave to my mother, by unplugging himself, because of his tribal marks. He had several straight line tribal marks on both his cheek. This was why I think he paid my mother a visit after I left Nigeria.

People should stop passing judgment about mental health sufferers it leads to stigmas which depolarise public users and providers; the book of the dead takes life while the book of the living gives life. Doctors' cares and social workers are there to cure, treat; and find solution to medical cure. Their involvement with patients should not lead to depolarisation.

If terminally ill people wish to take their own life with the consent of the government in relation to illnesses the government and NHS should not sullenly accept patients doing so though life is choice I recognise their freedom, individual should be free. Freedom is for all humans to the ends of all the corners of the earth to its thinnest details but is really the case. Nevertheless they should be advice to reconcile you might think you are doing badly but other people might be in a worse situation than you be careful you place is not easily taken by other people.

NHS staffs certainly know their rights and privileges for example NHS discount benefits since 2000 over 800,000 NHS staff save money through using employee benefits from NHS discount, they could shop online, print out vouchers, with free help services, booking of holiday, there are exclusive range of financial products such as bank accounts loans, insurance and mortgages services supporting reduced fee or cash incentives. Once staffs register, they are free to enjoy these benefits. They should not be taken by their service users taking their own lives because; it might mean they are no longer there.

There should have been thorough deliberation before it came this far; there is now a barrier within cares and patient relationship. The NHS might be privatised soon the issues involved should be looked at thoroughly if not taken too seriously, in time it might be tearing our communities apart. Deliberations are eminent they should not let their patients exile themselves from their services.

Freedoms have been granted to all human regardless if we experience a slave and a master relationship. Moral issues should be left for each man and women to decide. With regards to our environment and the recourses we are confronted with.

Plants and creatures are also waiting until our toils are over Heaven restored, to take its place and site. All things would remain that are right with God based on its need in Heaven. They would have a place for they have their own existence in relation for what God had created them for.

We just have to keep on trying, realising the purpose and full extent of the universe and its potentials. For some reason I think the illness schizophrenics is an illness, brought about by the effects of some related burden that are inconsistent through various inherencies through life incoherencies some of its anomalies are our own doing.

Our purpose in this world is to learn, understand, make amends for our right and wrong, become an entity, realise the concepts of existence of God the Author of all things this are why our existence is like the Greenwich housing authorities carrying out surveys if some council tenants should decide if they want private landlords, private owned companies should do the reaper service and own council properties.

Couldn't there be a means of compromise or peaceful measure of preventing the issues of conflict within the world's nation. Compromise, is a mixture of assertiveness and co-operation. Compromising individuals try to find mutual acceptable solutions, which result to both parties settling for something less than they really wanted. A compromise would address the issues involved more directly than an avoider, but not as mush in depth as a collaborator. Each party sacrifices something to end the conflict, or solve the problem.

The basis of a compromise is that a half a loaf of bread is better than none, which, I would use in describing one who shows concern but regarded as slow in action but moving towards a considerate action, since it involves that direct confrontation on the issue involved, is avoided and the issue are smoothed over in order to restore harmony.

Compromise brings temporary peace if steps are move in the right direction in facing the issue. It has a means of conflict resolution since, it is not very easy to handle conflict but using positive step by not avoiding the issue is right in conflict resolution

Compromise is usually bad; it should be a last resort. Excessive use of compromise stifles people or strangles might strangle situations.

People are often aware of conflicts if, they had been the responsible part and had put much effort in the issue with regards to contribution or efforts even if slowed or strangled in their efforts would always place his or her place solid with regards to accountability to be the winner to make everything work for the better. It would lead to assertiveness and co-operation.

An avoider pretends the conflict do not exist, repeated denial often leads to psychosomatic illness and other forms of psychological distress. Avoidance undermines a relationship and would lead to bleak, chilly distance. Premature forgiveness is one way of avoiding conflict I hope one would not confused being ambitious rather just avoiding conflict.

Avoiding conflict is a style which is appropriate occasionally but if repeatedly used, one may end up isolated. It is sometimes necessary to avoid conflict temporarily because of lack of information or bad timing. A person who don't want to be an avoider goes his or her own way to make friends, making others follow their ways which in some cases if not coursing, would lead to anti-social behaviour.

Competing style is often used by a person who is assertive, but considered as un-co-operative. Such a person tends to impose his solution on the other; he pursues his needs at the expense of the other person involved. He or she makes use of power strategies to achieve their objectives. Such strategies include the use of position, coercive measures, threats, or ability to argue.

An individual who tends to compete generally think they are standing up for their rights and are not always aware of the resentment they elicit from others i.e. emotional distance, and other destructive ways of striking back. A competing style may at times be necessary when quick decisive action is required, or when important, but unpopular action has to be taken.

Over-reliance on this style may cause sabotage, pilferage, work stoppage, passive resistance.

Accommodating may show too little concern for personal goals; this usually leads to a lack of influence and recognition. On the positive side, the accommodating style can be used in case where it is very important to maintain harmony. It can also be used in less important issues time is wasted and there are also struggles it's a sure way of being accommodating in resolving conflict. Allowing the other person the experience of winning, he may be more receptive when a more important issue arises.

An individual who is unassertive but co-operative will usually be accommodating in his style, his own concerns or needs are neglected in order to meet the goals or concerns of the other party or parties involved depending on needs if their needs to some extent is satisfied they borderless.

Being collaborative he or she is assertive and co-operative, they constitute the opposite of the avoiding style, and they try to work with each other until a solution is reached that satisfies the needs and concern of both parties.

For it to be effective, each party has to identify his or her underlying concerns, explore alternatives that are compatible, discloses a considerable amount of information. This means that there could be certain degree of trust between both parties.

Collaborative may include analysis of the disagreement to learn from the problem. This is usually a win-win way of dealing with conflicting needs. The collaborative way proves to be the most desirable style and the method that can be most often used can resolving conflicts.

Collaborating style enables consensus to take place and not merely a compromise. Consensus is defined as a decision participated in by all members of a group. Acceptance does not imply agreement; one may accept a decision as the best obtainable in that particular situation. An agreement is reached and the parties involve are reasonably happy with the final decision as no one's goals had to be sacrificed in the process.

In collaboration conflict is depersonalized and the emphasis is mainly on problem solving. No one is defeated. The goals, opinion, attitudes, and feelings of both parties are respected and accepted.

Whichever style of conflict resolution style we us in resolving conflict, these might be put into use because it contribute effectively whilst we are using the five conflict resolution style.

1. Active listening
2. Making assertive statements
3. The avoidance or use of fewer roadblocks
4. Effective tension release skills and methods
5. Increased tolerance and acceptance of others
6. They would be good at giving emotional support.
7. Being assertive
8. Ready to listen to avoid conflict

Bearing in mind people spend 24% of their time dealing with conflict of some kind e.g. intra- and interpersonal conflicts which could result in friction, wasted time, ill feeling, bitter divorces, bickering and back-biting.

I do enjoy some constructive criticism as far as the attitude used and implication of the criticism does not imply the other party is always displaying falsehood in being good, never in the wrong and never to be criticised. No one can be that perfect; moreover people will notice and quickly get fed-up with them.

In such cases, there are motives behind intentions of such individuals e.g. they are seeking a favour from someone else, before the end of such epilogues', people close to them might feel socially withdrawn, never too close or collaborative if conflicts of any kind should arise. Because they are faced with some incoherencies e.g. disbelief, surprise, shock, or taken aback because of the outcome of the situation. At the end of the day, one of the parties is likely to feel he or she had been betrayed.

A British old lady would go to jail for not paying her council tax bill, considering from her childhood she knows what life in England had been from her background she, her parents and grandparent had gone through a lot.

Most of such old ladies have contributed a lot into the UK I consider it most unappealing under any government should an old lady in any circumstances, especially an old pensioner go to jail for not paying her council tax. She should pay sending her to jail is too much to bear.

I am about to complete another 20 years of my life in the UK. Since 1995 to 2008, because of my illness, I could be on housing benefit, disability, incapacity benefit I just felt I should work with my job as a part time cleaner.

Prior to my arriving into this country my late father gave me money as bonus, I wanted to buy a television but, the amount was not enough. I had to go less for buying a radio, cassette recorder immediately in Nigeria radio licence was imposed or pay a fine or have your property confiscated.

One morning at work I told Mr. Joseph Olatunji my co-worker, how I felt about this lady who could not pay her council tax, and she was ready to go to jail. I told Mr. Joseph; you and I had been in this country, working for the same company before council tax was imposed have we ever paid council tax his reply was no we haven't.

1st May 2010 just five days before the general election the Conservative party policy pledge on pension are to restore link between the state pension and earning by 2012 and increase pension credit in line with earning.

To continue giving older people winter fuel payment, concessionary public and transport fares free eye test and prescription including free TV licence for the over 75. They would look at ways to abolish the default retirement age.

They would require employers to automatically enrol employees into either an in-house pension scheme or state pension account scheme. Give older people right to request flexible working hours if, they wish to look after grandchildren. And enable people aged 60 and over, claim working tax credit if they work at least 16 hours a week down from 30 hours.

This pledge by the Conservative is no different from the Labour party except that the Labour party would restore the link between the state pension and earning by 2012 and increase pension credit in line with earnings.

On this same day it was on the news people in the UK are facing a higher risk of early death than those in many other wealthy countries. It says while death before the age of 60 in the UK have nearly halved in the past 40 years as the rate for women remains similar to Slovenia and Albania.
Couple with these issues, it could be asked is Britain a land of promise if such an old lady should be sent to jail for not paying her council tax? Dose it signifies the UK and the rest of the EU as a place full of promise. Any way I do like them because they are people who, could enjoy some constructive criticisms otherwise, I would not be in a position to ask such questions.

There are people in the U.K who claim benefit for the rest of their lives, claim NHS treatment and prescription, A disable person could not only travel out of the U.K for family visit or occasions but some of them could drive a vehicle if, they are not wheel chairs users, the government should keep up the good work. At early and middle stage to my coming back to the UK I experience people with physical disabilities drive a car, go to work the present stance of immigration have change this it seems some people are happy when one cannot work. A schizophrenia cannot look good I mean for example well dressed at the same time not be a benefit cheat who are the people turning this country around from a place of love to hat?

- How do submarines get into water and emerge out of water while at sea?
- How do divers go below the see?
- There are many makes, brands of motor vehicles
- A West African god Shungo was the god of thunder and light lighting
- Ogun was the god of metal
- While Orunmila was patience, meekness, respect and power to achieve great intentions
- There are many food chains store in the U.K I worked at Iceland frozen food company
- I worked at B&Q Corydon
- I worked for Shell BP
- I worked at a brick making factory
- Now I work as a cleaner, a deputy cleaning supervisor and key holder
- My site of work, is an enlisted building
- My father was a middle class a managing director of a stevedoring shipping company in Delta state and Rivers state Nigeria
- Within the 1960 lots of vehicles where brought into Nigeria I was born close at this time
- Immediately in 1966 my father went back to Nigeria one of the first brand of cars was purchased by him a Renault wisely vehicle
- The present supervisor Mrs. Janet Clerk and her mother with her daughters work at the club. I and Janet's and her first daughter Joan Clark's birthday falls on the month of July.

I have the notion Miss Michelle Cook my co-worker at Iceland frozen food store in 1990 is the reincarnated of my father's mother, while Miss Joan Keeble first daughter of Ms Janet Clerk my supervisor at the Woolwich Gala club is the reincarnation of my grandmother, from my mothers' side. Both Miss Michelle and Miss Joan Keeble are of white English origin.

At the time I knew Michelle she was the only daughter of her parents within brothers she had, she showed me pictures of her mother and brothers when we were on one of our tea break.

Miss Michelle Cook before her reincarnation apart from my father had other children who were Miss. Sola Akinlami now Mrs. Tycos-lawson, Mr. Tamitayo Akinlami, Miss. Dake Akinlami now Mrs. Majekodunmi and Miss. Lanre Akinlami now Mrs. Charles. She was known as Mrs. Awoma Akinlami. Her origin was mixed British and African from my fathers' origin of Delta state Nigeria.

Early this morning 29th June 2006, I became unwell thinking of how, I would manage to wake-up each morning for work my illness had become worse.

I spoke to my eldest sister Mrs. Oritsegbubemi Ajagunla on this same day 29th July 2006 because; she had phoned me just after work on my way to W.H.Smith at Woolwich.
I told my sister, about my relationship with my immediate elder brother Mr. Omagbemi, the same thing I told Mr. Harry on the telephone and the effect of our relationship is getting worse than I expected. I had become too unwell to a stage I had not been able to visit Mr. Harry Gordon Slade as I used to.

One has to make a choice. We all have believes and knowledge of insight of what we want each and every one of us contemplating within ourselves reaching out from our soul towards higher level.

As long as this goes on regardless of pain and suffering Zion will not fall there is no better deal than this. The earth, the universe and all that is in it, are nothing but for a cry, each and every one of us to be the architects of our own lives. I frequently have hallucinations that I had seen myself die, I have watched myself die several different times until I cannot die, after each death, I go into oblivion remembering nothing, but all of a sudden, I rise again.

4th July 2006, space shuttle took off from Cape Canaveral into space the time is 8.30 pm as I washed it on television I contemplated on what happened that today at work, there was a torrential rain fall with thunder storm the Club was partly flooded preventions had to be taken to protect some of our cleaning materials, Mr. Amos did not turn up for work it was Daniela who turned up both of us had to do the job of three people which extended our working hours for the day on our afternoon job by one hour working time at our cleaning job at the Woolwich Gala Bingo Club.

Staff's of the Club Ms Mary Bright, duty manager, Cathy the current manager, Anthony and Sara's mum, with new vacuum and dryer Hoover had to be bought to tackle the inflow of rain water into the premise resulting to flooding which had been coursed by a blockage outside the premises drainage system.

At this time our company was looking forward to renew its contract with the Club, would the club have a chance our company is now a specialised notable and respectable cleaning services provider all over Europe. In fact the best in the whole of Europe if, they don't give it to us, they would be the one who lose out such as giving their contract to companies with less calibre and prestige.

I did not sleep one wink at night coming back from work, I went down to Erith looking out for Miss Loraine O'Connor if she was back at her flat in Erith, Before going out on my afternoon job I have had vision and illusion of hope that I and Loraine, would one day meet again in the future.

God gave Lucifer powers which were second only to God's powers. I was keen on my meditation to ascertain why those below power second to none, always want to attain more powers above those who have granted them authority when, they should be best of friends.

This was what happened with Lucifer and God in Heaven. It was Lucifer who carries out Gods commands, for this reason, many were below Lucifer, those who were below Lucifer, always seeking Lucifer's advice to carry out Heavens activities.

From my hallucinations, Lucifer began wondering where God got his powers from, and his week points where, God did many wondrous things, and deeds which amazed Lucifer and those below him.

It was not jealousy at first it was amazement but instead of bowing his head low before God, Lucifer pushed forward with an intuitions to go against God as if go on, Lucifer I am, I have powers and authority as well, Lucifer was of the opinion he, could do what God can do as well!

God knew all things, knowing where all things are placed in order or if things where not in order, knowing where mistakes could go wrong and if things could go wrong Lucifer went against God.

The alternatives God took, was to initiate the concept of as it is in Heaven from that time so it would be on earth. Gog looked for settlement that all in Heaven would understand him. Lucifer was cast down, since many chose to follow Lucifer, a great augment and conflict began.

Who could really say he or she has found the true meaning of trust in their lives since time began and in 21st century, very few. I have not found trust rather bewilderment at the rate of conflicts.

We have lessons to lean be tolerant about our ways of life and interaction, business, politics, administration and family life. We would keep the incident of slavery out of it, because all parts of the world have been under slavery at one time or another.

God trusted Lucifer, if things should turn round, there are ways of making dose who wanted to stick with God or, those who wanted to go on with, their disobedient with God understand, there would be no other powers greater, than that of God . Then, God created the earth and established the universe.

So that we those who chose to follow God, the angels, archangels, which we all as humans on earth are, would learn lesson through our own initiatives, through toils, pain and sufferings, thereby resolving through nature, he created all things on earth, for us to be self sufficient and reconcile to live and abide with God in peace until whenever protocol of Heaven is revealed that the conquest have been accomplished.

We would be ready having felt the effects of conflict would readily ovoid conflicts' for those who are ready taking up such initiatives in time; God and their quest would disarm conflict and suffering.
We might feel, we have been left in the hands of evil i.e. juju, witchcraft, worshiping the devil and all sorts of immoral act and so on. When Lucifer and the fallen angels, went on an uprising against God, it was a time when Heaven was established and was ready to stand on its footstool, invariably to stand on its feet as established it was about to be a time for celebration and thanks giving.

We had not been schooled or have experience to know right from wrong before times of creation, we had form we were not shedding blood we have to be put in a situation we would disregard evil to the very best, acknowledge God as author of Heaven and creation. Every one, the angels who are on this very day, still comes to earth to see that Heavens wish from the beginning is fulfilled to its defined purpose.

Though humans we were the same as who we were in Heaven since its very beginning. On earth, we are left as humans, to count the centuries, know the numbers of our hair, the blood that runs through our veins, knowing what happiness and sadness could be, pain and sorrow, knowing the reward of lies and truth so that, we would no longer be disobedient at any other time any more towards our existence, this is why, as it is in Heaven so it is on earth.

As I saw it in my hallucinations, several nights, it was as if, I was half asleep and half awake. Lucifer felt he had authority over many he could turn against God that he might become Like God, There were many who backed Lucifer up, If they seems to be in my hallucinations, a light flashes on them, their image, crashes or disappears.. .

Lucifer went to God and said I know not my father or mother , my powers and the rod you have given me is still with me, everything is still with me as it was from the beginning so what is there I do not have to make me be like you.

God said to him you are stupid. As God said these words, pronouncing the word stupid, he sparked at Lucifer. As he sparked at Lucifer it touched Lucifer like thunder and lightning, Lucifer no longer had form of who he was becoming something I would describe as stalagmites and stalactite Lucifer had a fit so did all his followers.

Lucifer and his followers began to melt like liquid dripping down to earth. It came down in colours like images.

Some of the faces I saw try to make gesture at me, but can't move their bodies. I perceived it as if it was all happening in the ice age, God then realised that this phenomenon had also taken over the Heavens. God had no intention of killing or destroying him at the time he rather, would educate him with what had been granted to him from heaven on earth.

This is what had resulted to the computer age, technology, cars, and industries. For then I question the form and origin of life that could have resulted to the pharmaceutical industries as a form of medicine and I wonder at what evil that has taken the whole forms of life. The feeling I had was if earth would come to an end, it would result that all things will subsume. All will not be lost we would encounter life we had lived before they would not be illusions.

God created the earth the stars, the planets and all that is in it i.e. the day the night and every living creatures I had a feeling God would not had created one man to be another man's slave rather, we are rather slaves to evil for as it was recorded in the bible everything was good and beautiful when God created the world..

If all these have happened in Heaven after God created all things from the way I see it did the serpent really tempted man to sin against God than Lucifer and those who felt they would be like God fell.

If they have chosen their own ways to rebelled against God, it was left for the serpent to say we humans God had created after such troubled times in Heaven should become like God, knowing well from evil.

I implied nothing was wrong about Adam and Eve eating from the forbidden fruit, for them to be like God not really like God, but knowing right from wrong. There are two perspectives to this predicament. It's either each of us, eat from the forbidden fruit, discerning right from wrong, by following God's own laws and commands, to remain blessed. It is my belief in time probably in space or another planet we would one day, find a peculiar fruit we would eat from through which for those who, have undergone their trials would wipe-out sin suffering illness and pain and all, we have been going through are not, for nothing.

If one cannot discern right from wrong, choosing to do evil, is for one to perish, without form, to be banished with Lucifer, Satan and the devil, who are already, without form or shape as they once were. It is time; realisation struck us about our faith on planet earth. Consider how long we have been one earth, with so much trouble, destructions, neglect, and disobedience on God's laws and commandments? We are all on earth to make a choice.

What led to the universe being created while men and women continue to live in a planet going through evolutions that man can learn and understand the concepts of God and his creation in a world of our own, where there is beauty, death and ugliness? I always have the feeling I had lived many lives to put myself at peace and within Gods concept in a whole universal creation of our God the architect of the universe.

Immediately Lucifer and his followers were called stupid he fell with the rod still holding the rod right from Heaven to earth, including all those who opposed God and the Heavens. Those who had feelings everything was perfect with them in Heaven so peaceful that, they chose not to question Gods order and authority did not fall realising that no one there defies God.

The word stupid followed those who defied God and his authority, they and their regalia's began to tricking down to earth. When earth was created it was to take another form of Heaven it became a place where all, who were involved would be called upon to face good and evil trials of life experience of the Garden of Eden is to remind us that we were holy when God created man but for the stalactite and stalagmite of Lucifer and his followers trickling down from heaven and their shouts for help we had to eat from the forbidden fruit to become like God knowing right and wrong to undergo trials we know how the evil going on in this world is manifest with our actions and deeds how it sometimes turn to something we ourselves cannot tolerate how far do we address ourselves in correlating ourselves against evil some of us in such respect have been called worse names like the Devil or with sinful words yet we are humans we know of being inhuman, dehumanisation should such word be used based on our behalf? We humans and Gods creation are now more blessed and powerful above Lucifer who remains to be educated suffering and pain is to close our eyes through ages past and consider God who we cannot see but go through all sorts of emotions and feelings that he is with us and had created all things. We are using Lucifer and his followers on a process of recreation we generate electricity, use fuel, science, spiritual gifting to power our course. May be one day a radio, television among other things would be capable of being powered for our use in heaven. Because of troubleshooting a man took his computer out and short it with a gun it doesn't all that sounds funny how many times had anyone bought and used several washing machine at on stage you felt you have bought the one compatible to you it checks you mood, timing of washing or gives you information or phenomena's of when it's about to complete a cycle wash with you having an huge of going out to do something or your TV knows when to tell you, to turn it on. I do not know if it's just me the world and everything in it seems to be in motion where every feelings count or have meaning but not all of them would be counted as meaningful.

Only God had overcome evil since earth's creation, or would God in the process of his creation accomplish all good knowing what was right, that he is all magnificent, we humans and all things are in such process as well because, we were all created in is image.
It was when the form of Satan and his followers began trickling down to earth though, it had no form, and the serpent besieged the law by tempting the woman called Eve to eat from the forbidden fruit. There is destruction in the animal kingdom, all creatures, as well stand the test of time and trials.

It was to be the evolution of man and woman who where also, the same host of Heaven to have dominion on earth, over all things with inclination as well to stand their test of time through trials. Those who do right, obeying Gods laws and commandments would be called upon into the celestial Heavens to wait until his kingdom comes by which time the form of Lucifer and his followers would have drained out of the heavenly bodies.

When Satan observed what God had done, Satan knew that God no longer deserve him, he chose to ruin man, because he observed man and all creation he would make the earth his own.

God told Satan you have disobeyed me, you seek to set yourself too high against me. You ought to have been more than friends with me, I don't deserve you.

The serpent is poisonous though not all snakes, when it bits, it could be poisonous and deadly, the way of preventing a person from immediate death from a snake bit is to inject it's gland into the person or to suck out the poison.

The mass of Lucifer, Satan and the Devil form and his followers when cast down became what I define as stalagmites found in caves. It had to be got ride off from Heaven from my hallucination, the gland and poison in a snake was better than what Lucifer had to offer.

It stood out shapeless without form, it was like what I read and saw in my secondary school days in geography class of stalactite and stalagmites in a cave in regions of the world. I thought to myself it could be the reason, why we humans are different in colours, race and creed it means we are searching for God the architect of the Universe, we are meant to search and on earth we would know who God and ourselves are!

How many times had you been some where before, you felt, you had been there before. You have seen a person for the first time; you have had feelings you known that person before, in some cases on one part of the world or another such realistic feelings might be true in once sub-consciousness.

It could be a feeling, yet it could be one can be certain they have come in contact with the person in their past. These same effects can result with furniture, a product, or technology as if; one was part of it before. Whatever gives me impression I was before television was made or that I had taken part in what brought television about. I don't know why, I have such feelings, but they are feelings I always have. I do have then about movies, dreamers, and films.

In my relapses as I lay in bed, a song I knew began ringing in my head and thoughts... O praise to the lord the almighty the King of creation O my soul praise him for he is thy health and salvation come ye who are here brothers and sister draw near praise him in glade adoration,

Praise the Lord who o'er all things so wondrously reigneth shelter thee under his wings yea so gently sustaineth hast thou not seen? All that is needful hath been granted in what he ordained.

Praise to the Lord who doth prosper thy work and defend thee surely his goodness and mercy here daily attend thee ponder anew all the almighty can do he who with love doth befriend him.

Praise to the lord! O let all that is in me adores him! All that hath life and breath come now with praises before him let the amen sound from his people again! Gladly for aye we adore him.

J, Neander 1650-80
Tr. C Wink worth 1827-78
And P. Dearmer 1867-1936

And another hymn also followed it was as if, there was a procession going on around me and I was part of it.
O worship the king all glorious above O gratefully Sing his power and his love our shield and defender the ancient of the days pavilion in splendour and girded with praise.

O tell of his might O sing of his praise whose rob is the light whose canopy space His chariots of wrath the deep thunder-clouds from and dark is his path on the wing of the storm.

This earth with its store of wonders untold almighty thy power hath founded of old hath established it fast by a changeless decree and round it hath cast like a mantle the sea.
Thy bountiful care what tongue can recite? It breaths in the air it shines in the light it streams from the hills, it descends to the plain and sweetly distils in the dew and the rain.

O measureless Might ineffable love while angels delight to hymn thee above thy humbler creation though feeble their lays with true adoration shall sing to thy praise.

Robert Grant 1779-1838

I remembered when got up from the slumber, it was as if everything around me was not in order my bed, the television, my carpets and chair all I realised later in the day, was that I began re-arranging my bed rooms, living room and my furniture's.

In my relapse, I shook, it was if, I was in my body but was not in my body I woke up more whole, light headed. It was as if, there was a big round hole in my whole being, serials of shiver runs through me. I remembered at this time, I was asking myself, why I was seeing these things, or heard voices.

We humans from every race and creed are all attached to all creatures, plant, minerals and metals, derived from earth and much more from other planets, wind, and fire. We could be vegetarians, carnivorous or herbivorous in our feeding habits. Did all these come from my own imagination? Moreover, human horoscopes are symbolised with certain creatures.

31st July 2008 water have been found in the planet mars. Water on Mars exists today almost exclusively as ice, with a small amount present in the atmosphere as vapour. The only place where water ice is visible at the surface is at the north polar ice cap.

I hallucinated during these periods It was as if my eyes were open to see planet mars a swan appeared from nowhere to have a swim and flex itself on the water on mars and latter shoot off further higher into the sky.

The hardest thing I ever do is keep believing that through temporary lives, there is some where special for everyone after our trials of life. Life on earth is not always a merry go round, it has purpose.

Developments, technology, or spiritual attainment, everything is for the architectural purpose and attainment for man by the end we would satisfy our souls in relation to our quest which has already been programmed on our behalf. The stronger we are in facing our reality each day of our lives, before we are called to an even higher sanctuary e.g. Paradise or Heaven, the better for us.

This earth and the universe have existed for so long, that at these stages of our existences, the less we seems to realise the wonders of God in relation to our existence. We should by now know why we are on earth, as our number one IQ. Information are out there to capture our interest we do not spend time considering.

For many of the elites in our communities it's all about how do they get more wealthy there is nothing wrong with it because it goes into deeper reality based on synergy in which we learn more about each other what is good or bad, whatever is conducive or not, it gives us purpose.

We do not just have government and elites in our communities we make them, infarct they are in a position, where they also can be used? We are all here to shape our destiny take it or leave it being gay, a lesbian, homosexual, a celibate, transsexual, illnesses, gain or loss within which comes different revelations that coincides with our existence our beliefs, culture and heritage. Why do we leave such notions as irrelevant? Centuries ago if a person is found to be a witch he or she would be burnt alive we have been somewhat living extroversion lives there is nothing wrong about it infarct it not only calls but lead to a change or direction to our destination. We are now living in a world where one person cannot judge another we are waiting for realities based on our existence.

For example when Moses showed Remises the Pharaohs father after he had built the city by Goshen, the Niles, and Cateress see he said to his son Remises and those around him as he exclaim in wonder magnificent, superb, 'Moses you have done well'. But it no longer coincides with Pharaoh when he discovered Moses was a levy an Israelite such are the same trilogy we under go on earth, until our work is done on earth for Heaven sake.

As for you or me, who think we are down-trodden, we must have something of ourselves to show for our existence that demonstrate our wiliness to have under gone life with suffering, kind of a way to be subjugated for example if am unwell, but can work with my illness, regardless of a welfare state, should I work or should I not work; If I can work, but do not work, it would be the same thing as stealing suffering cannot all that be a bad thing I am not saying it is a good thing for people to suffer, it adds to why humans are useful and creative. If you or I do not want to be subjugated we follow our own wimps or hid behind other people's integrity or do the will of God.

Human creativity have to some extent, created a true feelings of reality towards our destiny, we have been extricating from earth as it had been going on in heaven the demonic myth's of Lucifer, Satan and the Devil which have been right from time immemorial.

Yet human nature and awareness persist into the 21st century to our spiritual consciousness that Planet earth is subsuming drastically. No! Not yet, the world is not about to end, it would only subsume gradually am not afraid infarct after such events that would gradually free the world of evil then I would begin to live. Within 2006 to 2009 several astronaut have gone on space mission to various planets to search for other planet such as earth.

All hands are not equal but everything has its purpose and usefulness to each one of us, it could only take time, to circulate, at the end, would depict through our realisation that God really exist. If we could have been able to see God, we would have been less productive.

Think of earth as it was hundred of centuries ago and take a look at it now we have achieved a lot in respect of being creative. If God is hidden from our eye's he had given us hope and grace through our religion with faith, our courage to re-new our self to a new birth, gain and desire and a commitment to do right and not wrong. We have been subjected to doing right rather than wrong, when can it come to a stage of awareness that humans could be in control of everything in this planet, but only subjected to God the architect of the universe who has made man more than sufficient yet we have more to look up to regardless if since 1998 we have been shaken not steered with chaos and conflicts on all corners of planet earth.

He will unveil himself to us when our trials are over, and we would realise that God also had, work to be done, since when Lucifer was cast down from Heaven God knew after is creation of the universe and humans, the works of our hands and experience of what we have gone through would shape us, would have made men who had thoroughly under gone their trials irreplaceable to have and cherish a place in Heaven.

Man, no matter how great you are, you have been conceived by a woman, does it make you a human being, more powerful or relevant than a woman. As great as any man can be he had been conceived by a woman.

Some women are so powerful, not only with wealth, but with beauty, charismas, some women are a Devin sanctuary, straight to the point, they rule men and men do not rule them, they over rides every wimp's of so called great men.

Consider the rolls of women in this 21st century Monday 9th March 2009 1 in 5 says it is OK to slap women during crackdown on domestic violence aftershock surveys written by deputy political editor of the Sun news paper by Graeme Wilson. This article was attached with a picture of MP of the home secretary Jacqui Smith. The information on the article came after, MP Jacqui Smith ground breaking crusade to stop violence against women.

Religion, culture, tradition, and customs such issues should be based on reality. The creation of robotics in sciences could make some humans feel insecure, as for some of us, we are slaves to our desires at certain times in our lives it becomes clearer it's our desire that drive us!

Jesus Christ during his crucifixion cried out three times father, father, father, why had thou forsaken me. It was at this stage we all as one time already part and parcel of Heaven, become bona-fide citizens of earth after creation, we were not casted out from Heaven, through our rebirth to earth with commitment to live benevolent existence. the clouds, thunders, the firmament shaking above the skies, the rain that followed after the crucifixion of Jesus Christ, was for protocol Heaven should be made void a new beginning was about to start in Heaven and on earth the remains of Lucifer and his fallen Angels were cast out of Heaven to demonstrate as it was in Heaven so it is on earth or how come have we come this far it is the purpose that drives us if there could be no other route, we are likely to be sub-sceptical to conflict, suffering or condemnation.

It was recorded that Christ had no children recently it was contradicted by the Van dice-cod. If what the Da Vinci Code says is true, then the thunder-lightning, the earth checking and a voice saying this is my son with who am well pleased, identifies us all as the children of God. He knew he was going to die for our salvation and now, some say he had children, he had children and he said father forgive them they no, not what they are doing. If through Christ we are born again would it not give us the grace through his risen life and the blood he sheared for all lead to our salvation, not to live our lives in our own wimps but through the grace of God.

It becomes practical for us, having an understanding just as God under takes any venture on our behalf, so dose Lucifer and his fallen angels proceeds with their own undertaking, with the same precision having the ability to know right from wrong yet we still go into temptation or how come do schizophrenias hear voices to harm themselves? Certain aspects of human lives call for a deeper realisation of temptation to understand this phenomenon as schizophrenia, with such coincidence related to our illness, we must strive at the same time to be the master of our souls.

Trial is a very pleasant topic whether we like it or not, if we want to face up to its reality, every one of us will have to face a certain amount of trials and tribulations as we journey through life with no exceptions to its faith.

Unless we have full understanding as to why certain bad things happen in our world.

I believe one can learn to keep some of the adversity that may strike us in this life at a minimal if we learn and try to properly plead with our existence and endeavors'.

We have to learn how to become good soldiers then we can either keep a lot of storm and clouds from hitting us in the first place, or can quickly defeat them once they do come knocking at our door.

As a result of living in this world of conflicts the best of true soldiers will still have to face a certain amount of conflict and adversity from time to time. There is simply no getting away from it. Until we get the New Heaven and the New Earth, the curse of Lucifer will still continue to stay in place on this earth, and as a result, we will all have to face a certain amount of storm, clouds in this life with no exceptions to the cold, hard, brutal fact of their reality.

What gets many of us in trouble in this part of our walk is not having full understanding as to why this has to happen to us in the first place, at the same time, believing in God who is supposed to be all good, all loving, and all merciful.

Question many of us ask when we are hit with any kind of a trial and tribulation is why? How can an all-good and an all-loving God allow me or someone else close to me gets hit with such a severe trial or tragedy? How can God allow some of his own, especially the ones who are faithfully serving him, get hit by something that at times will literally come right out of the pit of hell itself?

If God is our true Heavenly and loving father who has nothing but our best interests at heart, then how can he allow some kinds of things to happen in our ways of life?

I could go on and on with some of the severe adversity that can hit anyone of us at anytime. No one on this earth is perfectly safe and immune from all of the different kinds of storm, clouds that can come our way.

When you really stop and think about this, and look back on some of the pure evil that a certain amount of people will have to face in this life, it is only natural to wonder how God himself could allow some of these bad things to happen.

How can God just sit up there and watch if he is all powerful, and there is nothing he cannot do, he superiorly operates on this earth, then why doesn't he protect more of his own from having to deal with some of these kinds of heavier trials and tribulations?

Why God allowed some of these trials and tribulations to come our way in the first place are for us, to become stronger and realistic.

Trials, tribulations, conflicts, and adversities are all a part of our lives and all a part of our walk with the Lord. As such, this should be something that should be talked about and taught on so the flock can be properly prepared and equipped to handle any kind of adversity that may come knocking on their doors no matter how uncomfortable this topic may make us feel.

There must be certain reasons why we have to face a certain amount of trials and tribulations in this life.

Distress or suffering that severely tests resiliency and character: no consolation in their hour of trial; the affliction of a bereaved family; the crucible of revolution; the ordeal of being an innocent murder suspect; a time of relentless tribulation. Great affliction, trial, or distress; suffering and tribulation would finally pass.

An experience that tests one's endurance, patience, or faith in God why are we born as babies, grow up, go to school, work the concepts are in our every way of life.

The natural response when faced with a situation that is unpleasant is to want that situation removed. If there is something that is causing you pain, you want that pain removed. It is natural.

However, according to the Bible, trials come into our lives to strengthen us. Trials are for our own good. We should not want them removed simply because they are unpleasant. We should bear them in faith, and seek God's wisdom to learn whatever God is trying to teach us during the trial.

Trials cause us to learn things which we could not learn otherwise we are extremely stubborn sometimes. Trials give us experience that back up our knowledge, and trials help us retain knowledge in a way that is unique and special.

Trials cause us to cling to the world and not its displeasures.

Trials cause us to be more useful to others experience is a great teacher, and it helps us to be sympathetic to others who go through it as well. The Scripture has a very interesting perspective on the problems we suffer in life. In other words, it should come as no surprise that if Jesus Christ, the Son of the Living, All Powerful God, suffered insults; criticism, injustice and death, then those of us who follow him are going to suffer, too. And just like Jesus, who arose from the dead in all his glory with nothing more than his scars to worry about, then we, too, can rest on the fact that our present suffering won't last forever we'll have relief on earth. If this doesn't seem to address the matter of those who suffer or have no religion it is about our existence.

There could be no pride in any one going about, attesting to his or her own existents that they live with pride being celibate's there is misgiving involved, in such a circumstances, there could be conflicts involved, or it is a process to correct some abnormalities. The sad story is that they are rather faced with prejudice, which shouldn't be the case.

If an individual chooses to be a celibate, or to commit their lives to euthanasia, surrogacy or the cloning of humans rather than such people being met with prejudice, questions should be asked they are as a result and causation of abnormalities related to our existence.

Considering most illnesses and some of our life experiences related to conflicts in certain cases do not permit us to live our lives the way we want to within ourselves and other people.

My parent's including step mother, brother, sister', uncles, aunties, niece, nephews, cosines could use me as whatever! If they wish, Africa is filled with rows and conflicts, which never subside each day, with conflicts that are unnecessary.

In Africa, we not only quarrel and fight all the time; it is common for each individual entering one or two misunderstandings. I appreciate Europeans involvement with Africa, especially the British and Americans relationship with third world countries, the reason and benefit are not far from realisation if not why do we choose to come here as immigrants though to some of us coming here we do not want to face reality, yet we are escaping from something.
Africa has changed over the years compared to what it was centuries ago in relation to our origin and history though we had been heady about change from the start but we should by now realise we have to change in line as the rest of the world change means progress and development.

It's not that we would lose our original conceptualization of life in relation to our origin and history; the effects are not farfetched, if one could observe most third world countries from its beginning to the present, things have changed. All that needs to be done is some home work with the right people holding military or political power. Third world countries have to come up with leaders, who have dreams.

Leaders who would thoroughly observe third world nations with pride at all level such as family relationship for example all head of African parents are god in their own right, culture; history, norms and religion have faculties. In the UK I cannot only make choices, I apply them to most experience and feelings of what I should do and not do based on my trials of life in facing life inconsistencies, and incoherencies.

Which does not overrule that my life in the UK has no bearing with some abnormalities, who says any one could have everything they want out of life? This is what drives us humans and give us purpose. Infarct residing in the UK I am still much attached with my African background. One thing am really enjoying, is freedom.

As an African British through naturalisation, I welcome everything that is happening to me with insight, I never chose to be born in the UK through my own wimp or caprice I was born here for a reason, of which, I see a basis of great insight, vision of the world to come in writing this book which started as diaries of a schizophrenia and saga of a Schizophrenic.

With my illness as paranoid schizophrenia having the tendency to under-go sudden unpredictable changes of attitudes and behaviours e.g. personality disorder, This capricious nature, coupled with my illness as a paranoid schizophrenia, within the month of May 2007 and April 2009 because of an era of the British economy, conflicts around the world, difficulty coping with my illness I became opinionated my illness had became worse but not in a state of calling anyone a monkey.

Every individual from all ethnic origin in the UK should be problem solvers within their own origin and within the UK. Because they also have problems of their own, regardless of this, Britain dose all it can to help other developing countries. Underlining questions are is it the same way these developing nations feel about themselves? They have wider audience because of their interaction expressing their own views aloud on a wider contest to the rest of the world. This had been the case since they have room for progress and development?

In some part of the world in some cases no one cares if you die, face an accident on the road, or you cannot fend for yourself to have one square meal a day? The scenarios is from the top to the bottom they are being sent out to still, if you have no food while there is someone who could provide you food for one day to do a favour even if it's to kill one might be obliged.

The press in Africa always have nothing bad to say about the wealthy members of the communities or the government of African countries regardless if they do, they are somehow connected to be part of it. They would only come out with stories if they would gain out of it the situation is changing.

There are little or no government stroke the general public of African views in leading to resolving problems apart from press reports. Majority live in these countries as if they are from nowhere or having no way ahead, or little or nothing to look up to in life each and every individuals are for themselves.

If a scenario should come out in the open it's with grudges or with conflicts, when are we Africans, when I mean African it includes Jamaican, Caribbean's, Trinidad, West Indians, and Barbados come out with our feelings about ourselves from which we could help ourselves? Such as coming up with good and thorough solution to our own personal problems, what we feel should be our values, attitudes in this ever constant changing environment within Europeans.

What are the opinions of Africans and its public views about commitments to extricate ourselves from self imposed slavery and delusion?

Until such a time arrives when Africans, Caribbean's, Trinidad, West Indians, Asians and Barbados take such issues into consideration, only then can we easily come to terms knowing what to do with ourselves and our identity which seems to be basically fragmented.

The world we live in today is an ever constant changing place, we need lots of solution, to many of our problems, involving each groups, sect, ethnic origin, religion, believes, creed and race. Most of us are observing ourselves with self pity and tears in our eyes, while we have all that it takes to make things better all we need, is motivation.

Let's deal with our bad side; it would do us better, in resolving our indifferences. With regards to our relationship with our allies or enemies, it makes it all easy for other ethnic origin not to observe, other ethnic origin with prejudice.

It's a difficult choice; It's something we have to recognise about ourselves to be part of our aim and accomplishment, if it could be said, we have insight into our future we need not worry because all ethnic origin have their own good and bad side. There is no wrong in any one facing his or her reality.

From the way, I observe Caribbean's, Trinidad, West Indians, and Barbados and Africans very soon, we all, would be seeking citizenship into Europe, where would it lead us to? Where would it take us to? I am not coming out with all these, with prejudice. We are in a state we have to reconcile.

The situation in developing countries needs to be streamlined in such ways that they would only receive help, if they are ready to help themselves. I cannot believe a man who cannot provide three square meals for himself a day with starvation and poverty has four children each with four different women and he is about having his fifth wife what do I call these genocide.

Are we, on the right approach to correcting our life incoherent traits and difficulties? Britain and America and the rest of the EU have, their own problems they try their best to handle different difficult scenario of which, they are still met with problems at least they are trying. If third world nations site down and do nothing towards their problems, they will deteriorate which seems to be the case.

Every day babies are born, the question is where are we heading to? They have problems of their own after

- Spying on nannies at children day care. The British always comes out with something, I mean anything rather than neglecting an epilogues or an issue, of great significances or scenario that are unfavourable within its communities or Borough and around the world, It's a good venture, which should be the same initiatives used by all third world countries to cooperate.
- It's not going to make us change from our own old accustomed, ways and background of living in our own land in e.g. Africa. But it simplifies we and the people from other countries, because of the affairs, we are obliged to co-ordinate relationships with these countries all over the world.
- What am trying to say in dept is that it is about time we stop being dependant, this is one reason why Senator Barack Husain Obama become the first African American to be the president of the united state of America. I would be more proud and happy, if we each day, out of our African history and background look up to ourselves. We treat each other in the UK with indifference. But who is being the odd once out, who is the weakest link?
- I have lived more than 21 years of my life in Africa, I have engulf myself in their residual image even to the extent of their birth, in the food I ate in Africa, the clothing I wear, I have under gone any difficult or degrading scenario any African could today admit in the UK, that he or she was faced with, that warrants he or her permanent immigration stay in the UK.

- Another irony is our intolerance of each other in the UK, we do not wish each other well, I have experiences conflict is inevitable within us in the UK! For years to come. With my illness as paranoid schizophrenia, Britain has given me opportunities to live my life as any other individual in his or her right mind, more in lifting me out of my illness
- Adopting a child, just to say, there is nothing happening here that are not also happening from our own origin is wrong, what, we do is always allowing our own epilogues to decay we have leant more from Europeans to better ourselves than we are. Here the UK within the European countries are calling for one common language.
- The British had always been, the once among European Union, commonly found to shear and rub bodies with third world centuries in good and bad times for centuries. They themselves have changed, over the years. For example an Irish family, Scottish, or Dutch families have been over the years obliterated from their speaking ascents, humans are prune to changes.
- The way problems are handled and tackled in the UK are awesome everybody is aware of what goes on around them and the rest of the world.

Do all EU member nation embraces third world nations, not all of them we should stop indulging ourselves in what breads hat and intolerance, which each day of our lives, creates greed, hat and conflicts, in our home, in all our works of life, and in our communities in Africa, Caribbean's, Trinidad, West Indians, and Barbados in our native origin and abroad we indulge in witchcraft, juju, voodoo in attaining our means it could be said its part of our nature or its in the blood at the same time being productive to meet our demands through such act is good a furniture, radio or a house we want out of such means do not just jump out of the cloud.

The situation each day in our daily lives, in Africa, Caribbean's, Trinidad, West Indians, and Barbados, leave those of us who would make it into Heaven, when the day of judgment comes within different scenarios each day because of our suffering and crying out tears based on evil trials through bewitching each other.

In a way we are prejudiced against ourselves, and do damages on those who are always trying to help us. E.g. who hears of driving offences in Africa, water shorted is a common thing in each community, there is poverty, cannibalism, child abuse, killing of people unlawfully? Why don't we unravel these or such problems of ours by ourselves right from our origins?

Who say there is no poverty in European countries, there is poverty, starvation, conflicts as in all parts of the world but take a look of how they conduct themselves amidst such occurrences.

Poverty is the state of one who lacks a certain amount of material possessions or money. Absolute poverty or destitution refers to the one who lacks basic human needs, which commonly includes clean and fresh water, nutrition, health care, education, clothing and shelter. About 1.7 billion people are estimated to live in absolute poverty today. Relative poverty refers to lacking a usual or socially acceptable level of resources or income as compared with others within a society or country.

For most of history poverty had been mostly accepted as inevitable as traditional modes of production were insufficient to give an entire population a comfortable standard of living. After the industrial revolution, mass production in factories made wealth increasingly more inexpensive and accessible. Of more importance is the modernization of agriculture, such as fertilizers, in order to provide enough yields to feed the population.

The supply of basic needs can be restricted by constraints on government services such as corruption, debt and loan conditionality's and by the brain drain of health care and educational professionals. Strategies of increasing income to make basic needs more affordable typically include welfare, economic freedom, and providing financial services. Today, poverty reduction is a major goal and issue for many international organizations such as the United Nations and the World Bank.

Fundamentally, poverty is a denial of choices and opportunities, a violation of human dignity. It means lack of basic capacity to participate effectively in society. It means not having enough to feed and clothe a family, not having a school or clinic to go to; not having the land on which to grow one's food or a job to earn one's living, not having access to credit. It means insecurity, powerlessness and exclusion of individuals, households and communities. It means susceptibility to violence, and it often implies living in marginal or fragile environments, with no access to clean water or sanitation.

Poverty is pronounced deprivation in well-being, and comprises many dimensions. It includes low incomes and the inability to acquire the basic goods and services necessary for survival with dignity. Poverty also encompasses low levels of health and education, poor access to clean water and sanitation, inadequate physical security, lack of voice, and insufficient capacity and opportunity to better one's life.

Poverty is usually measured as either absolute or relative poverty Absolute poverty refers to a set standard which is consistent over time and between countries. The World Bank defines extreme poverty as living on less than US $1.25 per day, and moderate poverty as less than $2 or $5 a day but note that a person or family with access to subsistence resources, e.g. subsistence farmers, may have a low cash income without a correspondingly low standard of living – they are not living 'on' their cash income but using it as a top up.

It estimates that 'in 2001, 1.1 billion people had consumption levels below $1 a day and 2.7 billion lived on less than $2 a day. A dollar a day, in nations that do not use the U.S. dollar as currency, does not translate to living a day on the amount of local currency as determined by the exchange rate. Rather, it is determined by the purchasing power parity, which would look at how much local currency is needed to buy the same things that a dollar could buy in the United States. Usually, this would translate to less local currency than the exchange rate in poorer countries as the United States is a more expensive country.

The proportion of the developing world's population living in extreme economic poverty fell from 28 percent in 1990 to 21 percent in 2001. Most of this improvement has occurred in East and South Asia. In East Asia the World Bank reported that 'The poverty headcount rate at the $2-a-day level is estimated to have fallen to about 27 percent in 2007, down from 29.5 percent in 2006 and 69 percent in 1990.' In Sub-Saharan Africa extreme poverty went up from 41 percent in 1981 to 46 percent in 2001, which combined with growing population increased the number of people living in extreme poverty from 231 million to 318 million.

In the early 1990s some of the transition economies of Eastern Europe and Central Asia experienced a sharp drop in income. The collapse of the Soviet Union resulted in large declines in GDP per capita, of about 30 to 35% between 1990 and the trough year of 1998 when it was at its minimum. As a result poverty rates also increased although in subsequent years as per capita incomes recovered the poverty rate dropped from 31.4% of the population to 19.6% The World Bank issued a report predicting that between 2007 and 2027 the populations of Georgia and Ukraine will decrease by 17% and 24% respectively.

Economic aspects of poverty focus on material needs, typically including the necessities of daily living, such as food, clothing, shelter, or safe drinking water. Poverty in this sense may be understood as a condition in which a person or community is lacking in the basic needs for a minimum standard of well-being and life, particularly as a result of a persistent lack of income.

Analysis of social aspects of poverty links conditions of scarcity to aspects of the distribution of resources and power in a society and recognizes that poverty may be a function of the diminished 'capability' of people to live the kinds of lives they value. The social aspects of poverty may include lack of access to information, education, health care, or political power.

Poverty may also be understood as an aspect of unequal social status and inequitable social relationships, experienced as social exclusion, dependency, and diminished capacity to participate, or to develop meaningful connections with other people in society. Such social exclusion can be minimized through strengthened connections with the mainstream, such as through the provision of relational care to those who are experiencing poverty.

The World Bank's 'Voices of the Poor,' based on research with over 20,000 poor people in 23 countries, identifies a range of factors which poor people identify as part of poverty. These include:

Precarious livelihoods
Excluded locations
Physical limitations
Gender relationships
Problems in social relationships
Lack of security
Abuse by those in power
Dis-empowering institutions
Limited capabilities
Weak community organizations

David Moore, in his book The World Bank, argues that some analysis of poverty reflect pejorative, sometimes racial, stereotypes of impoverished people as powerless victims and passive recipients of aid programs.

Ultra-poverty, a term apparently coined by Michael Lipton, connotes being amongst poorest of the poor in low-income countries. Lipton defined ultra-poverty as receiving less than 80 percent of minimum caloric intake whilst spending more than 80% of income on food. Alternatively a 2007 report issued by International Food Policy Research Institute defined ultra-poverty as living on less than 54 cents per day.

Before the industrial revolution, poverty had been mostly accepted as inevitable as economies produced little, making wealth scarce. The initial industrial revolution led to high economic growth and eliminated mass absolute poverty in what is now considered the developed world.

Research has found that there is a high risk of educational underachievement for children who are from low-income housing circumstances. This often is a process that begins in _primary school_ for some less fortunate children. Instruction in the US educational system, as well as in most other countries, tends to be geared towards those students who come from more advantaged backgrounds. As a result, these children are at a higher risk than other children for retention in their grade, special placements during the school's hours and even not completing their high school education.

There are indeed many explanations for why students tend to drop out of school. For children with low resources, the risk factors are similar to others such as juvenile delinquency rates, higher levels of teenage pregnancy, and the economic dependency upon their low income parent or parents. Families and society who submit low levels of investment in the education and development of less fortunate children end up with less favourable results for the children who see a life of parental employment reduction and low wages. Higher rates of early childbearing with all the connected risks to family, health and well-being are majorly important issues to address since education from preschool to high school are both identifiably meaningful in a life.

Poverty often drastically affects children's success in school. A child's 'home activities, preferences, mannerisms' must align with the world. They are at disadvantage in the school and most importantly the classroom. Therefore, it is safe to state that children who live at or below the poverty level will have far less success educationally than children who live above the poverty line. Poor children have a great deal less healthcare and this ultimately results in many absences from the academic year. Additionally, poor children are much more likely to suffer from hunger, fatigue, irritability, headaches, ear infections, flu, and colds. These illnesses could potentially restrict a child or student's focus and concentration.

How do we Africans Jamaicans, Caribbean, Trinidadians, West Indians in these European countries observe these countries, for example Britain are they hard or are they soft we can express freedom, freedom most of us cannot express in our native origin. What are our personal motives for interacting with them? It is evident that certain people change, while some people do not change, or recognises change, yet they are in power!

We must struggle in making things better in the right perspectives, the European part of the world is structured, doesn't it make us from third world countries dissolve ourselves in their own perspectives it will not all change to what they are; we would still be ourselves our origin, culture, tradition remaining intact. We have to be structured as well, we should not let our inconsistencies side to be more open than, the good side, nothing is ever too late to accomplish. In other to put ourselves in perspectives, i.e. (facing our own reality, to become constructive) we would discover our good qualities and realise, we have places in, Elysium from the Greek word which mean, dwelling place of the blessed after death on this earth.

Watching BBC two on television on the 28th of April 2008 at 9.45 pm, a documentary titled am I normal, it came into my mind when I wrote to Ms. Sally Bryden head of strategic information of the NHS, that the documentary should be classified. It not only tells but depicts all I have been word processing for years. Some of them, I had sent to her, my psychiatrist for consideration into their data base. If what had been shown on television, word by words could be precisely compiled into my word processed materials.

- 21st May 2008 Death of 7 year old girl in Birmingham, family charged with neglect because the child died from hunger and starvation.
- 18 year old man died after being stabbed in Sidcup, he enjoys a night out.
- Police investigates an explosion in Exeter
- A baby put up for sale in the internet
- 27th may 2008 Truckers calling for full oil tax rebate, rise in oil prices protesting to bring their message through to the government blockage in refineries, slowing down traffic in Cardiff, which also involves motorist.
- Violent crimes increasing within 4 years in the UK especially knife crime.
- 30th May 2008 Campaigners against 3rd Heathrow run way it led to a protest.
- Dose on 100% mortgage are in trouble.
- More help for carers, people living beyond poverty line and child poverty line is on the increasing in the UK.

- England worst secondary schools are close to being closed down because of poor performance.
- Arrangement of Britain holding world Olympics.
- Police will persecute any one found drinking on the tub in the UK
- Probe on spending of MPs through expense charges.
- 15th June 2008 two gay clergies had their civil partnership traditionally in a Church. Lots of people had something to say about the issue did it make a difference, it's not right for the Church, it's not acceptable morally. Everybody as individuals, have their rights. I here say, the world relationship is complicated enough. If we should view this issue with thorough considerations.
- Since every individuals have their rights, let's consider it, not breaching on other peoples disciplines by asking for some complacency 1) are any of such clergies once married, 2) have children, If not, they could just be expressing themselves, 3) The could be expressing their say within one being straight, gay, or a lesbians. Is it right under perspectives of religion?
- Such things happening within the Church and within the NHS who is really winning. From the NHS sex change, sperm donors, test tub babies, cloning, or a male human having a baby through sex change or cloning. All this events entering into the 21st century leaves every individual to, their own moral reality or concept.
- Humans using animal for testing, cloning, cross-breading, or for making cosmetics all have the some holistic approach of docile of deregulating universal moral principles in this changing world of ours, we should create a course, scene, and sense of directions for each month, years, and not divergence. There is no use in any one, family, society, or community living their lives with wimps there should be reason and explanation, I see it as diabolic, garish, dissimulation, dissonance and not genuine.

- With the issue of sperm donors, test tub babies, this could result in years to come to more rap in our communities also woman forcing men into sex, marriages, or rapping men. Which are uncommon in our communities today?
- Oil truckers still on strike
- Second time in a week of lost top secret confidential files in the UK.
- Tougher community sentencing.
- EU salvages the Lisbon treaty after Northern Island vote.
- 17th June 2008 food and fuel pushes inflation to 3.3% within the last twelve months, and for eleven years, above the government target. It resulted to high cost of living. The effect has called for global solution
- Safety at work, more work death than murder death

- 17th March 2009 a failing hospital caused death because of appalling emergency care resulting in patients dying needlessly said the NHS watchdog. 400 people died at Stafford hospital between 2005 and 2008 than would have been expected said the healthcare commission. It was said, there were deficiencies at virtually every stage of emergency care, while managers pursue target to the detriment of patients care. While health secretary MP Alan Johnson apologies, launching an enquiry into the incident at Stafford hospital.
- The dissident republican murder of two solders and a policeman sparked widespread public outrage. President Barack Obama said the people of Northern Ireland responded heroically to the recent murder in Northern Ireland.
- This is law, this is freedom, and such are the scenario that should be a part of all nations. If all third world countries, do not state doing something about themselves, I am of the opinion, very soon no one would take a second glance of third world countries anymore.

- There are no statistical record of employment or unemployment in developing countries, the idea of the general public of all third world countries have not been able putting such issues through to their government, or the government coming up with such polices.
- 18th March 2009 UK unemployment has risen.
- Police search for a missing florist and her disable daughter, the police recovered two bodies from a lake near their home at Gloucestershire.
- If it were in Africa, if the police have to do something a about a missing person, theft of property or assault, there would have to be a scenario of bribery, before the police, would do anything about a search, or complaint.
- Police agreed to pay £60.000 damages to a man arrested during an anti-terror raid. The high court heard he was subjected to serious gratuitous prolonged unjustified violence and abuse after his arrest. In my dreams would such a thing happen in third world countries, or probably in my next reincarnation?
- UK to set out anti-torture rules: New guidelines for intelligence officers on interviewing overseas detainees will be published in attempts to show the UK government opposition to torture. Prime minister Gordon Brown said he wanted to restore public faith in the security services of the UK and he absolutely condemns torture. This followed concerns about the treatment of former Guantanamo Bay detainee.
- Wouldn't third world countries also revamp their economy? Plans put forward for the bank by Lord Tuner did unveil proposals to overhaul the UK banking including measures to stop institutions from lending too much during boom years.
- The head of the financial services authority seeks to cut bank's ability to take excessive risks. Bonus systems at financial institutions must be overhauled. He recommended changes in the role of the FSA focusing on strategise of financial companies

identifying firms who are heading for trouble, before they get bankrupt.

- The financial service authority head Lord Turner says his plans for the UK banking would amount to a revolution. He called for better monitoring of credit conditions in the UK to assess if a dangerous boom would be approaching. Lord Turner was of the opinion banks should be required building up reserves in healthier economic times against future losses and be forced into holding more cash or liquid investments.
- Mental Health Investment Welcomed: Mental health charity mind did welcome the government commitment in investing £93 million on mental health services, Mind's chief executive Paul Farmer said; there had never been a more important time for such investment in mental health.
- The recession at the moment is not just affecting people's bank balances; it is rather having huge human cost too as well. Paul Farmer opinion was that we are in uncharted territory about how many people could be affected and the impacts this would have on mental health services.
- 19th March 2009 up to 1,000 Gambian villagers have been abducted by witch doctors to secret detention centres and forced to drink potions, so said human right group. Amnesty international said some are forced to drink the concoction through which, they developed kidney problems, with two people dead.
- Official in the police, army and the president's personal protection guard had also accompanied the witch doctors in the bizarre roundup, of which the Gambian government was unavailable to comment on the claims.
- These are the sorts of scenario we still choose to live in, all third world countries, yet we want to make Europe our allies,' such witch doctors would only extricate us from being productive. They should depend more on doing good jujus.
- I wonder what Dr. Gbadamosi one of my psychiatrist at the Fewryview mental health centre. An African

from my mother's origin in Nigeria would have to say, or give insight to in the UK while he works as my psychiatrist at the Ferryview mental health centre.

- An exclusive with Prince William Press Packers Alice and Oscar got to meet Prince William to find out all sorts of wired and wonderful things from one of the most famous people in the world.

Confrontation analysis known as drama theory is an operational analysis technique used to structure, understand and think through multi-party interactions such as negotiations.

It is derived from game theory but considers the fact that instead of resolving the game, the players often re-define the game when interacting. Emotions triggered from the potential interaction play a large part in this re-definition. Whereas game theory looks on an interaction as a single decision matrix and resolves that, confrontation analysis looks on the interaction as a sequence of linked interactions, where the decision matrix changes under the influence of precisely defined emotional dilemmas developing nations should take it up and access themselves.

Confrontation analysis looks on an interaction as a sequence of confrontations. During each confrontation the parties communicate until they have made their positions clear to one another. These positions can be expressed as a card table also known as an options board of yes/ and no decisions. For each decision each party communicates what they would like to see happen in their position and what will happen if they cannot agree to whatever threatens the future. These interactions produce dilemmas and the card table changes as players attempt to eliminate these.

Confrontation analysis then specifies a number of precisely defined dilemmas that occur to the parties following from the structure of the card tables. It states that motivated by the desire to eliminate these dilemmas, the parties involved will change the card table, to eliminate their problem.

Confrontation analysis does not necessarily produce a win-win solution although end states are more likely to remain stable if they do; however, the word confrontation should not necessarily imply that any negotiations should be carried out in an aggressive way.

The card tables or are isomorphic to <u>game theory</u> models, but are not built with the aim of finding a solution. Instead, the aim is to find the dilemmas facing characters and so help to predict how they will change the table itself. Such prediction requires not only analysis of the model and its dilemmas, but also exploration of the reality outside the model; without this it is impossible to decide which ways of changing the model in order to eliminate dilemmas might be rationalized by the characters.

Developing nations have their own culture, knowledge, tradition, conception of themselves true to very existence. We all have our own tears to give and take.

Slavery is not only the buying and selling of human beings, having a master over one, the illness schizophrenics is also a form of slavery, which I consider to be the last form of slavery on earth. I call the illness schizophrenia unnatural tendencies of humans subsuming, or going into extinction which has not yet been realised.

In many parts of the world it is found that the wealthy, leaders and government lead many into being disillusioned. They are all from the same race and ethnic origin, the wealthy lead many astray, and rob them of their livelihood.

Some parts say lets operate a welfare system, regardless if there are some wealthy once who clamour for all the lofty and good things for themselves, to enjoy themselves with, on the benefit of the disillusioned once, the poor and the needy still have something to hold on to as a means of their livelihoods by operating a welfare state but would they be ready to be tolerant.

In some case the poor and needy have opportunities to make their feeling heard about how the country should operate the result is that, the effect of poverty and slavery, is not felt such as within Europeans.

In third world countries, the poor and the needy have no means of making their feeling show but only in aggression, on how they should live their lives, from what, they know is limited of what they expect from the government but it isn't always forthcoming leading to conflict and aggression. Most of them are disillusioned, have no means of power over the bourgeoisies, because the poor and needy have been enslaved by not only government, the wealthy and those who seek more powers each day. Then some of them turn into rebels and guerrilla fighters but it doesn't help the situation people who are not involved are getting scotched while government feel they have someone to blame.

Life becomes boorish, leaving the disillusion once in most third world nations unable to fend or think for themselves; the bourgeoisies' do not fight in favour, or care to see to their welfare of the poor and needy, or their sufferings. They at the same time fail to see to the welfare of their country as sovereign nations, after freedom have been granted to these sovereign nations earlier. Are the people of e.g. West Africa really free and independent within themselves as sovereign nations?

Africans in the real sense never wanted to be under their colonial master. The wanted to be free what have they been doing since they gain independence I mean these are people who, wanted to be free to be free means you have something to offer yourself.

There is care for mentally ill person in Africa where there is care, is quite a state, what is left to such people is for them to walk in the streets if no one cares for them. It's as if, they have no life! A life of negligence is not always a blessing.

Though the Europeans would give the needy and those suffering whatever they feel they need, or are entitled to through their welfare state. Still, some of them are disillusioned with their suffering but not up, to a state at least, one can have three square meals a day. At least, there is hope for the needy and disillusioned once.

As long as such epilogue goes on in Africa and third world countries as they choose to neglect themselves, there are no justification on the part being played by the government and the wealthy based on whatever they are doing in Africa while we are meant to patronise ourselves with what dignity? It came to my realisation lots of people from their childhood in third world nations; grow-up becoming selfish or wicked it is hunger and feeling of being neglected and rejected.

It is also common among individuals who want to be successful by all cost or means those who hold a reign of power attention is only for themselves and not for their, family, relatives or friends often backed by them because they might want something from them as a result, they become powerful, and want more power over them by leaving them or their family in a state or emotional imprisonment but yet attached to them while there are a lot of things to do to help other people in Nigeria for example keeping it that way gives them authority they would not like to change the situation friends and companionship is now more important than a family unit nevertheless the situation of wealth and power gives them control over their family.

The government and elites in West African for example should become creative majority of African citizens are unable to emancipate themselves form social, political, cultural, traditional, religious constrain. From the top in hierarchy to the bottom in West Africans, every one want to be somebody of importance, if this are the case, why not become creative or use our full potential?

We have recourses and energy back home through which we could easily become creative; whatever is causing the drawbacks in West Africa is well known. I guess it's because of too many conflicts, greed, induced mannerism that causes indifferences or selfishness. My concerns are I see a dark side of an omen coming all the way to merge with the regions of Africa.

African culture involves the use of Juju's to do and undo, to have power through demonic means over one person or another, to make themselves rich, to outdo each other in e.g. students in education, work, family life. Some parents seems from the time of their children's birth, determine their course of action in life, e.g. how they would become great creating power struggle at home, school, work and socially within a situation one person is being downgraded or walking in the street naked some are left to suffer or neglected deliberately. West Africans and our native priest would never stop the use of Juju among themselves, to outdo each other.

Before my father and mother come to Britain in the early1960s, after which I was taken back to my father at the age of I year old. I experiences as I grow up in West Africa all sorts of cultural and juju practice.

After spending more than 20 years of my life in West Africa, I was to return to my place of birth. I would preferred my mother who was still alive should be the one providing me with pepper soup ingredients from my father's origin if it was really necessary into the UK but it was my step mother Mrs. Cordelia Megbele who was to be the provider of the pepper soup ingredients, why should it be when my mother was still alive?

A child born in the UK, after spending 21 years of his life in West Africa, my father was a freemason. It is all a scenario of my father and step mothers depicting me to come and live in the UK under their own repercussion. If they had children of their own with my father, what would have been their own expectations, would it be for their own children to go down, with me going up or vice-vase, take note, that within this family, am their step child! There are certain rigid system based upon recognition, division of labour, hierarchy of authority and officials collectively I mean some sort of bureaucracy which sometimes troubled me.

I might be fortunate am not selling gari, yam, maze grain or ice water in the streets or market place in Africa. It does not mean am not human within life trials based on what I had gone through it's how I feel and make out of it that matters. They could be down trodden, found begging in the streets, and hold their life with seals of salvation suffering in a way means we are being called upon, suffering is a trial in some case we might have what we want but it would not take us to our destination.

Through synergy interactions of the Europeans in third world countries have played a new foundation in all third world nations that should be accounted for through further progress or some people fear through Gods own magnificent judgment it might be the present infrastructures in e.g. Africa might belong to such poor, the needy and disillusioned once in the future because they have undergone their trials have humble themselves by placing themselves under trials of life.

It might be their dwelling tomorrow, because as it is in Heaven so it is on earth. There is nothing as a lost or fallen city, they will all rise again. It is the key that the architects of the universe, and the angelic host of God sent are waiting for! The wealth of having children or being in this world is different from material wealth there is spiritual, psychological, being who we are for now and what is known as emotional wealth based on reality of what is to come because the Universe is a system.

I believe this same world earth, we live in, is the same Heaven that would be accounted for as our home in Heaven!

Which will after being engulf in the rebirth as Heaven the whole world, becomes places in Heaven? It will be the dwelling place of those, whose names are not accounted for by the rod of Lucifer but written in the book of life, for them, it will be joy, happiness, bliss, which has been brought about through synergy. Then, we would have more than reason based reality of trials of life after being scotched from time immemorial.

I took my place in every step while I was in Africa based on my dreams, thoughts, and ambition to be in a position of which, I could do something for my native origin, but nothing was straight forward. My ambition would have come with the usual flashy cars, luxury house but I would never have been an individual who would have clamoured for power and not achieve something for the good of my native origin. I was born in the UK money is made with mercury imported from Europe psychological I wouldn't have gone far before the ill go-ten wealth do me in. I would never have been able to stand and watch to see people suffer.

I have an attitude of simplicity which wouldn't have helped much or pave the way for my dreams, conquest and ambition within my father and mothers native land. My mother said it out loud at one time of our conversation, that she feels she has a son, who cannot be jealous of any one.

In my own opinion of myself, am too religious based on my beliefs. As I dwell in the UK each day of my life, my simplicity is my greatest strength in life, through which I derives wisdom keeping peace and patience intact, moreover earth, life and everything in it, has its own law of governess through laws of nature.

Natural law or the law of nature is a system of law which is determined by nature, and is universal. Natural law refers to the use of reason to examine human nature and deduce binding rules of moral behaviour. Natural law is contrasted with the positive law meaning 'man-made law', not 'good law' of a given political community, society, or nation-state, and thus serves as a standard by which to critique said positive law. According to natural law theory, the content of positive law cannot be known without some reference to natural law (or something like it). Used in this way, natural law can be invoked to criticize decisions about the statutes, but less so to criticize the law itself. Some use natural law as having the same meaning with natural justice or natural right .

Although natural law is often combined with common law, the two are distinct in that natural law is a view that certain rights or values are inherent in or universally cognizable by virtue of human reason or human nature, while common law is the legal tradition whereby certain rights or values are legally cognizable by virtue of judicial recognition. Natural law theories have, however, exercised a profound influence on the development of English common law, and have featured greatly in its philosophies

The use of natural law, in its various embodiments, has varied widely through its history. There are a number of different theories of natural law, differing from each other with respect to the role those morality plays in determining the authority of legal norms.

The form of the Good is the cause of all things and when it is seen it leads a person to act wisely; the Good is closely identified with the Beautiful.

What the law commanded varied from place to place, but what was 'by nature' should be the same everywhere. A 'law of nature' would therefore have had the flavour more of a paradox than something which obviously existed.

The rise of natural law as a universal system coincided with the rise of large empires and kingdoms natural to being the result of divine, positive, legislation. Some asserted the existence of a rational and purposeful order to the universe (a divine or eternal law), and the means by which a rational being lived in accordance with this order was the natural law, which spelled out action that accorded with virtue.

The natural law was inherently teleological and deontological in that although it is aimed at goodness, it is entirely focused on the ethicalness of actions, rather than the consequence. The specific content of the natural law was therefore determined by a conception of what things constituted happiness, be they temporal satisfaction or salvation. The state, in being bound by the natural law, was conceived as an institution directed at bringing its subjects to true happiness.

A physical law or scientific law is 'a theoretical principle deduced from particular facts, applicable to a defined group or class of phenomena, and expressible by the statement that a particular phenomenon always occurs if certain conditions be present.' Physical laws are typically conclusions based on repeated scientific experiments and observations over many years and which have become accepted universally within the scientific community. The production of a summary description of our environment in the form of such laws is a fundamental aim of science.

The natural-law argument states that because there are consistent and predictable natural laws in the universe, there must be a law-giver who set those laws in motion. That law-giver is assumed to be God.

Natural law and natural rights follow from the nature of man and the world. We have the right to defend ourselves and our property, because of the kind of people that we are. True law derives from this right, not from the arbitrary power of the omnipotent state.

Natural law has objective, external existence. The ability to make moral judgments, the capacity to know good and evil, has immediate evolutionary benefits: just as the capacity to perceive three dimensionally tells me when I am standing on the edge of a cliff, so the capacity to know good and evil tells me if my companions are liable to cut my throat. It evolved in the same way, for the same straightforward and uncomplicated reasons, as our ability to throw rocks accurately.

The medieval/legal definition: Natural law cannot be defined in the way that positive law is defined, and to attempt to do so plays into the hands of the enemies of freedom. Natural law is best defined by pointing at particular examples, as a biologist defines a species by pointing. The natural world as it exists without human beings or civilization.

The elements of the natural world, as mountains, trees, animals, or rivers, Natural scenery, The universe, with all its phenomena, The particular combination of qualities belonging to a person, animal, thing, or class by birth, origin, or constitution; native or inherent character, Character, kind, or sort, Characteristic disposition; temperament, Biological functions or urges, The laws and principles that guide the universe or an individual.

The essential qualities or characteristics by which something is recognized a causal agent creating and controlling things in the universe, The natural physical world including plants and animals and landscapes etc, The complex of emotional and intellectual attributes that determine a person's characteristic actions and reactions, A particular type of thing, All the living things in the world and the environment in which they exist, The existing system of things; the world of matter, or of matter and mind; the creation; the universe. The sum of qualities and attributes which make a person or thing what it is, as distinct from others; native character; inherent or essential qualities or attributes; peculiar constitution or quality of being.

Physical constitution or existence; the vital powers; the natural life, Natural affection or reverence, Constitution or quality of mind or character to endow with natural qualities.

It's about time we start trying to get ourselves together, third world countries and their leaders have to talk, And future leaders of western hemisphere would help to make things work because we really need to talk. There are thing we need to do creating a better identity for ourselves such as to save and cherish our lives and the love we make.

Look at the situation in Somalia of children suffering from AIDs with no food available and starvation, yet more children are being born each day in Somalia. These are children we bear, but where is the love. Each child born each day is born into an inferno.

Let's say goodbye to isolation, segregation and disillusion, it's all the same as in any where... in the whole world, but in certain parts such issues should have limits.

You just came into the UK before one year; you are having children or just wait till you get a council flat bang again we are having children it's too obvious what your intentions are. Children would claim benefit for you when you cannot work at the age of 40 years when one can hardly work until they are 65 years as retirement age to claim pension.

The result could lead to anti-immigrant sentiments' in Europe it's not that these nations have not been generous enough there are limits to what have occurred in the past related to what relationship immigration now is.

As much as they seek their stay in the UK, they do not create bonds with each other worst still with children who are born through naturalisation of birth as British.

There should be some sort of attachment because no matter what the situation is in becoming British, we are all still from the same origin as Africans. If we cannot unit in Europe or in Africa where else can we be and live in unity while instead of using these open land of opportunity in seeking our goals and reality to be creative, we just go about basking in it.

Infarct these are the sort of things the British are good at, the works of the exorcist and archaeologist are always still taking place all over third world countries especially Africa.

A sentiment I hold is that those who are being granted stay in the UK, are those, who cannot divest themselves, so they are allowed into the UK, where there are face with an environment e.g. the weather, climate, a constructive charismatic, environment and situation through which, we are divested becoming spiritually psychologically whole or in some cases, after going through a devastating life experience.

If we feel the Europeans and Americans have got a well planed system of welfare is there anything wrong with third world countries having a welfare state of their own? They should do the little they can do man cannot live with hunger and live a decent moral life.

My father later gave me back the coral bead which, I had used to pay obedience to the Olu of Warri when he was made a chief in Delta state Nigeria in 1988. My father wanted the coral bead from me before the ceremony stated, was evident, at the time, he had the intention he was going to use me in his own way, I forced myself to deliberately bow to Olu immediately after my father bowed to him attaining his chieftaincy title I still remember the look my father gave me on that day and I noticed somehow the Olu of Warri noticed what had occurred. Within African culture there are different forms of slavery what I deduct from my illness is that part of my illness are as a result of it. I freed myself a little by bowing to the Olu of Warri.

My father had visited my flat three times on his last visits in the presence of my brother and his wife Nwamaka, told me I should go and buy him bear I told him the stores were closed he said I should go to a Pup so I went to the Greyhound Pub just by Kingsman street in Woolwich with a jar in my hand to buy him bear and bring it back into my flat, I did not see him ate the food I prepared for him drank and left this was before he handed me back the coral bead few days later in my brothers flat.

It is common for me not going down to Heathrow on my father's way in or out of the UK, Taking it by a taxi cab to my flat I became uncomfortable with it in my flat after a year. This prompted me taking the coral bead into the Woolwich Gala club for personal reason and witnesses.

It was already his intention of using the coral bead to reincarnate as a child at birth into the UK. At which time he was unwell suffering from diabetic receiving treatment at Ibadan where he died.

Photographs I took within 2004 depicted I had become frail something was living through my soul, body and spirit through African psychology concoction, Juju e.g. pepper soup ingredient that could have caused me concussion I began to take more of my father's shape and form in his resemblance. With the things I went through, I cannot stop having an inclination am superman, with the need to divest myself from my krypton crystal in other to become a spent force.

It's truly as it is in Heaven so it is on earth we are the same all over the world reincarnating through several repeated lives and trials to initiate or divest ourselves as to what it is in Heaven so should it be on earth. All we do is inter marry through insight and instinct.

I felt I should have to create a public awareness of what I am going through, awareness on the issues of mental illness as a sufferer and also other matters based on experience related to it.

When the re-birth of Heaven is completed inwardly I know this knowledge, would lead me and many other people to a true and coherent procedure of acknowledgement of our existence from some inward feeling in me all men, creature, everything would judge themselves.

There are reason why God provided us with Kings and Queen and leaders to acknowledge ourselves. If you were God, would you want another person to rule over your people? He is also a jealous God so the Holy Bible says in one of God's own commandments? Does this have meaning to our existence, do we really know God, what this kingdom of Heaven is, what it would look like, do our religious leaders give us insight into such issues?

That is when, we reason and understanding through inclination of why God gave us opportunities, If God is not happy with us why has he not destroy the world. We are already living under bitter blows to the extent of slavery within once self. If God had not destroyed this world, he is leaving certain things for us to understand for example after having lived such lives we live on earth is it likely, we would go further into being educated in Heaven?

No human wish to be another man's slave, If you do not want to be another man's slave, what would you like to be, what do you feel it should be, what changes would you like to see. What then are slavery, sickness, starvation, diseases, suffering degradation or unhappiness, are they all necessary? It's all solemnly for one to justify once self to once, true existence.

Though, the events of the world at just entering the twentieth first century have been filled of misshapes and events, in business, commercial, sport, entertainment, social, educational and family affairs are all in one conflicts or another.

Abeokuta as the state capital from which, my mother's family originates the Faneye's, Oshun and late politician Obafemi Awolowo, Olusegun Obasanjo and lots of other families, for a woman to have come all the way from Abeokuta to have had relationship with my father with children and not only having more children with my father in the UK, they got married in a court of law has left me some research to be done.

My grandmother from my fathers' side only had my father through her relationship with Gold Pin Megbele moving inward from Delta state inward into western Nigeria to Ondo state of Nigeria. I wondered how, my mother felt about marrying my father it could be regional, family background or interest. This meant my grandmother from my father's side married inward while my mother married outward. And my father already had a child Named Olu Megbele his first son before he got married to my mother.

I would have completed my B.A studies in Geography at Port-Harcourt, but my mother had made steps that I and my brother move to the UK.

My mind is at work most of the time thinking about all that has been happening to me since I regained consciousness from child birth among other things, the medication, unable to sleep well at times, having a job make me feel better about my well-being, because am able to work make me more resilient and the environment as well.

Because it prevents me from being on benefits, I do not pay housing benefit pole tax and council tax and my medications and health care are free because am on low income yet grateful about my ability to work part time as a cleaner and attending university. Everything an individual wish to achieve depends on the individual, if the facilities are available.

Polygamy has its disadvantages, I never wanted to be insecure, polygamy in which, I was born in have made me insecure I don't want to be bitter inside. I don't want to keep anything inside like grudges.

Each day of my life, if my dream, experiences becomes my reality on a basis of being alive, based on definite and appropriate purpose. the lord is my shepherd I shall not want, he necked me beside the steal water, he restores my soul he lead me in the part's of righteousness' for his name sake.

Ye do I walk through the valley of death I shall fear no evil for he is with me his rod and his staff, it comforted me for he had already prepared a table before me in the presence of my enemies for he had already anointed my cup with oil my cup runs over surly goodness and mercy shall follow me all the days of my life and I shall dwell in the house of God my author and creator Amen.

Within my background from a polygamous family, I experience my step mothers' would do anything, to make their children better, coming out in the limelight. In fact, we are always at a start of limbo within the family, because our mother was not living within our polygamous home within which our father teds to play politics within us.

I am more proud being my mother's child than to be an adopted child of a step mother or a step father except it is extremely necessary and there are reasons to justify it with good intentions such as death of a parent.

Regardless if I and my brothers and sister are from the same parents we could still be in antagonism. Do not bring food to me in my flat I told my brother, it has nothing to do with a disagreement, my brother says I should speak to his wife about it myself which is an inappropriate thing to say to her personally. I am on medication probably for life my brother works for Network rail while his wife works for the NHS or with children I ride on a bicycle or on bus regarding my plea I am not on medication for them. As family unit it's something they or a child would understand.

In the Holy Bible Abraham was in his old age when he had Isaac with Sarah on which account Hagar and her son Ishmael for Abraham were sent away. Abraham would have sacrificed Isaac who he loved dearly. Isaac had two sons Esau and Jacob with Rebekah, Jacob was the youngest he was the one reacting his mothers water was still flowing she helped him steals his elder brothers Esau's blessing from their father that God should decide because of her faith and plight.
Jacob stole his elder brothers blessing, when his brother grudged he ran with his mother advice to her brother Laban in Haran until his brothers grudge subsides. On his way in his sleep he saw a ladder through which angels were climbing into Heaven.
I began having feelings I have something in common with Jacob in relation to my family background in relation to my mother, my condition of birth that I was holding on to my immediate elder brothers heels when I was born, I should have children first before my immediate elder brother Mr. Omagbemi Megbele because am the last child of my mother with our father, and that my birth condition should have been clarified paving way for my brother Mr. Omagbemi. I am

more hairy and darker in colour than my brother who is two years older than me.

The scenario proved further in my life I should remain a celibate since my mother had another child a step brother Mr. Sola Awe with his father Mr. Gabriel Awe ironically I felt a female child with my mother would have been more pronounced than a male child for him proving his point it is natural for people thinking they are one thing or another which is typically natural we are all from one descendant or another.

At least it would have proved my mother's blood is still flowing it is my opinion since my mother death collapsing of heart attack all mothers do have them.

I do not see Mr. Gabriel Awe as a step father. He never got married to my mother, giving birth to my step brother Mr. Sola Awe makes it hard to understand polygamy or relationships. Mr. Gabriel Awe also would do anything to make his own son with my mother; more pronounced than me or any of my mothers' children. Women in this sort of situation are always at a limbo.

I do not think people feel glamorous looking after another person's child. Letting another person look after your children, is always an opportunity, for someone else using your children without second thoughts which may result to a devastating effect to your child's life!

It's often found families come out loud against paedophilias, child abuse, homosexuals, lesbians, gay people who are often confronted with negative remarks. If it is something we do not like let's consider how people get into such situation. They have been brought up in homes most of which are not happy once. They are all forms of created anomalies through relationships which at the end of the day would easily lead or termed as mental health in doing so; I hope those it concerns would do it with consideration through reconciliation that they do not go further in hurting people's feelings.

While all schizophrenic are not the same, much have to be done about stigma's attached to schizophrenic. To make matters worse each day mental health is a ground to hide after smuggling drugs, make a business go berserk, to the smallest detail to anti-social behaviours. It makes me feel, hunted.

Lots of such people come from broken homes, at their initial stage, with no body to look after them, or because they do not have the opportunities living a normal life, like anyone else. Getting such problems in our communities resolved, most start from our homes and background, which is the initial environment, where these problems states from.

I chose to be a celibate for simple reason at certain times in our lives. It comes a time, when one most encapsulate at one point or another. Because the situation we find ourselves in, requires we make use of our prerogative, or the circumstances requires a prerequisite because of our premonition or emotions.

We cannot choose to pass a choice we do not really understand; probably we have not yet assimilate the situations we find ourselves. Within the things we do these days, we should be more assertive. It is purpose and choice which defines any action to be taken. Choice is not an illusion because choice, are more than backed up primarily by motives.

The world is full of all sorts of predicaments, which we do not yet understand but go through but we are trying. It would be right to use the most powerful prayer patience and consideration. It is through patience and consideration we can reach the source of any problem we may have or see ourselves fall into. It is not all about life; it is also about existence where there is beauty, ugliness and death we all would like to live forever if this should be the case how do we go about it is by choice.

Based on this my present life, I have by choice placed myself, through my background, family, origin, culture, to undergo this my present life with some certain abnormalities, 90% of whatever I have gone through are by my own choice. It is sad to confess though I have been scotched, nevertheless, I not only remain resilient it gives me a part to transcend through apparent phenomenon's such as I have only one heart I should not loos it or my soul placed high within other planets or above the heavens.

Through my past lives, I could have chosen being white, Chinese, Indian but I have chosen coming from an Africa origin. It is experience, whatever we have endured, and what we have gone through on earth, which would enable each one of use stand the test of time in a new world. And make use worthy, filled with respect, joy, gladness and endorse our requirements to be at peace die or live forever.

What qualifies any one to be a parent is well known, except you become a parent, to look after your children and their are inherencies involved such as death of a parent, childhood should have advantages of looking up to their parents invariably you become a parent looking up to your children, who would access you, make up what, they think of you as a person or as a parent. From which they would either have respect for you as a parent or do it better through living under your care. They should not just be like friends but relatives with close ties not conflict parents contribute in making their children who they are.

Looking up to your children is good at the end of the day; it is whatever your children think of you that are most important. If they think right of you, then you have something to look up to. If they think wrongly of you, then you have failed towards your responsibilities bear in mind you are not God who would pass judgement within them, at this stage, you might be lucky if your child is usually shy and socially withdrawn, it means they are often caught-up in early signs with problems growing up based on certain problems of growing up in a family unit a sister would place are husband above her brother or a sister in-law would place her husband above her husband bother or a brother places his wife's brother above his own brother having lived in Africa and brought into civilisation who has time for that?

Most parents feel, they become parents in other to tell their children what to do yes, or how to grow up. At the end of the day it is whatever your children think of you as a parent that counts. It means more than anything to a parent, if the sun shines or it rains with thunders and lightning, or in stormy weather. It should be a place for holy matrimony. For better or for worse, till death do they part? This is how to create a constructive family unit or society.

Marriage break-up, polygamy resulting to neglects of marital vows and status are points in our life when things, do go wrong. If we cannot carry or see the problems through resolving family conflicts, do not go on blaming it on other people. Who are there to use our mistake, into creating devastating scenarios?

Most people say getting married and having children is the highest joy and exhilaration of man and woman. Or one is not yet human, until they experience marriage and raising up children. It's all a matter of choice, there are certain things we all can do or have, which we could prefer not to do, or have because of some life or natural incoherence's or just for the sake of being neutral.

There are certain times in our lives in this world at some point, if, we are not sure, rather than making a mistake, doing something we shouldn't do, which might result to our suffering as consequences of our action, we should rather secure our position or purpose in life with an indemnity or sacrifices the mode of sacrifices have now change we tend to do things for the better even if we lose out.

Schizophrenia hearing voices could lead to some insidious ways it could later be termed as this while the real search should be where and how the voices come about I feel some people know other people can hear their voices and they use it to their advantage it is enough to bear in a life time a schizophrenia having children growing up, later to be told, a parent suffers from mental illness is a scenarios that could be avoided with a little sacrifices on the part of the sufferer, if they had no children before they become unwell with the illness they could live their lives as celibates. If African children are spiritually or supernaturally gifted in some cases, more powerful than their parents or relative they are customary used for omens such children are their true children the others they come to do their own thing because they are omens for themselves. It is all written in the herbalist of African culture and native carvings depicted in natives or juju oracles something similar to the Book of Skelos or the living and the dead from which native doctors recites their incantations.

In <u>Classical Antiquity</u>, an oracle was a person or agency considered to be a source of wise counsel or <u>prophetic predictions</u> or <u>precognition</u> of the future, inspired by the <u>gods</u>. As such it is a form of <u>divination</u>.
The <u>Igbo people</u> of south-eastern <u>Nigeria</u> in <u>Africa</u> have a long tradition of using oracles. In Igbo villages, oracles were usually female <u>priestesses</u> to a particular deity, usually dwelling in a cave or other secluded location away from urban areas, and, much as the oracles of ancient Greece, would deliver prophecies in an ecstatic state to visitors seeking advice. Two of their ancient oracles became especially famous during the pre-colonial period: the Agbala oracle at <u>Awka</u> and the Chukwu oracle at <u>Arochukwu</u>. Though the vast majority of Igbos today is <u>Christian</u>, many of them still use oracles.
Amongst the related <u>Yoruba peoples</u> of the same country, the <u>Babalawos</u> (and their female counterparts, the Iyanifa's) serve collectively as the principal aspects of the tribe's World-famous <u>Ifa divination</u> system. Due to this, they customarily officiate at a great many of its traditional and religious ceremonies.
Am not saying they should not have children if, they wish and am not prejudiced against them if they watch their back their children would live healthy lives in the future. The ironic aspect of it is who is the weakest link as TV presenter Ann Robinson usually put it during her television show 'who within the team has been drawing the contestant backward'.

It is the same way, I observe polygamous families not making ends meet, broken home, couples breaking up and neglected children to be easily led astray in drugs, cocaine, ecstasy, anti-social behaviours homosexuals, lesbians, and paedophiles who should really be blamed for such incoherence's, nobody else can be blamed than the parents of such children. Any home without family love is always a disaster.

Pontius Pilate in the death and crucifixion of Jesus Christ, Pontius Pilate or other generals after his death would have been neglected, stripped-off from their duties and ranks during the persecution that followed after the death of Christ. To those he had asked to make a choice if they wanted Christ hanged who, is to blame.

27th of December 2007 I was at the Queen Elizabeth Hospital regarding my having pains behind my neck. I was told to stay on the Ibuprofen Dr Margery prescribed for me and ibuprofen ointment. 4th January 2008 I mentioned to Dr Jan Deacon I was seven months premature apart from other things we talked about with respect to my illness.

She said on our last meeting before this one, When I told her I had been moving furniture's in my flat and laying new carpet in my flat, and my work at the Woolwich Gala club lifting shutters whilst opening up for the past seven years, could be what have contributed to my having pains behind my neck it later came to my mind it might had been the effect of my freemason ring. She prescribed Diclofenac sodium E/C tablets 50 mg, to be taken three times a day and paracetamol tablets.

On my previous visit to her I told her about my job at Iceland frozen food plc, which was once known as Bigam, before, it become known as Iceland frozen food plc chain stores it might not be about just work I might have been working for a long time other things trouble me. She said the more reason it could be the result.

Heavy snow fall in Northern Island, traffic, road, houses affected, avalanched in Spain hit of-pate area, candidate for American presidency race election and the need for change in America in the present defining moment of history. Kenyan election rigging, caused mascara at least three hundred people where dead could be the result, we all have different temperaments for observing situations I could stay home all day without doing any work and still have back and neck pain.

It was one of my initiatives apart from wanting to join the Nigeria army; I also wanted to join the Nigerian air force. It was practically impossible in Western Nigerian because the only air force base I knew of in Western Nigeria was at Lagos collecting information in Nigeria if one have an interest is not easy. If I wanted to join the air force, I would have to go further in my army career in the North of Nigeria.

Apart from this I was biased because my origin from Mid Eastern and Western Nigeria with my mother coming from Western Nigeria would not have been considerate and favourable for me to come out with the best in me in my military career because of my family background and coupled with the relationship the three regions of Nigeria have within each other.

The situation calls for reaction because of feelings involved, it's about feelings common within the three regions of Nigeria they are always in antagonism.

Such antagonism is found in the UK within Nigeria I do not know how my sister in-law places our relationship. I have not made any response of being against her race or was it because she had given birth to my nice Lydia Omagbuse a Suzerain? Turning down my sister in-law Nwamaka open discussion, in my flat during a festive season during Christmas and New Year about my illness, in the presence of their children and my brother does not mean am against her she is part of my family it was about how I felt my mood was down it was just too dramatic.

There would have been nothing wrong if my sister in-law Mrs. Nwamaka Megbele simply just ask me how I felt. If it is about my illness and there was something of a problem or important to say, I have feelings they talk about me a lot within their home in my absence why not go straight to the point. Why discuses it for it to become a general dramatic thing all of a sudden for the first time. If there was anything bordering her about my illness, she and my brother can visit me privately and talk about it with me.

We all have times when it feels like things are getting on top of us, but it's important to recognize the signs that suggest what you're feeling have gone beyond the everyday ups and downs of life. Maybe you're having trouble sleeping, or you've lost interest in the things you usually enjoy. You might find yourself overreacting to things, or have difficulty concentrating.

I made a light matter out of my sister in-law discussion about my illness; instead I brought out my late father's hand book of his burial ceremony looked at it, taking note of their reaction.

My father's burial ceremony pamphlet with their presence in Nigeria during my father's funeral without my presence they did not bring to me in the UK, rather it was my eldest brother Barrister. Oritseweyinmi, who brought my father's burial ceremonial pamphlet and clothing's used for the ceremony to me on a visit afterwards in the UK.

I looked at my brother and his wife and children as if even if I wasn't present in my father's funeral they could have brought me the pamphlet it was a feeling I had. they are behaving as if they did not know my father was using me through the coral bead he gave back to me too late for it having much significance is what any member of my family would feel it is a common phenomena in Africa family a family member might even want the coral bead having meaning to them through me.

Other people within my family might want the coral bead for themselves. This is how cultural object of African are used when it has an over powering and effect on somebody else. They would want possession of the coral bead for their own use after my father's death, but they cannot have it from me.

Even if I wasn't going to keep it, I would be foolish giving it to any member of my relatives or selling it. The thought came to me of giving it to anyone of them as a gift but why, when it was something I wanted back from my father which he held on to, knowing what my father had used it for over me, to prolong his life, the more foolish I would be giving it to any other person if it has possession on it or phenomenon that doesn't seems right to me I rather get rid of it. While prescriptions is being bought from within the UK and sent to my father in Nigeria am not antagonistic about irrationality instead of me buying the prescription and send them to my father someone else is buying and sending it to him in Nigeria there are rituals in a religion understanding the position of the undertaker reality is very important.

This was my main reason for throwing the coral bead away into the central dirt bin of my number 1 to 20 Gorman road blocks of flat. So long I say to myself about culture and my traditional believes but I couldn't I now tend to see myself as strictly an observer.

Nevertheless I have gone through its theological experience, I have been used and I have had experiences of what culture could be. For me it's an experience for the rest of my life, I have been used, being used, I now have practical experience of what culture is, its effect of what culture could mean within my family.

It's not farfetched for me to have experienced that some people in my family uses culture and tradition to crave for power through blood ties in which rituals could be involved how can we create a better wellbeing, emotions, relationship within ourselves we cannot all agree with everything about life related to these in view of creating harmony we should not hurt each other's feelings or we would careless when other race, hurt our own feelings and not know how to react while the good and thoughtful once are left to be entitled with their burns in their face is written emotional scares or feelings of disillusionment within civilisation whatever affects our mind is who we truly are. About life and existence it's not merely a game for one for the money one for the show.

Asserting what we want effectively if the consequences are clear, definite, or concrete offer sound reasons for altering or not the behaviour. It could be extra cost, a waste of time, additional chores or damage to our personal possessions if the effects are tangible, if this is not the case, and we have to describe the inconvenience of dilemma.

If the relationship is close and important, the consequences are seldom tangible or concrete. We often want another person to change his/her behaviour because our needs are not met or we feel rejected or hurt. For the reason that there are no tangible consequences, we have to be careful not to impose our own values on the other person.

Communicate how we feel about the other person's behaviour on ourselves, the intensity of the feeling should be conveyed as accurately as possible because it is important that the other person is made aware of the effect the behaviour has on us and the emotion it brought about.

In describing the behaviour we consider undesirable in an objective, non-blaming and non-judgemental way. By being specific and accurate and not exaggerating or jumping into conclusions. It also involves being brief and no long-winded description.

Each one of the steps is important as far as we assert ourselves accordingly, for we will not fall into the trap of naming, blaming, or shaming the other parties.

Seven strengths of the driving interaction style:

1.	Strong sense of urgency
2.	Set clear standards
3.	Show initiatives
4.	Cool headed
5.	Assertive
6.	Attentive to details
7.	Commitment

Seven Weaknesses of the drivers:

1.	Intolerant
2.	Impatient
3.	Arrogant

4.	May over-react to critics
5.	Poor listeners
6.	Manipulative
7.	Become more egocentric

Seven Strengths of Analyst:

1.	Meticulous
2.	Good listeners
3.	Rational
4.	Tolerant
5.	Make quality decisions
6.	Not easily side-tracked
7.	Considerate

Seven Weaknesses of Analyst type:

1.	Stubborn
2.	Suspicious-minded
3.	Resist changes
4.	Undemonstrative
5.	Less risk-taking
6.	Tends to procrastinate
7.	Take no notice as (pretend)

Seven Strengths of Supporters:

1.	Democratic leaders
2.	Exhibit tact
3.	Co-operative
4.	Always trying to restore harmony
5.	Forgive easily
6.	People-oriented
7.	Creative

Seven Weaknesses of Supporters:

Too sensitive
Over elaborate
Too trusting
Avoid conflicts
Too idealistic
Over dependent

Always want to be trusted

Four Strengths and Four Weaknesses of Expressive

Strengths of Expressive	Weaknesses of Expressive
1. Socially responsive	1. Dislike routines
2. Quick-thinking	2. Over react
3. Imaginative	3. Tend to over-commit
4. Assertive	4. Idealistic

Is when we impose our values on another person for example children at home married man or parent having two or five children showing concern within the family one child is more loved or valued than the other, it leads to imposing our values on another person it could damage relationship. African parent do not customary portray tendencies of loving their children if a parent should send a child to be, educated abroad or run their business the parent want to use the child because the other children, are there to protect or wince, move closer to them. A father starts by loving a child by loving the child's mother this is wholly not customary in Africa and most third world countries. They do not portray affection for their women not even in bed when they are sleeping or making love they basically, do it to have children.

After a child become what he wants to be later in life or after helping a parent to run their business, they impose on their relatives who are less fortunate especially if one or both parents had passed away in some cases even to their parent when they are alive. That's why when children from African background are given such opportunity as education, run a family business they customary feel they are the head of the family. At the end of such family life span such children are only left with distance relatives their friends and associates have become more of a family member. To observe these all you need to do, is take a look at how the parents of such children became wealthy or famous. You have had problems in life, you have made sacrifices, took up endeavours in facing your reality within your family at the end of the day your parents or such relatives would have pulled strings within your life applying they are everything you have gone through or that they know better than you.

As for third world children who, are let's say fortunate to have been born in Africa and abroad, it is when they stamina courage to query their parent that, is when they start growing up that's when our parent would change we need to make them change the meaning of what my father or mother is to me, is quite different from what a brother or sister is to me or what a step mother or father is. If you are born in the UK and you have spent years living with your parents in their native land, you are for example in the UK just to be looked after take it easy calm down there are lots of things you can do in creating a better you.

It may, however, be appropriate at times to influence our children or spouse's values, but if we expect them to live according to our values, we are invading their personal space. If one child may feel he/she is more loved which could just basically politics while the other feels he/she is less loved would cause itra- and interpersonal conflicts which result to friction, wasted time, ill feeling and feeling, bitter, divorces, bickering and back-biting in our family or working environment.

Assertion those imply a pro-active behaviour and initiation of a verbal message, it involves communication of positive and negative messages. It enables us to express our needs, views, doubts, feelings and wants directly without violating the rights of others.

Social conflict is the struggle for agency or power in society. Social conflict or group conflict occurs when two or more actors oppose each other in social interaction exerting social power in an effort to attain scarce or incompatible goals and prevent the opponent from attaining them. It is a social relationship wherein the action is oriented intentionally for carrying out.

The pursuit of interests generates various types of conflict. Thus conflict is seen as a normal aspect of social life in some cases, abnormal because of its occurrence. Competition over resources is often the cause of conflict. Society is composed of different groups that compete for resources. While societies may portray a sense of cooperation, there is a continual power struggle between social groups as they pursue their own interests. This often means that those who lack control over resources will be taken advantage of. As a result, many dominated groups will struggle with other groups in attempt to gain control.

The real foundation on which arises a legal and political superstructure and to which correspond definite forms of social consciousness. Seeing Jonathan Goodluck as president from eastern region of Nigeria begins an era of social revolution. The changes in the economic foundation lead sooner or later to the transformation of the whole immense superstructure.

Jonathan was born in Otueke in Ogbia Local Government Area of the then Eastern Region, later Rivers State now Bayelsa State to a family of canoe makers. Jonathan holds a B.Sc. degree in Zoology in which he attained Second Class Honours, Upper Division. He also holds a M.Sc. degree in Hydrobiology and Fisheries biology, and a Ph.D. degree in Zoology from the University of Port Harcourt. After obtaining his degree, he worked as an education inspector, lecturer, and environmental-protection officer, until he decided to enter politics in 1998.

Jonathan and his wife, Patience, have two children. He is a member of the Ijaw ethnic group.

Rivers State is one of the 36 states of Nigeria. Its capital is Port Harcourt. It is bounded on the South by the Atlantic Ocean, to the North by Imo, Abia and Anambra States, to the East by Akwa Ibom State and to the West by Bayelsa and Delta states. Rivers state is home to diverse ethnic groups some of which include: Igbo, Ijaw, and Ogoni.

The inland part of Rivers state consists of tropical rainforest; towards the coast the typical Niger Delta environment features many mangrove swamps.

Rivers state, named after the many rivers which border its territory, was part of the Oil Rivers Protectorate from 1885 till 1893, when it became part of the Niger Coast Protectorate in 1900 the region was merged with the chartered territories of the Royal Niger Company to form the colony of Southern Nigeria.

The state was formed in 1967 with the split of the <u>Eastern Region</u> of Nigeria. Until 1996 the state contained the area which is now in the <u>Bayelsa State</u>.

The Eastern Region was one of <u>Nigeria</u>'s federal divisions, dating back originally from the division of the colony <u>Southern Nigeria</u> in 1954. Its capital was <u>Enugu</u>. The region was official divided in 1967 into three new <u>states</u>, <u>East-Central State</u>, <u>Rivers State</u> and <u>South-Eastern State</u>. East-Central State had its capital at Enugu, which is now part of <u>Enugu State</u>.

The region was what, later became <u>Biafra</u> which was in rebellion from 1967 to 1970.

In studying such transformations it is always necessary to distinguish between the material transformation of the economic conditions of production, which can be determined with the precision of natural science, and the legal, political, religious, artistic or philosophy in short, ideological forms in which men become conscious of conflict within them and fight it out. Just as one does not judge an individual by what he thinks about himself, so one cannot judge such a period of transformation by its consciousness, but, on the contrary, this consciousness must be explained from the contradictions of material life, from the conflict existing between the social forces of production and the relations of production.

Mankind thus inevitably sets itself only such tasks as it is able to solve, since closer examination will always show that the problem itself arises only when the material conditions for its solution are already present or at least in the course of formation. In broad outline while the bourgeois are the last antagonistic form of the social process, antagonistic not in the sense of individual antagonism but of an antagonism that emanates from the individuals' social conditions of existence property, prestige, and power the main influences to the conflicting behaviours of groups in society.

Stratification is the distribution of a valued good in levels, or could be looked as the inequalities among individuals and groups. It determines three levels of stratification they include property, economic class, prestige status, and power party. Property is related to control and ownership; prestige is the position that gains value determined by interactions with others; power is influence, relations, and position.

Psychology the study of the <u>mind</u>, partly via the study of behaviour, grounded in <u>science</u>. Its immediate goal is to understand individuals and groups by both establishing general principles and researching specific cases. For many, the ultimate goal of psychology is to benefit society classified as a social, behavioural, or cognitive science. Psychologists attempt to understand the role of <u>mental functions</u> in individual and <u>social behaviour</u> processes that underlie certain functions and behaviours.

Psychologists explore such concepts as <u>perception</u>, <u>cognition</u>, <u>attention</u>, <u>emotion</u>, <u>phenomenology</u>, <u>motivation</u>, <u>brain functioning</u>, <u>personality</u>, <u>behaviour</u>, and <u>interpersonal relationships</u>. It also considers the <u>unconscious mind</u>.

While psychological <u>knowledge</u> is often <u>applied</u> to <u>assessment</u> and <u>treatment</u> of <u>mental health</u> <u>problems</u>, it is also applied to understanding and solve problems in many different spheres of <u>human activity</u>. The majority of psychologists are involved in some kind of therapeutic role, practicing in clinical, <u>counselling</u>, or <u>school</u> settings. Many do scientific research on a wide range of topics related to mental processes and behaviour, and typically work in university psychology departments or teach in other academic settings. Some are employed in <u>industrial and organizational</u> such as <u>human development and aging</u>, <u>sports</u>, and <u>health</u>.

The word psychology literally means, 'The study of the <u>soul</u>, breath, spirit. These are effects I go through more in the mind and thoughts coupled with my activities I choose to go through each steps from stages to stages in my hallucinations though my thoughts are distorted at certain times in the day or at night the idea of such thoughts through reliance and positive thoughts put me in a more positive temperament but, it takes effort.

I feel the Islam washes their hand, leg, face and pray three times a day, to unveil or to divest themselves our soul and body are the temple of God,

We Africans who where Christian should focus more on being Christine's, tradition or juju just as Jamaicans are to voodoo were repressed and delusion about the effects of voodoos and jujus it is about time we start divesting ourselves of it. It's only natural we now unveil to reveal a new Heaven. Our body and soul with the irrationalities we face on earth, before the coming of Christ, for which reason we have in the New Testament of the Holy Bible in the book of revolution ending with Amen. The gods and deities originating juju is as a result of a breakthrough through their own divine self at first they gave it out through their own inspiration and self, later there was a breakthrough of offering creatures as sacrifice now it's a breakthrough of using ourselves taking from one person and giving to the other while human sacrifice has been abolished but still goes on in certain parts of the world. It is all a paradigm like in a cup that would gradually corrode but have meaning based on life and experience through existentiality. These gods and dirties were not given an opportunity to express as Christ did this is body this is my blood they were not Jews but Christians or pagans they came to Africa our mode of living and environment, culture, heritage and tradition might have express this as also attached to the gods and deities but are left to drift through their interference we still held on to our beliefs and then, came Islamic religion. Life experience and religion is like a cloth being washed and wiggle by hand. With the Arabs', they wash hands, leg and face three times daily, and pray three times. Days are gone when war lords or men of power raise insects, snakes in multitudes to or guard or fight on their behalf such are powers now lucked intact by such creatures by omens and realisation of science and technology which no man should unveil anymore but rather use science to represent by now, we should be living in the age of reasoning which has taken its effect through science and technology whereby it is left, for moral virtues' to uphold humans with a sense of reasoning to do just. If the age of reason has already taken place by now, we should show awareness to making amends to related inconsistencies of the world that is to come. In this age of reasoning it's not just to read books or one enjoys reading it is to read and capture the full meaning of what the book entails.

It should all be a distension of Europeans, Middle East, and Africans right from the time of human evolution after Lucifer, the Devil and Satan was cast down from Heaven. Every parts of the world sought out what Heaven wanted of them.

No matter what religion we belong to, race, creed or beliefs we all originated and lived within the Heavens and the earth. The Islam originate and live within the earth and the abyssal, this was why the archaeologist did lots of work and findings in these region of the world, which were occupied by the Arabs.

What where the interest of European centuries years ago in the Middle East, Afghanistan Lebanon, Cairo, and Egypt. While the Arab parts of the world should be asking, what are the interests of the Europeans Astronauts are venturing through desperate endeavours into the moon and planets of our universe? There is no reason for anyone to be a Pagan on the face of the earth. Every one of us should have a religion or beliefs. In my case, my conscience is my God if I have a body and have to interact not only with my environment but with other people there must be something of belief if, there are no beliefs, the world would just be about like and dislike with a hole at each stage asking who are we. In our beliefs we may have likes and dislike in certain beliefs we are content with and some of which, we are not or find difficult to apply but with not putting ourselves in the position of God. Nobody can live in this world and not contemplate on or find out who God is there are lots of reason to ask why certain things are the way they are.

Being a Christian, of many different denominations all over West Africa, I am in no way biased but left thoughtful about any other religion, many of us should be aware personally and spiritually, how long have the earth been occupied by we humans? Being able to discern, or incapable of discerning right from wrong, truthfulness from falsehood are all I need to go through any religion. Contrary to expectation within the elite and the down trodden once on earth, it is the down-trodden once who have much wisdom, experiences of life inherencies and causation than the elites this makes them viable to concepts of reasoning if they cannot, it is because of hat cheating, backbiting, kicking, slapping and hitting.

All this attributes should all be self contained in all humans in terms of our human awareness, consciousness and sub-consciousness through repeated trials to transcend or upgrading our civilisation not basically having to do with material effect but about our inward being. We ask questions such as; why are we here on earth, why do humans suffer, with wonders untold including those of science and technology, unfolding each day in our lives. Through many years, decades, and centuries, we are prone to ask questions why this or that happened with our memories emotional feelings affected yet, some of us could easily forget, if today or yesterday was a Monday or a Wednesday.

Life on earth is always a changing process, such as comparing the era of, e.g. Conan the conqueror acted by Arnold Schwarzenegger is quite different from what our lives is today in the 21st century. I reckon the story must have been written many years before it became a tail on cinemas movie or before, the European became Christian's in the Western hemisphere.

For these reasons, thanks to does who invented television, radios, hydro-electric power, after many years of isolation in many under developed parts of the world, these inventions, now have one or two things of significance attached to their ways of life culture, history and customs of people's lives it should be used to upgrade heritage, history that applies to our conformity about life.

Many of us do emphasis on the present, or the future, technology is now an aid to our memories, the more we observe ourselves, as having something in common as we dwell on earth, within different race and creeds. Differences not only in technology but other things i.e. the cloths we ware, banking, the way we care for ourselves, the effect of synergy in our lives, the food we eat, or even the made of the house and bed we sleep on.

Within Africa alone it is quit natural we look at ourselves with indifference, with technology of television and radio, our culture, history, our ways of life, tradition are more in focus, to be left open for the observation of the rest of the world. In Africa, we are incapable of recording Omen e.g. the birth of the antichrist, but the whole idea of Africa, is to get rid of all demonic powers, or anything that has the attributes of evil let us concentrate on our consciousness, doubts, and taste.

The intervention of technology is good towards our own endeavour if our motives in Africa are true and sincere especially within the African government and its elite. Under developed as it may be, having the most divers of race, culture, tradition, compeered to the rest of the world we would eradicate ignorance and doubts that it is not good to be wealthy or associate ourselves with Europeans. Let us get rid of this devil and evil spirit or witch doctors sucking objects out of peoples head and stomach it is exorcism but it's out dated cloning, surrogacy, sex change are exorcism of the present age and era.

With the intervention of technology in all third world countries, i.e. the use of television, radio, telephone, mobile phones, and a recognised banking system to explore our wealth, we are now prone finding lots of similarities within ourselves as Africans and the rest of the world to be united under one body through intervention, within ourselves if we wish. I look forward to such an era. Nobody can change you from who you are you will always be a part of yourself.

Most people are of the opinion, including myself, that there is a relationship within Britain and America, with such a long distance apart. But all Europeans are the same, they even have skin colour, speech, language differences, which is also common in Britain today within the Scots, Irish, Welsh, and Dutch.

It is through their creativity e.g. technology, cinemas, air plans, science and medicine, they have structurally presented themselves to the rest of the world to gain recognition. China is the only third world country to have been found utilising such development to some full potentials India and Nigeria in their movie and cinema industries, and it is doing them much good in getting recognised around all corners of the Earth. You still have the choice of not believing in everything you see, let us make it for the better the road is long and head let us make it easy for ourselves by now, we should have exposed our indifferences.

Am not a child to have grown up within my family in Africa, who would because , am British and am residing in the UK, would have done any such thing like speaking to any of my parent aloud with disrespect! African children never have such chances and never, in an African child dream could he or she take such an action towards their parents. Something was wrong; and it was confusing.

28th July 2007 UKTV History at 11.15 featured on television Sahara with Michael Palin. After watching the documentary about Omar in Timbuktu east to the nomadic headers of Wodaabe, who had numerous wives and children how does he fend for his wives and children they should not be partly born to be his slave but with a dignified meal each day for himself and family

The same thing applies to most parents in Africa, though my father had something to offer but not until my father receives a depressed temperament from me or gets a rubbing on his head that's when we are likely to receive favours from our parents.

I thought to myself when next I see Miss Loraine O'Connor, what is happening in our lives I want to shear my views with her on what could likely be the cause of my illness? I still wonder why she went to Egypt, before we become friends. I reckon it might have got to do with what the Vikings or Normans did in Europe centuries ago. I have feelings she has interest in Africa.

After each day of my word processing, I am faced with racing thoughts in my mind and thoughts, e.g. what did I say, why did I say this or that and why didn't I say this or that. It always makes me feel less conscious of my illness keeping a good frame of mind I am fortunate to have insight into my illness as a schizophrenics? Not many sufferers have insight to their illness but just go through them what creates temperament of awareness starts from early childhood identifying once self with their experience at that stage is very important at this stage they have eyes, legs can speak they have started encapsulating themselves and their environment the kind of people around them other experience that follows at such stage, should make them more focus to expressing their thoughts, feelings and emotions.

It is true am schizophrenic related to certain symptoms not all of them are bad we live in a world of beauty, ugliness and death do not pass judgment on any one in a world like ours if you do apply reason not all that with resentment, people are of the opinion being a schizophrenia means one cannot prepare meals, have a bath, he or she have to be on drugs, cocaine, marijuana, anti social behaviour est. its far more than that we live in a world where other people might use your predicament to make a pass because of their own wish for empowerment or to redress their own feelings or emotion we are all here to put ourselves in perspectives of what is left for us to find out that's why we have life its one reason why we are who we are being capable of understanding such paradigms is a blessing. Could it be all true if one is a schizophrenia they are incapable of looking after themselves, the idea of the illness, is never to let the illness and symptom take control over the life of a person. You do not have to be on drugs to be termed a sufferer.

It is often the case, of people like me, who could be termed as doing all I can to manage the illness who takes the bitter blows from whatever goes on related to the illness certain aspects of it are mistaken or the real issues involved is being avoided by cares. Because of our illness some of us could be mistaken from what we really are or are going through this can cause breakdowns.

I am capable of doing the things I do regardless of my illness, I mean being able to braze myself up within the community I dwell in, living a life, like every other individual partly because of my background or because of who I think, I am. Having spent part of my life in West Africa, I do not think my illness would reach a point where I would not be resilient to outlive the illness infarct I would be found to be much stronger in certain aspects related to my illness.

At mid life, we reflect on not just occasions, but on paths and opportunities we have missed at certain times in our life, what we must do in our more years to come. This in some cases might be uncomfortable we might come to conclusion we have been hurts, suddenly past experiences we could have long forgotten suddenly resurfacing, catching us on the way.

I feel am being bewitched or be in a condition that I am under a spells or evil forces around me. These are what I want out of life; my super human strength is too much for me. I want and choose to divest myself of my strength certain reality of transubstantiation lies with me.

Through this process, I grow attitudes of acceptance, putting my past in a microscope setting, seeing what I could acknowledge as blessings or burdens which are part, or have been parts of my life, believing in God, my own and other people's existence that worked all things promises, mistakes, and misdirection together for good.

I spoke to Dr. Banjac on my appointment at Ferryview mental health centre about these I told myself; since this is a process symptom I suffer from, I try to control myself, make use of self made therapy as much as I could, e.g. not neglecting my every day activities and choir as would any other person in my community, and writing, without forcing my pace. I feel I would reach a pace I would move more freely as well as accept my limitations as the psalmist declares 'The boundary line have fallen for me in pleasant places; I have a goodly heritage' Psalm 16:6.

It could not be described as the same as it was in 1994 with me telling my father to step down, smirching an empty bottle not really to hurt, but to show my distress of how I really felt, shouting at him, I was his last child with my mother he did not see me whilst, I was born in the UK in 1966 because my father had to be in Nigeria because, he had lost his mother, Mrs. Awoma Akinlami to call for a redress when you really love somebody there could be certain things one understand or go through you feel the other person would understand in some case might have gone out of limits.

I lost my mother in 1993, my father never wanted me to be at my mothers' funeral, what else does my father wants me to do for him, with the normal Itsekiri pepper soup ingredient he brought, and left outside my flat because I would not let him in did I know if the pepper soup ingredient had been prepared by Cordelia or Tsainomi Megbel? This time around, with his fourth wife, Mama Bawo as she is called within the family her name is Mrs. Tsainomi Ayo Megbele, whom, my father recently married just after, my mother's death.

With four wives only one of my father's children at that time was a graduate, which was my elder brother from my mother Barrister. Oritseweyinmi, with all the wealth my father had all being spent if not on his numerous lady friends, on his chieftaincy grand occasion in Delta state with backbiting, bickering going on.

Heaven helps us all in our family, my actions towards my father was not to us conflict for personal gain, there is nothing, I would had gained by talking to my fathers, the way I did in London 1994 with my father, wearing his traditional regalia, with his new wife he brought with him on his visit she was not present with him when he visited me at my flat.

This new wife of my father who came to the UK with my father in 1994, would have been, another lady from Rivers state, she was a custom officer in Rivers state Ports Authority. My father rented a flat at Port-Harcourt Township for her, fully furnished and in my room at Port-Harcourt there was no radio or television I had to buy mine myself from minimal pay I could hardly save within which politic is involved within me and my brother with his family partly neglected at Warri and where was my mother at this time or what is expected of me to think of my mother? Do we actually bring into focus what it takes in Nigeria to create an additional state in Nigeria Then the Federal capital is being moved from Lagos to Abuja a question to ask is what is it that is causing so much intolerance among us within the black communities.

Wouldn't my earthly father late Chief Dr. Frank Anirejuoritse Megbele the Agbueju of Warri from Delta state might had felt intolerance if somebody else did the same thing to him? This is where wealth or prestige comes in they hardly react openly but us bias politics through their influence there would be one person within a celebrated party because of immigration who would make the situation worse feeling he has influence to make him or her have their stay in the UK this mind you is a conflict within a father and a son. Regardless if he was my father, his actions are also open to scrutiny. With me life on earth becomes like to wonder on Gods creativity, Gods might, his purpose, my purpose, the mystery and motives behind my creation in comparison to my earthly father.

Coupled with human creativity pros and corn e.g. the European electricity compared to that of Nigeria, which never goes off. If we should be without electricity power, we would be informed before hand in the UK at any time.

In West Africa e.g. Nigeria the electricity power supply can go off at any time. The creation of electricity in West Africa and the introduction of the use of computers, only infers that Africa could by this time have been able to generate electricity supply by the 21st century but rather still prefer jujus and evil spirit which has always be a part of us.

My earthly parents, family, relatives, friends and neighbours, and all things created by God are open to scrutiny. These are why it is through significances of freedom with the introduction of synergy, we all would proceed following the parts of the architect of the universe and not the parts we have chosen for ourselves nevertheless we would still do so but less in misdirection. Also to consider Psalm of King Divide chapter 24 the earth is the Lord and the fullness in it.

I had taken driving lessons in Nigeria, got my driving licences, and helped my mother more than twice in changing her Toyota car registered LA car tier when it got punctured.

I carried bucket of water on my head, when I go out to fetch water for our household use; I was the only child in my father's household who rode a bicycle.

I was the only child among my mother's children who during our secondary school years who went to missed school or who haven't been to boarding school all his years in Africa.

In my school years in Nigeria, I was always with grades; no lower than just within four of the most brilliant students in my class, while I was at primary and secondary school at Lagos and Ibadan, in my class in form 1st to 6th form at school. Never was I below in scores in each unit of 9 subjects within any 4 pupils in my class in my first year to six years form, in the following subjects Chemistry, biology, physics, agricultural science, English language, arithmetic, geography, apart from statistics and Yoruba studies. Each case of my education, I was always my class prefect, and at primary school until my final year at Eyinni High school Ibadan; I was my school head health prefect.

As far back since my youth I always feel am a miracle of some sort, attached to so many people who, I also observe as miracles as well. Heaven help me, through my co-worker at Iceland frozen food plc Lewisham I have the inclination Miss. Michelle Cook her name was Awoma Akinlami before her reincarnation as my father's late mother.

Miss. Michelle Cook's height was just about my shoulder, she had red hair like a fairy tale representing, one of the crystal of the planet Krypton. My father's mother died during the time of my birth, for which reason, my father had to travel out of the UK for his mothers' funeral.

Miss. Joan Keeble, Ms Janet Clerk's first daughter I have this notion is the reincarnation of my grandmother from my mother's side, who my mother's first born son Mr. Oritseweyinmi and my sister Miss. Oritesgbubemi Megbele were under her care while my parents where in the UK, during which I and my brother Mr. Omagbami Oluwagbenga Megbele were given birth to in the UK.

My grandmother from my mother's side, died few years later, when we went back to Nigeria, as for my relationship with Miss Loraine O'Connor she took me as a friend that's nice but we need to understand each other better. My father and mothers relationship I feel was something special I wish it had worked out. Miss Lorrain O'Connor was an only child of her parents.

Knowing these people through greetings e.g. Christmas and birthday greetings with exchange of gifts, words, laughter's in my life time, I was going to do something more than spiritual, i.e. to dance to all the tunes song by the late musician legend Bob Marley {This was what late popular musician legend Bob Marley sang i.e. you will know your own on earth, then you will know where you are coming from and what life is really worth.

Bob Marley's dreadlocks and words of his mouth are nothing more than the same implication to the Tower of Babel as recorded in the Holy Bible; it has a big picture, implication and reality. Dreadlocks are the home of some people e.g. people who are spiritually dead leaving Omens, as for me, it's the home of superman, I was not born premature for no reason; it had implications.

For example the illness schizophrenia has implications that are crucible of dreadlocks which represent mental illnesses or wellbeing within Jamaicans or Caribbean's, Within the UK and at home in relation to all ethnic African background its time, to have your say. When I say African this includes Jamaican, Caribbean's, Barbados, Trinidad's and mixed race all over within black origin.

People with tribal marks on any part of their body, the something are the repercussions are scars in our physical body, and memories left with scares but they are in print by tradition that signifies belief, identity and culture. What could be the representation that had represented my birth in the UK as a premature baby?

With my condition of birth my life in Africa to represent the tears of humans the Arab world represent it as the tears of

Allah meaning the tears of Gods with implications relevance to heritage representing tears of God.

Every existence has come into this world, to reverend creation where Lucifer, Satan and the Devil have been cast down, a place which lays beauty, ugliness and death. In this planet the theology of greatness of any kind have meaning of significance that our heads are lifted high in respect to our endeavours, it is time to appreciate that we have come this far.

Why should we have the sun by day or the moon by night? Taking nothing or everything for granted, why can anyone impress or inspire you and it could meet your eyes without limitations? How did man come this far to have invented a mirror to see our reflection? In the Book written by William Shakespeare Julius Seizer said to Bateaus gentle Bateaus if, a reflection cannot sea itself, why not eye your glass. If we have come this far, have most women come about what would make them feel like a natural woman? If, I am who I am, I should basically see myself in my own reflection?

I am related to an aunty with an open middle set of teethes who is married to a doctor living at Ibadan with one of the first houses built by a Yoruba ethnic family in Oyo state with a swimming pool. Reflecting on it I see my life as a needle passing through a camel's eye starting from the day, I was born.

What is yet unknown that could be recognised yet, history would have spelt it. What is the greatest thing that brings about recognition of truth, or what has been left behind? How do we define legacy that has been left behind should be left to Gods magnificence of judgment children are born each the world is constantly changing and there is death.

I suffer from what I call medication fever where one can easily drop medication foils that comes with the medication into their internal system this in my own case, I have to keep a close eye otherwise I end up in hospital for an operation.

On the 6th of May 2010 I received a communiqué from the Ferryview mental health centre that as from 1st June 2010 I would no longer be seeing Dr. Bhatnager as my consultant but with a new consultant Dr. Sujaa Rajagopal all these where happenings falls on the month of May which happens to fell, my mother's month of birth.

I had an appointment to see Dr .A. Bhatnagar on 17th May 2010 to discuses my eating problems as a result of my recently changing my diet from English food to Nigerian diet I have not only been in the state of a coma I was also suffering from general body weakening I am just a residual image. I have resemblance to my grandfather from my father's side.

Friday 21st May 2010 I was going for a dental appointment at N. Karia and Associate dental practice at 23 Calderwood Street Woolwich to have a molars tooth extracted for the second time. This came within a week after I received a phone call from my brother Mr. Omagbemi his youngest son Zack had lost his two front teeth. During the time Mr. Zack was given birth to I was an alcoholic. As a young lad on the second time of seeing my late grandfather from my father's side there was nothing I noticed more than his rugged and a couple of lost teeth's in his mouth as if, I saw a hole inside the Moon. Which I felt right from that time had been inside my stomach when he visited his son and children at Lawani street Yaba Lagos, after which through certain experience such as my father at certain times when he is having his meal calls me and put a small bit in my mouth. Or when I grow up to live with him at Port Harcourt he insists I eat with him on the same table and from the same plates. I grow up to realise it became a family secret inside me other people or members of my family wanted it so much that they fain a lie under circumstances that I fondled my cosine Layiwola Akinlami or at that stage of my youth they tried to convey to me I should live the life of a celibate probably because culture or the science of medicine have other use of what I felt the experience is. The first time I met with my grandfather from my father's side was in his village at Obonteghareda at Delta state Nigeria when I was a young boy where he baptised his son's children before we moved to Port Harcourt in the early 1970's. It was just about after that his visit to his son family at Lagos in the mid 1970's I moved to live with my mother at FESTAC Town Lagos. My mother told me the grinding stone she uses in her kitchen was given to her by my grandfather Mr. Goldpine which I made use of while helping her out in the Kitchen when living with her at Lagos and at Ibadan Oyo State.

My late father had several little doted stabbed of tribal marks on his back which in his Ogboni cult could represent the number of children he should have if he had cared for his children and wives, it would had been something different infarct, I had to summon courage to intervene on their behalf. It might have been customary once again as a chief the local government would had provided him with land to shear among his children which would represent the tribal marks on his back it is a ritual the earth, is the Lord and the fullness thereof the world and they that dwell therein. I was born premature in his absence in the UK in the year 27th of July 1966. Sometimes existence can deal one a blow with history repeating itself why not uphold it with caution?

My father with my mother including other step mothers of mine had relationship with lots of female friends including young girls my age groups. At the end of the day, he might want people to believe, the girls where after him for something he had behind his back or his bank notes, what would have been, in my back that could have made me in a foreign land and hospital outside my parental origin to have been born premature? As Orunmila the tribal marks on my father back represent my (Awo Ifa) while the tribal marks on his father's face represents the bead used on the Awo ifa in consulting the oracle. The Awo Ifa is a dish which native doctors use flat on the ground on top of it, is placed the bead during consultation.

In Yoruba religion, Orunmila is the Yoruba Grand Priest and custodian of Ifá. This source of knowledge is believed to have a keen understanding of the human form and of purity, praised as being often more effective than remedies; his followers and priests are known as Babalawo.

Among West Africans, Orunmila is recognized as a primordial Irunmole that was present both at the beginning of Creation and then again amongst them as a priest that taught an advanced form of spiritual knowledge and ethics, during visits to earth in physical form or through his disciples.

In Yoruba mythology, Orunmila is the spirit of wisdom among the Irunmole and the divinity of destiny and prophecy. Orunmila is considered a sage, recognizing that Olodumare placed Ori (intuitive knowledge) as prime Orisha. It is Ori who can intercede and affect the reality of a person much closer than any Orisa. For this reason it is important to consult with the Babalawo in other to know one's direction and the wish of one's Ori.

The Yoruba believe in the duality in life males exist because of the female essence and females exist because of the male essence, so every major rite or ceremony includes both genders. The traditional religious point of view includes similar privileges accorded to women as priestesses of Ifá and women's societies.

Babalawo claim to ascertain the future through communication with Orunmila. This is done through the interpretation of either the patterns of the divining chain, or the palm nuts on a traditionally wooden divination tray.

Because of spiritual development they must dedicate themselves to improving their own understanding of life and be proper examples for others. A person who does not hold his own behaviour to the highest moral standards will fall out of favour with his or her community, thus creating a situation where he will be judged more harshly than others would be for like transgressions.

Some are initiated as adolescents, while others learn as full adults. In either case, training and years of dedication are still the hallmark of the most learned and spiritually gifted. This is why on average; most initiates train for as long as a decade before they are recognized as 'complete' Babalawos.

While Ogun in the Yoruba and Haitian traditional belief system, Ogun is an orisha who presides over iron, hunting, politics and war. He is the patron of smiths, and is usually displayed with a number of attributes: a machete or sabre, rum and tobacco.

Ogun is the traditional warrior and is seen as a powerful deity of metal work. As such, Ogun is mighty, powerful and triumphal, yet is also known to exhibit the rage and destructiveness of the warrior whose strength and violence must not turn against the community he serves.

He gives strength through prophecy and magic. Therefore, he is often called in the contemporary period to help the people to obtain a government that is more responsive to their needs.

In Yoruba religion, Ogun is a primordial Orisha whose first appearance was as a hunter. He is said to be the first of the Orisha to descend to the realm of Ile Aiye or the earth to find suitable habitation for future human life. In commemoration of this, one of his praise names is Osin Imole or the 'first of the primordial Orisha to come to Earth'. He is celebrated in places like Ekiti, Oyo and Ondo States. He is believed by his followers to have wo ile sun, which means to have disappeared into the earth surface instead of dying, in a place named Ire-Ekiti. Throughout his earthly life, he is thought to have fought for the people of Ire thus known also as Onire. He is the god of war and patron deity of smiths and craftsmen. He was sent to earth to make it a nice place for people to live, and he has not yet finished this task.

In all of his incarnations, Ogoun is a fiery and martial entity. He can be aggressively masculine much like the spirit Shango — but can also rule the head of a female or effeminate male initiate to whom he takes a liking. He is also linked with blood, and is for this reason often called upon to heal diseases of the blood.

Ogun comes to mount people in various aspects of his character, and the people who venerate him are quite familiar with each of them.

His possessions can sometimes be violent. Those mounted by him are known to wash their hands in flaming rum without suffering from it later. They dress up in green and black, wave a sabre or machete, chew a cigar and demand rum often, this rum is first poured on the ground, then lit and, finally, the fumes generated by this are then allowed pervading the peristyle. The sword, or much more commonly the machete, is his weapon and he often does strange feats of poking himself with it, or even sticking the handle in the ground, then mounting the blade without piercing his skin.

Ogun is the lascivious (unruly) Orisa; one that would take multiple enclosures to the battle-front; some filled to the brim with gunpowder; pockets full of miracles; allowances of wine and others sealed-tight in polished minerals.

What more can my earthly father meant to have had enough wealth, to have both ten plots of land, not only that he would have built houses on them but wasted time and money to had built just two houses on just one plot of land.

Gone are the days when men would have ten wives in a home and still call it a home but he as a god in the home education regarding such issues is still ongoing in some parts of the world. If you are a gay or lesbian clergy not in the church take it somewhere else. One might say why should one not be a womaniser when a man could be gay or there is cloning and surrogacy? It's no excuse it is moral virtues that are considered justified not immorality. The same applies when same Africans complain it was when the Europeans' brought material goods, politics and their system into Africa it became a place of hat, greed and lies it has nothing to do with it, it is the way we have been applying ourselves it is time to make a difference.

What were my father's achievement as a freemason or why should he had ever wanted to be a Freemason, what could have driven him to be a member of the African Ogboni cult member and a Christian where he could define everything he wants to be? The disposition I viewed my father is within all these he had everything and much more at his disposal to be a Nigerian president or state governor just like any most Nigerian men.

It is often thought your organisation is discriminatory towards non-members for instance you have many members cutting across the Judicial System from top Judges to Police officers or the likes perception are that if a non-member finds himself in court against a member, he will never win his case against the non-member if the Judge happens to be an Ogboni member a fellow member will be protected by the Judge as demanded by the oath that binds them together true or false why do they hold their ceremonies secretly, no one is allowed into their meetings or place of worships if he or she is not a member they know how to schedule their meetings to suit their activities?

Don't know much about Ogboni fraternity Nigerians are scared of them there are supposed to be ritualistic, witches, blood suckers have you heard there fraternity members exchange their heads with those of friends and family to extend their life span every once in a while the cult might demand you sacrifice a loved one in return you would become more successful and more powerful in society. Customary when eating with their children a child dear not stand up from the table until the parent stand up after their meal. In Nigeria Ogboni fraternity members do not pretend or hide the fact they belong to such cult, or so much for it being a secret society they are usually feared.
They strive for immortality an ability to live forever they practice act of not dying or not being subject to death.

It is not yet known if human immortality is achievable. Eternal life can also be defined as a timeless existence, which is also not known for certain to be achievable regards to this reincarnation can prove otherwise and then lead to it. Physical immortality is a state of life that allows a person to avoid death and maintain conscious thought. It can mean the unending existence of a person from a physical and spiritual source.

Through their practices it spells how Ogboni fraternity members are capable of prolong their lives, their influence cuts across all works of life like family the police, army, judges, universities, government officials, their members are protected against non members weather wrong or right and are always favoured in court.

Membership generally signified a high level of power and prestige, the society held pre-eminent political authority among decentralized groups where they were intimately involved in the selection of regents to date Ogboni members command great power and influence in the affairs of the nation you can join at any level and become empowered.

Various fraternities in Nigeria have incorporated references and insignia from the original Ogboni, including the Reformed Ogboni Fraternity, the Indigenous Ogboni, and various others. Many of these contemporary societies combine elements of Ogboni's historical functions with superficial similar functions.

The question has often been asked by various groups and people: what is a secret cult? A cult can be said to emanate from great and excessive admiration or belief in a person or idea. This could be manifested in rituals, praise songs, chants and worship. It is an unquestionable practice that may be difficult to dislodge even with superior argument.

Secret cult could therefore be defined as a set of practices, belief system or idea whose essence is known only to the inner members and excessively admired and defended even to the point of laying down one's life.

Renowned Secret cults in Nigeria includes the Reformed Ogboni Fraternity at least within each tribal clans within the Itsekiri's of Delta state you would find one or two prominent members of the reformed Ogboni fraternity my father, was one of them, Ogboni cult has always been known among varied cultures in West Africa some of them are infarct very serious with their ways as a cult fraternities. Their meeting places are ascribed to names of deities or a group such as the (ille di Oduduwa) at Port Harcourt. They have ranks held by members such as (Apena). My father as an Apena has a rod on it is a caving of human head made of gold with two horns he takes it along with him during processions such as when a cult member dies when he or she, is being buried all members go on procession match on the street with their regalia of traditional costume with the Apenas in front leading the procession. The Olori Apena's wear (Shaky) on their shoulders with a tree leaf hanging on their ceremonial hat made of white fluff.

Their secret cult are defined as a set of practices yes, belief system or idea whose essence is known only to the inner members and excessively admired and defended yes even to the point of laying down one's life. They go into the cult for reason they want something, they have to give something.

They can sign time of their death, they can sign a member of their family to take their place after their time expires in some cases they can sign a family member to be used either a wife, a child this is by way of giving something in return. Some members could sign their whole family away for prestige and when, they die the family is empty. To be a member, you most have something the cult wants before they sign you in as a member. It is such doggedness and strong conviction demonstrated by members that reinforce the importance of and awe for the group especially among non-members.

Not all members ask for wealth and prestige these are members you could find anywhere walking in the street of Western or Eastern Nigeria they have asked for power you would know them when you see them they are characterised by strong and stern physic you look at them once and you know there is no time for nonsense attitude.

The once who have asked for power are the gate keepers of their meeting places they make the arrangements they are the once more involved in background cultural activities, they are the once who know what goes on within the local communities which group are doing this or saying this or that they report to the once with wealth and prestige while they in high places feed them with information about social and political matters. One thing about this arrangement of the Ogboni cult is that no one is highly placed which implies their secrecy because each one of them had become a member by asking for something and giving something in return they more each members needs and requirement are met and respected and their secrets hidden from outsiders who are meant to be afraid of them.

The one who have asked for power would had gone in through their background or with experienced in juju they could invoke or revoke juju practice they are the once who keep the once with wealth and prestige to focus on the right, laws, ceremonies, rituals of the cult the implication is all members are in as one body undivided they all have to give, shear something e.g. educate a members child at university, find work for members or give them work through influence that binds them together whatever it is that could binds them together might be something sown within secrecy. If you had asked for wealth part of the wealth go into the cult needs, if you ask for power you use it to protect its members. Educational, career, the type of work a members dose whether as a business man or woman, a top politician still meets such requirements.

Members of the reformed Ogboni cult are very secretive even to their families and relatives. No wonder an African child could live within their parent home and hardly know them one day all you know is that they are dead. Naturally all African parent are swan into something it's typical of African background. How do young girls find themselves into the hands of herbalist, native witch doctors? Within the cult in some cases, the requirement might be a member should loose a child. It's part of why life in Africa one cannot bank on anything you must be part of something with all the bustling going on with things happening or taking place in secret is all part of a communal life.

In another case a member could be given the number of children they should have if they have not asked for a long span of life in their initial stage of entry a member could prolong his or her life by giving birth to the children in no disperse format in doing so prolong their life. Before you join a cult such as the Ogboni be very careful, be wise of what you ask for because after this comes in what you should do and what you should not do and you only have one chance to make your wish and it cannot be changed. You do not have to be rich to be an Ogboni member. They have friends who are not members in lots of places to an extent of even a groundnut seller in the street of Nigeria.

They do have their own conflicts not to be domineering over each other but if a member infringes on right, rituals of another member or the cult itself there are constrains an enigma about them is that they could be frighten of each other. Do not get me wrong this does not mean if you are not a member you can get around members easily when in conflict.

There are terms to the cult such as in relation to their children in some cases when a member dies the rest of the family dies with him this, is common among the influential once. It's not that the children would die they crumble with the member or rather the system of being a family would collapse or why did they became their children they tend after a members death to live on proceeding in some cases laid down before their death.

Rituals are set of actions, performed mainly for their symbolic value. It may be prescribed by a religion or by the traditions of a community. The term usually excludes actions which are arbitrarily chosen by the performers.

The initial function of ritualistic behaviours in human evolutionary prehistory was to achieve the altered state of consciousness in order to transform individual into groups of dedicated individuals with a single collective identity.

A ritual may be performed on specific occasions, or at the discretion of individuals or communities. It may be performed by a single individual, by a group, or by the entire community; in arbitrary places, or in places especially reserved for it; either in public, in private, or before specific people. A ritual may be restricted to a certain community.

The purposes of rituals are varied; with religious obligations or ideals, satisfaction of spiritual or emotional needs of the practitioners, strengthening of social bonds, social and moral education, demonstration of respect or submission, stating one's affiliation, obtaining social acceptance or approval or, sometimes for the pleasure of the ritual itself. But what are the correlations within Celestial spiritualism in Africa and native witch doctors? They are basically different in origin and culture the Celestials deal with Christianity, they commune with the spirit world as they imply good spirits they worship in groups as a Church, they believe in what is contained in the Holy Bible, in Christ, spiritual healing, moved by spirits, prophesies, speak in different tongs. Revelation through dreams and visions are made and they can foretell the future using spiritualism. Traditional doctors use traditional medicine which in reality is out dated traditional witch doctors may be viewed different from the use of traditional medicine but they seem the same. They use leaves cut off from trees, herbs and crude methods with rituals using goats, snails, and snakes for sacrifices while some culture keeps them as pets may be if they could use more refined ways they could authenticate their practice to please the public eyes and critics. Some say it may lead to paranoia if something goes wrong with the rituals.

There might be hardly any limits to the kind of actions that may be incorporated into a ritual. The rites of past and present societies have typically involved special gestures and words, recitation of fixed texts, performance of special music, songs or dances, processions, manipulation of certain objects, use of special dresses, consumption of special food, drink, or drugs, and much more. Religious rituals have also included animal sacrifice, human sacrifice, and ritual suicide. Ritual songs performed with weeping in some societies were regarded as required to ritually carry the departed soul to a safe afterlife enough to divest Superman from his strength and Krypton.

Rituals of various kinds are a feature of almost all known human societies, past or present. They include not only the various worship rites and sacraments of organized religions and cults, but also rites of certain societies, purification rites, oaths of allegiance, dedication ceremonies, coronations and presidential inaugurations, marriages and funerals, school club meetings, sports events, Halloween parties, veterans parades, Christmas shopping and more. Many activities that are ostensibly performed for concrete purposes, such as jury trials, execution of criminals, and scientific symposia, are loaded with purely symbolic actions prescribed by regulations or tradition, and thus partly ritualistic in nature. Even common actions like hand-shaking and saying hello may be termed rituals.

Prophecy is a process in which one or more messages are communicated to prophets which is then communicated to others. Such messages could involve divine inspiration, interpretation, or revelation of conditioned events to come divine knowledge as well as testimonies or repeated revelations that the world is divine. The process of prophecy especially involves reciprocal communication of the prophet with the divine source of the messages.

Various concepts of prophecy are found throughout all of the world's <u>religions</u> and <u>cults</u>. To a certain degree prophecy can be an integral concept within any religion or cult. The term has found deep usage in two of the world's largest religious groups, <u>Christianity</u> and <u>Islam</u>, along with many others. There must be differences in prophecies within Christianity and worship they both basically come with instruction to harder to and they are both acts prophecies has more to do with religion, juju enforces how do they make one believe in something that would come true, they initiate it. Let's say someone becomes a chief its part of culture and juju there becomes an imposition to enforce his or her calibre, stamina that enforce cultural rituals and juju. Black magic could be obtain by other people through it.

In psychology, the term ritual is sometimes used in a technical sense for a repetitive behaviour systematically used by a person to neutralize or prevent anxiety; it is a symptom of obsessive compulsive disorder.

Ritual actions are not characteristic of human cultures only. Many animal species use ritualized actions to court or to greet each other, or to fight. At least some ritualized actions have very strong selective purpose in humans and in animals. For example, ritualized fights are extremely important to avoid unnecessary strong physical violence between the conflicting animals.

Social rituals have formed a part of human culture for tens of thousands of years. The earliest known undisputed evidence of burial rituals dates from the Upper Palaeolithic. Older skeletons show no signs of deliberate 'burial,' and as such lack clear evidence of having been ritually treated. Anthropologists see social rituals as one of many cultural universals.

Rituals can aid in creating a firm sense of group identity. Humans have used rituals to create social bonds and even nourish interpersonal relationships nearly all fraternities and sororities have rituals incorporated into their structure, from elaborate and sometimes secret initiation rites, to the formalized structure of carrying out a meeting numerous aspects of ritual and ritualistic proceedings are engrained into the workings of all societies could our existence be based as a ritual considering we exist in a planet where there is beauty, death and ugliness?

Where there are coffee machines, computers, a sleeping bed attached with a TV and Hi-Fie system, luxury cars, working practices, new roads and bridges scientific development culture and human ritual in the 21st century is taking a new meaning without our awareness. We are forgetting culture and rituals as it uses to be in the old days they are now represented in other forms.

Focusing on inner life also offers a way to base personal values rational to nature or independent on phasing whims and desires while earth exists to reconnect people with their natural environment in order to restore their well-being, their health and their capacity for wisdom. Earth is our healer, companion, teacher and provider it is our home, our natural setting.

It has much to offer us, from side-effect free treatments for stress and depression, to a context for growth in spiritual maturity, to more harmonious teams and wiser decision-making.

Traditionally, many religions have regarded spirituality as an integral aspect of religious experience. Among other factors, declining membership of organized religions has given rise to a broader view of spirituality. It emphasizes qualities such as love, compassion, patience, tolerance, forgiveness, contentment, responsibility, harmony, and a concern for others, aspects of life and human experience which go beyond a purely materialist view of the world, without necessarily accepting belief in a supernatural reality or divine being. Spiritual practices such as mindfulness and meditation can be experienced as beneficial or even necessary for human fulfilment without any supernatural interpretation or explanation. Spirituality in this context may be a matter of nurturing thoughts, emotions, words and actions that are in harmony with a belief that everything in the universe is mutually dependent.

Belief is the psychological state in which an individual holds a proposition or premise to be true. Mainstream psychology and related disciplines have traditionally treated belief as if it were the simplest form of mental representation and therefore one of the building blocks of conscious thought. Philosophers have tended to be more abstract in their analysis and much of the work examining the viability of the belief concept stems from philosophical analysis.

The concept of belief presumes a subject (the believer) and an object of belief (the proposition). So, like other propositional attitudes, belief implies the existence of mental states and intentionality, both of which are hotly debated topics in the philosophy of mind whose foundations and relation to brain states are still controversial.

Our common-sense understanding of belief may not be entirely correct, but it is close enough to make some useful predictions. Understanding what your values and beliefs are is an important aspect of personal growth and to outlive mental illness. So what are values and beliefs? We all have an internalized system of values and beliefs that have developed throughout our lives. People use both their values and beliefs to guide their actions and behavior as well as helping to form their attitudes towards different things. However, values and beliefs are different.

Our values are things we deem important and can include concepts like equality, honesty, education, effort, perseverance, loyalty, faithfulness etc. Our values are very much individual and they affect us at a deep subconscious level. Every decision we make is based on our values and either we use them as avoidance or for aspiration.

Our beliefs on the other hand are assumptions that we make about the world. They grow from what we see, hear, experience, read and think about and they apply not only how we see ourselves but also how we see other people. We tend not to question our beliefs because we are so certain about them and many of them stem from childhood. Our beliefs can be changed or turned round by re-programming of our subconscious. Like values our beliefs can be split into two different types empowering beliefs and limiting beliefs.

An Orisha (also spelled Orisa or Orixa) is a spirit or deity that reflects one of the manifestations of Olodumare (God) in the Yoruba spiritual or religious system. (Olodumare is also known by various other names including Olorun, Eledumare, Eleda and Olofin-Orun). This religion has found its way throughout the world and varieties or spiritual lineages as they are called are practiced throughout areas of Nigeria, the Republic of Benin, Togo, Brazil, Cuba, Dominican Republic, Guyana, Haiti, Jamaica, Puerto Rico, Suriname, Trinidad and Tobago, the United States, Uruguay and Venezuela among others. As interest in African indigenous religions (spiritual systems) grows, Orisha communities and lineages can be found in parts of Europe and Asia as well. While estimates may vary, some scholars believe that there could be more than 100 million adherents of this spiritual tradition worldwide.

An entity possesses the capability of reflecting some manifestations of Olódùmarè Yòrùbá Orişas (translated 'owners of heads') are often described as intermediaries between man and the supernatural. The term is often translated as 'deities' or 'divinities'.

Orişa(s) are more like 'animistic entities' and have control over specific elements in nature and are better known as the divinities, and yet there are also the Orişa that are more like ancient heroes and or sages and are best addressed as dema deities. Even though in the basics of things, the term Orişa is often used to describe either of these entities it is mainly reserved for the former.

The Yoruba belief in Orisha is meant to consolidate not contradict the terms of Olódùmarè. Adherents of the religion appeal to specific manifestations of Olódùmarè in the form of those whose fame will last for all time. Ancestors and culture-heroes held in reverence can also be enlisted for help with day-to-day problems. Some believers will also consult a geomantic divination specialist, known as a babalawo (Ifa Priest) or Iyanifa (Ifa's lady), to mediate in their problems. Ifa divination, an important part of Yoruba life, is the process through which an adept (or even a lay person skilled in oracular affairs) attempts to determine the wishes of God and His Servants. The cultural and scientific education arm of the United Nations, declared Ifa a Masterpiece of the Oral and Intangible Heritage of Humanity in 2005.

Oduduwa is considered as the first of the contemporary dynasty of kings of Ife. Cosmicists believe Oduduwa descended from the heavens and brought with him much of what is now their belief system. Migrationists believe Oduduwa was a local emissary who it is said have come from an all, too earthly place to recount the coming of Oduduwa more likely signifies the region of Ekiti and Okun sub-communities in north-eastern Yoruba land and central Nigeria.

Whatever the case may be, all of the Yoruba traditionally believe that daily life depends on proper alignment and knowledge of one's Ori. Ori literally means the head, but in spiritual matters it is taken to mean an inner portion of the soul which determines personal destiny and success. Ase, which is also spelled 'Axe,' 'Axé,' 'Ashe,' or 'Ache,' is the life-force which runs though all things, living and inanimate. Ashe is the power to make things happen. It is an affirmation which is used in greetings and prayers, as well as a concept about spiritual growth. Orisha devotees strive to obtain Ashe through Iwa-Pele or gentle and good character, and in turn they experience alignment with the Ori, or what others might call inner peace or satisfaction with life.

The Yoruba theogony enjoys a Pantheon of Orishas, this includes: Aganju, Obalu Aye, Erinle, Eshu/Elegba, Yemaya, Nana Buluku, Obà, Obatala, Oxossi/Ochosi/Osoosi, Oshumare, Ogun/Ogoun/Ogunda, Oko, Olofi, Olokun, Olorun, Orunmila, Oshun, Osun, Oya, Ozain, and Shango, among countless others. In the Lucumi tradition, Osun and Oshun are different Orishas. Oshun is the beautiful and benevolent Orisha of love, life, marriage, sex and money while Osun is the protector of the Ori, or our heads and inner Orisha. The Yoruba also venerate their ancestral spirits through Egungun or Eyo masquerades, Orò, Irumole, Gelede and Ibeji, the orisha of Twins (which is no wonder since the Yoruba are officially known to have the world's highest rate of twin births of any group). In fact, the world capital of twins is the Yoruba town of Igboora, with an average of 150 twins per 1 000 birth.

The clearer we can be about our values and beliefs, the happier and more effective we will be. One option is to look at our own values by completing a range of exercises designed to draw out and clarify the things that are most important to us. These will help show why we make certain decisions.

In a wide variety of traditions, spirituality is seen as a path toward one or more of a higher state of awareness, perfection of one's own being, wisdom, or communion with God or with creation and the things we go through in life.

Spirituality is necessarily bound to any particular religious tradition.

Spirituality has played a central role in self-help in relation to my illness if spirituality is understood as the search for or the development of inner life or the foundations of happiness, then spiritual practice of some kind is essential for personal well being.

If consciousness exists apart from the body, which includes the brain, one is attached not only to the material world, but also to a spiritual world as well which could be on the basis of individuality since we have different religion, creeds and beliefs system.

In human communities, intent, belief, resources, preferences, needs, risks, and a number of other conditions may be present and common, affecting the identity of the participants and their degree of cohesiveness.

A spiritual discipline is the regular performance of actions and activities undertaken for the purpose of cultivating spiritual development. A common metaphor used in the spiritual traditions of the world's great religions. Spiritual practice moves a person along a path towards a goal. The goal is variously referred to as salvation, liberation or union (with God).

Spirituality and psychiatry some people say on the face of it, do not seem to have much in common I do not shear the same views as much as psychiatry deals with the thoughts in a person head and mind so dose spirituality infarct, both are somewhat psychological. We are increasingly becoming aware of ways in which spirituality offer benefits for mental health. This may involve anyone who has an interest in spirituality and mental health or have mental health issues or explore mental health with spirituality. How mental health and spirituality connects, how to help people with mental health spiritually.

Spirituality often becomes more important in times of distress, emotional stress, physical and mental illness, loss, bereavement and the approach of death.

This may involve helping people with mental health have deep sense of meaning and purpose in life, a sense of belonging, a sense of connection of the deeply personal with the universal, acceptance, integration and a sense of wholeness.

Spirituality is not tied to any particular religious belief or tradition culture and beliefs can play parts in spirituality, every person has their own unique experience of spirituality it can be a personal experience for anyone, with or without a religious belief. It's there for anyone. Spirituality also highlights how connected we are to the world and other people.

Spiritual issues can be therapeutic such as asking questions what is my life all about is there anything that gives you a sense of meaning or purpose? Emotional stress is often caused by a loss, or the threat of loss. Have you had any major losses or bereavements? How has it affected me and how have I coped?

Do you feel that you belong and that you are valued? Do you feel safe and respected? Are you and other people able to communicate clearly and freely, did you felt that there was a spiritual aspect to your current problem?

A spiritual assessment should be part of every mental health assessment. Depression and substance misuse, for example, can sometimes reflect a spiritual void in a person's life. Mental health professionals also need to be able to distinguish between a spiritual crisis and a mental illness, particularly when these overlap.

Spiritual practices can help us to develop the better parts of ourselves. They can help us to become more creative, patient, persistent, honest, kind, compassionate, wise, calm, hopeful and joyful. These are all part of the best health care.

I feel I had at one time made a wish out of the statue of Zeus what, was granted to me out of the statue of Zeus had been on behalf of the land my father built his house on?

We now know how come certain parts of the world could receive snow and other parts harmattan which is common in Nigeria that comes from the North in the month of November and December or sand dust such as it is found in the desert how come did king David said if I have the wing of a dove, I would wonder of, to the desert to find myself shelter which is what every man who want peace and happiness seek from the time King David used these words what has humans been striving to achieve we all know what we want out of life lots of things happening to make our dreams come true and Christ said seek and ye shall find.

As the space mission through NASA continues I wait for their findings if I live long enough as the space mission continues I appreciate the presence of the first black woman to have under taken space mission in September 12 1992 without being biased it was not a black man. More so with interest it falls within a time in the history United State of America a mixed race African is the president of the United State of America.

Or why during the election debate for the first time in the history of the British people where just after the election in the second week of May 2010, David Cameron and Nick Clegg want to form a coalition government after the debate.

I am two years older than Miss. Michelle Cook, but much older than Miss Joan Keeble. I and Miss Joan Keeble both worked at the Woolwich Gala club. I know these would call for some psychiatrist scrutinized with a bit philosophical schizophrenic's paranoia.

Every individual have realities to keep intact, to perceive, all true intention of reality through experience related to love, joy, peace, patients, kindness, generosity, faithfulness, gentleness and self-control and their opposites as well in a way that ask or explain why things happen or why are things the way they are. Existence is a quest when it is backed with enough food, clothing's and shelter then reason and purpose could takes its place.

At University I was provided with a computer installed for me in my flat to get on with my studies, because of my illness. After my studies at University, I bought my own personal computer installed for me in my council flat by Curry's store in Charlton. If there are opportunities, people would do better in life.

One thing about these Universities in the UK is that, they give thorough and precise information and introduction on the various courses they offer. There is an enrolment day, the course starts and there are time table when class would be held with different time slot.

I have this feeling my mother was sad at the time she gave birth to me while, I was asking through my condition of birth what was wrong I gesticulated! It would have been considered a serious condition then but know, the science of premature birth is has been much more developed.

Medical practitioners and science of medicine have done a lot I still have to do a lot for myself. Before cloning began I had worked in a cold store making sure, I remain self contained at this time, I was somehow reacting, protective and rationally over my system. What do they do with sperm donated for cloning humans, they freeze it? It is the same reaction that triggered me living in a male only hostel.

Thursday 26th February 2009 Astronomers took stunning photos of a Heavenly Eye watching us on earth from outer space, very soon they would not only be taking stunning photos of the eyes of Heaven watching us on earth, but the pillars that holds the universe! Life is complicated enough but we have to start from somewhere understanding life and our existence.

When Jesus Christ disciples were filled with Holy Spirit, they all began to speak in different languages. Each having a unique language, in their own unique way being filled with Holy Spirit began to communicate Heavens love to people they should turn to God.

Could the disciples in their dreams, vision probably, in their prayers had envisage the use of technology as it is on earth in this world of today, e.g. the use of vehicle, air planes, photography, science or the earth's current infrastructure.

What if Moses hadn't been educated and trained as an Egyptian Prince, would Moses have been able to have the stamina, courage, temperaments to withstand the miracles God did through him within the Egyptians and the Hebrews?

Feeling the way I do, regardless of being schizophrenics. Each of us has ways of our own communicating who God and the Heaven is, and what we are, or pensive about ourselves and our existences, which is unique in each and every individual in different ways. I believe in reality most of what we do has to come out through reality its one reason why we are who we are going through certain things we later tend to understand. Always searching is a good temperament, a gift of facing reality based on life's trials sometimes we would found making mistakes open to advice, opinions of other people might help us further.

It's good to search for what life and death is then we might understand immortality we all have spans of life to be viewed under different scenarios. Slavery is not just chains in legs and hands we should not take our existence as a form of slavery it has been based on precondition. We could be slaves to our own desires, or the way we shape our lives depending on our stand in life, we reincarnate through birth and rebirth to earth, again, and again to undergo our trials through perpetual pilgrimage, just as study skills count, so those life experiences count and how it relates to Heaven we wait for. In Heaven, we would become spent forces with our lives persistent with relentless spiritual glow cycling our repeated life's while on earth but in different dimension such as in all goodness.

I often ask why do people have resemblance is it because we are all part of one body through repeated life and trials, In Freemasons the universe has only one eye through which all things are perceived persistently, because of their beliefs in symbols they, are open to divesting based on paranormal, superstition or phenomena's if it is realistic.

Our whole life, communication, personality, synergy, creativity and reality is to communicant's realism of God based on what our universe and we wants it to be, before, we took form. In due course what we would accomplish on earth through human endeavours would be the Heaven we have attain for ourselves with the help and blessing of God who is willing to give us time in undergoing our trials.

Our existence, is always taking something from us in otherwise bad things happen that we persevere making use of our endeavours based on what are left at our disposal for good. A new Heaven we have to face a new reality which best soothe us that we have given ourselves to God goodness of humanity or face eternal extinction. There are only two forces on earth good and evil. We all have multiple choices but predominantly two choice, Our existences leaves us with choices e.g. being a parent, celibate, being an elite in our communities, going for sex change, being gay or a lesbian, being unwell, being the down trodden once are all by precondition that we make choice or change the choices is for us to find out.

We made the choices ourselves under a conceptualised, catalysed e.g. food, nature, qualities from childhood to adulthood, endeavours, dreams cyclised understanding under subconscious's mind and through the effects of what we find on this planet. They are trials we have to undergo in making choices; we are driving the point of good and evil home. I walk my way into life on earth, and make my way back to where ever I presume to have originated from, because I have reason believing I am living in a world, with certain attribute or tendency deflating about my existence is always a journey made by choices yet I continually come back to it.

I found difficulties walking to the Ferryview mental health centre I had to book an earlier appointment for me to see Dr. .A. Bhatnagar before the one that had been booked for me on the 7th of April 2009. I have been under the Ferryview mental health centre since 1995 to 2009; I had not been under a care co-ordinator since I was under the care of Dr. Mazaroli too much fuse under different cares make me unsettle under their care.

From what I experienced at the Ferryview mental health centre, for some reason in my past experience with my uncles in Nigeria living within my family, I realised I have to consider my uncles action for confronting me I had fondled my cosine.

The reason that brought me to the conclusions was because of a young man around my age group, also a patient; he was a dreadlock Rastafarian very much in resemblance to my uncle Mr. Tamitayo Akinlami my father's half brother.

The Rastafarian was also suffering from mental health issues, and then I began wondering what my late uncle's reality was all about. Could something about my being born premature have had something to do with my late uncle? Yes it probably could be as I took another look at the Rastafarian he looked haggard and not well cared for.

I find it heard but true to believe I had relationship in teratology to this particular Rastafarian, the branch of science in medicine concerned with the development of physical abnormalities during my fatality, or early embryonic stage of my life while I was born in the UK.

This Rastafarians was seating by the entrance door, by the tea and coffee machine table. He even gestured me into the reception area by pressing the internal entrance door latch for me to enter the Farryview mental health centre with Ms Barbra as the receptionist for the day.

My reason for being at the Farryview mental health centre that particular morning was because of how I was getting on with my recent change of medication. My medication had changed from Quetiapine tablets 25mg to Olanzapine.

In my past reviews I had been on Quetiapine 25, 50, 75, 100, and 150mg. I was getting on well with my Quetiapine 25mg, medication hoping it will then, be increased gradually. I look forward each day to be tranquil.

Why should I be on higher dosage of my medication? I see reason believing I thrive very well with minimum dose intake of my medication at my initial stage of being on new prescriptions. For which reason; I preferred 25mg of Quetiapine. But to my psychiatrist and cares, I should be on higher dose or the medication, will not take effect.

I had to be there for a review as well because I was suffering from the following side effects of Olanzapine e.g.
1. Eating too much
2. Breathing with difficulties
3. Difficulties in grasping breath

4. Pain within my chest
5. Pains in all my body joints and
6. When I walk a short distances, I get a contraction within my chest unable to breath with ease.
7. Going through such phase I realise suffering with some psychologically emotionally related issues.

Cares I spoke to that morning at the Ferryview mental health centre were Esther and Ms. Marcie Brian.

Emotion is a complex <u>psycho physiological</u> experience of an individual's state of mind as interacting with <u>biochemical</u> and <u>environmental</u> influences. In <u>humans</u>, emotion fundamentally involves '<u>physiological arousal</u>, expressive <u>behaviours</u>, and <u>conscious experience</u>.' Emotion is associated with <u>mood</u>, <u>temperament</u>, <u>personality</u>, <u>disposition</u>, and <u>motivation</u>. Motivations direct and energize behaviour, while emotions provide the affective component to motivation, positive or negative.

There are basic and complex categories, where some basic emotions can be modified in some way to form complex emotions the complex emotions could arise from cultural conditioning or association combined with the basic emotions. Further to this, relationships exist between basic emotions, such as having positive or negative influences, with direct opposites existing.

Distinction is made between emotion episodes and emotional dispositions. Dispositions are also comparable to character traits, where someone may be said to be generally disposed to experience certain emotions because of their experience. For example an irritable person is generally disposed to feel <u>irritation</u> more easily or quickly than others do. Finally, some theorists place emotions within a more general category of 'affective states' where affective states can also include emotion-related phenomena such as pleasure and pain, motivational states for example, <u>hunger</u> or <u>curiosity</u>, moods, dispositions and traits.

My parents came into the UK in the 1960s to engulf themselves in the English man and European ways of life. I hope one of my psychiatrist at the Ferryview mental health centre Dr Gbadamosi and many others some of them have tribal marks on their face we have to realise the opportunities given to use as Africans that we should understand each other.

What are the significances of a UK born African, some of us had lived part of our lives in Africa? We should encourage pleasure of culture, do away with the dark side of culture rather than practicing Juju's against each other, be united as one, understand each other in relation to our culture, tradition, custom and what rolls it play in unifying us within our cultural background and how it coincide with the rest of the world since they have their own culture as well.

From the book of Colossians on the new testament of the Holy Bible chapter 3 the rules for holy living verse 12 to 17. Therefore as God's chosen people, holy and dearly loved, cloth yourselves with compassion, kindness, humility, genteelness' and patients. Bear with each other and forgive whatever grievance you may have against one another. Forgive as the Lord forgives you, and over all these virtues put on love, which binds them all together in perfect unity.

Let the peace of Christ rule in you and me in our hearts, since as members of one body we were called to peace that we be thankful, let the word of Christ dwell in us richly as we teach and admonish one another with all wisdom and as we sing psalms, rhymes and spiritual songs with gratitude's in our hearts to God, whatever we do, whatever words or deeds, we should do it all in the name of the Lord Jesus Christ giving thanks to God the father through him...

Early morning 24th of March 2009 I was at GLLab in Woolwich Powis Street to speak to Mr. Terry McGinness about work placement for the second time, to really show how interested I was to have work placement in housing not particularly in housing but in administration.

Mr. McGinness was straight to the point, giving me all the information I need to know about, e.g. founding from the government, how much was being invested, the founding have already been acquired, the project is about to be given the go ahead and he would be contacting me as soon as a place is available in work placement for me.

Speaking to Esther and Ms. Marcie Brian on the 23rd of March 2009 because I wanted a quick medication review with Dr. Bhatnagar at the Ferryview mental health centre, earlier than on the 7th of April, which had already been booked for me Ms. Marcie Brain told me according to what Dr Nair told her, I should stay on Olanzapine 15mg in the morning, whichever is right for me either in the morning or by night.

I felt I would be more certain of what to do about taking my medication and symptoms I suffer by speaking to my psychiatrist as much as I felt about having an earlier review, there wasn't much they could do. My appointment had been booked for the 7th of April that was all.

This was the same occurrence which, happen in 2007 when I had a breakdown or rather relapse, at the same time, having problems with an over payment of housing benefit, which had been recorded by Riverside housing benefit office, because they were of the opinion that I was on receipt of disability living allowance, which I wasn't.

With my illness and relapse, I was left alone to deal with the matter myself, e.g. Ms Marci Brown, Mr. Akim, Carty and many others, where among those visiting me regularly at my flat from Queen Elizabeth hospital home treatment team in 2007.

I was at the Ferryview health centre on the 26th of March, to see Dr Hughes, he was the one who introduced Quetiapine tablets to me, which I found very favourable to my getting better from my illness, but my psychiatrist says I could not be put on Quetiapine 25mg, it should be above 100g. I would not mind the medication of Quetiapine being increases gradually after some time, I surly prefer Quetiapine than Olanzapine.

I do not take drugs; I have quit smoking and drinking, for some time. Dr Hughes checked my weight gain because I have been eating too much. He would not add my continued intake of Co-Danthramer capsules on my repeat prescription emphasising it is a medication that should not be taken continuously.

Any way he did prescribe some Co-Danthramer capsules, with my other repeat prescription, that have already run-out. One other prescription Dr .A. Bhatnagar prescribed for me to take along with my Olanzapine tablets, was Clonazepam tablets 500 micrograms, one to be taken twice a day, Clonazepam makes me feel better each time, I take the medication, because it relaxes me and makes me sleep well, regardless that it has an effect of making me unable to sleep on certain nights all because, I wasn't doing too well with Olanzapine which makes me over eat even at night sometimes I find myself preparing something to eat.

The illness schizophrenia is not only psychiatrist illness, it is also a psychological illness but what are the conflicts behind such an illness?

Day by day babies are being born, but where are we going to? Mind you, the sins of my fathers and forefathers', will always visit we who are their children. This underlines, that celibacy now has a strong and powerful implication in the life of human.

Questions should be asked why am I a schizophrenia sufferer it's a question I continuously ask myself it always ring in my ear, what are the causes, reasons for this illness after many years of my suffering as a Schizophrenia. Or what are the meaning behind my common sense, making a choice of being a celibate and not being a parent.

Or what is the meaning of my father holding back a coral bead of which, I have used paying homage to our making of a king Godwin Emiko the Olu of Warri Delta state Nigeria. Of which my father held back the coral bead, which was my father's intention for it, to be used after his death, in other, for him to reincarnate into the UK. With me deputing form him.

A LETTER OF LIFE WELL SPENT MY DEAR FATHER

The celebrations of life of chief {Dr} Frank Anurejuoritse Megbele the Agbuejule of Warri part of once Bendel state of Nigeria now known as Delta state of Nigeria within Warri Kingdom 1936-2004 {68 years} From the Ayeye Dudu family of Oleyo in greetings to Mr. Chief {Dr} Megbele's family you will forever remain evergreen in our memories signed all children.

The programme and official ministers where
Pastor Ayo Oritsejafor------Word of life bible Church in Warri.
Bishop B.O Jolomi------Foundation Faith Church Port Harcourt
Pastor Sam Aboyeji------ Foundation Faith Church, Olu of Warri Prince Godwin Emiko's Palace
Ven. P.J. Agbolayah------Christ Anglican Church Warri
Reveren. Opeyemi Ehinola------Christ Anglican Church, Warri
Rev. Best Agbolayah------Christ Anglican Church, Warri Delta state Nigeria.
I did not attend his burial because I am unwell the Friday 22nd of October 2004 service of songs at 35 Mabiaku road opposite NANA MODEL COLLEGE G.R.A WARRI delta state Nigeria was when the saints go marching in Ho when the saints go marching in.

On Saturday the next day, at 12.00noon commendation service was held at my father's resident 35 Mabiaku Road with interment at 2.00pm on Sunday 24th October there was thanks giving. His burial fell during the Nigerian Independence Day celebration Late Chief (Dr) Frank.A. Megbele was born on the 14th of October 1935 his burial was held at African Church Warri. As I was word processing, the phone rang picking it up, the voice said am calling from talk, talk they are my telephone and broadband service provider they want to know if am the account holder I continued all it means to me is an extempore prayer so I continued telling myself am not alone. At the same time I heard this voice calling me talk, talk my father was dead and buried why not let it be am the only one in the family, who is broadcasting his memoirs. Why not he was born on the 14th of October 1935 his burial took place within the month of October what a coincident.

I hope probably reaching the end of my own time my mind would be open to reveal the order of outing and thanksgiving service for my father's burial i.e. processional hymn-IYHM-IHB 209/A&M 240 introit, praise worship, HYMN – IHB

124/A&M 135, special PSALM – chapter 6, lesson – revelations 21 vs. 1-7, HYMN – IHB 80/SS&S 38,, creed to grace, announcement, general thanksgiving, sermon, hymn/the collection- IHB 61/SS&S 488. The sermon was read by Ven. P.J Agbolaya followed by social thanksgiving while his family lead to the closing choruses, closing prayer and benediction as time goes by, I felt I was the watchword for a peace greeting the, I looked forward for the processional HYMB – H.C. 203.

As I was later in the day reading the hand book of my father's burial ceremony memories came back to me about my background and experiences since whilst I was a young, question to be answered such as why was I born into this particular family, what has the picture of being born in the family left for me to hold on to? I felt I had been born within this African background, before my birth, considered my family disposition, mistakes, where things have gone wrong, for I dwell within this particular family for the sake that, they come out better and not self indulge themselves in ironies of situation and comparison. I never knew it was directed at me to understand probably I would had viewed the scenarios differently, lots of us grow to imply we are better, than another member within a family, which create a situation and the impression every situation within our family is up for grab.   Such might only be found within friends, and not within a family because a bound is needed within every family they, can speak in one voice.

West Africans should cultivate principles to see every dead person receives a burial considering the mode of rituals, slaughter house and the way poultries are sold in Nigeria also, the works of native and witch doctors their ways of practicing native medicine, the way houses are built and accommodated, environmental pollution, lack of good water supplies and hygiene standard our dead should be given proper burial.

African ways of livelihood are accompanied with diversity, quarrels, and disagreements. Self righteousness is always a key word within members of the same family, e.g. doing things and saying words such as I am the one mummy or daddy loves more than anyone else, or I am the one who always does the right things within the family, or from a parent if you do not agree with what I want or say and do there are many others like you, There are little or no room for attachment to initiate family bound.

For many years, Africa has always been polygamous, it was common for the head of the family raising children to look after the firm i.e. till the soil, clear the firm, plant seed and crops,. This over the years had changed every one wants to be free of one situation or the other and would love to do things in their own ways, this does not mean going beyond boundaries within your family children are born with different temperament within all family units.

The scenario of dependencies is the amour of the head of any polygamous family. With the head of all polygamous family always raised high in their family because they have scattered their seeds (children) all over the communities with propagandas whether they are looking after their family or not or care about their feelings. Dose this add much into the livelihood of African children? Its power, empowerment, survival for the fittest within which conflicts becomes inevitable you hardly can be you, you must be someone else.

The situation is so awkward because it creates situation of why is it that, it is only the good once that faces the worse scenario and loos out within a family and their community. As for me, faith has been kind to me and I would be the last person who would use other peoples predicaments, making my own way to create outraged. According to the Psalm of King Divide blessed is the man who follows the parts that God have chosen for him or her.

There is no pride in any one going about, attesting to his or her own existents that they live with pride being celibate's the situation is proving different. The sad story is that they are rather faced with prejudice; it should rather raise concern or interest why one chooses to be celibates. From my part, born into the European hemisphere, the question is what could have gone wrong.

There is no question of doubt from African origin; I have been compelled to write this book because I have knowledge of my background. Or what would you say if, I told you one of the reason my father wanted to be conferred a chieftaincy titles had been because the African cult of the reformed Ogboni fraternity once a member dies before their burial, all the thumbnails of their hands are cut off, my father did not want this to happen as is customary of the Ogboni cult in which, he was an Olori Apena title holder. Children of Ogboni members are a representation of themselves in relation to their heritage, culture and livelihood heritage would call it symbolic representation of configuration if you understand its somewhat no different from scientific configuration but having to do with culture.

Anyone who, could ham children of Ogboni members is someone who must have accepted gifts from them they are very generous in their ways infarct if you have conscience, you would question their generosity. Why because they believe if you ham something about them, you are wicked than them which, is a getaway for them their humbleness is being question while you do not know what they do in doors in secrecy. It means on the other hand your juju; witchcraft is more powerful than theirs or you tend to call for their acumen in their practice they have means to fight back. No wonder Africa is so very divers in nature do not take them for not knowing what they do culture and heritage are divers by nature resulting as a consequence of their doing juju to themselves is wrong why not do it to eliminate conflict.

There are doctors, lawyers, native witch doctors, religious leaders, business men and women involved and people from all works of life and it does not mean they agree with each other on everything. Thoughts feeling and premonitions' are divers so, what is the way forward towards development, first of all tidy the area they have huge stacks of land and forestry, animal conservation and we need not only depend on petroleum, stop turning any new settlement as villages, huge initiatives needs to take place such as building of houses and infrastructures and make their own few housing and caring necessities, market places where we sell meat and fish should be kept clean and tidy and make sure they sleep well at night. Take a look of how African poultry and food stuff are kept in the UK very presentable when those from other part of Europe such as Greek, Span, France or Italy there are sits for science comes into the UK from the way we Africans live our lives from the onset are in relation to our environment, culture, heritage and ways of life so do origins from other continents of the world, people are prune to change do not let other people tell you what you should know about yourself. We are juju orientated it was inevitable. I have come across Europeans who have fed on African diet. It's a flog gate to understand culture while if only some of us will realise the Europeans brought Africans to Europe to make us and the world a family this we have to realise if this, is really the age of reasoning. Before slavery Africans who have come across Europeans' would not have had the incline they would one day test or feed on African dishes.

Children from African and West Indies background born in the UK and the rest of Europe are looking forward to work in catering, carpenter, painters and decorators, qualified cleaners can you imagine; qualified cleaners some people would be asking what for. While in Africa for example those who have qualified as gradates in Europe who are now back home in their native land, should display knowledge of education received then, we would not only appreciate their worth but also the worth of education.

I told Mr. Harry about what I felt about Mrs. Mary Rodney my co-worker at the Woolwich Gala Club giving birth to the reincarnation of my late father Mr. Harry asked me if Mrs. Mary Rodney won't be embarrassed. I told him what for he should not underestimate the level at which West Africans uphold culture? In this case, I am rather patronising Mrs. Mary Rodney. After slavery in Africa which as of today Africa is an inferno when dealing with scattered members of the same families, someone tells you, you have given birth to his late father, it means the person knows who you are. I have a slight resemblance to Mrs. Mary Rodney.

Considering most illness or experiences, could not permit some of us to live with pride within probably ourselves and other people in several relationship race, creed or culture. Nevertheless, nobody enjoys being alone, being a smoker, a drug addict, unwell or a celibate.

My parent's including step mother, brother, sister', uncles, aunties, niece, nephews, cosines could use me as whatever in this case, I have made a choice of being who or what I choose to be, Africa is filled with rows. What could I get from it, if it needs to change and there are no changes coming forth, nobody needs tell me what to do if I have a choice but first, it has to come from me because I have an inclination of who, I want to be. It is not from the wish of other people; I become what I want to be, but being myself realistically. I thank my stare of being able to see through the arena of my family, my background and Europe.

We always seems to quarrel within ourselves, vastly arrayed in culture if is so great and beautiful we should be happy finding peace within, I thank the Europeans for coming into Africa the reason is not farfetched we can through information technology look into the beginning of our past very soon, with optimism it might be a case for tete'tet'e to greater prosperity as the French would say that's if we choose to change.

Born in the UK, I am not against everything that is happening to me it gives me insight.

Born in the UK taken away from the UK by sea passing just by Ghana, to Lagos in Nigeria for every step I made as I grow up in West Africa where trials. I know not how to hat, create enemies or conflict. Life with me in Africa wasn't all that difficult it was something I had to go through. If one is upright in Africa seeking only to do right with less wrong, your deeds are never justified but if, you have lived to follow Christ one just has to bear with it and it does not make you the more, happier.

It is very difficult a thing to do or accomplish with ease in Africa because life out there is full of constrain such as a young lad growing up within an environment where all sorts of things happen. they do witchcraft to anyone who speaks against them, or are hindrance to them having their way with anything they want. Or wish for. Wives do witchcrafts', cast spells and jujus at their husband or close relatives.

I observed my predicament at some stage of my youth now that am grown up I feel the right thing for me to do is to make atonement. Some of us on earth do change, but for some people, do not seem to change.

What most people want out of life is for them to have everything they want regardless if it destroys other people's lives how can life be more meaningful this way?

They are not aware there are cosmic laws implying no one can cheat or escape laws of nature if soils have different texture, color all lands have its laws. For those who are watchful and diligent. They get wiser remain firm each day, with much courage and strength facing much more and overcome difficult problem because they have chosen to undergo their trials but there are less room of laying good examples.

My grandfather from my father's side also did practice his own juju on my mother, myself and other members of the family before his death in 1990. Immediately I moved in with my mother at FESTAC town in Lagos, in 1979. I was grinding the pepper, onions and tomatoes for my mother with a grinding-stone preparing the soup for our evening meal, which is mostly done in Africa, by female members of the family.

My mother told me one evening, the grinding stone was given to her by my grandfather from my father's side, I realized how powerful a grinding stone can be because it had effects on my life. Later, the benefit of me using a grinding stone was unveiled; I discovered the grinding stone had some significance in my life one of which was while sleeping not to lay down flat on my back but sideways. I have to seat up straight when sitting down for me, it holds something against possession it had effect on me from traveling outside my body, as in astral traveling and am never moved by spirit violently whenever we attend our

Aladura Church for Sunday and Wednesdays service at Mercy Church of Jerusalem Ibadan where I was ordained as a centurion.

I arrived at the conclusion it was something that could replicate Superman Krypton crystal but it hold memory and provides immunity towards my thoughts and belief related to Rastafarianism. My being born coming to earth was a call and based on a purpose through protocols to immerse myself into African spirituality and tradition it also did held me down as a seismograph.

I guess my mother off handedly told me, just to make a light conversation but knew its full implication, probably to make me feel at ease because, I was a male and not female. I guess it meant something to both my mother and grandfather before she accepted it from her husband's father then she was no longer living with his son he gave the grinding stone to her in my absence afterwards I moved from living within my father's dwelling with his wives and children at Lagos to live with my mother at FESTAC town Lagos.

Whilst I was residing with my father and step mothers at Lagos much younger, my step mothers also had grinding stone. I used the grinding stone some time with an effect or feeling dizzy after each time I use their grinding stone. I never had such feelings whilst using my mother's grinding stone at Lagos and Ibadan. Does it have anything to do with why West African mothers carry their children behind their back? To my surprise, some of them do so in the UK where it is common in the UK to use baby-prams.

A premature child growing up whiles in Africa, I felt virtually carrying the grinding stone behind my back, The grinding stone is made up of granite , with shining, dazzling crystal , I would describe, like fallen stars shining on the front of the grinding stone the bottom part is flat with rugged sides because of the uneven cuttings.

Before I left my father's home at number 2 Lawani Street Onitiri Yaba Lagos to live with my mother at FESTAC Town, we had a visit from our grandfather from my father's side by name Mr. Gold Pine Megbele all the way from my father's home town Obonteghareda (Dudu Town).

I never knew my grandfather visited my mother privately. If he did, he most has just given my mother the grinding stone through that visit which was the first and only visit I knew Mr. Gold Pine gave to his family whilst we were residing at Lagos. The relationship with my father and his father was not that very close his wives may know why, but not any of his children. As a young lad, I kept on wondering why the older generations of my relatives were not all that very close it most have been, as a result of their childhood and upbringing.

Our grandfather had tribal marks on his face. At this time of my youth, I considered it unusual for my grandfather to have given my mother a grinding stone as a gift during our grandfather's last visit to his family while we were residing in Lagos. The use of grinding stone is common among the Yoruba origin of which, my mother Mrs. Tomori Abani Megbele originates from but the impact is now clear.

After this episode of using the grinding stone at Lagos and at Ibadan Oyo state Nigeria, no other thing did I consider unusual about the grinding stone until years after I came back into the UK as resident working for Iceland frozen food plc. The grinding stone is believed by Africans to be part of what governs culture it is cut out of granite stone.

The few years of I and my brother Mr. Omagbemi staying with our father at Port-Harcourt and Delta state at the times, there was all sorts of occasions e.g. the making of a king in Delta state, my father becoming a chief, before this we had to travel to Ibadan to see my mother as, she made arrangements for both I and Omagbemi to have our British passport, through Oyo state British consulate.

After my arrival into the UK, I wrote to my mother several times and got replies at number one Searles road close to Old Kent road whilst living with a private landlord through an agency at Camberwell Green just by my working place at Iceland Frozen food plc Camberwell, I was transferred working at Iceland store at East Dulwich and went back to Camberwell store as part of my training where I was transferred to Iceland at Lewisham where I met Miss. Michelle Cook by Miss Caroline S the assistant manager. In my mother's replies to my letters from Ibadan she told me my grandfather Mr. Gold Pine visited her at Ibadan again just after we left Nigeria! I consider his visit dramatic. As I gathered, it was the last time they both saw each other because my mother and Gold Pine both died two years within each other. Then I felt each time Mr. Gold Pine visited my mother, there was something wrong and he was using my mother as an excuse I considered I was old enough to have told him it was enough, using my mother as an excuse. It was no use for Gold Pine going to Cordelia then I understand why Cordelia my father's second wife had always used the excuse it was my father's mother Ms Awoma who wanted our father to have a relationship with our father. The reason behind this was the relationship within son and father was not all that good in this case, within the son's father and mother who would Cordelia choose if the relationship with son and mother was good? Infarct why should late Ms. Awoma later marry Mr. Akinlami after giving birth to my father for whom, she had four children with and a Yoruba man for that matter how close could she had come to such a conclusion my father and mothers relationship should not continue my mother was also Yoruba.

Could these had led to what made my uncle egocentric within my father's house implying I fondle my cosine Layiwola Akinlami his daughter who was my age group at our tender age what happened was that she come to the boy squatter after being warned they should not be found there in my experience of living at the house, apart from my eldest sister not even my step mothers except once when Cordelia gave me a bath while I was unwell before the experience occurred this was before my uncle moved in with us. Apart from this never once had I experience any female venture towards the area except my eldest sister it was mainly occupied by male members of our family at intervals we had several male helpers in the house.

Could the relationship within both my father and my uncle have changed if my mother was still living within my father's house and my father had not married Cordelia or Aya Megbele? I presumed it would have just all been a Yoruba do on my father. Mr. Akinlami had other wives with children all Yoruba's what pushed my uncle to such an extreme he was shearing my father's dwelling with his wife and children with both my step mothers doing the cooking if, he was not pleased with the cooking he could had asked for permission for his wife to do his cooking for him in our kitchen. He needed money and I think frustrated and it turned to a situation even if my mother was in the house he did not care. He and his family just came back from America by the time he could pay for import tax on luxury furniture's he imported from America to Nigeria from the beginning it was all planed to be a show off. If it were only my mother who was within my father's house on my father's part it would had been all too good and calm for my uncle and not distress for my mother if I were to speak behalf of both brothers it meant, this two brothers had been quarreling from when they were young. After my uncle made his accusation at my tender age of within 8 and 9 years my father did not call me talked to me or ask questions I looked up to him to say something my father said nothing. How could a young lad of 8 and 9 years feel about such an experience? I grow up looking up anxiously regardless of difference to great expectation within my family as far as I remembered I was excited when I heard my uncle and his family who I would meet for the first time were in Nigeria from America they were going to stay with us.

For the last time I set eyes on my grandfather one evening when he busted into the family home at Warri he had to spend the night. I had to leave the family spear room for my grandfather to spend the night this was just after my father had been made chief.

Apart from one other thing my grandfather asked me for a handkerchief I always have on me? I told him my handkerchief was not with me, I asked my grandfather, if he would use tissues papers? He replied no! To me the implication of this was an omen I would have to pull through his son had moved closer to his homeland rather than father and son becoming friends, there was conflict. The handkerchief holds something of an enigma when the Olu of Warri came to Port Harcourt on a visit before my father become chief a strong wind took the handkerchief off me left it laying on the center of a motorway I put myself in danger whilst trying to retrieve it from the middle of the road.

I would have sheared the family spear room with my grandfather for the night. I considered it quite queer of my step mother Mrs. Cordelia Megbele asking me to shear her room with her for the night. I was no longer a child at that time of my life; I was over 21 years of age.

The first thing that came to my mind was to make excuses but I would sound untrusting, or being withdrawn. It was not appealing for me spending the night with my step mother on the same bed and not with Cordelia. I had to turn the table round but how would I make the excuse I had sensed, the way Gold Pine came into the house, something was wrong. This was a year before I left Nigeria. I never slept a wink I found it uncomfortable I was the first person who woke up and worked out of the bedroom. To me the whole experience were all rituals as when my uncle felt he was going to make good impression with his imported goods coming from America when he moves out of our accommodation it was going to be a good show off. Cordelia knew as our father had become chief he was going to make all effort to build his main house apart from the bungalow yet to be completed. Shearing her room with her was something she would use as an impression on my father or she was concerned about him building a proper home for
the family. He had waited too long and she was going to have a big role to play such as attracting attention to herself she had to use me as an excuse shearing her bedroom with her.

What else could be reasons why I should shear her bad room with her or she wanted to unfold a tale about Native Duck, Electric Fish but a Guinea Fowl in particular, brought in to our home by my father at Lagos one afternoon before my uncle Temitayo and his family moved in with us at

Lawani Close also known as Lawani Street which later escaped that afternoon before it could be slaughtered for a meal or that she knows am moving out of the family home a celibate for the rest of my life. Africans parents, especially nations of the Commonwealth do inquire through native oracles and rituals to ascertain everything about their livelihood before they occur. Issues like Mosquitoes bites, when groups of birds cluster suddenly on a roof top relates to spirituality, beliefs, witchcraft or juju in Africa based on reality in details of their relationship and impacts to their beliefs in superstition. Illness such as Malaria to science of medicine its cause and medications used for its cure. I have this feeling mosquitoes do not sting Europeans' in Africa for us they are rituals because we are natives of Africa.

I could have gone to spend the night at my father's other quarters in Warri where lies his office and three bedroom I wanted to be close to the rest of the family. The other two bedrooms apart from the one used by our father were not furnished and the mosquitoes there, are like masquerades I rather spend most of the night at the family homes as a matter of fact on that very night, it was too late going down to our other quarters at Apoyan Street way out of GRA Government reserved Areas. Europeans have been going to Nigeria for centuries for several reasons visit, business or enterprise ventures one could imagine some experience they encounter when they get there while at the late beginning they are there to assist in shipping which has become wide spread and easer with the use of mobile phone and computers. In the early 1970s of cause, business owners are usually their guide getting to know the environment better, there are other guides who they find at hotels and business environments.

When they arrive they are treated with respect and liking in time from what they experience they would decide if they like the place and they need not act, as if it were strictly all business like. In some case they get to know families of their business associates, leaders or government officials where they pick up several guides.

Some Europeans who like the place get to know Common Wealth nations live with all kinds of rituals practically everything has to do with jujus, witchcrafts and spells for some of them to their amazement Christianity for example are not as they find it in Europe they have to understand our cultural background and essence that entwine with Christianity in our way of worship. Most of them who live quiet lives there are respected that is what entice me about the white race living in Nigeria it is as if nobody occupies the house they live there but it's as if no one is there except when you see them come out of their home.

Take for instance when they get close to their associates at hotels they are introduced to some females who take their fancy if they do not approve then they get, to know what African witch doctors could do with mosquitoes. All she needs do is tell the witch doctor the White man did not take her fancy. When he gets to his lodging at night by morning he is all red complaining of mosquito's bits. But it wasn't the first night he had spent at the lodging why the mosquitoes bits. They get to know and accustom themselves with the people and environment. Rather than showing signs you do not take her fancy buy her drinks, dance, tell her about yourself then she tells you about the place and environment. Do not drink bear have whisky if she is becoming too intimate show yourself more as an English man there are others go for the best, become more businesslike, call up your reputation pretend you are drunk or tired at least it shows you are friendly. Association with men is always business like or to show their own influence they use juju against themselves to have their means they would customary introduce you to one or two women. Your guide would let you know such things get even closer, he would tell you about the woman who bewitched you because you did not show signs you liked her and how, they do such craft. They may be superstitious, the English do not believe in superstition you would be, when you get there.

Culture varies also dialects they would treat you differently do not worry there is always respect for you

Gold is mined in Ghana while Petroleum is drilled in Nigeria; Traditional Clothing is a major business of the Ghanaians some of which are imported to Nigeria used flamboyantly more by Nigerians. Is based on superstitious beliefs Nigerian have more Mosquitoes bits than the Ghanaians have or white men and women in Africa are not customary bitten by mosquitoes except somebody terribly wants something from you that has not been given to them or they are not liked by the people around them.. More killing since time goes on in Nigeria than in Ghana through religious conflict does it have anything to do with why more of such conflicts relating to killings dose not prevail in Ghana because of their clothing industry? But if you steal in Ghana your hands can be cut off. Ghanaians are more bodily built and hard in their physics' while Nigerians are delicate is it as a result of Gold in Ghana and Petroleum in Nigeria? such issues are based on Beliefs, culture, tradition and cultism on which certain basic reality lies when it comes to asking questions such as within Ghana and Nigeria which region is more a suspension bridge to an Earthquake then it has to do with science at the same time has a lot in common or in similarity in perceptions as natives their beliefs in native medicine, juju, witchcraft and Christianity within which they view themselves as occupants of Commonwealth nation. The same applies to Cattle, sheep, goats rears all the way from Mali, Togo to Nigeria. I could go on and on narrating various fixations but most people might feel it's because they are still primitives but they are not it has to do with their culture and heritage its Gods own making. Superstitious belief varies in Africa and other parts of the world.

Superstition is a belief in supernatural causality: that one event leads to the cause of another without any physical process linking the two events, such as astrology, omens, witchcraft, etc., which contradicts natural science. Opposition to superstition was a central concern of the intellectuals during the 18th century Age of Enlightenment. The philosophies at that time ridiculed any belief in miracles, revelation, magic, or the supernatural, as 'superstition,' and typically included as well much of Christian doctrine. The word is often used pejoratively to refer to religious practices (e.g., Voodoo) other than the one prevailing in a given society (e.g., Christianity in western culture), although the prevailing religion may contain just as many supernatural beliefs. It is also commonly applied to beliefs and practices surrounding luck, prophecy and spiritual beings, particularly the belief that future events can be foretold by specific unrelated prior events.

Superstition in some ways is a deviation of religious feeling and of the practices this feeling imposes. It can even affect the worship we offer the true God, e.g., when one attributes an importance in some way magical to certain practices otherwise lawful or necessary. To attribute the efficacy of prayers or of sacramental signs to their mere external performance, apart from the interior dispositions that they demand is to fall into superstition *Matthew 23:16*.

Woe unto you, ye blind guides, which say, whosoever shall swear by the temple, it is nothing; but whosoever shall swear by the gold of the temple, he is a debtor! Ye fools and blind: for whether is greater, the gold, or the temple that sanctified the gold? And, whosoever shall swear by the altar, it is nothing; but whosoever swear by the gift that is upon it, he is guilty. Ye fools and blind for whether is greater, the gift, or the altar that sanctifies the gift? Whoso therefore shall swear by the altar, swear by it, and by all things thereon. And whoso shall swear by the temple, swears by it, and by him that dwelled therein. And he that shall swear by heaven swears by the throne of God, and by him that sits thereon. Considering humans and all things are the temple of God his spirit lives in us the choices we make about the use of our physical temples will affect us throughout eternity.

Whenever I start hearing voices which makes feel distress, paranoiac or emotionally disturbed if I should touch anything religious I do have this feeling sometimes I would be punished made holy and Devin or being punished for something afterwards after my contact with religious object.

Witchcraft, juju, voodoo, sorcery and magic are still part of our lives infarct we live through it each day of our lives still gradually sliding down through effect of science and technology needs to be address. It's still part of our lives and daily activities. Suicide, murder, conflict cases has effect of witchcraft gradually; we would outlive such destiny as we live through the effects of our modern day world of greed, hat lasciviousness, sin, far away from God and his commandment within which we are called to show our true worth.

Some symptoms of mental illness are as result of witchcraft infarct, there diagnosis relates to witchcraft. Level of income also has effect and they way we live our lives through religion, culture, tradition and creeds in every part of the world which each day entwines creating other effects even on television and on Movies 50% of what we see in such as Lord of the Ring, The Omen, The Devil's Advocate are issues having effect of witchcraft from our past to the present but in different dimension phase on reality most of the stories did not all happen in one day, it takes a lot to have occurred coming down to a story or written or in film industry tales how are we living our lives are no fairytales if the gravity of what goes on in our lives based on experiences are actually brought to the open just like religion most people do not pay attention to them or realize people go through such tails or experiences.

Modern World do not permit us using the word witchcraft religion put such aspects of our lives is coined dramatically though different in practice and beliefs coined into sin, such as greed, jealousy, lasciviousness, hat, lies while human law puts it down as mischief, Love, peace, craving for Gods commandments we consider as living good moral lives which is very open. There is no other way a court of law can term witchcraft, juju, voodoo, the use of talisman other than as mischief considering when it's depicted in a court of law as witchcraft; In what other ways do we describe what juju, voodoo and talisman are used for if, not to get what you want from supernatural sources while not all humans believe in the supernatural? We are now living in a different world really the same but in different perspectives on how they are practice one has to be vigilant and watchful it takes experience to be aware of or how do we describe such issues if the people who practice it do not come out openly that they ascribe themselves to its practice. To my amazement if you have experience, witchcraft and juju or voodoo, you would be shy, confused with fear coming out in the open with it even about our religious views and beliefs with regards to its practice. We are found of avoiding open discussion on witchcraft though it is a criminal offence but very difficult to redress in a court of law mischief's involve could be quite unique, awesome and strange.

Let me put it this way how would you feel if your local food chain store sells you out dated product knowing they are out dated product it would be said it's as a result of greedy profit making business men who careless for the interest and health of their customer yes, but it's modern day witchcraft and not under mischief it is called sales promotion while beneath is inducement some customer may worry over why they haven't got enough money   purchasing goods or services it could lead to theft the beauty of sales promotion only applies when customers have enough money to buy such goods and services commonly termed as in low price. The supernatural forces of witchcraft, juju, magic now considered as tricks over decade have been divesting itself from human existence because of religion, science, business, wealth, luxury goods, working practice, the environment we dwell in and technology through which it is taking a new form which humans enforce against themselves through modern day ways of living and culture of business, personal relationship. Witchcraft, juju or voodoo since time was handed over to generation some of us are born with it while others initiate its practice and rituals. The modern ways of living prevents them from enforcing the will of witchcraft and voodoo since money is concerned it gives those who practice it to enforce their will not the supernatural forces which has taken a new form of what I call spiritual harassment based on omens they initiate. This somewhere along the line, mental health comes in and you can hardly take such issues to court because of difficulties in explaining the situation due to secrecy and paranormals involved which have close ties in relation to paranoia.

Buy one get one free, half price, and double sales, a particular branded product sold at three different companies whether in goods and service is sold at a lower price than in another store, are all forms product promotion it is also modern day form of bewitching and charming customers. You have more income than a friend or relative or who is, on benefit each time you go out to the pub because you are well off you buy less expensive type of drink for this your particular friend because he or she is good as a companion or through him you have just met a new girl friend while at the pub, you often buy yourself a more expensive bear, it's a good offer and your are being a good friend for all your friend knows but you are winging him or her at each case, it is customary you are the only one doing all the talking and smiling its bewitching simply because your friend or relative felt like having a pint but had no money. The same applies if someone is caring for you and makes you feel low its bewitching and also winging get out of it considering such act, could be deliberate.

Can it be said more children from African decent whose parent are in the UK through seeking for their stay are oblivious of what are shown on television how witchcraft in Seri León, traditional faith healers in Zimbabwe there are Nigeria dramas on DVD sold in the UK expressing such issues of the different ethnic cultures of Nigeria on the dramas elaborating on DVD sold in the UK it also happens here but in mild or different perspectives experience this and you would observe no fixation of the different ethnic cultures of Nigeria on the dramas elaborating on witchcraft, juju and native doctors but at the same time it enlightens not only these children but the Europeans what goes in Africa where such beliefs are in effect where it took its stance from their history and tradition. It now depends on how these children view their parental background which they have no experience of. What they experience here in Europe about their culture is quite different from what their parents went through back home. Considering their living in Europe their parents would want to bring them up in relation to certain traditional setting or stance.

since I believe in reincarnation to certain extent some Native Africans use juju bearing on their children in the UK then such scene on DVD's are welcome but not all these children appreciate the effect because it makes them bias, leg behind in education within the UK and their profiles are diminish because they want to be educated elite. In the case of what disposition I have of my father what life has he comes into the UK to live? Once you take part in witchcraft, juju or voodoo in another life, you still remain the juju or voodoo artifact you have practice in your past life. So, why should we be shy about such issues? If I am truly the reincarnation of Orunmila could my illness and family trials and experience in life imply I am suffering from mental illness as result of once being an artifact of juju, its one way I could describe the reason for my illness. Then to my understanding it could be an illness but also a life trial to ascertain certain faculties. Because people do not just become powerful to become powerful, you need to attain it. Attaining it there must be a drive and willingness, courage, resilience and the supernatural force that lies behind my past that drives me. Being able to word process is like a miracle to me with clarity and agility regardless of my illness and condition of birth but in this case an artifact not made by human but by a supreme forces if not, why else do I believe in God or can do the things an doing?

This 21th century one needs to be spiritually and psychologically aware of the significance of witchcraft and possession. Some people like to leave their homes untidy; some would rather always want their homes clean and spotless. With the huge impact of science, engineering and technology my experience is that a tiny sport of dirt, stained clothing, small debris in my flat could mean sings of witchcraft or possession, having strange effect or even an insect that finds its way into my flat.

Anyway that's one reason Africa might have been rich in wide areas of culture, rituals and traditional representation such as masquerades dance and carvings, ritualistic ways of paying obeisance to their deities and gods and how they keep their homeland. Politics and technology is the Englishman's representation in which they need to enlighten themselves which takes time they need to take up the Krypton factor or they would wallow in the X-Men Factor which is an interesting television series for example what do the X-Men want in Lagos, what were they doing there?

Am a mental health sufferer I do not eat well, dress well, I drink and smoke. I suffer from paranoia, am on medication probably for life are wide areas of the X-Men factor.

The X-Men are a <u>superhero team</u> in the <u>Marvel Comics Universe</u>. They were created by writer <u>Stan Lee</u> and artist <u>Jack Kirby</u>, and first appeared in <u>The X-Men</u> #1 (September 1963). The basic concept of the X-Men is that under a cloud of increasing anti-<u>mutant</u> sentiment, <u>Professor Xavier</u> created a haven at his <u>Westchester</u> <u>mansion</u> to train young mutants to use their powers for the benefit of humanity, and to prove mutants can be heroes. Xavier recruited <u>Cyclops</u>, <u>Iceman</u>, <u>Angel</u>, <u>Beast</u>, and <u>Marvel Girl</u>, calling them 'X-Men' because they possess special powers due to their possession of the 'X-gene,' a gene which normal humans lack and which gives mutants their abilities. Early on, however, the 'X' in X-Men stood for 'extra' power which normal humans lacked. It was also alluding that mutations occurred as a result of radiation exposure.

The first issue also introduced the team's archenemy, <u>Magneto</u>, who would continue to battle the X-Men for decades throughout the comic's history, both on his own and with his <u>Brotherhood of Mutants</u>. The X-Men universe also includes such notable heroes as <u>Wolverine</u>, <u>Storm</u>, <u>Colossus</u>, <u>Nightcrawler</u>, <u>Rogue</u>, and <u>Shadowcat</u>. Besides the Brotherhood of Mutants, other villains that the X-Men have fought include the <u>Sentinels</u>, <u>Apocalypse</u>, <u>Mister Sinister</u>, and the <u>Hellfire Club</u>.

The X-Men comics have been adapted into other media, including animated <u>television series</u>, <u>video games</u>, and a commercially successful <u>series of films</u>.

The Krypton facto in my opinion is for Commonwealth nations to clear the area make it tidy; improve amenities for its people, good and viable politicians good living and environment.

27th of December 2007 I was at the Queen Elizabeth Hospital because I was having pains behind the back of my neck. I was told to stay on Ibuprofen Dr Margery; had prescribed for me with Ibuprofen ointment. 4th January 2008 I saw Dr Jan Deacon I told her I was seven months premature it was the first time I had mentioned to anyone I was premature at birth apart from my brother Omagbemi, I told her I had been moving furniture's in my flat and laying in new carpets, my work at the Gala club lifting shutters whilst opening up might have contributed to the pains I was having.

She prescribed Diclofenac sodium E/C tablets 50 mg, to be taken three times a day and paracetamol tablets 100 quantities in tablets. This was when on my previous visit to her I told her about my job at Iceland frozen food plc. Regardless I was born premature and had been working hard for many years I had not suffered much pain the effect might have drawn on my health. Dr Deacon took me off deep heat ointment I prescribed for myself. Since then, she becomes more sublime about my care. Drawing to 2009 my general practitioner Dr Robert Hughes asked me one afternoon if I had a shorter name or English name I told him I was not going to answer another name but Oritsesemisan or if, I was going to answer another name, it was going to be Kuntakinte he smiled but I was relieved.

Heavy snow fall in Northern Island, traffic, road, houses affected, avalanched in Spain hit of-pate area, candidate for American presidency race election the need for change in America the current defined moment in the world's history. Kenyan election rigging, cause and mascara at least three hundred people are dead.

At work apart from feeling giddy, dizzy spells, I was shaking all over. I had to see my GP and psychiatrist immediately. Informing the receptionist of my intention to see my GP I did the same to see my psychiatrist.

By the month of July on which falls my birthday, My psychiatrist Dr Banjac came to the conclusion to refer me to Queen Elizabeth hospital mental health home treatment team. At this time, I was doing all I could to avoid my being hospitalized and wondered why I always get unwell during my birthday.

Queen Elizabeth mental health home treatment team reviewed my medication they were in my flat, to hand me my prescription at the same time, I had to write letters for reconsideration on my overpayment of housing benefit, Going down to the housing benefit office personally.

Riverside housing office is by once sit the University of Greenwich used as a computer and library room, before the

University recently pulled out of the location. The housing office has moved of Riverside house to Wellington Street in Woolwich.

I was no longer a student at this time; I had taken two student loans, one while I was at Greenwich University, the other while I was at South Bank University. I have taken student loans of over £5,000.00, which I should pay back. At this time before and after 2005 I had been making one off payment back to the student loan company, with money earned whilst working at the Woolwich Gala club under Initial Rentokil cleaning services each month on direct debit and through the telephone.

Riverside housing office was of the opinion, I did not inform them within 2nd May 2005 until 24th October 2005 after several consultations and appeals from me, that I informed the housing office I wasn't receiving DLA, I did inform them before the month 24th of October 2005 settled that I had informed them in October 2005 I waited for their conclusion.

On the same day I also remembered informing the council tax office at Wellington Street with my pay slips, the council tax office told me their conclusion after an assessment, I am on full housing benefit I need not pay. I was never aware it was being recorded at the Riverside housing office I was on DLA; it was a benefit I was never in receipt off. 2006 and 2007, I was never sent a form for housing benefit reassessment then I got this letter from them.

Through appeals I made personally confronting these problems with my illness, whilst going through various medications to keep me stabilized, with visit to the hospital for examinations while at the same time under Queen Elizabeth mental health home treatment team.

Further to my letters of reconsideration to the Riverside housing recovery team with regards to pay a recovery of £4450.34 for the period of 2/5/05 to 9/7/07. A decision was made that for the period of 25/10/05, to 9/7/07, they would not be recovering an overpayment of £3493.84. But however, for the period of 2/5/05 to 24/10/05 an amount of £956.50 was recoverable.

From the month of May 2007 when these issues of overpayments of housing benefit occurred, I had to put in a claim for DLA, income support and after my SSP stopped, I began claiming incapacity benefits because. I was so unwell; I could hardly work, or keep my job

Speaking to a social worker at the Ferryview mental health centre Ms Cathy, She told me sorrowfully, that she had been filling benefit forms for a lot of patients, but recently her manager told her not to fill in benefit claim forms for patients. It was through Mr. Dotun Sobowale's help I was able to get bye at these difficult times as a paranoid schizophrenia. As difficult as it was for me to get by, I remained resilient.

Britain is not a place where people are wholly deprived and repressed as in West Africa. It should be a general opinion, that in my case, regardless of an illness, I was still geared intro actions against all odds' of not being deprived or repressed, The British system has avenues to make people live with less anxiety.

Some mental health problems are described using words that are in everyday use; for example, 'depression' or 'anxiety'. This can make them seem easier to understand, but can also mean people underestimate how serious they can be. Mental health issues make one feels just as bad, or worse, than any other illness which cannot easily be perceived though mental health problems are very common affecting around one in four people in Britain. There is also a lot of controversy about the way mental health problems are diagnosed, what causes them, and which treatments are most effective. Despite these challenges, it is possible to recover from a mental health problem and live a productive and fulfilling life. It is important to remember that having a mental health problem is not a sign of weakness. Never be ashamed of having bad days, weeks or even months – because they show your inner strength.

Depression lowers your mood, and can make you feel hopeless, worthless, unmotivated and exhausted. It can affect sleep, appetite and self-esteem. It can also interfere with daily activities and, sometimes, your physical health. This may set off various cycle, because the worse you feel, the more depressed you are likely to get. Depression can be experienced at different levels for example, mild or severe, and can be related to certain experiences.

Anxiety can mean constant and unrealistic worry about any aspect of daily life. It may cause restlessness, sleeping problems and possibly physical symptoms; for example, an increased heart beat, stomach upset, muscle tension or feeling shaky. If you are highly anxious you may also develop related problems, such as panic attacks, a phobia or obsessive compulsive disorder.

Fear becomes a phobia when you have an exaggerated or an unrealistic sense of danger about a situation, you might often begin to organise your life around avoiding the thing that you fear. The symptoms of phobias are similar to anxiety, in severe forms one might experience panic attacks. Schizophrenia is a controversial diagnosis. Symptoms may include confused or jumbled thoughts, hearing voices and seeing and believing things that other people don't share. If you have these symptoms you might also become confused and withdrawn. There is debate about whether schizophrenia is actually one condition or more of a collection of symptoms.

A personality disorder doesn't mean personality change very much in most cases it does. It does develop as people go through different experiences in life or as their circumstances change. If you have a personality disorder, you are likely to find it more difficult to change your patterns of thinking, feeling and behaving, and will have a more limited range of emotions, attitudes and behaviours with which to cope with everyday life. Eating disorders can be characterised by eating too much, or by eating too little. If you have an eating disorder you may deny yourself anything to eat, even when you are very hungry, or you may eat constantly, or binge. The subject of food, and how much you weigh, is likely to be on your mind all the time. Your eating disorder is likely to develop as a result of deeper issues in your life and is possibly a way of disguising emotional pain.

Anorexia, bulimia, bingeing and compulsive eating are some of the most common eating disorders. In addition to the more formal issues above, there are some behaviours and feelings which are strongly associated with mental health problems.

Self-harm is a way of expressing very deep distress. You may not know why you self-harm, but it can be a means of communicating what you can't put into words, or even into thoughts, and has been described as an 'inner scream'. After self-harming, you may feel better able to cope with life again, for a while, but the cause of your distress is unlikely to have gone away. It is common to have suicidal thoughts if you are experiencing mental health problems especially if you have diagnosis depression, borderline personality disorder or schizophrenia. The deeper your depression, the more likely it is that you will consider killing yourself. However, you can help yourself and you can get help from other people. A great many people think about suicide, but the majority do not go on to kill themselves.

Panic attacks may result when people make one feel unexpected bouts of intense terror. If you experience an attack you may find it hard to breathe, and feel your heart beating hard. You may have a choking sensation, chest pain, begin to tremble or feel faint. It's easy to mistake these for the signs of a heart attack or other serious medical problem. Panic attacks can occur at any time, and this is what distinguishes them from a natural response to real danger.

There are many opinions about what causes mental health problems. This is part of a wider debate about whether personality is shaped by life experiences, or determined by genes. The following are some of the factors that may play a role in the development of mental health problems.

Difficult family background coming from a difficult background where you have experienced neglect, violence, and abuse or been overprotected can make people highly insecure and more vulnerable to mental health problems.

Stressful life events may be traumatic events, such as the death of someone close, or longer-term struggles, such as being the victim of some form of harassment or oppression.

In recent years, research has shown that being made redundant or spending significant periods out of work can also have an impact on your mental health, fear, insecurity, knowing what you want out of life but you can't make it through worse if the situation gives you hits that your dreams can become reality but yet pose as a stumbling block.

Your body chemistry can affect your mind. For example, if you are frightened, it triggers the body's 'fight or flight' response to produce a hormone called adrenalin. If physical activity doesn't use up all the adrenalin, the body remains tense and the mind stays over-active.

Social factors such as poverty, domestic violence, isolation, poor housing and addiction have been associated with mental health problems. These factors trigger the problems, leading to social problems you might not otherwise experience or expect.

If you receive a diagnosis, you might feel relieved and be glad that you can put a name to what is wrong. However, if a diagnosis becomes a label, it can be very damaging. For example, instead of being seen as a parent, writer, mechanic or student who has schizophrenia, you may be seen as 'a schizophrenic', anti social behaviour, drug addict, alcoholism as though this diagnosis is all that you are.

Many people prefer to see mental health problems as part of human experience rather than distinct illnesses. Why a diagnosis should determine the whole course of once life and may come to be a relatively major part of once identity or history.

It is not about being classified by your mental illness: it is about learning to accept yourself and seize the day for all it is worth because tomorrow might be different.

As I was word processing one morning, an issue of the Greenwich Time's news paper was pushed into my flat front door.

I picked up the times news paper, made myself a cup of tea, with snowfall outside in the South East beginning to melt down, I am not going out of my flat, to Reed in Partnership or the Charlton disability centre, to surf the internet and check my e-mails' account.

I sat down in my living room reading the Greenwich times. Something of interest cut my attention an article of

Greenwich NHS teaching primary care trust by Pat Greenwood. 'It was titled changing our minds about mental illness to backs campaign to end stigmas and discrimination. It said time to change is England's biggest ever national campaign aimed at ending the stigmas and discrimination surrounding mental illness. It was being backed by charities e.g. Mind and Rethink, as well as comic Relief and the national lottery. Millions of people across the country live in the shadow of fear.

The numbers of people suffering from mental health issues are dramatically increasing in the UK. As the stresses of our daily life increases, with contributing factors like the credit crunch, job losses, relationship break-up's.

High profiled entertainers like Stephen Fry and Ruby Wax, political commentator Alastair Campbell were among the well-known personalities who were to speak about their personal experiences. Every little thing helps in other to challenge attitudes and dispel the myths of stigma and discrimination among people with mental health problems.

As I continued reading the Greenwich times, I took note that in the next few weeks, Greenwich teaching Primary care trust (the GTPCT) will be joining forces with other organizations to support Time to Change and promote well-being of people living in the borough.

Greenwich council did put up adverts in bus-shelters at various locations promoting the campaign which went on for a fortnight, poster where also at community buildings bookmarks and drinks coasters distributed locally throughout Greenwich borough in a way of raising awareness.

Looking out for National TV, radio and press advertisements as part of the campaign launched asking question e.g. would you date someone who is a schizophrenia?, would they trust anyone, who was convinced that the world was out to get them? Would they be prepared to employ someone who had been signed off work for several months because of stress?

These are challenging questions found on national thoughts-provoking awareness how people feel about the illness with quiz for anyone to try and answer with details of special events taking place across the country within our community on website www.time-to-change.org.uk, anyone interested, could contact Alexia Fergus or Alex Parish in the mental health promotion unit at GTPCT.

Helping people with disability going back to work employers should think it thoroughly and work it out its good for our wellbeing.

I know what it feels like for one to suffer from fit because on two occasions I have seen people suffering from severe fit one experience was of a close relative, I do not suffer from such fits but experience general body weakening.

Or I drowse off into controlled hallucinations, I am a very quite person living a lonely and isolated life that morning, without a phone call or knowledge of their coming to my flat with their intended visit,, I was in my flat, in such a state of drossiness, hallucinating with a spider right on top of the ceiling in front of me in my bedroom, as I was lying down on my bed. I could hardly move. I merely tried opening the door of my flat for them.

When my door bell rang, it was my brother Mr. Omagbemi and his wife Nwamaka, with my nice Miss Lydia Omagbuse Megbele. It was an unexpected call from them which took not more than five minutes, before they walked of my flat. The experience troubled me for years; I have been asking myself what was the true reason for their visit?

My sister in-law greeted me with unexpected cheerfulness, my brother told me they were just passing by and they just dropped by with a jeer of laughter on my brothers' face with my sister in-law caring my nice Lydia on one side of her hand I walked back into my bedroom.

Straight, they walked into my bed room, I could not stand on my feet, went back, straight on my bed as they walked into my flat. Immediately, my sister in-law spotted the spider stretched out her hand, with a tissue paper in her hand, and picked up the spider from the ceiling, smiling at my brother and said with an unexpected cheerfulness to my brother that

I have company. This was after just two weeks when I came out of hospital having my appendicitis removed.

As she picked off the spider from my bed room ceiling 'my sister in-law used an African terminology of words in pigeon-English said to her husband 'Your brother is keeping company'. Within five minutes, they walked out of my flat. Whatever, my sister did with the spider in her hands on the tissue paper I never knew, but why? Considering what they had done with my birth certificate in 1995 while I was in hospital, when I gave my brother the key to my flat, to get me some cloths. There is one thing about me and any insect's which comes into my flat I do not kill them I always hush them out alive the once which makes me go into trance or hallucinations always comes in unnoticed. You don't do that I wanted to tell her I was in trance they just came and break it and walked out. I do not wonder why I keep on hearing peoples voice there is always something they had done which makes me hear their voices. I felt I was a schizophrenia going through strange phase with my illness they are also, doing strange things they were both traditionally dressed on their visit.

I am always unsettled of being hospitalized at any stage of my illness,
At one point, I lost track of the most important schedules, and details I should keep for five days. Indeed the spider was a visitor as she well knew, I had company she should had also known she had broken my concentration and meditation being that, I was using the spider traveling into other world or spiritual realms through which, I was receiving massages and I dear not tell her in particular that, she was an intruder or it would mean I was calling her a witch she already knew I was having company. Centuries ago such encounter of communicating with the spiritual world would have been done through chanting incantations songs and display of rituals to communicate with also deities involved usually done as piecemeal to show your presence there is no doubt through all the stages I go through feeling am Orunmila is to assimilate myself with the spiritual world at the same time changing with the rest of the world. Close to that time I received two different set of traditional Yoruba

clothing's from my brother and his wife I did not make the mistake of not wearing them to Saint John's church Lewisham and taking photographs with them one reason for my doing this, was to detect any personality disorder while I hope this might not be a case of the only Yoruba clothing my father made for me and some other members of his family at my early years of 7-8 years for Christmas celebration while we just moved from Port Harcourt to Lagos state could till this very day be inside one of my stepmothers wardrobe. These are issues I would find reasons applicable of why I should be under care with a psychiatrist from an African background and they understand such things or why some Africans mostly adults who one might say have some solid, strong family background and understanding of culture, juju, witchcraft, magic over some years might have reason to have moved from Africa to make Britain or any other part of Europe their home or that they are running away from such effects but it is dealt with, with ignorance, politics, a game or further harassment coming from people of your own race or background.

I go through phase observing people as if they are from my own world and planet in the UK, they are the once who have built Great Britain, and the rest of Europe to where it is today, yet they are the once who are being stripped from whatever, they have.

It is only natural for them under going such a peril, because, they choose to be spent forces; they know themselves too well, why they are on earth this is why they are with acumen. They have all had a bit of who God the architect of the universe is, before they make their way and presences into earth, holding themselves as seals of the universe.

Not every soul's dose this before they are born into earth such as when I went out of my flat to the Greyhound pub at Kingsman Street to buy my father bear to drink with meal prepared by me. All he was doing was to snuggle into my system while in the UK through which, he would reincarnate into the UK after his death. And on his last visit, my father did hand over to me a box filled with traditional cooking ingredient including rice I could easily obtain within the UK. I consider it branding, branding into let's say a vampire diary it was the last gift I received from my father which I took from my brothers accommodation in Pulton House in Brockley all the way with a taxi cab about 9.30 PM to my flat and the last I saw of him because he died few years later.

Some of the items in the box contained Ogbono, ground crayfish, hot pepper, Iteskiri paper soup ingredients they are spices, for preparing soup which goes down the stomach with Gari made of Conserver shoot, Amala, Pounded yam both made from Yam shoot one can buy in the Woolwich African market. Rice, Palm oil I guess my father was already divulging into his naming ceremony here in the UK before he died at Ibadan except for the Kola nuts, Atariko, honey and salt that weren't in the box. And he never explained why he gave them to me from which I could go into paranoia all this taking place within a home where he had more than three wives in Nigeria, my brothers accommodation from which this event took place, with a wife who, had already been spoken for before he moved in with her it was all like an episodes of witchcraft in the making. At one point I felt the Pepper soup ingredients Cordelia gave me whether in her own accord or my father was involved in it which I flow into the UK with was enough to imply any other requirement they wanted to make. Under such circumstance it becomes a fix or going through a paranoia of paying homage as in relation to culture and tradition. In my observation I experience Mrs. Cordelia Megbele is powerful in her own way. My late uncle Temitayo went through the same experience whilst shearing home with his brother two wives of his brothers had to prepare his meals. You come into your brother's house all the way from America trying to find you own level two wives of your brother prepare your meals its African language within two brothers.

While I frequently suffer from phobias as of if I feed on African food or on English diet there was no time I and my father sat down at any time to discuss the impact in my life as to my being born premature in this case, he could he have been making decisions for me or putting me in the right perspectives of what to eat and not what to eat for handing me what was in the box he brought from Nigeria on his visit.

Not when it's a repercussion within his family when one child would consume what he brought and pray for him while another child, would use it to empower his or herself. Cordelia handing the bottle of pepper soup ingredients might have meant to free me within a position she holds in his family or for me to be committed to her at last I thought my father surrounded to her when he gave me back the coral bead I had used in paying homage to the Olu of Warri and a photograph of Mrs. Cordelia Megbele on his last visit to the UK. I felt at that point members of my family realized no matter whatever kind of juju is done to me I customarily use it in some ways to enhance myself or rewrite its proverbs. The meanings of some African traditional proverbs have changed or shifted over the years since some people find reason in worshiping mix religion. Proverbs and sayings are short statements of wisdom or advice that are transmitted from generation to generation and passed into general use. In most traditions in Africa, people explain proverbs with their life's trial it is usually typical, for one to tell an African proverb and still be the one to explain its meaning in another life.

Could it be possible someone went to length in reversing or crowning his or her self with a prayer I made to mean something else or for themselves? The experience left me unable to feed on goat meat recipes for quite some time. An experience I had which am still trying to respond to was when my father was being conferred his chieftaincy title revealed a strange phenomena after I had drank so much alcohol moved by an uncontrollable spirit to say prayers for my family on the sward chosen for him on which his conferment was made afterwards it meant they should kill a goat for the ancestors which I found the head of the goat dripping with blood on the old rusted sward the next morning in the living room with its both horns gouged out. Was this the devil's trick so that I can worship them instead of worshipping God. The goat was used for preparing an Itsekiri traditional soup with Yam called 'Epuru' which Cordelia offered to me personally on the day after the ceremony. I remember the experience in a way that Mrs. Cordelia Megbele as at other time I had spent living with her if she did something in good turn on my behalf that evening by offering the prepared meal of Yam and soup of 'Epuru' all mixed together but did not include any parts of the goat meat on the plat of 'Epuru she offered me I still ask myself why did she offered it to me and made sure I ate the Epuru in front of our family home just after the celebration the next day. I have the feeling it was taken from the bottom of the pot when it was all most all served to other people. I discovered eating from the bottom of the pot is best since I choose to follow the path laid down for me by God and not as I choose. I go through phase of a nature I am called upon through certain prerequisite to grant members of my family their own wish. I found out the spirit of my family ancestor who summoned itself was ready to give through me but cautioned me I should not take from the ritual and reassured me then that for what lies ahead I should ask for my peace of mind. Through the experience I believed I was clothed in the 'Amure' in Yuroba meaning 'Armor' in which I was provided with emotional, social, or other defences of my Itsekiri ancestors. In which I became an 'Emere'.

An emere, in traditional <u>Yoruba</u> culture, is a child who can travel between the spiritual and physical world at will. A negative connotation is associated with the word, as it implies a family's child may disappear and reappear at will. The patient emere's wants the best of heaven and Earth. An emere is a spirit in disguise, misrepresenting death as life, and is clever enough to disguise his objectives. Believed to be more powerful than witches, they most often die on a particular day of joy. On wedding days, when having their first baby, graduation from university etc. depending on the degree of happiness the event might cause. They are also believed to be extremely pretty, and have seductive powers. The emere gives unconditional support to heaven while on earth, asserting the balance of power or sequence betraying earth, annoyed that earth did not allow or welcome visitors from heaven. Whatever cause people to live unhappy lives, or when situations like my experience occurs family members or friends might use it to invoke their own personally course or self gain.

For some reason I put it down to some reason as to what propels me to being a smoker. Considering I had worked in several food chain stores for Iceland Frozen Food Company I had some ideas of why my father brought food to me from

Nigeria other than making avenues for himself considering he is a managing director of a Stevedoring company based at Port-Harcourt Rivers state Nigeria. Before my father's business started he worked with European business men as formed joint company owners in clearing and forwarding. I see not much reason why he chose coming to the UK bringing me foodstuffs of West Africa origin I could easily buy in London its implications could mean lots of different things from the look of it such as deliberating causing what occurred within he and me relating to my living the life of a celibate as a resort for his own wish depicting I have purpose in life on his behalf or coming into the UK or that it is meant for me to understand my working life or what it is meant to be.

We talk of herbalist, juju and native priest, witchcraft, black magic, sorcery practiced in all race and creed when I was a young lad while my father his having his bath once in a while he calls me if any of his wives are not around to scrub his back while having his bath in our family bathroom. At Lawani Close Yaba Lagos the main house had an English bathroom at the boy's quarters it was plain flooring. Living with my mother at Lagos it was English bathroom both house we occupied at Ibadan Oyo state, was plain flooring imagine a four story building and a one story building at Mr. Osibowale's house and the other owned by a man and his family who owns bread making factories while I was residing at Port Harcourt the house I and my brother Omagbemi occupied belongs to a popular and wealthy friend of my father known as Mr. Agoro. My father's office and living quarters a two story building with English bathroom and toilets belongs to an Okrika lady and her husband Okrika is a port town in Rivers State, Nigeria, capital of the Local Government Area of the same name. The town is situated on a small island just south of Port Harcourt, making it a suburb of the much larger city. I remember the house I and my family lived in while I was young boy at Warri before we moved to Port Harcourt it was slightly appalling with English bathroom and toilets. It was an old building with English bathroom and toilet as far as I could remember the part of the house we occupied was.

Juju has meaning and education I mean something to learn from what it is yesterday is no long what it is today nevertheless it has this yearning for give me, give me we are bound to change as the world changes meaning our environment, culture and tradition at the moment its playing a huge part in politics. How do we apply politics and science should be our focus polygamy, having a male or female child, who should go to school and who should not go to school imply meaning to culture based on what a parents feel should be their natural selection what does it imply a child born in Great Britain in the mid 1960 from a polygamous family realize that because of a conduct of a step mother among others living in the UK I cannot have my bath at the same time us a sponge is it part of my own juju or a juju of my step mother or my late father?

Definition of sponge: A primitive sedentary aquatic invertebrate with a soft porous body that is typically supported by a framework of fibres or calcareous or glassy spicules. Sponges draw in a current of water to extract nutrients and oxygen.

A piece of a soft, light, porous absorbent substance originally consisting of the fibrous skeleton of an aquatic invertebrate but now usually made of synthetic material, used for washing and cleaning.

Obtain or accept money or food from other people without doing or intending to do anything in return.

My father is also a spent force from a different perspective from mine. What is the true insight of me and my father relationship as father and son? There is more in life than my ordeals to say prayers for my soul to keep watch being good and living the good life is by choice not everyone wants to live the good and virtues life because they have choices to have it their own way it might upset you if you choose to live the good life therefore it is part of your ordeals in reality if you are good it is part of your own making, if you understand African rituals the implications are vast and could be rigorous. Because there is a light in you to be good in a world of beauty, ugliness and death where you can only set things right summing all you can, you could do things for better and not for worse you are not in position to judge others for this reason, some of us put it down to the existence of God. It is not fear or the lack of confidence in ourselves for such reason we believe in God's grace because in reality every wonders which encapsulate our life the wonders of the world if we really have consideration for life and what comes after death in us there is a God, he is merciful this is what the spirit world holds. Human have all it takes to do and undo every aspect of their livelihood for better or for worse with little or no retribution for their deeds it's a fixation being who we are knowing right from wrong while there is pain and suffering that we forage, having all it takes to act on them why, aren't we making it any more better for the sack of beauty in the world infarct why do children come into this world?

Within few years after my fathers' death in Nigeria, after years in my flat of the episode of the spider, my sister in-law and my niece, in which my sister in-law lost a pregnancy for my brother after they had Mr. Zack and moved from Brockley to Kent. I remembered I drank excessively during that period.

My first step mothers Mrs. Cordelia Megbele first daughter for my father after a first relationship with two children before, she moved in with my father, now Mrs. Anita Oritsewarami Timile made a visit to the UK she is my immediate younger sister in our family.

She was pregnant on her visit to my flat, after haven't seen me for years the words which came out of her mouth where words of bald remarks on entering my living room. I was taken aback I felt like saying if she had nothing sensible to say, she could at least keep quiet and let other people do the talking moreover she was pregnant it is not customary in African culture for women during pregnancy to talk the way she did. You do not hold grudges I offered her food and drinks she did not touch them. I sometimes remember the two children Mr. Tenye and Ms. Cibella Mrs. Cordelia Megbele had before moving in with our father we hardly see them or hear about them yet, they are part of the family. I was informed they had moved in with Cordelia in our father's house after his death. All children needs both parents as I grow up questions need to be asked such as was Cordelia really happy looking after children that weren't her own bearing in mind she had two children in her first relationship who she hardly see or hear much about. Within our family what would be paramount to her of cause was her own children without second thoughts if, she was a slave to my late father because he would have been the first most important person before her children to see her through her ordeals in life. Considering the situation did I have a voice in the family I take things as they come to me and I there not complain. Dose the situation produce a concept or picture of what is a true family and a happy family.

In retrospect when I summed up each experience it draws a line for me remaining a celibate and find my true self and I have this illness of paranoid schizophrenia. What I sort for since I was a child was happiness and one big happy family. A family I thought I had and hoped for what it would be that never was. At least every one of us has an idea of what their family should be or, is it just me?

Happy families have certain traits in common. Communication, togetherness, sharing activities, affection, support, acceptance, commitment and resilience are typical in families that function well. Children benefit from regular mealtimes, affection, play, traditions and outings with the whole family. Unhappy families may not benefit from professional help if there is any. It might be valuable to occasionally evaluate the dynamics of your family to ensure that everyone is as happy as they could be.

A happy family is where the mum and dad are together, and the sisters and brothers feel safe and can talk together. You need to have a loving and caring family that will support you and trust you. Sometimes you need both your parents. The best thing to connect with your family is love. Help each other and don't love one person more than the other it is basically out of family politics that makes one person egocentric. Being a happy family is about being able to look ahead, to be able to find a good thing about every bad thing that comes up. I think you need to love and trust each other, and if you are always yelling at each other then maybe you need to talk. Are all families in such a disposition if they just listen to each other they will get along?

A family in my opinion is really a family when their souls and body can reach out to each other it is usually the parent who should make such standings. It does not have to be a standard setting but creating a feeling no matter what the situation, you all are one family failing for parents to achieve such setting would be the failure of what conceptualise it as a family more so if it were a polygamous family you have much more work to be done. Families where there is just both parents and children, it is easy and natural for them to remain united as a family, they would have their disagreement but remain peaceful to shear their ups and downs and generally look up to each other when something is bordering them I mean, things you would not normally take to a friend but first of all discus with a family member. I mean you do not only have brothers and sister we have aunts and uncles, cosines and niece.

- Concepts of a family and what makes a happy family differs across countries, regions, race, culture and creed and it defines us as each individual. Difficult it might be to categories families across countries race and colour anyway it makes us who we are. I come from a background of rituals to the extents of growing up that are left for me to put into a perspective that's if I have the mind to owe it to myself not to someone else or beat about the bush.

We are an immersed forces, having put immersed efforts through synergy making ourselves whatever we are today on earth. It seems to me sometimes as if Planet earth is subsuming, why are more people each day in Europe could so many people be found suffering from mental illness.

Spiritualists believe that we all die physically and some aspect of our personality or mind survives this and continues to exist on a spirit plane, sometimes referred to as the spirit world. It describes all minds and entities that have entered into the spirit world. The purpose of the medium is to provide some evidence that a human has survived by describing the person to their surviving relatives. The degree of accuracy with which the deceased are described goes some way to convincing the living relatives and friends that the medium has some contact with the spirit. Spiritualists describe this as 'survival evidence'.

There have been a number of famous practitioners of spirit communication connected to Spiritualist churches. Mediums develop their ability by sitting regularly in development circles. Meditation usually plays a large role in Spiritualist practice used calming modern, hectic life so that the practitioner can better hear his or her guide. Meditation often includes the breathing practices. The Spiritualist also focus on their chosen religion to help them attain higher existence prayers may be included as they attempt to contact with the spirits world.

- Healing circles within the churches

Spiritualist healing, as practiced in some Spiritualist churches during services some of which involves technique of directing healing energy to a person from a higher source.

Many mediums work at spiritualist churches bringing through messages from spirit beings particularly loved ones who have passed over to members of their audience.

Nowadays spiritualism is practiced in a wide variety of venues when would we strive to follow the principals of Spiritualism.

Spiritualism is a belief system; inferring spirits of the dead residing in the spirit world have both the ability and the inclination to communicate with the living.

Anyone may become a medium through study, gifting and practice as little as when they are still children in Africa. They can attain growth and perfection, progressing through higher spheres or planes. They dream, they see vision and they prophecy. Give them food, clothing and shelter they would do better.

Spiritualism was equated by some Christians with witchcraft. As Spiritualism emerged in a Christian environment, it has features in common with Christianity, ranging from an essentially Christian moral system to practices such as Sunday services and the singing of hymns.

Christians, generally speaking, accept and believe that Jesus Christ died on the cross to pay for all the sins of all humanity from the dawn of time to eternity. The great majority of Spiritualists do not accept that the death of Jesus Christ on the cross was to pay for all of humanity's sins. Instead, they believe that each individual is personally responsible and may have to answer for all of their own thoughts, words, and deeds after death upon their return to the spirit realms.

In the same way that Christians have the guidance of the Ten Commandments, Spiritualists follow a number of principles, which are different depending on the tradition followed.

There are quite a number of Spiritualist churches which are explicitly Christian in theology, forms of worship and praise, and orientation. Among these Christian Spiritualist groups are the historically African American denominations collectively known as the Spiritual Church Movement, a group which includes multi-church organizations such as the Metropolitan Spiritual Churches of Christ, and Pentecostal Spiritual Assemblies of Christ International.

Spirituality means something different to everyone. For some, it's about participating in organized religion: going to church, synagogue, a mosque, etc. For others, it's more personal: Some people get in touch with their spiritual side through private prayer, yoga, meditation, quiet reflection, life experience or even long walks even with mental health. This world is partly created for us to envisage Spirituality, Paranormal, Philosophical and the Supernatural.

Demonic possession is held by many belief systems to be the control of an individual by a malevolent supernatural being. Descriptions of demonic possessions often include erased memories or personalities, convulsions, 'fits' and fainting as if one were dying. Other descriptions include access to hidden knowledge and foreign languages, drastic changes in vocal intonation and facial structure, the sudden appearance of injuries (scratches, bite marks) or lesions, and superhuman strength. In other forms of possession, the subject has no control over the possessing entity and so it will persist until forced to leave the victim, usually through a form of exorcism. Spirituality itself are all things that exist this include metals, bricks or the cutleries we eat with substantiated they exist because for example above them all humans exist what is existence is still yet to be known if understood which must be, because we have life, we are progressive would it really become finite? Whichever way we carry out spirituality the experience is life itself while we are yet to really define right from wrong and we say God doesn't exist it all depends on his own magnificence judgment.

Many cultures and religions contain some concept of demonic possession, but the details vary considerably. I believe all diseases of the body and mind are caused by sickness demons there are levels of tolerance. Most spiritual Church's practiced exorcisms; many contain prayers asking God for protection from demons, while others ask God to expel demons that have invaded their homes and bodies. If the effect of The Da Vinci Code is real it in effect means that we could over centuries have been reading, exploring and cultivating and also practicing that the ten commandments of God over centuries have been read and ordained and could be read, and practice forward and backward also, the Holy Bible. The novel is part of the exploration of alternative religious history, whose central plot point is that the Merovingian kings of France were descendants from the bloodline of Jesus Christ and Mary Magdalene, ideas derived from Clive Prince's The Templar Revelation and books by Margaret Starbird. The book also references another book, The Holy Blood and the Holy Grail though Dan Brown has stated that it was not used as research material.

The book has provoked a popular interest in speculation concerning the Holy Grail legend and Magdalene's role in the history of Christianity, our existence, work and the life we live.

Cultures also believe in demon possession and perform exorcisms. In some of these cultures and some Churches diseases are often attributed to the presence of a vengeful spirit or demon in the body, head and minds of people some of them could be attributed to mental health patients. These spirits are more often people wronged by the bearer, the exorcism rites usually consisting of respectful offerings or sacrificial offerings.

Christianity holds that possession derived from The Devil, Satan and Lucifer, or one of his lesser demons. In many Christian belief systems, Satan and his demons are actually fallen angels which have relevance to Gods covenant of circumcision which is huge and more reason to understand such issues of being gay, lesbian, transvestites, transsexual, surrogacy, cloning. Science over centuries has left lots of issues for us to understand or put into perspectives as we enter this age of reasoning. Everything we go through are the making of God that we may understand ourselves better and owe him gratitude.

What follows are concepts that would make me determinate whether there is a psychiatric problem or a demonic one or both could be involved.

The use of condoms, steroids, medication for men having erections or to increase women huge for sex they practice, all sorts of sexology at home sometimes, in the street considering our environment the houses we live including insets sex of all nature are all forms of possession and we have the ten commandments to live by you and I know when we are living the good or bad life but why is demonic possession craving for its part on all this. How do we define it, to be honest how varied is culture and how does it represent our existence if, there are no demonic possession or spirit world, would culture really represent our existence dose it has a vice against reality.

The vice cannot be the food and water we eat and drink what then are diseases fungi's are used for curing disease, spells against juju or for juju and witchcrafts nature of their growth are awesome one can only appreciate fungi's which are not classified as plants if you have reaction to it you might address what it means by spent force by nature how do I explain this further, if I emphasis am really Superman no one would believe me what then are diseases' if food products and the food we prepare could get rotten in our homes and fridges with varied sex acts performed, food therefore can be possessed and therefore different from diseases what then are disease they are Lucifer, Satan, the Devil and their fallen angels because, they have no form but want to take form trickling down from other planets where our souls and spirits once occupied you do not have, to believe me, it's just a feeling I have let's wait till life is found in planet Mars if living plants could be found in any other planet, I have the feeling, they would look like fungi's in my imagination.

A fungus is a member of a large group of <u>eukaryotic</u> organisms that includes microorganisms such as <u>yeasts</u> and <u>molds</u> (<u>British English</u>: moulds), as well as the more familiar <u>mushrooms</u>. These organisms are classified as a <u>kingdom</u>

Possession is a common phenomenon. Although it happens more often that people realize, it is still considered common. To my own understanding, most diagnosis of mental illness thoroughly considered implies they are being possessed. Science has swept away much of what is used to be considered as demonic possession. Diseases of the mind such as Schizophrenia, bipolar syndrome and various forms of psychosis are sure-fire signs of possession or diseases of the mind they could be about life, our environment. Lots of people suffering from such illnesses do live active lives while on medication.

It is true that in past centuries, mentally ill people were subjected to difficult exorcisms and the results were poor. Science took over for some reason it works the food and medication component we take in are all one or another form of minerals and chemicals they give life. Whatever takes away life or is obstacles to life resist such consistencies in which case it could be said sciences has effect. Demons do not like seeing light most medications are heated up in strong heat. Why could one be on medication for mental illness at unusual times, they do not want or feel like taking their medication how can such problems be resolved? During each stage of the seasons especially during winter my medications have to be reviewed and changed as I endeavoured to ask my psychiatrists Dr Tariah from an African background and Dr Singh from an Asian background at my Ferryview mental health centre if they understands issues of vampires my experiences had something of such nature Dr Singh and his associates directed me to see a psychologist Michelle McCartney at the Heights at Charlton in Greenwich.

A problem is an obstacle, impediment, difficulty or challenge, or a situation that invites resolution; the resolution of which is recognized as a solution or contribution toward a known purpose or goal. A problem implies a desired outcome coupled with an apparent deficiency, doubt or inconsistency that prevents the outcome from taking place for instant if at one time men had have been cannibals it might have been as a result of possession from hunger. While at the moment in my origin regardless of illness and diseases some of us see no justification for English mans medication through science while they need to understand jujus has repercussions they cannot handle in retrospect for which, there is less and thorough retribution. Centuries ago I would accept there were reasons for it to be so because we were isolated from the rest of the world our lives and ways of living have changed over centuries improving it further to meet a required standard light can be sheared on our own methods now, it should be plan culture and tradition that implies our background which is beautiful while time and relationships have changed. The food we eat, the clothing we wear have not changed because, they signify our culture which is what I believe in. We should develop what we have if it's any good to many extent it would use them more for justified purpose based on cultivating and preserving our heritage we act, feel and react differently whichever the case let's make what we have a blessing to ourselves.

Since religion came to Africa, all sorts of Christine denomination sprang up against witchcraft and demonic possession in a land where hunger and poverty lies we are from the soil we should not stop going back to the soil without uphold spiritualism where our spirituality lies we should tend to deal with our existence out of poverty you can have three square meals a day someone's has none. All nations have poverty and diseases, sadness and sorrow varied by culture if they are doing well in Europe it means they are doing something about something which becomes like solving the problem of Heaven and Earth. If Africans are sons and daughters of the soil rub the earth with good juju, not blood that would infect dried woods and sacrifices that would drain downward and would not please the soil, the gods or deities that makes our skin rough and dryer a times comes, when such experience change it should change in the sense of direction not dramatically left with exposing dark side.

When the English men came to Africa to cut down the trees still use in making juju's it were not brought into Europe to be used the same way as it were used in Africa. Till this century when the sons and daughters of the juju priest were brought into Europe their children are pleased with good schools, education and food brought in from Africa to Europe why not try the same ventures in Africa in ways of modernizing Africa. When young star from African background go back From Europe to Africa or for visits they complain their skins become dry and rough they are calling for changes such changes needs to be implemented.

Every theoretical problem asks for <u>answer</u> or solution. There are many standard techniques for problem solving. A problem is a gap between an actual and desired situation. The time it takes to solve a problem is a way of measuring <u>complexity</u>. Many problems have no discovered solution and are therefore classified as an <u>open problem</u>.

Problem solving is a mental process which is the concluding part of the larger <u>problem</u> process that includes <u>problem finding</u> and <u>problem shaping</u> where problem is defined as a state of desire for the reaching of a definite goal from a present condition that either is not directly moving toward the goal, is far from it or needs more <u>complex</u> logic for finding a missing description of conditions or steps toward the goal. Considered the most complex of all <u>intellectual</u> functions, problem solving has been defined as a higher-order <u>cognitive</u> process that requires the modulation and control of more routine or fundamental skills. Problem solving has two major domains: <u>mathematical problem solving</u> and personal problem solving where, in the second, some difficulty or barrier is encountered. Further problem solving occurs when moving from a given state to a desired goal state needed for either <u>living organisms</u> or an <u>artificial intelligence</u> <u>system</u>.

While problem solving accompanies the very beginning of human evolution and especially the history of mathematics, the nature of human problem solving processes and methods has been studied by <u>psychologists</u> over the past hundred years. Methods of studying problem solving include <u>introspection</u>, <u>behaviourism</u>, <u>simulation</u>, <u>computer modelling</u> and <u>experiment</u>.

Being possessed means one is being invaded pretence are not involved one is likely to feel depressed and unsure of themselves then to help them, virtues and morals become a discipline on which they could find solace in meditation, belief or religion, what it means to be intolerant or do things that are not consistent some of which people may observe as unusual it's all a disposition of life any way not a situation others should use to make their own fixation or to make profit.

We are here to face our trials of life every individual would have to make and face a dictionary of their lives involved are many inconsistencies come to make sense of it, we are in each other's lives even the dead though dead are still with us and here we are making planes for the future.

Some mental changes affecting people are changes in personality, becomes extremely quiet. Someone who are normally very active suddenly becomes isolative, avoidance, observable changes in personal hygiene, changes in sleep patterns, sudden weight loss or gain, changes in the way the person dress, evidence of occult materials in their homes; they could display positive or negative aversion to religious objects with obvious changes in their features,

These are psychological or psychiatric changes; they are in some ways signs of possession or to reconcile. All of the above can be cries for help or signal the beginning of drug use or mental illness. As you will see, there are many other indications of possession. Look for some of those before you give credence to the idea of possession. In addition, never mention to someone undergoing personality changes that they might be possessed rather give hint for consideration first. You can plant a dangerous seed by doing that. Not even psychiatrists do this very often even if there are signs. The Church has completely avoided such stance while some of us are so self cantered we live our lives by possessing other people such people live only for themselves some culture across the world are grounds where they can get away with it.

If we could help it, we would really share our things. We would really want to think about others and sacrifice something that could've been all ours. While we live in a society and societal rules, nomenclature demanding we share, care, empathize and such and such. So we learn these are all positive traits a good human is one who has a profusion of these positive qualities. Of course, there are times when we show traits of negative behaviour in the way of selfish behavioural patterns.

But this does not all become part of our behaviour and merely limit itself to select occasions. And then there are self-cantered people who do not exhibit any of the above mentioned positive traits and thereby affect other people's adjustment in society. Dealing with self-cantered people can get tough if one does not know how to go about it. In extremes this can turn out to be a personality disorder and can be very draining for those who give or deal with it. Why do we know people for various reasons I suppose my advice; is do not get yourself too involve with people who think or react at the very last minute they are signs of possession if their reactions show signs of evasiveness when it comes to dealing with reality worse if they show singes of being egocentric and no signs of self consciousness.

Egocentrism is when one is over preoccupied with their own internal world. Egocentrics regard oneself and one's own opinions or interests as most important or valid. Self-relevant information is seen to be more important in shaping one's judgments than do thoughts about others and other-relevant information. It also generates the inability to fully understand or to cope with other people's opinions and the fact that reality can be different from what they are ready to accept despite any change in their personal life anomalies or belief.

During childhood, the child is unable to distinguish between what is subjective (things that are strictly personal or private) and objective (what is public knowledge). Essentially, children believe other could have different perception than their own.

Egocentricity in children involve language and morality when communicating with others, a child could believes that others know everything about a topic of discussion and become frustrated when asked to give further detail.

This might affects a child's sense of morality a child is only concerned with the final outcome of an event rather than other intentions. For example, if someone breaks the child's toy, the child would not forgive the other due to the child not being able to understand that the person who broke the toy did not intend to break it but if the person makes the child in any way feel, it was intentional the child becomes frustrated worse it would be if this happens at the last course of the action. Take for instant my father initiated I and my immediate elder brother as freemasons we were meant through our initiation to take up celibacy after a period of over seventeen years before our fathers death I have kept my vows even based on personal reasons of my own who among both brothers should receive encouragement or enlightenment in view of our fathers disposition to have initiated us into freemason? If it's what I want to do most people might consider it bleak why should he rally round his family and make faces at me to do exactly this if the initiation was of good intention or motives is left to me. An irony could be due to his ritualistic ways my father has a hold on me or maybe I have a hold on him he would motivate me in any way carrying out the real rights of my initiation into freemason that he shall rise. How, would I feel at the very last minutes I got to be aware, there are certain rituals carried out in West African culture that requires certain age of children within a family to cross over that is when the rituals can be renounced? In view of the situation it is left for me choosing a prerequisite of being my own master.

Egocentrism is thus a child's inability to see other people's viewpoints. The child at this stage of cognitive development assumes that their view of the world is the same as other peoples', a little girl does not see that taking another child's ball is wrong because she does not understand that taking the ball would hurt the other child's feelings.

Accordingly, since she fails to differentiate between what others are thinking about and her own mental preoccupations, she assumes that other people are obsessed with her behaviour and appearance as she is herself.' This shows that the adolescent is exhibiting egocentrism because she cannot clearly identify another person's perception.

To help describe the egocentric behaviours exhibited by an adolescent population such as what is calls an imaginary audience and personal fable. Imaginary audience refers to the idea that most adolescents believe that there is some audience that is constantly present that is overly interested in what the individual has to say or do. Personal fable refers to the idea that many teenagers believe that they are the only ones who are capable of feeling the way that they do. Egocentrism in adolescence is often viewed as a negative aspect of their thinking ability because adolescents become consumed with themselves and are unable to effectively function in society due to their skewed version of reality.

Reasons as to why adolescents experience egocentrism adolescents are often faced with new social environments (for example, starting secondary school) which require the adolescent to protect the self which may lead to egocentrism.

Development of the adolescent's identity may lead to the individual experiencing high levels of uniqueness which subsequently becomes egocentric this manifest as the personal fable.

Parents not facing their family responsibilities and commitments may lead to their children experiencing high levels of self-consciousness, which may lead to egocentrism.

A study was completed on 163 undergraduate students to examine the adolescent egocentrism in college students. Students were asked to complete a self-report questionnaire to determine the level of egocentrism present. The questions simply asked for the reactions that students had to seemingly face embarrassing situations.

Results from other studies have come to the conclusion that egocentrism does not present itself in some of the same patterns as it was found originally. More recent studies have found that egocentrism is prevalent in later years of development.

The prevalence of egocentrism on the individual has been found to decrease between the age of 15 and 16. However, adults are also susceptible to be egocentric or to have reactions or behaviours that can be categorized as egocentric.

Test on adolescents (14-18 years old) and adults (20-89) on their levels of egocentrism and self-consciousness. Found that egocentric tendencies had extended to early adulthood and was that these tendencies were also present in the middle adult years.

Looking at 153 participants and tested to see how the presence of depression affected egocentrism. They tested adults between the ages of 18 and 25. It was found that the participants with depression showed higher levels of egocentrism. Therefore, this would suggest that a mentally healthy individual evolves out of most of his or her egocentric habits. Which could mean at certain point in the life of a mental health patient fear and uncertainty are involved which make them depress they could mean signs of egocentrism, possession such as socially withdrawn, they find it difficult to communicate at some point, they could hardly express their feelings or put themselves into actions of activities because of negative bias.

An individual cannot be mentally unwell infarct very fit because the person is egocentric or with fear of mentally being unwell could be driven to work in mental health care. It might be fear or you are running away from yourself or something you might become egocentric on getting into mental health care to work, you are in time possessing the place because, you have been condition by emotion to go in there and work everything you encounter there might not seem as you want it to be or thought it would be bear it in mind you have already been conditioned to go in there and work but on what stance?

Your motives for going in there might be dashed as time goes by in your working life since; you have developed your own motives for going there to work. Definition of motive is something (as a need or desire) that causes a person to act yet you want to care for people with fundamental derangement of the mind (as in schizophrenia) characterized by defective or lost contact with reality especially as evidenced by delusions, hallucinations, and disorganized speech and behaviour moreover in a place where people even go there to divest themselves of their internal organs to add to this, is there any good reason why hard drugs should be handed over to drug addicts in hospital environment yet the NHS is advising some of the general public to quit smoking and there are needs to improve hygiene standards? Couple of these concepts can be related to medical or psychological conditions most of them fall outside the realm of science some people say, I say thanks to science and technology because in our past our existence were part of witchcraft, worshiping the Devil, magic and sorcery symptoms of these, still remain with us till this century but how do we describe them? At some point when science came into shape. Some believed it was out of magic and witchcraft those times, were troubled times with people worshiping all sorts of omens to attain power such as make magic portions in some cases for healing or curing demonic possession or other illnesses myth were involved in some parts of the world.

Science brought in new meaning to all these based on practical experimenting and observation. Take a look at the huge effort of science today consider what it has brought to us, consider architectures, consider technology the homes we live in hot water running, washing machines in our homes, fridges, television sets, these are just a minor few of them consider information technology.

Science over the years have coexist with religion our lives are less possessed consider the amount of power struggle still going on in our world today if we have been left to summoning the Devil, witchcraft and magic our lives would have been more chaotic what we have left today, is greed, hat, winging and lies. Science has changed Africa from what it used to be. The same applies with superstitious belief this, does not mean they still do not exist.

What we have now is going to meet juju, voodoo priest for jujus and talisman that would make one become wealthy, succeed in education, business should flourish. The stance of science and technology is bringing a new meaning to our lives a radio, television, modern ways of building infrastructure and ways of life what we have left is lies greed and hat. This does not mean being possessed has not implications in the world we live in today infarct the implications are much more different in every aspect of our lives. Because of the things we do or say, how we live has changed, how we perceive thing is moving towards clarity and conformity. How dose lies, hat greed, jealous employs itself and the effect in our lives if not through being bewitched with simple advice, one can be bewitched.

There are lots of implications I can imply including experience but it would not accredit me because of the nature of my background and how other race terminals them in Europe coming out with it as they happened would be sour, some might accredit me of being unreserved to my race creed or colour in due course some of them get away with it especially in Europe because in retrospect especially critics whether genuine or not would not count it in the interest of let's say; children while it befits parents or children from my background who say, they have come to live the better life in Europe a good question to ask is are they genuine would it call for better change for example consideration for ourselves within each other?

If it would help in solving problems of mental illness like schizophrenia from level of family, environmental, societal context. We should be speculating on the real courses of schizophrenia witchcrafts, magic, juju, voodoo and sorcery including sin are involve because, blood is thicker than water synergy, our environment, government and politics, our life style have become different t where most anomalies causing mental illness, suffering and pain are hardly brought to the surface considering it gives stance to other people to move on in life. In Britain you do not really come out with the true implications or how one emotion drives one into madness because of some feel good, all good factors the inherencies dose not really speak for itself in the real perspectives of whatever, the situation really is we call it civilisation or using caution.

But the message would really get to those who, understand the true implications involve when it is not all about feel good factors one might be raising secret enemies or critics. For using such a word some would say it is madness but its reality or that we still worship the Devil in the 21st century. British people do not always deal with strange things when they happen but only when it comes out in the open. In this respect, I do not mean any other thing but strange things or phenomena because of technology, engineering and science they should move towards reality by making a choice within science and phenomena the Americans are good at it anything initiating something of a nature of welcome to the real world.

Africans who could be said to have lived in somehow the real world within good and evil when they came into Europe they dramatically change accompanied with yet anomalies or inherency in different dimension such is life. Schizophrenia is not all that a bad illness in some case it is what people turn you into that is a problem. It deals with perception, query, reason, magnitude, calls for explanation and existentiality. People who such issues should have meaning or inclination to care for us should have the right attributes. Some of them are partly the once who, had already laid down some effigy for its occurrences and they might be from your own race we should in no way be stigmatised because of our illness or suffering.

For some of us coming to the UK we digress before making turns or watch closely before using the roundabout. It leaves us emotionally to do right, not wrong but when relationship get sour or problematic emotions become difficult to overcome if it gets worse one might become paranoid anger may set in not knowing one is just being bewitched. One race or culture within the UK should watch out, how they imply themselves to other race the situation could lead to schizophrenia. It is common for men to rule each other, use vice, control and commands. It is therefore quite simple understanding why people generally suffer.

Drug addicts, anti social behaviours, schizophrenia, bipolar, paranoia, counselling in prison all these people come from within families, you might find yourself caring for them how, did you make your life better while they could not make their life own better? How easy can you convince majority of British and the rest of the world that the illness schizophrenia is genetic? If someone implies this to me I would question the person if he or she is trying to test, question my faith, life experience, what I think or make out about life involving all sorts of scenarios, experience or paradigms that creates mental illness. But if I should imply people are being bewitched in this century I might be doubted termed as am not living in the real world. Some of us suffering from mental health issues might be holding the reign of witchcraft, juju, voodoo, God, mysteries of life, faith and emotions but we fail knowing how to control them or use them for good purposes. There are several different spiritual lives, level, attainment, alignment we go through in life, we practice our religious rights, our beliefs, conscience and consciousness should be made sound and clear why should anyone want to use talisman, juju, magic, sorcery or witchcraft it's partly through such creative process we can understand mental illness behaviourism, attitudes, concepts of rationality and irrationality. You are using worldly artefacts you could through it initiate other peoples live for better or for worse. Do you ever think of what you are moulding for someone else to use in attaining their purpose through your own initiatives? For example juju ironically depends on the implication of your spiritual self or implications when we through stages of existence divest ourselves since some of us believe in reincarnation.

If it is through you requirement at one point, it has to come where, you show your true self what, would it be? Some of us believe in Heaven some believe in hell some people see hell while living on earth while some people see Heaven knowing what it contains, knowing what it entail is a gift would we actually be judged? Or couldn't it be said we are judging ourselves through our life experiences based on repeated lives in a world of good and evil, love, hat, peace, war beauty, ugliness and death? To the end of time our achievement would be our rewards. Everyone wants the all good, feel good factor where dose wrong comes from drawing close to our modern world of advance human technology and engineering, entrepreneur, business, working environment what has synergy since time brought to us, if you believe in the social aspect of existence the age of reasoning, what are the inherencies are more than mental illness and we take no notice of it. It is through one way we could know those who still really cares, love, and hat or are peace makers.

There are different level of initiating anomalies, if I as a schizophrenia going through such memorise what do you as a care, family, friends make up of what am going through emotionally. Nigeria is not a welfare state after over 21 years of my life spent there when it could be said I would had gained enough perception, become a man or have come of age attributed by all sorts of rituals Britain is a welfare state there is no cries for hunger but emotionally one can be disturbed should I pass it on to my children?.

Humans use all sorts of powers and calibres we yet to achieve the greatest of all human endeavours going into Heaven the road is hard and troublesome some humans use magic, juju, witchcraft, sorcery and voodoo, cultism, spirituality, beliefs, myth attaining human fame the greatest of all achievements is what money cannot buy. The architects whose glory it is to wear the privileged rob is identifying himself in Zion before our wear and tear divest in time through means by choice to be in Zion deliberately we willingly give in to our divesting at such a stage more in what we know, what we believe in and what we understand.

History comes and go whatever is left at each stage for example is more than schizophrenia applied to culture or tradition we go through different eras in it we achieve goals this is certainly not an era for stigmatising people suffering from mental illness we should be rejoicing in our achievements. How do we eradicate self wimp we all want the feel good factor, dress well, eat well. Within this, we might want to show off. While others probably from the same origins within the land you have made your dwelling go on drugs why aren't they going for the all good, feel good factor, while you might just only be a chipping in factor within an establish system. What makes some people suffer from less self esteem? I await my critics but think of why they or I should suffer from schizophrenic and who, are those caring for me? This part of the world is a place where we bring out the best out of ourselves.

In Nigeria the Ibos and Yoruba's have been quarrelling for decades over lots of issues in religion juju versus Celestial and Aladura worship. Fighting over culture making fixations on each other is the latest form of juju while progress do not take place if not in religion and beliefs but why not in human advancement why the customary conflicts and accusations instead of social enhancement e.g. food shelter and clothing civilisation, wellbeing and education. Juju worship is quite different from Aladura and Celestial worship it's all basically a problem of peace of mind and a relationship with God but problems keep piling up from different directions it becomes a thing to be enjoyed by some people because it gives them room having things their own way by any means. The Gospel and Evangelicals play their own roles. There is more of claiming one faction is better than the other meanwhile Zimbabwean, Serial Leon, Uganda in times like these when there is conflict relating to politics, religion, a time of moving towards science and technology or knowing the implications that might be right for Africans through our natives ways in such time choose to move e.g. towards native medicine.

 Antagonism should not be involved, moving towards factionist in relation to the whole African continents why not stand or space each viable as they are related and move towards a dignified whole of not conspiracy but interrelationship. Where does it place the relationship within Africans and the Europeans? In relations to Jamaicans,

Caribbean's, Barbados or Trinidadians and its Voodoo in relation to science and technology for them and the rest of Europe, who have spent more years in Europe than the Africans? Science and technology over time have become more complex and easy to build. Culture, tradition changes over time because while playing the culture other overturns takes place through e.g. reincarnation, condition of birth if inscribed might incur divesting ourselves going through repeated heritage likely different while lines, would rationally be drawn to accept or reject us to meet the current era. it is not all inevitable man is moving towards space missions for third world countries it is time to use the Krypton factor try and develop, live decent lives in a place like Africa where rituals, witchcraft, cultism, conflicts, antagonism, misshapes, juju, sacrifices to pay homage to the soil, the gods or deities it can all be portrayed in all sorts of dignified ways for the better not all juju, witchcraft are bad. The concepts of culture is huge and divers a place to be justified in our act, deeds and reason behind our ways make it a place and call it a name, a home where everything had not gone wrong but has meaning and would end well. Such should be the motor for Africa the rest of Europe should join in and help them the soil is firm after decades of cultivation, climate diversity, drilling of petroleum and shipping it is time for the Krypton factor to set in.

Religion is enlightenment because of something you and I perceive in time, one can realise it's a key. In another aspect one might think of getting hold of the key and its all through phenomena how could one get hold of the key is through perception of reality in somewhat a trouble world? Greed, hat was not impose by God it's all imposed by man later resulting to conflict, diversity drawing to business and political avenue led to maladministration mind you, we have all been programmed into this world using the term this world mostly mean not only planet earth. We have been going on space mission discovering other planets and galaxies what is on planet earth might be what, would be on these planet in the uprising of Zion at all stages whatever is visible to the architects is more than phenomena's what should be preceding planets earth is that it should be termed the planet of reasoning.

Some culture depicts from their childhood children are given tribal marks as branding, ethnicity, diversity or initiation or circumcision it's what I have dedicated my existentially on, divest myself through this present life with an inherence of being born premature one other inherencies I would have to put up with is schizophrenia these are reasons why I wanted my father to become a chief I had at one time in Nigeria filed an application form through JAMB I wanted to study psychiatry at university of Ibadan. It's the same way some Europeans use their lives being creative in making chair, tables, medicine, engineering modelling of such products in wide varieties as for food, its food that is culture in my terminology we are what we eat, wear as to each race and ethnicity,.

They make instruments for music some through or as part of cultural orientation some of which we now use but are not creative at making though we might have, their own traditional instrument which does not have, the same effect as the once we use back home in our homeland but are present within other countries of the world. Our using them through their own creative process how it rimes into our own culture entwines depending on the joy it brings to us food also entwines, as to race if it brings the race joy and happiness when it comes to being stingy with food the sky would strict back on such race without food there is no happiness.

The Europeans used their wisdom in being creative in making household goods for feel good factor while some developing part of the world use their manual labour such as China they have their culture strong and determined they have suffered loss in turning to modern science and technology loosing their old heritage this those not mean they are not still Chinese.

Living in the old ways invariably their culture has not changes there is still some to make their parents and the spirit of their forefathers uphold them as to whom, they have always been life is always a blessing if you continually turn it into blessing and gifting. Nature provides for China and its history that they do not uphold evil witchcraft invariable sooths them becoming manufactures which has not wiped-out the Shoaling dynasty. How do we change by using reason, caution and discretion or we would not have started from where we began the realisation is that it bring happiness, fulfilment or there would be nothing like death.

The earth crust of West Africa and its soils after centuries of being battered by climate change still convenient in many ways for us considering after many years of petroleum drilling, intense farming, I believe the earth crust is now firm using the Krypton factor that's by planning and development manufacture whatever is convenient and necessary. It might wipe out some diseases or stabilise the surface of the earth, keep it tidy, keep some idle hands busy and enhance our wellbeing the government should protect and avoid death on the road and highways of West Africa, all dead bodies should be buried without rituals, use good juju make it viable if it is our belief children are being born into the world to face a different era do not block our journey from the world we proceed from because some of us believe in the supernatural and spiritual to drain down the blood of life from Heaven call it from the sky if you like but lets us not enjoy the feel good factor we should look up to each under with understanding. Man had started from something we believe would not have added up to what the world is today.

In such respect, what is schizophrenia the inability or constrain leading to less enjoyment, become disturbed, suffer from distorted thoughts that leads to emotional suffering while the background, culture, environment add up its own effect to what makes a sufferer less resilient to life constrains. Going through such emotional phase, if no notice or concern are taken by the sufferers family, friends or government agencies understanding what is going on, the sufferer at say the initial stage might put themselves in harm such as drugs, alcoholism or go about with gangs and get into trouble but a short while ago, nobody would had expected him or her to be of such a kind. How can anti social behaviour be mental illness? It's an abuse terming in such a way. It is an opportunity for people to get away creating antagonism.

I do not agree with the aspect of anti social behaviour it's all a cover up from dose who want to enjoy the feel good, all good aspect from other peoples inside out and they may be our cares. Cares make things up because they want to create impressions about the services they provide. At the beginning, how do some people viewed certain strict actions in working places or the start of women right activist some say it was out of anti social behaviour now, it all has new meaning to our lives as a democratic action.

Schizophrenia has a lot to do with moral values, rituals, sacrifices, witchcraft, spell casting, social programming or way we change and live our lives it could even be as a result of programming through the effect of Science, technology, engineering, our environment and livelihood. Some of use might want to programme ourselves but cannot what is holding us back where dose the all good, feel good factor comes while in some cases some people are not allowed to fit in? The effect could make us problem solvers are we, being given the right chance or opportunity or there is none at all that has driven us into such a state of mental illness. It's good to train up a child religiously because when faith, religion comes in handy because of once religious undertakings time might have run out it only leaves one resilient to carry on further into the unknown which are always hard and difficult times.

We all have different temperament to food regardless in all creatures it has already been determined if we are carnivorous, herbivorous or vegetarians in all expect regardless either one you are in preference to certain food in such categories and its now difficult living marital lives, a child to grow up, work and enjoy life, it is the age of reasoning it is time of getting to know and understand what people are like what they could be while there are many factors to choose that would last one until Zion is restored we are also living in dreadful times of trials sex, business, work, environmental and social life be it celibacy, moral, caution, dedicated parenting, work committed to what you can do to achieve not other peoples disposition made worse because of you but justification for a life well spent. In the world we dwell in today it is difficult knowing a fool when you see one.

Lies are easy pass for any given situation that beguiles our livelihood we are still yet realising the impact of democracy and its gifting. Some of us do not know what it is to love yet faced to live the all good, feel good factor it deepens democracy, relationships that result to conflict more of humans are prune living emotional lives if they have harts the effect is schizophrenia which can turn them to having no heart at all. The world and the entire Universe is entwine as all things good or bad, religion, culture, faith, myth and our ways of life entwines with the things we do even with languages, I do not see any reason why we should quarrel among each other. The human tongs in our mouth could have different shape you can speak one language some of us can speak five different language how could it be if not for a good reason languages entwine in this age of reasoning you do not differentiate languages from dialects its politics it could be dangerous. If I can speak your language, intermarry. It means I can do things your own way and I could do mine it has impact on synergy for good intentions if this is the case why should we quarrel.

In West Africa being possessed has moved on to a more celestial spiritualism that confirms to religion such as Christianity there are good and bad spirits. Out of the spirit they could prophecy, make revelations, warding off evil spirit give thanks and praise to God and ask for Gods protection in the name of Christ. This has ward off the use of juju and native witch doctors but with continual disagreement lack of peace, food cloth and shelter life becomes more of a burden we do not even care about our wellbeing but except some few and for themselves only.

We talk of being possessed what about people who, display pathetic attitude, disposition and morals yet they are not observe as being possessive or antisocial.

More still have to be done through education in my stand as a mentally ill patient as for my cares I would like to address this that it is not when one is looking haggard, smoking alcohol in one hand walking in the street that's when someone is suffering from mental illness. Drug abuse, antisocial behaviours are just stigmas attached to mental illnesses. Some people are of the opinion certain men most treasured inventions were carried out through madness, strain and difficulties process through mind and body, there certain things or issues that can be very delicate to handle that is all they were not madness when one takes a real view how good are most underdeveloped nations good at tackling problems. It was the motive behind it that had paved their way. If one has good motives or mentally but unwell they could slightly manage the illness this depend on lots of factors social, environmental and not only the way people live their lives in the community in which the mentally ill person resides but also the kind of people around them such as relatives and friends. If it is failing, much does not count as the fault or failure of sufferer, not being able to outlive the illness but on the society, the environment and people living around them.

Lots of medication have come through for cure of mental illnesses at the time such medications where being considered through various diagnoses of patient and experiment think of the effort those patient put in detailing to their practitioners how mental illness affects them and remember centuries ago mentally ill people were locked up, exorcism where practice look at mental health today and the people who care for people with mental health its going back to such settings.

You do not go and see your practitioner tell them you want to do your shaving instead of using shaving cream you hear voices telling you, you should use bathing soap instead in our world of today if you tell somebody such a thing what are their responses, they do not look at you as if, you are being possessed, someone stabbed himself with a knife they do not look at it as if the person is being possessed what then can make someone do such harm to themselves all they say is that its mental illness.

You want to go out to do your shopping knowingly or unknowing because your hands aren't looking smooth you peak up your hand cream to moisture your hands. On second thought you say, I am going to the shops I have to peak up foodstuffs you do not want hand cream on the products at the shop considering you are not the only one who, would be doing their shopping at your Supermarket well considered. But you might not care, your hands are more important to you. Or you might be hearing voices say look your hands are more important who cares what it means to other people. This are sings of sin, possession or temptation to your values and morals. If you are not a bad person you keep on hearing these voices what does it mean. You might not care for other people but you might in time be leading yourself to being possessed.

Put such a matter through to the Church they would say it is sin what makes people do this things are life inherencies you are a Christian because it does not affect you in such ways most Christine's are avoiders of most of the issues we face in life for example, they fail to see our lives and existence are based on trials you do things to make people change their ways if it is bad, you do not only talk you cultivate do not hid the bad things bring them to the open then more pressure would be applied in sorting them out. Our world is taking on a new meaning ahead religious leaders have to preach rationally we are not fighting for God he has authority over all things we are fighting for ourselves. We commune with God to make reason out of ourselves and the world we live in religious leaders should add more to our confronting our life's trials they should not tolerate hat or sin the problem is how do we lessen the burden of sin and hat. As Christine's the problem we have constantly been faced with is how we can exorcise sin and hat out of this world.

It's time we think it over; our hearts should reach out to each other's feelings and emotions' nothing should hold us back darkness follows light if we make up our minds, do rethinks we can go forward instead of backwards we cannot live in this world and just keep on believing it is turning into a bad place such feelings would only hold us back.

In time hatred would never pass this place again we would become friends having felt all the pains we have been through these feelings have been going on for too long I know but we should not let it take us far from our realties they are our trials. It can't be the end; even if it ends something better would turn up. As we go through life we should accept each other as more than friends we should not be thinking of how we are going to make it no matter your situation or position do the right thing encourage others to do the same let us encourage each other to move more towards positive affiliation. These are the kind of words I want religious leaders to preach on during Sunday sermon they are biased about coming out with the truth about life most people are getting fed up it most relate in ways that would not only moved but encourage members of the congregation. There is nobody who doesn't know what sin is even children can discern right and wrong ignorance is becoming a thing of the past in our world of today.

Mental illness and drug abuse, antisocial behaviours, alcoholism, divorce, marriage and separation, child custody, adoption, mental health and in prison are issues religion and culture should act on, you do not go to them and tell them about sin and hat you can't do this, when you are going to them as personal advisers such issues are very complicated and you do not make them feel you are telling them how to live their lives, they are a failure or there is something wrong with their lives and remove stigmas attached. Mental illness can mean in life you have done all you need to do the present life you are living is your last life. They know they have problems at such trouble times one could be on edge because they are more conscious of issues concerned in their lives not all of them might be good build courage in them. It is a time one is most conscious of their lives and the issues involved and they are looking for way out instead of making them run initiate ways to make them relax and confront their problems.

There are tension between the complex narratives patient brings into consultation room and a doctor's understanding of what is really going on as formulated in a diagnosis or an idea about mental illness. Which is a 'truer' account of reality: the patient's or the doctor's? Can both be true if so, how? Before we can address this there should fewer drawbacks but understanding within patient and cares relationship.

These questions are particularly relevant in mental health care for a number of reasons. Firstly, sociology and ethnography have identified psychiatry alone among the medical specialties as peculiarly culture, social, environmental and religious bound but religion does not want to accept this. Psychiatry lies in an uncomfortable no man's land between conventional medical science and the search for meaning which may extend into political and religious domains, mental health professionals often seems to use confusing and contradictory language to describe their observations if the patient has no idea or awareness of what they are saying except how the illness affects them that, is if they can explain. When compared with explanatory models which often seem to disqualify each other or which may simply be a way of asserting the therapist's power such are relevant the same way when advising sections of the general public or patients to quit smoking, drug abuse or alcoholism how far those this draw the line in dealing with people in prison or in prison with mental health. The professionals own story more often gain authority and seem sane than that of the patient. Finally, psychiatry is the only area of specialist medicine in which talking and listening are explicitly understood to be therapeutic.

The success of 'talking cures' depends on their ability to give coherence to the client's experience of physical or mental illness and to enable the construction of a narrative of healing or coping

The narrative approach to mental health is concerned with the question of how a patient and clinician working together can construct a story that makes sense such as antisocial behaviours are antisocial behaviours mental illness is mental illness they are both different things. Or the more patients would hit back that they are being stigmatized.

In general practice doctors may make useful contributions to patients' stories although such contributions are not seen as superior truth then, they should make the patient more aware and constructive in their approach social, religion and culture can help to achieve such approach. Patients should not be treated in ignorance if, they are well aware, they would contribute more to themselves in their recovery. The problem is like dealing with any other problems in our community. The ways some mental health patients behave with their cares are as a result of their cares imposition. And there could be inclination involved there is possession in relation to mental health. Some patients see a psychiatrist for the first time and the psychiatrists are amazed the patient could express things their psychiatrist had not told or have the slightest inclination the patients know about their care or medication. Some of them could display certain level of clairvoyance and telepathy if it is in any way distorted or give them impression they do not know what, they are talking about or signs of tolerance by those who care for them some patient could display sings of defence or create a defence around themselves limiting cares and patient relationship.

The term clairvoyance is referring to ability to gain information about an object, person, location or physical event through means other than the known human senses, a form of extra-sensory perception. A person said to have the ability of clairvoyance is referred to as a clairvoyant ('one who sees clearly').

Claims for the existence of paranormal and psychic abilities such as clairvoyance are highly controversial. Parapsychology explores this possibility, but the existence of the paranormal is generally not accepted by the scientific community more work will have to be done probably they can ascertain why people with mental health suffer from hearing voices could it be an ability one could develop for useful purposes?

Within parapsychology, clairvoyance is used exclusively to refer to the transfer of information that is both contemporary to, and hidden from, the clairvoyant. It is very different from telepathy in that the information is said to be gained directly from an external physical source, rather than being transferred from the mind of one individual to another. Could this be true?

Outside of parapsychology, clairvoyance is often used to refer to other forms of anomalous cognition, most commonly the perception of events that have occurred in the past, or which will occur in the future (known as retrocognition and precognition respectively), or to refer to communications with the dead.

Clairvoyance is related to remote viewing, although the term 'remote viewing' itself is not as widely applicable to clairvoyance because it refers to a specific controlled process.

Clairvoyance has come to be indicative of most forms of purported mediumship.' There are four primary channels, clairsensing, trance, healing and physical, plus a whole raft of others that do not fit neatly into any one primary channel. Clairvoyance (seeing) and clairaudience (hearing) for example are both kinds of clairsensing. Many mediums who are good clairvoyants may well have little or no clairaudient capability even though both 'gifts' belong in the primary channel of clairsensing. Remote viewing is a facet of clairvoyance and usually appears in practitioners suffering from arrested development.

Trance is the ability to communicate with, and mainly to receive from, other entities, incarnate and discarnate, and may sometimes be independent of time; it is usually divided into deep trance (obliterative and so dangerous, where the operative abdicates the throne, quite common) and light trance (a high or even total degree of awareness and thus safer for the practitioner, and extremely rare when well-done).

Healing is the ability to induct health benefits from some usually unspecified higher source where the healer can direct the effects to the beneficiary. Contact healing involves the healer being in the closest proximity but not necessarily touching. Absent healing is explained by its alternative name of distant healing and is independent of spatial distance.

There have been anecdotal reports of clairvoyance and 'clear' abilities throughout history in most cultures. Often clairvoyance has been associated with religious or shamanic figures, offices and practices. For example, ancient Hindu religious texts list clairvoyance amongst other forms of 'clear' experiencing, or 'perfections', skills that are yielded through appropriate meditation and personal discipline. But a large number of anecdotal accounts of clairvoyance are of the spontaneous variety among the general populace. For example, many people report seeing a loved one who has recently died before they have learned by other means that their loved one is deceased. While anecdotal accounts do not provide scientific proof of clairvoyance, such common experiences continue to motivate research into such phenomena.

Clairvoyance was a reported ability of some mediums during the spiritualist period of the late 19th and early 20th centuries, and psychics of many descriptions have claimed clairvoyant ability up to the present day.

Sceptics say that if clairvoyance were a reality it would have become abundantly clear. They also contend that those who believe in paranormal phenomena do so for merely psychological reasons.

Telepathy is the transmission of information from one person to another without using any of our known sensory channels or physical interaction. The term was coined in 1882 by the classical scholar Fredric W. H. Myers, a founder of the Society for Psychical Research, and has remained more popular than the more-correct expression thought-transference. Many studies seeking to detect, understand, and utilize telepathy have been done within this field. Claims of telepathy as a real phenomenon are at odds with the scientific consensus. According to the prevailing view among scientists, telepathy lacks replicable results from well-controlled experiments.

Telepathy is a common theme in modern fiction and science fiction, with many superheroes and supervillains having telepathic abilities. In more recent times, neuroimaging has allowed researchers to actually perform early forms of mind reading.

According to Roger Luckhurst, the origin of the concept of telepathy (not telepathy itself) in the Western civilization can be tracked to the late 19th century. In his view, science did not frequently concern itself with 'the mind' prior to this. As the physical sciences made significant advances, scientific concepts were applied to mental phenomena (e.g., animal magnetism), with the hope that this would help understand paranormal phenomena. The modern concept of telepathy emerged in this historical context.

The notion of telepathy is not dissimilar to two psychological concepts: delusions of thought insertion and removal and psychological symbiosis. This similarity might explain how some people have come up with the idea of telepathy. Thought insertion and removal is a symptom of psychosis, particularly of schizophrenia or schizoaffective disorder. Psychiatric patients who experience this symptom falsely believe that some of their thoughts are not their own and that others (e.g., other people, aliens, or conspiring intelligence agencies) are putting thoughts into their minds (thought insertion). Some patients feel as if thoughts are being taken out of their minds or deleted (thought removal). Along with other symptoms of psychosis, delusions of thought insertion may be reduced by antipsychotic medication.

Psychological symbiosis, on the other hand, is a less well established concept. It is an idea found in the writings of early psychoanalysts, such as Melanie Klein. It entails the belief that in the early psychological experience of the child (during earliest infancy), the child is unable to tell the difference between his or her own mind, on one hand, and his or her experience of the mother/parent, on the other hand. This state of mind they called psychological symbiosis; with development, it ends, but, purportedly, aspects of it can still be detected in the psychological functioning of the adult. Putatively, the experience of either thought insertion/removal or unconscious memories of psychological symbiosis may have led to the invention of 'telepathy' as a notion and the belief that telepathy exists. Psychiatrists and clinical psychologists believe and empirical findings support the idea that people with schizotypal personality disorder are particularly likely to believe in telepathy.

Various theories have been advanced to try and explain telepathy. A physical theory of telepathy whether described as traditional or by other terms assumes that transference is effected by means of a vibratory current linking one brain to another. William Crookes proposed a 'brain wave' theory in which he claimed telepathy might occur due to high frequency vibrations of the ether. Crookes stated that there may be parts of the human brain that may be capable of sending and receiving electrical rays of wave-lengths.

In the early 20th century there were two other theories of telepathy, the spiritualist theory which claimed telepathy was the result of external spirits and the subconscious mind theory which claimed telepathy occurs due to contact between two or more subconscious's. The subconscious mind theory was advocated by psychical researcher Thomson Jay Hudson who wrote that the mind is a duality and actually consists of two minds the objective mind (conscious) and the subjective mind (subconscious).

Psychiatry has improved the average levels of happiness and well-being in the general population, with vast expenditures on prescribed drugs and, treatments. The practical outcome of psychiatry to improve well-being and not focus on stigmatizing aspects of mental disorders and the neglect of methods to enhance positive emotions, character development, life satisfaction, and spirituality.

Simple and practical approach to well-being is described by integrating biological, psychological, social, and spiritual methods for enhancing mental health. Evidence is presented showing that people can be helped to develop their character and happiness by a catalytic sequence of practical clinical methods. People can learn to flourish and to be more self-directed by becoming more calm, accepting their limitations, and letting go of their fears and conflicts.

People can learn to be more cooperative by increase in mindfulness and working in the service of others. In addition, people can learn to be more self-transcendent by growing in self-awareness of the perspectives that lead to beliefs and assumptions about life which produce positive emotions and limit the experience of negative emotions.

The personality traits of self-directedness, cooperativeness, and self-transcendence are each essential for well-being. They can be reliably measured using the temperament and character inventory. A psycho educational program for wellbeing has been developed, called 'The happy life: voyages to well-being'. It is a multi-stage universal-style intervention by which anyone who wants to be happier and healthier can do so through self-help and or professional therapy. Keywords are well-being, character development, spirituality, happiness and psychobiology

There has been as yet no substantial improvement in average levels of happiness and well-being in general populations; focus of psychiatry has been on mental disorders, not on the understanding or development of positive mental health. Morbidity and mortality are more strongly related to the absence of positive emotions than to the presence of negative emotions.

Focus on discrete categories of disease provides an easy way to label patients with disorders; as a result, many people are ashamed of being mentally ill and avoid treatment. A focus on universal interventions to cultivate healthy mental health for everyone should not be stigmatized, by recognizing that all people share much in common with one another.

In my youth I had worshiped in Cherubim and Seraphim Church with my mother at Ibadan in white rob and red band tied around our waist to signify our ordination and rank. At Port Harcourt apart from other Churches I attended I did also worshiped at a Cherubim and Seraphim Church where remarkably, worshipers could be possessed by Holy Spirit without my late father's knowledge I was attending such Church.

Here I am in the UK considering my environment whilst I was in West Africa here in the UK one queue when you go out, to do their shopping. There is provision for housing and health care. You treat other people to some extent with equality and farness compared to some parts of the world. It is said it is alarming the way Britain is moving considering the rate of mentally ill people increasing. There, are degrees to the effects of mental illness all around the world With effect in some parts of the world, some patents could manage while in some parts of the world the degree of the effect of mental illness on people is as if, there is no point of outliving some mental disorders, diagnosis are not made, some have no food or shelter.

Considering the circumstance I had worshiped in Cherubim and Seraphim Church and what some critics say about them, the environment I had lived in the UK I was provided with a one bedroom flat, hot water, gas and electricity running, with no pips sticking out. Bathroom and Kitchen, wall paper if I want wall paper in my dwelling, floor carpet and furniture though, it would be difficult to acquire them if am on benefit but I can. And the Royal borough of Greenwich is getting tougher with tenants who trash their council homes before they move out is all part of spiritual awakening.

I can acquire them for my own use which is not that easy for me to acquire whilst I was in my past environment the idea of a plumber, digital television connected would be jubilation because it lightens the burden of my soul. They could be as a means of therapy, resuscitation to get me out of my mental illness and if, I don't tough.

An English man who had lived in the UK all his life could say to me you can manage the illness and if am not, could it be, am anti-social after living all of my years in the UK based on the changes or negative aspects that confronts the environment, ways of life e.g. climate, whether, constructions and renovations. Or as a freemason the symbols and allegories of freemasons might tell on me if I am just being anti-social or community life can tell. If it is about getting a job, I know when to go out and get a job I need not to be stigmatised before I do so those who show such signs of stigmatising people like me are the ones who, are causing the problems because they want other people to feel they are doing better than people like me some of them could my cares.

Why all the kicking and hitting its mental illness why should they be found of hitting back it's not a solution to any social problem. If it is a matter of being grateful I know I should be committed to being grateful to my cares. They also should show appreciation if, it is for a simple reason that they are working on my behalf if so, the more I would appreciate them. Credence should be applied with transcendent when it comes to patients and cares relationship there does not seems to be any bound within them if cares cannot create bound with their patient I wonder where we are heading to while they tend to always push they are doing something if made clear to the patient and not to be viewed with suspicion it result o close understand attachment based on cares and patient relation it's frustrating to leave someone hanging in a limbo as far as patient and care relationship is concern I do not think patients would deliberately think less of their cares.

Caring for people is just a small fragment of the whole social contrast but of very important significance. There is nothing awesome like helping someone when they really need you. There should be more Gospel on the joy people bring into each other's lives rather than fear. If this world was mine, I would bring it down to your feet God has done exactly this. Would you compare God to any other thing or person you are a care; it is a disposition of cares and patient relationship to be blessing to other people's, a parent, government should endeavour to bring joy into the lives of children and the community we should appreciate their worth for better than for worse there are always sacrifices involved to give and take what more can I say other than our existence can be no other thing but based on trials.

We go through countless trials in life there are things that tells on us in our various ways of life such issues are what religious leaders should authenticate about our existence through which they could demonstrate by words true gifting of the Gospel on the basis of how we live our lives. Here is the future tomorrow some of us would be going on space mission, galaxies are being discovered and explored in time they would be holding holy sacrament in one of the planets are we saying we are yet to understand science and religion coexist?

Some distribution of characteristics limit the availability of effective treatments around the world while treatments are highly expensive, there should be openness in all areas of dealing with caring.

Treatments of the body should not be anti-spiritual in their orientation human beings are spiritual beings who spend more time in prayer or meditation than they do having sex. Cultivation of spirituality provides an inexpensive and powerful way to enhance well-being. I am a celibate with no intension of having children and I have the intension of working in a hotel in Woolwich after it has been completed it is to raise self consciousness if I could get employment in cleaning, as potter, kitchen assistant and making beds it would give clear indication I could get a job well-done without me or my employer being biased about my illness but rather related to my wellbeing. My employer could inspect my work and easily ascertain I could do the job well enough rather than working in an office because of my illness my employer could feel not at ease of my keeping clear records and details because am a schizophrenia. These are some of the issues people with health problems go through these days when considering moving back to work. We suffer lots of self consciousness to certain point we feel our illness is a misgiving up to a point of paranoia's.

Self-consciousness is an acute sense of self-awareness. It is a preoccupation with oneself, as opposed to the philosophical state of self-awareness, which is the awareness that one exists as an individual being; although some writers use both terms interchangeably or synonymously. An unpleasant feeling of self-consciousness may occur when one realizes that one is being watched or observed, the feeling that 'everyone is looking' at oneself. Some people are habitually more self-conscious than others.

Unpleasant feelings of self-consciousness are sometimes associated with shyness or paranoia. According to Schopenhauer, man can, through self-consciousness, make a choice between affirming and denying the will.

When feeling self-conscious, one becomes aware of even the smallest of one's own actions. Such awareness can impair one's ability to perform complex actions. Adolescence is believed to be a time of heightened self-consciousness. A person with a chronic tendency toward self-consciousness may be shy or introverted.

Unlike self-awareness, which in a philosophical context is being conscious of oneself as an individual, self-consciousness, being excessively conscious of one's appearance or manner, can be a problem at times. Self-consciousness is often associated with shyness and embarrassment, in which case a lack of pride and low self-esteem can result. In a positive context, self-consciousness may affect the development of identity, for it is during periods of high self-consciousness that people came closest to knowing themselves objectively. Self-consciousness affects people in varying degrees, as some people are constantly self-monitoring or self-involved, while others are completely oblivious about themselves.

Psychologists frequently distinguish between two kinds of self-consciousness, private and public. Private self-consciousness is a tendency to introspect and examine one's inner self and feelings. Public self-consciousness is an awareness of the self as it is viewed by others. This kind of self-consciousness can result in self-monitoring and social anxiety. Both private and public self-consciousness are viewed as personality traits that are relatively stable over time, but they are not correlated. Just because an individual is high on one dimension doesn't mean that he or she is high on the other.

Different levels of self-consciousness affect behaviour, as it is common for people to act differently when they 'lose themselves in a crowd'. Being in a crowd, being in a dark room, or wearing a disguise creates anonymity and temporarily decrease self-consciousness

These considerations have led me to develop simple approach to help myself to be happy. My approach is integrative, combining biological, psychological, social, and spiritual approaches to my mental health because of the positive side it shows on how conscious I am.

Now I am writing a more oriented book to explain how to apply approach in psychological and am developing a series of modules where I will summarize available data about the need to reduce discomfort and give credit. The spiritual needs of people, and the effectiveness of spiritually-oriented well-being therapies. Then I will describe the key spiritual, social and environmental concepts about stages of self-awareness.

The treatment of mental disorders has been improved with the introduction of medications and psychotherapy techniques that show acute benefits in randomized controlled trials. Nevertheless, available treatments are unfortunately associated with frequent dropout, relapse, and recurrence of illness. For example, in the treatment of major depression, the acute response to antidepressants or cognitive behavioural therapy is only moderate.

Substantial improvement occurs in about 50% to 65% patients receiving active treatment, compared to 30% to 45% in control subjects. Relapse is rapid in subjects who drop out or prematurely discontinue treatment, because the interventions are directed at symptoms and do not correct the underlying causes of the disorder. Most patients with major depression who do improve acutely have recurrences within the next three years despite use of medications and cognitive behavioural therapy which I do experience.

Well-being is not all enhanced by wealth, power, or fame, despite many people acting as if such accomplishments could bring lasting satisfaction but it underlies positive emotion in some cases. Character development does bring about greater self-awareness and hence greater happiness. Fortunately, recent work on well-being has shown that it is possible to improve character, thereby increasing well-being and reducing disability in the general population, and in most, if not all, mental disorders. The most effective methods of intervention all focus on the development of positive emotions and the character traits that underlie well-being.

Randomized controlled trials of therapies to enhance well-being in patients with mental disorders show improvements in happiness and character strengths that increase treatment adherence and reduce relapse and recurrence rates when compared to cognitive-behavioural therapy or psychotropic medication alone. Such are evidence in my life after having lived years in Africa and now, am residing in Europe. A consideration is going through such experience without food, shelter and clothing would become even far more difficult.

The methods of improving well-being can be understood as working on the development of the three branches of mental self-government that can be measured as character traits using the temperament and character.

These character traits can be exercised and developed by interventions that encourage a sense of hope and mastery for self-directedness, kindness and forgiveness for cooperativeness, and awareness and meaning greater than oneself for self-transcendence.

Improvements in each of these areas is beneficial, but emotional consistency and resilience depends on the balanced development of all three major dimensions of character Western concepts of mental health usually emphasize self-directedness and cooperativeness, but neglect the crucial role of spiritual awareness and meaning based on self-transcendent values.

Most psychiatric patients want their therapist to be aware of their spiritual beliefs and needs, because human spirituality has an essential role in coping with challenges and enjoying life. My experience and advice I would give on spirituality is if for example you are a Christine at young age when you cannot afford to buy yourself a Holy Bible your parent may buy one for you buying a Bible for you, is their blessing from them to you such as their parental guidance, and the blessing of God be upon you as their child.

In time when you are older working and can afford to buy one for yourself do it probably with your first wages then you are summing your consciousness up as contained in your spirituality and belief you owe to yourself. Do not let a stranger buy you, your bible or religious materials. Rituals are held every were in the World, rituals are part of our everyday life and it differs across race and creed some of them, are to possess or enslave you buying your spiritual needs with your own earned money would be a blessing against such stance. From my own background a child first wages either goes to your parents or giving part of it to a younger relative.

Human consciousness is characterized by a capacity for self-awareness and free choices that are fully determined by past experience. The great mystery of neuroscience is that human consciousness cannot be explained or reduced to materialistic processes if only more emphasis would be laid on belief and spirituality, what are expected within a society and the world as a whole, life, existences, what are happening around us, how far has the world changed, the way we see and observe our world and environment what, do most people think of science and technology.

As a result of the fact that human consciousness transcends spiritual and self consciousness and explanations on which religion now finds itself at an important crossroad. The fostering of spirituality and well-being is crucial for psychiatry to achieve its meaning and purpose, but spirituality and well-being have been neglected because of a tendency toward materialistic reductionism. Psychiatry has now the opportunity to promote a broader understanding of what it means to be a human being. Humanity cannot be reduced to matter, as in behaviourism or molecular psychiatry. Humanity also cannot be reduced to the dualism of body and mind, as in cognitive- behavioural approaches.

Self-awareness requires an understanding of the physical, mental, and spiritual aspects of a human being. To foster fuller self-awareness, added focus on existential issues, such as finding self acceptance and meaning in coping with life challenges. Meaning can be found by encountering someone or something that is valued, acting with kindness and purpose in the service of others, or developing attitudes such as compassion and humour that give meaning to suffering.

Possession is common it's taking new meaning in difference and terminology except for cultures that still use old tradition and culture cures of illnesses probably due to my condition of birth I feel there is slight possession on science when a computer or mobile phone has contacted viruses it is possession the manufacture has to make a new model. Holding a Mobil phone or a wristwatch within often dirty or unsafe environment often contact virus easily, a manufacturing plant having been in a place for decades could contact virus people become conscious of the effect depression sets in the place is possessed.

The Indian moon weakens or regenerates my body or spiritual system depending on my mood, the rainbows make me feel better, livelier or a mood to correlate my life and purpose the moon dose the same the sun feels me with vigour some rain and thunderstorms makes me feel peaceful, calm and reassured while at some others times could make me feel disturbed.

Frederic William Henry Myers (1843–1901) was a poet, classicist, philologist, and a founder of the Society for Psychical Research.

• Early life

Frederic William Henry Myers was the son of Rev. Frederic Myers and Susan Myers (born Susan Harriet). He was a brother of poet Ernest Myers (1844-1921) and of Dr. Arthur Thomas Myers (1851-1894). His maternal grandfather was the industrialist John Marshall (1765-1845).

Myers was educated at Cheltenham College and at Trinity College, Cambridge where he received a B.A. in 1865, and university prizes, including the Bell, Craven, Camden and Chancellor's Medal: however he was forced to resign the Camden medal for 1863 after accusations of plagiarism. He was a Fellow of Trinity College from 1865 to 1874

In 1867, Myers published a long poem, St Paul, which became very popular. It was followed in 1882 by The Renewal of Youth and Other Poems. He also wrote books of literary criticism, in particular Wordsworth (1881) and Essays, Classical and Modern (in two volumes, 1883), which included a highly-regarded essay on Virgil.

- Psychical research

Myers was interested in <u>psychical research</u> and was one of the founder members of the <u>Society for Psychical Research</u> in 1883. He became the President in 1900. In 1893 Myers wrote a small collection of essays, Science and a Future Life.

In 1903, after Myers's death, Human Personality and Its Survival of Bodily Death was compiled and published. It was two large volumes at 1,360 pages in length, which presented an overview of Myers's research into the <u>unconscious mind</u> Myers believed that a theory of consciousness must be part of a unified model of mind, which derive from the full range of human experience, including not only normal psychological phenomena but also the wide variety of abnormal and 'supernormal' phenomena.

Frederic Myers may be regarded as an 'important early depth psychologist', and his significant influence on colleagues like <u>William James</u>, <u>Pierre Janet</u>, and <u>Théodore Flournoy</u> and also <u>Carl G. Jung</u> has been well documented.

Melanie Reizes Klein (30 March 1882 – 22 September 1960) was an <u>Austrian</u>-born <u>British</u> <u>psychoanalyst</u> who devised novel therapeutic techniques for children that had an impact on <u>child psychology</u> and contemporary psychoanalysis. She was a leading innovator in theorizing <u>object relations theory</u>.

- Life

Born in <u>Vienna</u> of Jewish parentage, Klein first sought psychoanalysis for herself with <u>Sándor Ferenczi</u> when she was living in <u>Budapest</u> during <u>World War I</u>. There she became a psychoanalyst and began analyzing children in 1919. Allegedly two of the first children she analyzed were her son and daughter. In 1921 she moved to <u>Berlin</u>, where she studied with and was analyzed by <u>Karl Abraham</u>. Although Abraham supported her pioneering work with children, neither Klein nor her ideas received much support in Berlin. However, impressed by her innovative work, British psychoanalyst <u>Ernest Jones</u> invited Klein to come to <u>London</u> in 1926, where she worked until her death in 1960.

Klein had a major influence on the theory and technique of psychoanalysis, particularly in Great Britain. As a divorced woman whose academic qualifications did not even include a bachelor's degree, Klein was a visible iconoclast within a profession dominated by male physicians.

After the arrival of Sigmund Freud and his psychoanalyst daughter, Anna, in London in 1938, Klein's ideas came into conflict with those of Continental analysts who were migrating to Britain. Following protracted debates between the followers of Klein and the followers of Anna Freud during the 1940s (the so-called 'controversial discussions'), the British Psychoanalytical Society split into three separate training divisions: (1) Kleinian, (2) Anna Freudian, and (3) independent. This division remains to the current time.

Apart from her professional successes, Klein's life was full of tragic events. Allegedly the product of an unwanted pregnancy, she had little affection from her parents. Her much loved elder sister died when Klein was four, and she was made to feel responsible for her brother's death. Her academic studies were interrupted by marriage and children. Her marriage failed and her son died in a climbing accident that may have been a suicide, while her daughter, whom Klein had analyzed as a child, the well-known psychoanalyst Melitta Schmideberg, fought her openly in the British Psychoanalytic Society. Her daughter's analyst at the time, Edward Glover, openly challenged Klein in the British Society meetings. Mother and daughter were not reconciled before Klein's death, and Schmideberg did not attend Klein's funeral.

- Thought

Although she questioned some of the fundamental assumptions of Sigmund Freud, Klein always considered herself a faithful adherent to Freud's ideas. Klein was the first person to use traditional psychoanalysis with young children. She was innovative in both her techniques (such as working with children using toys) and her theories in infant development. Strongly opinionated and demanding loyalty from her followers, Klein established a highly influential training program in psychoanalysis. She is considered one of the co-founders of object relations theory.

Klein's theoretical work incorporates Freud's belief in the existence of the 'death instinct', reflecting the fact that all living organisms are inherently drawn toward an inorganic state, and therefore, in an unspecified sense, contains a drive towards death. In psychological terms Eros (properly, the life instinct), the postulated sustaining and uniting principle of life, is thereby presumed to have a companion force, Thanatos (death instinct), which allegedly seeks to terminate and disintegrate life. Both Freud and Klein regarded these biomental forces as the foundations of the psyche. These were human instincts ('Triebe') unrelated to the animal instincts of ethology. These primary unconscious forces, whose mental matrix is the 'id,' sparked the ego—the experiencing self—into activity. Id, ego, and superego—to be sure—were merely shorthand terms (like the 'instincts') referring to highly complex, mostly uncharted, psychodynamic operations. Freud and Klein never abandoned the terms or the conceptualizations despite protests and controversies by many of their adherents.

While Freud's ideas concerning children mostly came from working with adult patients, Klein was innovative in working directly with children, often as young as two years old. Klein saw children's play as their primary mode of emotional communication. After observing troubled children play with toys such as dolls, animals, plasticine, pencil and paper, Klein attempted to interpret the specific meaning of play. Following Freud she emphasized the significant role that parental figures played the child's fantasy life, and considered that the timing of Freud's Oedipus complex was incorrect. Contradicting Freud, she concluded that the superego was present from birth.

After exploring ultra-aggressive fantasies of hate, envy, and greed in very young, very ill children, Melanie Klein proposed a model of the human psyche that linked significant oscillations of state, with whether the postulated Eros or Thanatos instincts were in the fore. She named the state of the psyche, when the sustaining principle of life is in domination, the depressive position. This is considered by many to be her great contribution to psychoanalytic thought. She later developed her ideas about an earlier developmental psychological state corresponding to the disintegrating tendency of life, which she called the paranoid-schizoid position.

Klein's insistence on regarding aggression as an important force in its own right when analysing children brought her into conflict with Freud's own daughter, Anna Freud, who was one of the other prominent child psychotherapists in continental Europe but who moved to London in 1938 where Klein had been working for several years. Many controversies arose from this conflict, and these are often referred to as the Controversial discussions. Battles were played out between the two sides, each presenting scientific papers, working out their respective positions and where they differed, during war-time Britain. A compromise was eventually reached whereby three distinct training groups were formed within the British Psycho-Analytic Society, with Anna Freud's influence remaining largely predominant in the US.

Today, Kleinian psychoanalysis is one of the major schools within psychoanalysis. Kleinian psychoanalysts are members of the International Psychoanalytical Association. Kleinian psychoanalysis remains a large and influential school of psychoanalysis within Britain, in much of Latin America, and to an extent in continental Europe. Within the United States of America, the Psychoanalytic Center of California is the major training center that follows the work of Melanie Klein. Kleinian psychoanalysis with adults is characterized by a 'classical' analytic technique using an analytic couch and meeting four to five times a week. Kleinian analysis focuses on interpreting very 'deep' and primitive emotions and fantasies.

Sir William Crookes, OM, FRS (17 June 1832 – 4 April 1919) was a British chemist and physicist who attended the Royal College of Chemistry, London, and worked on spectroscopy. He was a pioneer of vacuum tubes, inventing the Crookes tube.

- Early years

William Crookes was born in London, the eldest son of Joseph Crookes, a tailor of north-country origin, and his second wife, Mary Scott.

Career

Meteorologist and lecturer at multiple places

Sir William Crookes

By Sir Leslie Ward 1902

From 1850 to 1854 he filled the position of assistant in the college, and soon embarked upon original work, not in organic chemistry where the inspiration of his teacher, August Wilhelm von Hofmann, might have been expected to lead him, but on new compounds of selenium. These formed the subject of his first published papers in 1851.

Leaving the Royal College, he became superintendent of the meteorological department at the <u>Radcliffe Observatory</u> in <u>Oxford</u> in 1854, and in 1855 was appointed lecturer in chemistry at the <u>Chester Diocesan Training College</u>.

Married now and living in London, he was devoted mainly to independent work. After 1880, he lived at 7 Kensington Park Gardens, where all his later work was carried out in his private laboratory. Crookes's life was one of unbroken scientific activity. The breadth of his interests, ranging over pure and applied science, economic and practical problems, and psychical research, made him a well-known personality, and he received many public and academic honours. In 1859, he founded the <u>Chemical News</u>, a science magazine which he edited for many years and conducted on much less formal lines than is usual with journals of scientific societies.

Crookes was knighted in 1897, and in 1910 received the <u>Order of Merit</u>.

Discoveries

In 1861, Crookes discovered a previously unknown element with a bright green emission line in its spectrum and named the element <u>thallium</u>, from the Greek thallos, a green shoot. Crookes also identified the first known sample of <u>helium</u>, in 1895. He was the inventor of the <u>Crookes radiometer</u>, which today is made and sold as a novelty item. He also developed the <u>Crookes tubes</u>, investigating <u>cathode rays</u>.

In his investigations of the conduction of <u>electricity</u> in low pressure gases, he discovered that as the pressure was lowered, the negative electrode (cathode) appeared to emit rays (the so-called <u>cathode rays</u>, now known to be a <u>stream</u> of <u>free electrons</u>, and used in <u>cathode ray display devices</u>). As these examples indicate, he was a pioneer in the construction and use of <u>vacuum tubes</u> for the study of physical phenomena. He was, as a consequence, one of the first scientists to investigate what are now called <u>plasmas</u> and identified it as the fourth state of matter in 1879. He also devised one of the first instruments for the study of nuclear radioactivity, the <u>spinthariscope</u>.

• Legacy

Crookes worked over both fields of chemistry and physics. Its salient characteristic was the originality of conception of his experiments, and the skill of their execution.

- *Chemistry*

Crookes was always more effective in experiment than in interpretation. The method of spectral analysis, introduced by Bunsen and Kirchhoff, was received by Crookes with great enthusiasm and to great effect. His first important discovery was that of the element thallium, announced in 1861, and made with the help of spectroscopy. By this work his reputation became firmly established, and he was elected a fellow of the Royal Society in 1863.

Crookes' attention had been attracted to the vacuum balance in the course of thallium research. He soon discovered the phenomenon upon which depends the action of the Crookes radiometer, in which a system of vanes, each blackened on one side and polished on the other, is set in rotation when exposed to radiant energy. Crookes did not, however, provide the true explanation of this apparent 'attraction and repulsion resulting from radiation'.

He published numerous papers on spectroscopy and conducted research on a variety of minor subjects. In addition to various technical books, he wrote a standard treatise on Select Methods in Chemical Analysis in 1871, and a small book on diamonds in 1909.

- *Physics*

Crookes investigated the properties of cathode rays, showing that they travel in straight lines, cause fluorescence in objects upon which they impinge, and by their impact produce great heat. He believed that he had discovered a fourth state of matter, which he called 'radiant matter', but his theoretical views on the nature of 'radiant matter' proved to be mistaken. He believed the rays to consist of streams of particles of ordinary molecular magnitude. It remained for Sir J. J. Thomson to discover their subatomic nature, and to prove that cathode rays consist of streams of negative electrons, that is, of negatively electrified particles whose mass is only 1/1840 that of a hydrogen atom. Nevertheless, Crookes's experimental work in this field was the foundation of discoveries which eventually changed the whole of chemistry and physics.

In 1903, Crookes turned his attention to the newly discovered phenomenon of radioactivity, achieving the separation from uranium of its active transformation product, uranium-X (later established to be protactinium). He observed the gradual <u>decay</u> of the separated transformation product and the simultaneous reproduction of a fresh supply in the original uranium. At about the same time as this important discovery, he observed that when 'p-particles', ejected from radio-active substances, impinge upon <u>zinc sulfide</u>, each impact is accompanied by a minute scintillation, an observation which forms the basis of one of the most useful methods in the technique of radioactivity.

• Spiritualism

In 1870 Crookes decided that science had a duty to study preternatural phenomena associated with <u>spiritualism</u> (Crookes 1870). Judging from family letters, Crookes had already developed a favourable view of spiritualism by 1869. In this he was possibly influenced by the untimely death of his younger brother Philip in 1867 at age 21 from yellow fever contracted while on an expedition to lay a telegraph cable from Cuba to Florida. Nevertheless, he was determined to conduct his inquiry impartially and described the conditions he imposed on mediums as follows: 'It must be at my own house, and my own selection of friends and spectators, under my own conditions, and I may do whatever I like as regards apparatus'. Among the mediums he studied were <u>Kate Fox</u>, <u>Florence Cook</u>, and <u>Daniel Dunglas Home</u> Among the phenomena he witnessed were movement of bodies at a distance, rapping's, changes in the weights of bodies, levitation, appearance of luminous objects, appearance of phantom figures, appearance of writing without human agency, and circumstances which 'point to the agency of an outside intelligence'.

To find support and assistance for his research, he joined the <u>Society for Psychical Research</u>, becoming its president in the 1890s: he also joined the <u>Theosophical Society</u> and the <u>Ghost Club</u>, of which he was president from 1907 to 1912.

His report on this research in 1874 concluded that these phenomena could not be explained as conjuring, and that further research would be useful. Crookes was not alone in his views. Fellow scientists who came to believe in spiritualism included <u>Alfred Russel Wallace</u>, <u>Oliver Lodge</u>, <u>Lord Rayleigh</u>, and <u>William James</u> . Nevertheless, most scientists were convinced that spiritualism was fraudulent, and Crookes' final report so outraged the scientific establishment 'that there was talk of depriving him of his Fellowship of the Royal Society.' Crookes then became much more cautious and didn't discuss his views publicly until 1898, when he felt his position was secure. From that time until his death in 1919, letters and interviews show that Crookes was a believer in spiritualism.

• Personal life

In 1856 he married Ellen, daughter of William Humphrey, of Darlington, by whom he fathered three sons and a daughter.

He died in London on 4 April 1919, two years after his wife. He is buried in London's <u>Brompton Cemetery</u>.

Thomson Jay Hudson (born <u>Windham</u>, <u>Ohio</u>, <u>USA</u>, February 22, 1834) Chief Examiner of the US Patent Office and Psychical researcher, known for his three laws of psychic phenomena, which were first published in 1893.

Refusing his father's wish to become a minister of religion, Hudson funded his own study of law at college. He began a law practice in <u>Port Huron</u>, <u>Michigan</u>, but, in 1860, he began a journalistic career instead; and, in 1866, unsuccessfully ran for the <u>US Senate</u>. From 1877 till 1880 he was Washington Correspondent for the <u>Scripps Syndicate</u>. In 1880 he accepted a position in the US Patent Office, and was promoted to Principal Examiner of a Scientific Division, a post he held until the publication of his remarkable book The Law of Psychic Phenomena in 1893.

He wrote and lectured on this subject until his death from heart failure in 1903.

Hudson's theory

Thomson Jay Hudson began observing hypnotism shows and noticed similarities between hypnosis subjects and the trances of <u>Spiritualist</u> mediums. His idea was that any contact with 'spirits' was in fact contact with the mediums or the subject's own subconscious. Anything else could be explained by telepathy, which he defined as contact between two or more subconsciouses.

Hudson postulated that his theory could explain all forms of spiritualism, and had a period of popularity until the carnage of the <u>First World War</u> caused a fresh interest in spiritualism again as psychic mediums emerged to meet the demands of grieving relatives.

- Hudson's three laws

1. Man has two minds: the objective mind (conscious) and the subjective mind (subconscious).

2. The subjective mind is constantly amenable to control by suggestion.

3. The subjective mind is incapable of inductive reasoning.

Happiness is a mental state of well-being characterized by positive emotions and intense joy. Existence in varieties of ways such as biological, psychological, religious, and philosophical define our happiness in a world we dwell in, in beauty, ugliness and death our sources of happiness is derived through our interaction, the way we view ourselves and the environment we live in.

We would for countless generation try in defining, understand, express what it is to be happy and what it is, to be unhappy because we live in an ever changing planet there are always questions and answer of what happiness is correlated to the nature of our world can happiness be contained, could there come a time of everlasting happiness if you and I have dwelled on this planet we would know what joy it would bring after our lives of happiness, sadness, beauty, ugliness and death.

Philosophers and religious thinkers often define happiness in terms of living a good life, or flourishing, rather than simply as an emotion. If happiness is termed as living the good life, it would be a matter of virtues and ethics to describe what are character of a moral agent as a driving force for ethical behaviour, rather than rules. The derivations would be to derive rightness or wrongness from the outcome of the act itself rather than character while happiness is something emotional.

I was born to a family who with all sorts of uncompromising experience which I went through within the family, for which reason, on my father's part, he should have brought up his family to be united, each individual with his or her own conscience and identity with love for each other, which would have made my father stronger with unity among his family.

Rather my father was a self centred individual with the result his children become self cantered with competition within his family. As part of his family, I did not see myself going into competition with anyone there are other people to correlate such temperaments with, in spite of the scenario I admit with no regret in spite of the situation, we are still a family.

I loved my father very much; I would not be concerned with competition within our family, with self wimps and antagonism within which, made me in some ways unhappy. But for my resilience, with little strength I had with no comfort coming from anyone, with less room to find myself comforted from members of my family with my father monopolising the whole situation as head of his family while his wives and children follow sooth. What I am saying is that I was never left to be what I wanted to be though wincing for what I want it to be its just that I do not fancy the idea of one parents taking from one child to please the other.

No child need to be brought up in such a way; no wonder with my immediate elder brother Mr. Omagbemi from the same parents under polygamous family, living in the UK, we might just like two complete strangers, while friends use us to be domineering over us with either of us as brothers being domineering over each other.

The situation in some case might be found very confusing; I do not see any reason why relatives should be competitive over each other. As for my step mothers, brothers and sisters since my mother was not present within my father's house, I was left to be used, with other people being advantageous over me. It goes on further at the moment misunderstanding after our father's death result to manipulation within our family.

On one of my visit to my brother and his wife, with gifts for his children, he accused me of buying inexpensive gift for his children; could it be because of my being a celibate at one point he told me out of the blue that his children are all now grown up was it out of things I should imply or not imply about our family background now that we are in the UK if so, why should he be worried. I should be more worried because of my illness and looking after a family of my own.

Elder brothers and sisters comes first before their younger once within families is it really as consideration the older once are subjects over them in this case, I and my brother had lived under our parents with step mothers; am over 40 years without children would my brother admonish me they way he did in front of his wife because of what I bought for his children as a gift without me obliged pointing out my views in relation to our relationship as both brothers. His children would normally honour him, before giving me consideration but I have my view points as to our relationship as brothers I have gone through lots of experience with my brother coupled that I understand our background and the way we had lived our lives back home in Nigeria. In a case, were am suffering from schizophrenia is no place for competition within we two brothers of the same parents within a polygamous home of who is buying the best birthday, Christmas or Easter present I felt I was being stigmatized if they do not like the present they at least just get rid of them rather than an outburst am buying dirty, deity things to give to his children as gifts.

I asked myself if he should come up with such words, how I could be happy for him if he told me he bought a house hoe does he expect me to feel or what does it mean if he bought me expensive gifts, even if to him the joy of raising up children on his part should be based on competition such statement should not come from a brother I am not living my life to be what he wants it to be because of conditions beyond my own control other people contributes into making you, who you are.

I am not compelled for any reason living my life the way he wants situation are not bound to be the same for all people. Is there anything wrong for being a celibate it is more than my just being a celibate at least he should grant me receptive for my choice nevertheless, I guess after more years to come he would give me recitation for my not being a parent as my choice. Couldn't we all living our life with different result makes the world more interesting? And I do not think it was because I was a celibate or not living up, to expectation why those words should come from him it is as a result of him being egocentric.

I visited my brothers dwelling just about the time before I stopped going to see them at Brockley it was his wife who was at home I had not sat down she asked me if I would have pepper soup even if I would in my mind say no I said yes, I would have some. She went into her kitchen came back with a small bowl having the pepper soup I got hold of the meat cut in four tiny bits to put in my mouth to my amassment it was bone not meat fleche. This was just after our father's death and her mother paid a visit to the UK that was when I saw her for the first time meeting wither something came over me I went straight to their kitchen had a glass of water greeted her once again and left their dwelling coupled that I began hearing all sorts of voices. It can't be to make sure I held each piece in my hand into my mouth it was only four little tiny beat on the plate they were bones. It came to my mind it's a start of troubleshooting in my family this was around 2004. I did not tell my brother about the experience but simply withdraw from him because I did not want an outburst to occur as much as the incident and others which did occur troubled me. The relationship within a father and a son is now a situation a step brother or sister who at their tender age I have at numerous times fetched bucket of water by carrying on my head for their mother to prepare meals and bath them with the absence of my mother in my father's house I would be in trouble if I should be in Nigeria after the experience.

Shortly before the experience of pepper soup my sister in-law served me I went to visit my brother when I went into their dwelling, As I was about to greet my sister in-law who was in the living room she bloated out this words 'Am a Monkey' she called herself a monkey in a sarcastic tone of voices. No I said to myself she could not be calling herself a monkey it's a joke. I steered at her a little bit confused and then I said am a gorilla jokingly at this point my brother came out of one of the bedrooms I was going to comment further I meant no harm by asking my brother if he remembered when he, our mother and myself went to Ibadan zoo I am the gorilla call Aruna my bother just said to me in stain sarcastic tone 'do not insult my wife' I was completely taken aback demoralised. What a set-p if it's what is going on behind my back in the relationship they are having together that concerns me I see no reason why I should not stop visiting them.

Then the incident of the pepper soup occurred I just withdraw from visiting them in their family home since 2004 I wonder what they wanted me to make out of it when within 2005 and 2006 my brother informed me they had bought the property in which these experience occurred. I might be a paranoid schizophrenia, I had been the one who signed their marriage on behalf of my brother as his closest relative at their wedding at a district at which she made comment at the district during the wedding someone else should sign the contract on my brothers behalf I would not have played such part in their wedding ceremony and years later walk into their dwelling and call her a monkey I was very traumatised by the incident on the other hand, I felt I was just being persecuted. The next time I went to see them at their dewing they were all in the living room rather than seating on a settee I sat down on a rest chair by a corner my brother bloated at me asking me why I was seating on his chair he went into the kitchen came back towards me directly with just three little piece of fried sausage and gave it to me. Our father his late I experience he is inside me customary as I use to know him and am going through such experience within his family after his death is a dilemma he left behind while they use what is going on here calling for attention within family and friends back home it is left for my readers to ascertain the kind of representation my father made here in Europe during his visit and what it had represented with I and my brother, his family and friends relationship. It's now 2015 never once had I introduce anyone to my brother Omagbemi in the UK since we came back as a friend of mine except one person. And I have been to several parties with him to have fun with people he calls friends and relatives of his and his wife.

The best thing to do I thought is I should go and calm down and think about it. On the other hand she might not mean it as it is maybe she probably wanted me to ask for more or the better part of the pepper soup or she wanted to ascertain if she had prepared her Itsekiri pepper soup very well or up to taste. One thing about my sister in-law is that she has this affinity to keep me silent if I feel, I should say something relevant to our relationship how come? It come to me it's likely what those suffering from mental illness go through in their family I wonder if cares understand such underling occurrence within family members and when they imply we should get our family members involved in our care. On the other hand my sister in-law was studying health care at the time it might be I was under experiment and observation. I have spent years living in Nigeria am not a stranger to such phenomenon. I have never once spoke against their relationship such as in Africa it is customary for men marrying younger women you do not marry women older than them I was never aware of the gap within my brother and his wife's relationship as in some region of other cultures in view of this, your wife or husband would be just about the same age with your younger brother or sister coming from hospitals at birth where they had knocked their head about in their mother's womb before being born to entwine or align their Ori in relation to their cosmos. We grow up together from childhood with different experience where culture, tradition and inherencies differs if am civilised I would take a brothers wife as she presents herself or as a brother presents himself where things go wrong or if, there are misunderstandings would my cares, families or psychiatrist in anyway imply in writing my books, I have been consulting my imagination or intelligence on the other hand it is an emotional state. 2007 when I became unwell and out of work my brother his wife and children visited me at my flat one of the things my sister in-law said in the presence of my brother and their children was that her children should not eat anything in my flat which means I should not give them food to eat in my flat.

I have lived in Nigeria to be precise where I have seen doctors, nurses, pharmaceutical environment and observe family relationships I do not misunderstand the concepts of the type of individuals from Commonwealth nations who deal with my care of psychiatrist illness I have respect for knowledge Africans should be doing well back home when it comes to education it should payoff there and in European based on productivity on the other hand regardless if you had lived in Nigeria, born in the UK or come here to live for any other reasons you should think twice before becoming a care in mental health nursing, dentistry, nutritionist and pharmacy etc if you choose going into such practice, you should have the qualities and would do all you can to do it to the best of your abilities most people are born to be physicians.

Dose from Commonwealth nation coming into Europe's bringing all sorts of conflicts within themselves and apply them here in Europe on basis of their race, culture and creed leading to more conflict especially at work which goes deeper within family in a place where I could be British you are not or I have had my stay and you haven't these are drawbacks to progress or wellbeing. Coming from any Commonwealth nation to reside in Europe anyone coming to live in through immigrations comes to be contended with a little happiness at heart, honest and tolerant and think of how the situation back in their mother land should become better than they left it. Most of our educated elite who over the year as far back as when I was young who had become educated should now be depending more on educational interest within native medicine and science to define clarity, purpose or improvement of their use.

Madness, sadness, mental illnesses are means impending misshapes due to misrepresentation that comes in almost every form applicable to human existence how could such phenomena be interpreted in our daily terms in some cases, only time and positive application would tell.. Nature of being egocentric does not come with sudden outburst it develops over time and years in human and animal nature timing is an important aspect in human lives growing up attaining or going through certain aspects of our lives, the way we go about it could be termed as our degree in relation to our beliefs and spirituality through experience I accept applying nature of being patient is one of human most greatest virtue and answer to many prayers through race, culture and creed.

Children do not cry into this world that, they are in need of medication rather, they want purpose if one becomes mentally unwell had to be put on medication for life with people having all sorts of views about you what kind of prayer can get you out of your mental illness? You need to recall your life experience regardless if you smoke, on hard drugs in hospital or in prison do the rest of the world and dose caring for you apply your experience to your mental illness? It should not all be about power, money and politics. How about living with an experience where you in hospital diagnosed with mental illness during which period your brother's wife after having a child in her first relationship gave birth through Suzerain section and I have all these to say.

We are whatever we are partly because of our past, it needs not to be the same for every one of us the word individuality is a concept on which our ideologies are based on If you know happiness and you know how you have achieved it and what it means to once true intention and reality, other peoples impression is not that important it is what it means to you that matters and the joy it brings.

It would be quite difficult tagging along other peoples delusion of which they have deliberately inculcated. Of which, if you follow them you might have a price to pay or it could lead to habeas corpus this is natural and have ever been so since time began while there are laws governing all parts and undertaking of our lives.

There are no good reason living out of somebody else dreams or there initiation into whatever, because you have your own life, dreams, disposition, prerequisite, what ought to be. For example it would be difficult for me having a child if I know the unfailing they would encounter in the future and probably, I might not be around to help them through, moreover I want to find peace in my grave. On Monday 20th July 2009 on Sky news it says that suicide cases are as a result of mental health patients who hang themselves who, were supposed to have been kept under observation in hospitals according to new reports.

I find myself each day running from something which ought not to be in the dark, I want to look at myself in the mirror to be me and not someone else.

The last thing I want to see happen is to be hospitalized because I feel it would make me less resilient coping with my daily life, no longer would I be able to beat the relapse I go through at each stage through my own personal efforts initiatives that would get me out of my worst feelings about mental illness is of concern to me.

I find the voices I hear instigating sometimes, with concern, how do I feel about it when we live in a world, each individual could seek to use the next person to pave their way either through predicament it is common within all race relation if I begin to hear peoples voices depicting such nature preventing some of us from attaining the best of our wellbeing.

With part of the world having different times of sunshine and darkness, while another part of the world wakes up from their sleep, another part of the world is going to their night sleep while other's experience midday! I do not see reason, why we all should not live a democratic life. Schizophrenia is an illness taking liberty at people's lives, our eating, sleeping, and our emotions makes one feel out of order. Are they as a result of other individuals, a demonic possession, witchcraft, juju spells? Or is it, that our souls and bodies are being called for a new order?

I do not see any reason why I should wake up each morning to find myself being dominated over by other people's voices, going to bed and find myself screaming for help unable to sleep well at night while no one can hear me.

Until humanity unfolds all they myth and mysteries contained in this world, this world would wait for its accomplishment meaning we would continue to exist... until we create the right order.

Nevertheless our ways of life within my family if we had lived under both parents would had been like having a debit card with a pine number if, it weren't a polygamous family in which my father would have been the debit card, while my mother be the pine number. What use is there having a debit card without a pine number for transactions? Within such a family, with both parents present, you could swipe your card at any time whichever way or at any time.

While if my mother is not present I can hardly complain by entering your pin number, you just have to oblige or if you complain you could get hurt, with other relatives pulling their weight on you. Africa most change, most people from third world countries are here in the UK for a better life so they say, not all of us can bury our past.

Look at the state of Africa, e.g. starvation, malnutrition, diseases, and aids yet; more and more children are being born in each day with men having more than three wives, men who can hardly look after themselves. For example for all my late father had been, who in Nigeria is looking after one or two of his last children, except my mother who is dead, all of my father's wives are still alive, who is caring for them at the moment after my father's death?

They are all left to be used in Africa after my father's death in indigent. Because my father left no indemnity, it was all a life, lived and centred on himself which had resulted to conflicts after his death for what he left behind.

A child would want their parent's marriage to breakup; it is common for parent separating, to break a child's life in a family history. The effects are that there is no cohesion within children and their parents or with their relatives but only to be used. It becomes a case for those who should be the strongest like become the weakest link, who is a child that would live in cohesion with a step mother or a step father, you would only pretend to live in cohesion with them when you get to know them meanwhile they may have other children to look after it makes one shy and uncertain in life. After our fathers death that's when step mothers begin to really let you know what it feels like to be child of your own parent or examine who your mother or father are who might be dead. There are racial and ethnic conflicts coupled with intermarriage family members distancing themselves from each other because they want their own private space or peace of mind in West Africa this those not come easy the place is always bustling one must mingle with other people to move on in time, that's when you begin to really know the people within your own family it might be likely close members of the same family are more closer to friends than their relatives sometimes I wonder what the situation might have been if blood is not thinker than water.

It is a concept for African to enhance themselves with dignity and respect from all corners and within their children, since these are the case, a child, from an African parent could spend their life time trying to know and understand their parent's, without getting anywhere while there are some who are born underprivileged in a way no different from each other but slightly different one would not customary spent years climbing elders getting to position of prestige while others your age group who might have attended the same school with them suffer.

If a person travels within Africa, it is a perpetual travelling to live or visit relatives, if you travel, it is for a purpose to live with an uncle, aunty, travelling to a place like Great Britain is considered travelling to a special place opportunities are wide and varies, how come most of us are now found of deserting Africa this dose not only concern Africans the issues involved are now filled with complexity, doing this would not sorts out the incoherencies.

Britain is no longer a place where third world countries come to for a visit unlike what it is with the British travelling around the world for the simple sake for fun, experience, interest meeting new people in their own country for the sake of experiencing their ways of life or business.

From the way mental health care workers position themselves when ever patients with mental health issues inform them of how the illness affects them some of our cares seems from the way they listen show the empathy with etiolated expressions.

The irony of it is if a sufferer tells them how they really feel and how the voices they hear affects them, the voices are emotional and can hardly be explained our cares need to show more concerns, this as part of their care is very important in getting to know if they are frustrated with hearing voices that could lead to their harming themselves or other people we all seems to be on a delicate scale based on how we live our lives how things affects us, mainly to get along in related issues of our lives the negative effects seems to boiled down on those suffering from mental illnesses'.

It need not be whenever a patient tells them; they feel like committing suicide or could harm others that are when they show some concern. Such observation should really starts from the literal outburst of hearing voices understanding their feelings about hearing voices is very important because it has relevance if it could be harmful to them or others.

No patients come out easily with their intention to commit suicide or herm other people. NHS mental health care workers and social workers should by now have developed techniques in making mental health patients come out in the open of how they really feel and how their illness, life, feelings, background, the way their mind, thoughts operates, how they feel about life, the community in which they live, the things within their communities that affects them most.

Such as factors that might increase vulnerability in developing mental psychotic illness mine are my background, culture, what I think of myself, experience and memories such as childhood experience etc.

What might increases my chances of developing psychotic episodes are my thoughts, what other people think of me as a person and my perception; my environment, conflicts and lack of support.

Things which made me stressed could be vulnerability, lack of confidence, lack of using self initiatives resulted to my not eating or sleeping well. Sometime when about to dish food on my plate voices tell me the amount I should take from the cooking pot preventing me from taking the part of the food I like best. According to what I told Dr Singh and Dr Tariah, I associated it with Vampires implying it through their voices. Demonic possession is involved in mental health and it should come up onto the surface. Little thing I want to do, they would not let me do them well or have basis or right initiatives to do them how the voices get me emotionally involve I cannot describe but try to overcome at my early stage of hearing voices which was quite disturbing.

Some of the strength and resources I have that might decrease my risk of becoming unwell are self initiatives, therapy and resuscitation, advice and encouragement.

The underlining facts is at times mental health care's and social workers show signs of bias towards us besiege our illness and emotion with stigmas attached anytime there are bad news about mental health they go cold on us or withdrawn.

It's because they are yet on focusing on the right manner or approach to mental health treatment, knowing the right ways of handling different kinds of mental health case situation which covers a wide range of issues they are still studying the illness not yet with real understanding of e.g. what schizophrenia is all about is it getting worse why is it getting worse, what are coping methods gathering their information and findings should not be in a hurry from what they know the more we are informed and made aware some of us might find our own level in reducing negative aspect involved.

For example, the illness depicts an individual under the influences of the Devil, how does this relates to patients what sorts of enslavement is it, is it beyond their control or they can mange. If the patient as a suffer is under the influence of evil forces; whilst communicating with either their cares or social workers or their psychiatrist or under observation in hospital care, the patients realises that they are under the care of someone who deliberately do not show signs of rejecting the evil forces in them, they create a barriers with such cares.

If the care worker show sings that they also are hearing whatever the devil inside a patient is saying to the patient and the effects of evil force within a patient, without going into antagonism with the force while the patient are being cared for, the patient creates a barriers within such care worker, social worker or psychiatrist which underlines to hearing voices as we all know could be voices of people they have met and those of people they do not know or have met we are yet to know, if they are voices of other people or the devil but tell this to a care, psychiatrist or social worker they imply, it is our own voices it goes deeper than being our own voice in my case because of what I hear, what the voices say.

If while they are being cared for, a patients feels their cars are more interested in whatever the devil inside the patient is saying to them or without showing signs of <u>malice's and resentment</u> towards the force might make a patient feel carers are in line with the voices or evil force and not respond to treatment. It is important cares are relaxed, make the patient feel relaxed without being biased in any way look each other in the eye. Few patients reach such level at understanding certain important aspects of their illness which depends on their level of care how do they come out with it if they are not listened to or have opportunities to voice them out dealing with mental health patients it is good to use friendly approach if not friendly at least try to be open it bears good effect when a patient tries to be resilient while at that stage tiny negative effects could make them feel bias intimidated, uncertain or withdrawn.

If they are not made to feel they themselves as cares are not speaking for the voices, patients would feel reassured to communicate with their cares what are the actual facts surrounding their mental health problems of schizophrenia in relation to hearing voices?

This may involve experiencing voices or disturbing beliefs some people hear voices and are quite happy with the experience; I am sometimes in some case happy about my hearing voices sometimes, I could be confused or annoyed or uncertain. Apart from other symptoms I suffer such as feeling tired with lack of motivation, depressed mood, anxiety, trying to figure out my moods, not being in a world of my own.

The voices may be coming from out of my head or in the air or in my body, they are voices of someone else, it may be critical or friendly sometimes with whistling and may be in different frequencies or cross linked I mean saying things in union with other voices. But they are never, my own voices they are voices of other people. Sometimes the voice goes away then comes back at certain episodes it could go on for several days and night when am awake.

Psychiatrist cares and social workers should by now know what mental health patients go through, during the course of their illness i.e. hallucination, hearing voices, feeling suicidal, aggression and aggravation just to mention a few. Dealing with such issues patient who are really suffering would not recent you as a care if you spend more time and consideration with them discussing such issues. Some of us may even be shy or timid; it is a starting point of wanting to come out, with how our illness affects us.

I am fed up of some patients my benefit this, or my benefit that. But from some patients telling you my benefit this or that is not their major concern it is about their suffering with mental illness.

Involve me about the company I keep why am I not close to my families if the voices cheer me up or make me annoyed sometimes it dose how and why, or how am coping with bad emotions yet they are mainly focused on anti social behaviours, alcoholism, drugs why should some of us be given little amount as benefit to live on we spend more of it on tobacco, alcohol or drugs.

28th June 2009 on Sky news Doctors want right to talk faith, demanding NHS staffs should be given right to discuss spiritual issues with their patients, as well as being allowed to offer prayers to patients. Medic will tell the British medical association conference during the week that staffs should not be discipline as long as they handle the issue with sensitivity. Doctors say's recent cases where health workers got into trouble makes workers fearful.

The atheist says its wrong involving religion and health care. In my opinion, it's like what if a patient expecting his or her benefit to come through, but hadn't come through in time, leaving the patient with no money, to buy food for the day or the next day because spirituality helps Heaven is for the taking not for the giving in reality you would attained it before it proves worthy in your life then you resuscitated yourself as you live with your illness.

It so happened that this patient on this same day, would be having an already booked appointment with his or her social worker. On his or her social worker hearing about the patients' financial difficulty, the social worker gave the patient £5.00 to buy food.

All patients would like to see their cares and social workers spiritually fit and considerate. At least this social worker who through his or her private pause gave a patient £5.00 without doubt, such a social care worker, I would consider mentally and spiritually fit as an individual, whose care, I would be confident, happy to be under. I am in no doubt that all my cares should be religious, very religious caring for people pain or suffering is not only spiritual, emotional it is also about existentiality.

It is a test of faith, motive with good intention on the part of the social worker and in this case, race, creed, sex or gender was not a part of the whole scenario but simply a care looking after his or her patient. But reflects religion or a test of good faith involved, which is better than abuse some patients or cares mate to each other.

Helping patients spiritually is more nicer encounter taking places then we each month hear of patients abusing their care or cares abusing their patients.

On Monday 20th July 2009 Sky TV news says more than a third of mental health patients who commit suicide by hanging themselves were supposed to have been kept under observation in hospital.

I wonder what kind of people I am living with in this world who make me lay down on my back on my bed thinking of the evaporation of my life, so sad since, I want so much to believe in them.

What more can the Church come up with when churches would vote gay people as priest? The US Lutheran on the 23rd of August 2009 split over gay clergy.

I find myself each day running from people I should be close to for one reason or the other or because of the comments I hear them make from the voices I hear from them. I have observed in many cases that I am not the only one hearing their voices.

The last thing I want to see happening to me, is to be hospitalized, it would reduce my self esteem of which I am of the opinion if I should be hospitalized, I would become less resilient, no longer would I be capable of using my own initiatives assisting myself in getting out of the reverie of my illness through my own personal efforts.

About my health my stomach has been protruding out because of my eating too much whilst I am on Olanzapine 10mg tablet. I was on 15mg Olanzapine before I was put on 10mg because, I could not stand my eating problems with 15mg, waking up each night around 1 or 2am to eat within short periods I have to go back to bed without the food digested in my stomach which I find difficulty sleeping well at night. It is customary for patients to be depressed, when one is depressed, the person might eat too much, which leads to obis, overweight leading to diabetics.

Anything is true to an individual are what one could find complaisance with. But could the voices I hear from other people really be their voices?

It's so surprising to me because I always seem to oblige my father. Whatever he says or does goes! He is the head of the family. I am the one who is always sublime in respect to my father while the others are domineering, which never went un-noticed by my father. At certain point I felt if my father had not pampered me, when I needed to be pampered it had made me stronger confronting my life for certain things I had not expected but had come to be part of my life for example I am no longer in Africa, I am a schizophrenia living in the UK.

Within all aspects of physiatrist treatment, psychiatrist, cares and social worker, should allow patients coming out of how they really feel how, their illness as their patients affects them, It becomes easier informing them of dangers the patients should take precautions on regarding their medication, life style of which most patients no matter how they try, still find it difficult to come out with based on their own opinion what brought about their illness how, they themselves can with help with outliving such inevitable problems they are confronted with regarding to their illness for example eating problems, drug abuse, depression, neglect, stigma, abuse or antagonism.

Psychiatrist, care and social worker should give patients avenues for them to come out with how their illness affects them from the patient's points of view on how through for example therapy; they could initiate gear themselves to outlive their illness. Britain is filled with most of the world's multi-cultural race. Mental illness differs in respect to race, creed or beliefs!

For example, the illness schizophrenia is a trial of life so are many other illness and disabilities. Mental illness are a test into human existence within Gods creativity, the under takings of humans existence on earth, their purpose, intentions, the human soul, mind and spiritual abuses that are parts of us. Rather than looking at them with stigmas, they should be tolerated and observe as a test of love faith, integrity empathy. People with mental illness should be consoled not abuse or seen as a stigma it could become an erratic situation that could burst care and caution should be taken when dealing with mental health cases!

It is all as a result; we are not ready to bend our waist in service against human injustice is what has brought about mental illnesses chronic and manic depression. While those who are still haughty looking for riches or, to be in high places leave most people as fools on earth who pushes more and more people into mental health and spiritual slavery. The problems is life can sometimes be a bondage to bear to set ourselves free from through which we become rich in other ways intelligent and wisdom perseverance, controlled emotion, temperament are human wealth as well it come in handy in a next life. In reality everybody should be doing better in one thing or the other we should find common grounds as human beings for the pleasure, peace, unity, beauty on this planet. If death or bondage is better than life we would not have hospitals we would not have love, emotions, understanding to express within ourselves.

I just came back to my flat after doing the shopping ho I need a fag! I would do it after unpacking my shopping.

I have to do the shopping and cooking before I would reward myself with a fag I told myself encouraging myself.

I had been observing myself while I was doing my cooking how did I have so much strength getting my cooking done? By this time, I was perspiring and was very tired, I made sure the gas cooker was turned off after preparing my meal, do the washing up straight away before going to bed to lie down and it was not yet night time; I had to have some sleep because of exhaustion.

Lying in bed I had a voice say if I had put so much effort preparing the meal, I should at least eat before going to bed but I couldn't.

I only put such effort preparing the meal because it is through one of these ways, I resuscitate myself from eating out side any way, I wasn't hungry whilst preparing the meal it was because I had the strength. I might be a schizophrenic I can still help myself. It's just that it took me twice the effort getting it done. It's about using my common sense before I go into relapse or psychotic emotions I am never aware when it would occur, it just comes all of a sudden. Being prepared is one way of outliving several effects of schizophrenic.

Stressful events or circumstances in a person's life such as family conflicts, illness, employment difficulties or bereavement can place extra demands on a sufferer leading, to feeling of more stress, frustration, being anxious, angry or sad. Even positive events such as starting new relationship, burden of having a new Capet placed in your flat, not having good appetite, having children or moving homes could result in lots of stress which could be chronic or long standing example of a more chronic stress could be in a unhappy relationship or living in affixed income or living in an unsatisfactory accommodation risk factors are also involved. Or other people giving you impression you are not doing fine most of us experience such stance in our home land we come into the UK implying the same effect really it depends on you and I to make a change. Have you lived a religious life from which no one can deter you from being only constructive to your spirituality and peace of mind?

Mental illness is a state of the mind you could add fuel to it or make it subside. Depending on whichever way you want it, you could listen to positive voices you hear or listen to the negative voices you hear. Some times because of your illness your strength is limited. You could confront your thoughts with the feelings of your mind.

You were walking on the foot part getting to a road crossing, you hear a voice saying you do not have to look left or right cross the traffic there is no motorist coming what would you do? Consult your mind is the voices telling me to do the right thing or the wrong thing? At this point, you have consulted you mind. You better hold yourself and think twice before you cross or you get yourself hurt. Be positive avoid such accident by not listening to negative voices or do what it tells you to do. For the amount of motorist on the way it poses how carful pedestrian the amount of effort they put in to walk and cross the roads.

During an appointment with your physiatrist you were given a new prescription you hear voices saying do not go and collect it immediately you should immediately tell your physiatrist or ask yourself why not. Why shouldn't I go and collect my prescription immediately?

How could I break the mould of hearing voice to harm myself or other people cry, or listen to you mind if, it doesn't help in breaking the mould consult your conscience. You and I as a mental health sufferer have to wait for foxy who, is waiting for the bride or a wedding waiting for the bride.

I ask myself why should the voices I hear not ask me to tell them about myself. No voices we hear should make us feel like bacon about to be fried.

The medication we are on should reflect in our personality that we are getting better.

Since 12pm I have returned back from my shopping and prepared a meal its now 5pm I have not been able to have a meal even from what I had prepared I had finished half a bottle of whiskey I brought to my flat with my shopping.

Its Christmas nights with a black coffee in my hand I reminisced, since I became unwell my heart is breaking. I see lovers walking hand in hand all around me. I was all on my own it's just not right all the lights and Christmas ornament celebrating the Christmas hoping, the angels would hear our prayers.

Regardless if you suffer from mental illness if you use your initiatives to understand certain things to keep it real, you would find out that 60% of what we go through are realities with meaning.

Why should we hear voices of people who are not in harmony with us telling us to harm ourselves or other people? Something most have gone wrong somewhere while everything we have just seems to us like they are here, just for the day. For some of us, I know our lives, are different from the voices we hear, How can we be and no longer shear tears of hearing this voices it seems it's going to take a life time I have accepted hearing voices as a common thing on the other hand it is why, we are being put on medication but medication is not everything to mental illness but very important that should cross our mind is being mindful of outliving the illness?

Our cares are going to take a life time understanding how we feel it is a feeling we only can express because, we are the sufferers. Only if we can make them understand, it is through mental illness we can make people understand that this world partly reflects evil that could deteriorate humans physics to an extent of being unable to care for the tiniest detail of human care yet one can be fit able to walk in the street with no one noticing. When one is not suffering from physical injuries it's rather an illness besetting the human mind, soul and ways of thinking, feeling while at the same time devastating once emotional drive.

The voices I hear are of people who have demonstrated their lives in teams I have accepted it is their voices. Hearing voices can create good feeling at times but not that a sufferer should feel they are demonstrating their voices as we should be slaves to their unrighteousness. Mental illness is not all that about committing suicide, causing harm to yourself or to other people it is more a means of communicating with you thought, feelings, and your understanding from what is right or wrong.

At least, it makes us happier when we hear voice that puts us in right perspectives rather than voices that tells us to harm ourselves or other people. We could be customary prone to hamming ourselves and not necessary to harming other people.

Such as it is necessary to stop smoking when we suffer from a blocked nose we can hardly breathe we hear voices telling us, that we should smoke even header than before. The same experience applies to alcohol during such a state; we are customary losing our sense of taste or reasoning if we still continue as the voice tells us to continue smoking and drinking. Sometimes the effect could be overpowering because you and I cannot control ourselves or the thoughts in our mind. What drives one to such an extent while we are not strangers or thoughtless to how harmful they are to our health?

May be some day we would be lucky enough to know and understand how the brains of a mental health sufferer works in accuracy how such thoughts, comes into our mind and head without warning signs! How have we become slave's to alcohol, smoking, hard drugs sometimes to a state of paralysis while it doesn't mean, there are no hint of righteousness in our lives.

How could the heart of a mental health sufferer be mended? We cannot waste this precious life going back, to where we started or into a pit hole. The life of a mental health sufferer is as a result of tragedy. It's the world and people we have to put up with, our environment trials of life; we cannot stand up with or fight against and it's as if there is a battle going on inside us we cannot arrest. For some of us, it is only if life has been kind to us. We all have dreams may be we lost it somewhere; there is no reason why we should be crying. Or is it that old times have been frustrating us rather than smiling or should have been kind to us.

These days it is difficult to ascertain or understand an evil minded individual on the other hand an evil minded person is observed as the mind of a mental health often termed as a mental health sufferer. Nevertheless I consider hearing voices a gift and a blessing upon me.

It is time to think about how the world is going to get better in this age of reasoning it is now evident for each sufferer to lend a helping hand to change the world. Could it have been our faults why we suffer from mental illness and if so why?

I do not observe myself as a devil incarnate to have become a paranoid schizophrenia it is what keeps me resilient without considering seeing myself capable to commit suicide, murder or harm anyone. Rather I confront my illness with resilience regardless of my existing within other people's psychosis. Suffering from mental illness one is either living with psychosis one has created by themselves or initiated by other people, or both.

Whatever the case, it depends on how you hold or commit yourself for example being resilient enough of being able to conduct yourself in your daily life of being able, even if it's slightly having a chance of coping with your condition of mental illness would be up to you as a sufferer. Apart from other problems when under care a mental health patient could be reasonable enough; reducing excessive smoking, drinking of alcohol and drug abuse for the sake of being able to us their common senses do they receive encouragement for trying to do so?

Some patient virtually do not know what to do, with themselves each day; I sometimes go into such mood swings am a kind of person who broad over things a lot because I enjoy positive outcomes it is a good sign on my part of outliving the illness because it gears me up into actions or endeavours to motivating myself. May be it is a nature that had paved way for me to outlive the illness to some degree! I am not one to believe that money could grow on trees; since this 21st century, it is the Benefit money or to have their stay through immigration that drives some patients into the illness.

I do not eat or sleep well especially at night at certain point of my illness it has now all changed because of my own personal efforts I could be depress, stay awake all night, lonely and confused not only in the way I live my life, but also, from the voices I hear. In African terminology it could be considered am being bewitched or used for juju purpose.

From the voices I hear people talk about me, some people say good things about me, quit different from those who wants to be the hypocrites just for the sake of hypo personalising themselves with the situation with false impressions and information some of them are true and direct in some cases making my mental illness get worse at the same time pretending that those involving negative voices I give less attention to since the voices are not giving me a good tune.

The illness is more of an emotional state then can lead to psychosis it could be negative or positive. Negative, virtually means caring for such a sufferer might lead to aggressive manners, not conducive to problems solving they would rather feel hurt other patients are doing fine while they are not. Positive relates to being timid, unstable or being uncertain. If such patients had been resilient, accommodated lots of bad memories over a period of time, insecure in life meanwhile have advance their moral virtues or conduct they may be resilient and think positive to outlive the illness.

VOICES I HEAR:1) I should not take my medications in the morning whenever I have an appointment 2) I should use my prescriptions even if, they are out of date 3) other effects, lethargy, confused, feeling of being let down, feel insecure, feel downgraded, socially withdrawn because of intimidation, swaying and dizzy spells, unable to control my mood with different periods of mood swing, difficulty explaining to other people, how I really feel in view they might not understand what am going through. THERAPIES so as a means of therapies I listen to music but not very frequent, food, appetite is weird, confused as to what to eat or being happy about what I eat.

I have the feeling it depends on each patient through their own initiatives of self developed therapies resuscitating ourselves our moods, coming out of reveres based on how the illness affects us. Otherwise one could go down wrecked it really depends on the patient. Most of us are more withdrawn because of stigmas attached to schizophrenia manic and chronic depression.

Any form of disappointment could trigger a patient coming out worse at the same time most of us feel we are being used by opportunist. Or how else would you feel as a sufferer finding out that your soul is being used against you by other people, not spiritually but dominating you or accrediting themselves based on wired feelings? It should not be the case more therapies with such experiences need come into light.

While other people impose on your thoughts tell you to do things, some of which could be harmful therapies such as do not be a danger to yourself or to other people take your reveries seriously I would rather not own or drive a vehicle but walk, use public transport rather than driving a vehicle.

I hear voice I should not wash or iron my clothing's before I wear them in such disposition I rather would help myself by asking questions why I should not iron my cloths such as, is there any reason why I should not iron my clothing's, uplift yourself from any voice that insight negativity.

As for resuscitation, through faith, religion, spirituality, beliefs, meditation do not think, because you are unwell with mental illness it's the worse for you. Trust is also very important because it builds a right frame of mind through concept one can overrule hearing negative voices. One can mediate, build up good and healthy thoughts and a good frame of mind, we all have to start from somewhere it helps if you have no one to depend on at least trust and mediate within yourself its one way of approaching the right people for help.

I suffer from two mood swing about my medication one I hear voices at certain times I should not take my medications. While at other times, I suffer from medication fever, agitated to take my medications.

23rd March 2010 a survey found out that 65% of doctor's question could rarely offer psychological therapies to depress sufferers within two months of their referral. The Royal collage of GPs studies as part of a campaign by mental health charity Mind called for better access to therapies.

All who took part in the debate placed great stress on the need for talking therapies in which patients would be encouraged to express them and face whatever troubles them. Depression affects one in 10 people a year with more than half of those experiencing more than one episode.

I went for a therapy session after being referred to a special clinical psychologist Michelle McCartney by the recovery team at Ferryview mental health centre. I go down to the mental health centre in the Heights in Charlton Greenwich once a week where, I had appointment with Michelle McCartney. what could had led to my having appointments with a psychologist was because of my resilience on my part in outliving mental illness it was a crucial time for me because I needed someone to talk to about my illness and some of my trials.

Recent work suggested that taking therapy is effective in tackling depression in the short term and better in the long term. Mind campaign challenged all political parties indulging them to come up with a manifesto to guarantee offering therapies to all those who need them within 28 days of requesting referral.

In 2007 the government earmarked £173 million to boost the number of therapists on the NHS It did aim to treat 900,000 extra people in England by 2010/2011 with half of them moving to recovery and 25,000 fewer on sick pay and benefits. The Royal Collage of GPs chairman Professor Steve Field did say there had been substantial improvement in the last years but there was more to be done and a long way to go! If patients could be treated early they could be left to work, with help for them to get on with their lives.

Mind chief executive Paul Farmer said talking therapies could save lives; it was crucial patient who needed help receive it as quickly as possible. The department of health said more than 230,000 people had already benefited from the improving access to psychological therapy programmes with still more work and research to be done. Tory shadow health minister Anne Milton said mental health condition might deteriorate in the same way as physical condition if not treated.

MP Anne Milton they would make sure GPs have better information about the effectiveness of talking therapies. The Liberal Democrats say they are totally committed into giving people with mental health problem guaranteed access to the treatment they need. Talking with Michelle McCartney was a relief to some of my emotions. She was the one person I encountered as a care and patient relationship that made me came out with most of my feelings about my emotional life and how my illness affects me. We constructed a diagram of my family, talked of some of the issues surrounding my background and life experience, how I felt about my illness and how, difficult it was for me expressing certain aspect I also filled some questioners with her help writing my books at the time also did encouraged me to listen and pay attention.

One of the causes of schizophrenia is as a result of their having been bitten by vampires who have sucked the blood of your patients and left their blood in your patients. The symptoms of schizophrenia are as a result of sufferers being victims of vampires. Some patient can coup if they have strong religious or vampire background that's if there is one in their family. Africa its part of culture to drink bottled concoctions from dried woods, sticks and plants in some cases, they use animals. My father drink the once made from dried woods, sticks and leaves mixed with whisky or brandy but not from animals he would rather use them for rituals.

The bit of a vampire could make a victim hear voices to harm themselves or other people, to do things; they are not expected to do because after the bit, they start living in the world of the vampire. They could suffer from abnormal feelings, tendency or feel they are not themselves through vampires bite. They could begin to have strange thoughts. For example they came from a higher authority such as paranormal psychotic inclination to different degree or level it becomes a check on who you really are. Or that they are god or God have sent them to do what they do. Which are customary to the thoughts, symptoms and feelings of most schizophrenics? One the other hand it could all be true because one has transcended to a higher level based on reality of their life experiences.

There are two category based on such assumptions related to victims of vampire one the patients themselves could be vampires they are the once usually associated with aggression while the once who are not vampires but victims, are found suffering from lethargy, dizziness headaches, loss of memory, agitation, stress and body pain. They would use twice an effort to do whatever, they want to do and three times, the effort any normal person can do whatever they want to do because of showing signs of withdrawal from a vampire diary.

It is common for them to be depression, confused; feelings of uncertainty, reserved, self withdrawn they are accustom to make facial expression, agitation not with violence. If cares notice any sign of aggression within such patent it calls for concern in most cases, it is because the patient have suffered a disappointment or something have triggered or disturbed their emotional state. Something had occurred that had disturbed their state of mind. It is a critical stage in treating a mental health patient. The worst any of such patients should meet at such stage is antagonism which could harmful, very harmful if their cares are not experience enough.

A defect about their care in such a critical stage is that their psychiatrist, care worker and social workers give them little attention or no attention at all they might tend to feel nobody cares. No mental health case can be predictable. It is wrong for cares having their own opinions of what a schizophrenic should look like expect based on observation findings and theories this those not mean they should not have an open view.

Psychiatrist, cares, social workers dealing with mental health have their own private lives I intended writing my book in terminologies of such as madness is all over the world fixation is paramount in every lives and environment, evil prevails religious leaders cares less and make fixations about their private and family lives, their children comes first more of those holding their zeal and trials of life are being let down.

Experts are predicting the only privately-owned version of Edvard Munch's masterpiece The Scream could fetch $80m (£50m) at auction in New York in May. The work, which is one of four versions of the painting created in the 1890s, is going on display in London ahead of the sale. The BBC's David Sillito spoke to Philip Hook from Sotheby's about one of the most famous images in the world. It portrays a view of certain aspect on planet earth.

The painting reflects reality through its imaging is essentially the basic premise for painting in general. The form, method, content and reason for making the depiction are at least significant. The question today about art is actually about depicting reality based on what is going on around us,

It provided outstanding and very distinctive answers to aforementioned questions. The exhibition has its own inner story. It conceptualize reality of which the surface, through all of its traceable connection to concrete reality, is also a gateway or window to a world within a time with an evocation potential that breaks the possible references to the here and now. It is evident the invention of the painting of the historical need to come to terms with seen reality, the need to constantly return to narrative realism and the attempt to create as faithful representation as possible. It is able to be the bearer of many meanings; something which could not be achieved or accented using other methods of depiction.

Virtually all the artists represented at the exhibition construe images of obvious reality. This new reality through the credibility given by its high quality, mostly illusionary painting, not only faithfully imitates reality, but it is through this fidelity that they provide insight and guide to a world outside reality. This is a world that may be imaginary or sensed, but also often seen either in a dream, in everyday reality, or even in old art gallery; a world that has more than a superficial dimension, a world that is often a very complex, intellectual structure based on creative thinking about the world and providing space and incentives for richly structured thinking about reality in details.

In most cases, cares are wrong in believing it is when the patient is tattered, he had not had a bath for a whole week, or there is always a can of bear in a patient's hand that is when a patient is suffering from mental illness. Whereas it is the socially withdrawn patients who would not display such characteristics who are the once who unexpectedly might commit suicide, self harm with no knowledge from their cares or family members that they could do such a thing unexpectedly.

If at such time, the mental health patient is pressed with difficulty or disappointment or that nobody seem to cares as a result become withdrawn depress moods might stretch further, socially withdrawn or be in the defensive which leads to what psychiatrist call disorder which are varied depending on the patients background, upbringing, race, creed or religion, temperament or emotions they are going through because they give toughs to certain aspects of life this is where cares come in.

It is with such patients psychiatrist often found to the least of detail capable of explaining how, their medication affects them. Some of them because of the effect of the inherencies are found to be smokers but not drug addicts because the inherencies have contributed to their inclination to crave. We all know smoking is associated with craving. They crave because, they want to set themselves free. But of what we never know even me myself I do not know probably because we are showing signs of withdrawal from vampire diaries. Or we have supernatural powers or ability we want it spent! We want to outlive connect to the force of nature that are superficial that binds us to the supernatural. Could it be the same reason why people become cult members or secret societies? It does not authenticate such logic because they go there to attain privileges like wealth, prestige through rituals what could be driving the lives of mental health patients down the drain. Where one is physically fit all of a sudden one is looking tattered on drugs or unable to care for themselves its unnatural every individual wants to look cute, come out into the street and showing signs of happiness.

While some patients lack such temperaments they are prone to be drug addicts, they breathe down hard on you whenever they talk to you and they look aggressive. If they are not victims they are associates of vampires.

They are often found to have created mental disorder or they create the disorders which are some of the behavioural pattern associated with mental health illness most people view with stigmas attached.

In the case of victims of vampires I associate certain mental health or personality disorders associated with the patient because of the reign of vampires in their heredity. Such as when the sun shines, it shins because of them, they have supernatural powers, they could have strong personalities at certain times with charismas' attached to their behaviour or characteristics. They always seem to be in control. An irony is that most cares do not pay them much attention or view them with an enigma. My advice is that they should study the war within vampires and werewolves it has been going on for more than a hundred of centuries.

The recognition and understanding of mental health conditions has changed over time and across cultures, and there are still variations in the definition, assessment, and classification of mental disorders, although standard guideline criteria are widely accepted. Or could it be the residual image through practicing of witchcraft, magic, Voodoo, juju, spell casting, medieval, and cultism including science and technology that has for thousands of years been a part of human existences.

Since the year 2004 I have been given opportunity to stand for election as part of a team as governors with Oxleas, I wrote to Ms. Sally Brydon stating if I or any mental health sufferer should stand as candidate for election as board of governors, they would have to know or understand us better for example there should be something behind each candidate that make them tick or stand out as the right person to be elected.

It could be sport, therapy, keeping records of minutes during meetings; it could be socializing, bringing out hidden feelings on how the illness affects most patients.

Some critics are of the opinion the voices associated with schizophrenia are the thoughts of the sufferer. If it's true they would not be in conflict within themselves and the voices they hear infarct they wouldn't need to hear voices at all and they wouldn't need discussing about the voices they hear with their cares.

As a mental health sufferer, it could not be the thoughts of my mind that can gear me into having thoughts of committing suicides it is imposed through paranormals that can't be fought against to reach such a level, understand what it takes for a sufferer to makes it a most to have a whole packet of 25g of tobacco alcoholic drink before other consideration such as food or pressing their clothing's find difficulty in preparing my daily meals, not being able to watch my clothes or clean my flat being unable to do these are from the voices which are controlling, drives us into motives and then actions due to emotional harassment.

It leaves most of us depress, to a state of chronic or manic depression. It is a matter of the Devil, Satan or Lucifer tormenting our lives. We go deeper each day suffering from such issues without our being able to control it. Yet we know excessive smoking drinking and the use of hard drugs are no good to our health and wellbeing infarct I would describe the situation as if, spells have been cast upon a patient.

Each day a life of a mental health sufferer goes down the drain some of us, are aware the tax payer and government have to make sure such sufferers receive their benefits the most important issues is that the illness have to be understood. The worst thing that could continue going on is stigmas attached to mental health. It worsens any progress being made by some sufferers to outlive the illness whilst under care. That's if there are signs of outliving the illness. We need to show them what efforts it takes to display such initiatives of outliving the illness related to its disorder.

Infarct I cannot understand the difference within a schizophrenic sufferer and a murderer, or someone just out of prison or, anti-social behaviour or theft the excuses or often mislead terms associated with mental illness is any murders, offenders to a simple petty theft or even paedophile and benefits fraud given for their action are now all under the influence of mental illness.

It would be interesting to know how cares, feels about these happenings and its effect. If they are doing their job the first thing, they would have done is to keep close to their patients, reassure them such times of contacts are always very good for understanding issues of mental illness. Especially for dose who are doing their best to outlive the illness.

Not all mental health patients are the same Great Britain is a highly multi-racial nation with people from different races, creed and religion. These are not time for mental health care's isolating themselves from their patient not when their predicament could be used by opportunists!

As much as the illness of schizophrenia is a deadly illness some sufferers are battling on how to outlive the illness. They should be given all the help and support they need in other to outlive the illness the more sufferers endeavour to give clear indication related to symptoms of the illness the easier it might lead to a cure.

Segregating labelling of patients within cares and the community should not go on I understand conflicts have always been a part of every life or environment use it for creating better understanding and harmony. I am your patient you are my carers who, among both of us should be more obliged should not be confused we are both obliged to each other.

No matter what the situation cares should get more closer, to their patients without being biased if the effect of stigmas attached to mental health makes any one of them segregate themselves from their patients, such a care is not ready yet to be a mental health care in my opinion. I would advise you please find another job because, it is obvious the road ahead in relationship to mental health issues are going to be difficult very difficult it would be no ground for any care, who is an hypocrites. The illness could drive one to various emotional stages they should be doing more for those who show positive signs rather than negative signs.

As far as am concerned I see my future related to my illness as very bleak and I feel bad about it. Over the years I had written to Oxleas they should involve patients in the care it would create a common ground, for both patients communicating real experience that are crucial in their mind but difficult to tell cares.

It is about time we put blockage against those who would always want to use our predicament as excuses for their evil intents.

All mental health sufferers are being labelled with stigmas because; we are constantly being used by opportunist. I have the filling this would go on for years and would get even worse while the innocent once among us continue to suffer the effects. We feel heartfelt about being stigmatized in our community for those who do not know how to love teach them how to love, recuperate adjust to life's anomalies not all of us have the same strength towards facing life trials.

Each day we want to come out with good intentions, be creative, if it could be just for the purpose of outliving our illness, or to contribute to our community for example to work even if its voluntary work. The numbers of the unemployed 2010 have risen considerably. There is much competition among those looking for work because of our predicament; we are less likely to be employed. We should not allow ourselves to be grouped as social outcast.

Our chances of standing up to look for work or getting employed, better understanding of ourselves or community should not go down the drain. In most cases some of us who get employed must have lied about our illness. Our lies relating to our mental health slow us down while at work.

It makes some of us less functional in our work because we might be afraid our employer might find out we have mental health problem. We are tensed while we are at work the strain on certain individual sufferer contributes to their likely chance of suffering from deeper level of depression.

As sufferers we are faced with problems that could sometimes be difficult to explain no wonder most of us, our conditions out of the ordinary gets out of hand sometimes. We feel we are being segregated, left out, look down upon and intimidated. Tell them one crazy thing you are doing to outlive your illness such as playing a guitar you hardly know how to play all day it makes no impression but tell them about drugs, sex, suicide thoughts that's when a patient is responding it rather inculcates such thoughts and activates in patients who have no such thoughts thinking this, is what mental health is all about.

We have to stand up to these challenges; we have to confront the issues. There is enough reason understanding why all of a sudden some things out of the ordinary do occur. For example a patient commits suicide or goes on the rampage an over dose of harmful substance our cares view us, with suspicion the most annoying part of it, is that they are always on the defences in relation to themselves and our care does it have to show.

The more this situation goes mental illness still remains uncertain. Mental illness is not all about drug abuse, alcoholism and antisocial behaviour. What can be the cure if they are ready to support us, listen to us? While we come out with initiatives for our general community having a second view of us, as mental health itself.

We hear of entertainers making millions through enhanced drugs. While we, mental health patient take hard drugs for what? Very soon it might be a common thing for patients with drug problems having their joints in NHS environment.

Within a patients on drugs and an entertainers on enhanced drugs who suffer most when it comes the effects of using drugs? Going out if one is aware informing the police of every angle where the sales of drugs are or are used puts one's life in danger. Those who make the drugs available get away with it without being disturbed, harassed or stigmatized. Our illness is always on constant reviews. What have we got to give in relation to the effects of hard drugs and not undermine mental illness is being open minded with your cares.

Could it be right as a drug addict we are privileged within the NHS to have joints here is an opportunity turning conflict into collaboration.

Drugs as most people know are for enhancement, why is it not enhance patient to clean themselves, wear clean cloths, at least it most lead in some ways of getting patient to do better things than being associated with anti social behaviours.

Let's contribute on the knowledge on the effects of head drugs because while you go on depicting such attitudes, some people are using it, to make millions on the bottom line it all boils down to you or me being the black sheep in the family.

Here is what we should do; we are going to form a football, table and lawn tennis club with terminology e.g. medication, chronic football club, manic football club players names would be different types of diagnosis. Cares more focus on care for those in prison and care less for those in open community I observe it as an omen that could go terribly wrong at some point.

We do not have to play as normal football players do but have fun with some of the funniest gestures, it would be customary to score twenty goals, we can demonstrate break dance, within a match, nine players would be replaced because, they are no longer feet to play.

We can have a music band of our own called mental health group musical band. We would play during carnivals and charity. We could have our own drama series on television to capsulate members of our community understanding more about life of those living with mental illness.

The television series could contain strong language For example we have not had sex for the past one year. I do not know what is wrong with me. By the time I have my joints; I can hardly have a hard-on.

It's about time we stand up for changes we should not let other people spell out our lives based on our predicament we would rather find ourselves being used.

It would not only create reality based on the illness, it would create better understanding on issues of mental illness! The harm of stigmatising such people might be understood. It would remove stigmas attached to mental illness.

It would take time and efforts but its reward would be great very great because, it would make most of us feel free discussing our problems It would portray a reality of ourselves the. It would spell out how people with mental illnesses live their lives on a daily basis, the problems associated with their illness such as stress, depression, relapses, frustration and disappointments. There are certain things there are that are not meant to be the way they are they could be difficult to analyze because we forced to be confronted with it might not be all that a good experience.

What are the positive or negativity associated with our illness. Effects of drug, medication abuse what are the issues preventing some of us displaying positive mental attitudes. How to overcome stress, what are the disappointments contributing or preventing people from living happy lives? How come can a person not value his life or the life of other people could be because of human nature what brings it about covers lots of issues not everyone has time or interest in. What could contribute to our keeping up appearances with a positive mental attitude how do our cares feel about us infarct our community as well view dose with mental health issues?

What are the dark side associated with mental illness, manic and chronic depression? For most of us who embrace ourselves regardless of our illness, such as keeping ourselves clean and tidy we have to show or give in to one or two things that we are spending our benefits wisely.

In relation to these our cares should keep an open mind towards our care. The illness is unpredictable.

Our cares do not have to wait until we display involuntary movements, Jacky movement, and depressed mood before they start taking action in our care our care should be monitored in every stage and most importantly, before it gets out of hand. As far as there could be segregation within cares and patients in my opinion a course for improving lives is not involved. Most of our cares are very judgmental.

My reason for having such an opinion is that situations sometimes seems to be falling apart the future might seems to be bleak because you give in to thoughts some of which can be quite positive but gets nowhere, each time a patient breaks down or something tragic happens, our cares seems to break down as well and who takes the blame?

As much as I try continuously to express myself they say to me, you are doing fine I could be doing worse than they think for my resilience could break at any time or unexpectedly. No mental health case it is said can be predicted but cares ought to be able to predict them if they understand issues surrounding mental health problems another mistake they make is that they have in their own mind with enigmas attached of what they feel the illness of paranoid schizophrenia is most of which makes us unsettled we want to see the bright side that the illness can really be understand leading to a cure.

The present government under David Cameron is making it a matter of more people having more choice.

In some cases one could feel one is being demonised the only thing a sufferer have left is their mind, body and brain but sometimes could be fragmented if they are resilient enough to outlive the illness, show self control develop way to help the mind or body through therapies, be cognitive show signs of overcoming repressed mood rather than show how high you are on drugs. I do not know how to explain it to my psychiatrist because it in the bottom lime symptoms of schizophrenic is rather embarrassing to tell.

It's a battle based on human existence within the mind, soul and thoughts the mind, soul and thoughts of a sufferer are being torn apart the way some evil mind now operates is not only through juju or witchcraft it's through other effects e.g. global effect. Its only when a sufferer fights back positively the illness would not be a threat to their life. The dark side is that to do this you have to use twice your initiatives putting yourself in a positive mental attitude while at the same time a sufferer might be prone to being depress. No matter how a sufferer outlive the illness they will for certain period go on mood swing example being unable to wash their plates after a meal or just not feeling good because of different level of temperament.

After the washing-up, you find out that you have not done the washing up thoroughly. A sufferer at such stages no matter what they do becomes more depress with lethargy among other things you have to do for the day that's if, you care enough and concerned e.g. you have not washed the plate after your meal thoroughly. Trying to do it thoroughly is a best option it would make you feel much better later and put you in the right frame of mind when you least expect.

If they look easily to become agitated look for signs if they are harmful to themselves or would be to other people. If they look serene with sings of notable relapse or disappointment calm the patient down do anything quickly to getting them out of their reverie. As for me, it's only to sleep and write; come to think of it, we all do things in different ways. I find it very unveiling, it relieves me of my depressed thoughts, thinking, overreacting or hearing other people's voices.

Some patients over the years feel science have gone too far in dealing with issues of mental illness I wonder why this could be the case peoples feeling differs about everything or how it relates to them. Some of the carers apart from their studies in mental health are inadequate with their talent to care for their patients.

Things like care for the eyes, diet, cleaning our teeth and general cleanliness should be part of our care programme in therapy sessions for some of us; we should take it up as a means of therapy or resuscitation. There is no way to outlive mental illness except, the patients themselves are ready to outlive the illness. You should give attention to those patients who are responding to treatment because, for them it might take twice the efforts to get anything right done.

Some side effects of some medications is over eating their stomach just keep on churning for food; they eat a lot within a short time without the food digesting before they go to bed to have some sleep before the food, digest in their stomach. I do not think the word churning is in the dictionary to me it means 'hunger'

Those with such eating problems should not be put on such medication but to patients who have no appetite for food.

It might be right to give patients the right to choose those who care for them. One of the causes of mental illness is because people suffer from social, environmental, physiological and philosophical downsizing; As a care what do you make out of a patient you are caring for whom for the sixth time wearing the same cloths and have, not had a bath since the last time you saw the patient calls for concern.

How are some cigarettes, drugs embezzled out of its warehouse some of which might had been confiscated as not fit for sale which are later sold at low prices? They make huge amount of money through the sales of such cigarettes or drugs which are smuggled out from their warehouses. Why and how do these drugs, marijuana, ecstasy and cocaine operate in our communities?

It's a common thing to be found in almost every company especially common within developed nations I call them Staffs undermining local enterprise. They have to be apprehended by the police and border force; rather than our communities putting all the balm on addicts. The illness schizophrenic is a challenge to each sufferer. Over the years in my studies and contemplation on mental illness I have experience fear of stigmas attach to mental illness, you feel people are conscious of you or that you could be harmful to them. Which you could find uncomfortable sometimes, it could seems as if people are talking about you behind your back.

The idea that as a sufferer you are going to be on medication for the rest of your life in some case, there could be signs of paranoia such as other people giving you the impression you are not in control of yourself, feeling insecure, afraid for your life and in some cases depress. Such issue drive sufferers feeling low in emotion or aggressive in certain cases. We can hardly come across patients who could outlive mental illness if you come across one or two who could manage the illness, they would tell you that it is a tough experience.

Emotions are the various bodily feelings associated with mood, temperament, personality, disposition, and motivation. Motivations direct and energize behaviour, emotions provides affective component to motivation, positive or negative. It defines the states of our feeling which coexist with our physiological, cognitive, and behavioural components. Strong emotions arouse autonomic nervous system the greater the arousal the more intense the emotion. It also appears that the type of arousal affects the emotion being experienced. Although the word emotion might seem to be about feeling and not about thinking, cognitions-particularly interpretations of the meanings of events are important aspects of emotions. Fear, which usually occurs in response to a threat, involves cognitions that one is in danger as well as arousal of the sympathetic nervous system.

In 1972, Paul Ekman developed the following classifications of basic emotions: anger, disgust, fear, happiness, sadness and surprise. Robert Plutchik developed the 'wheel of emotions', suggesting eight primary bipolar emotions: joy versus sadness; anger versus fear; trust versus disgust; and surprise versus anticipation. Some basic emotions can be modified to form complex emotions. The complex emotions could arise from cultural conditioning or association combined with the basic emotions. Alternatively, similar to the way <u>primary colours</u> combine, primary emotions could blend to form the full spectrum of human emotional experience. For example interpersonal <u>anger</u> and <u>disgust</u> could blend to form <u>contempt</u>. Relationships exist between basic emotions, resulting in positive or negative influences.

A distinction is then made between emotional episodes and emotional dispositions. Emotional dispositions are also comparable to character traits, where someone may be said to be generally disposed to experience certain emotions. For example an irritable person is generally disposed to feel <u>irritation</u> more easily or quickly than others do. Finally, some theorists place emotions within a more general category of 'affective states' where affective states can also include emotion-related phenomena such as pleasure and pain, motivational states (for example, <u>hunger</u> or <u>curiosity</u>), moods, dispositions and traits.

We try to regulate our emotions to fit in with the norms of the situation, based on many (sometimes conflicting) demands upon us which originate from various entities. These entities are studied by sociology on a micro level, such as social roles and 'feeling rules' the everyday social interactions and situations are shaped by, and on a macro level by social institutions, discourses, ideologies, etc. For example, (post-) modern <u>marriage</u> is based on the emotion of love yet the very emotion is to be worked on and regulated by love. The sociology of emotions also focuses on general <u>attitude changes</u> in a population. Emotional appeals are commonly found in advertising, health campaigns and political messages. Recent examples include no-smoking health campaigns and political campaign advertising emphasizing the fear of terrorism.

Mental wellness and mental health to a large degree results from an adequate amount of self-helping, flexible, logical-empirical ways of thinking, emotion and behaviours when a perceived undesired and stressful activating event occurs, and the individual is interpreting, evaluating and reacting to the situation rationally and self-helpingly   the resulting consequence is likely to be more healthy constructive and functional this does not by any means mean that a relatively un-disturbed person never experiences negative feelings it is questionable people normally do not go on debilitating on un-healthy emotions which is subsequent leading to more of our self-defeating behaviour to a minimum humans tend to be running away from deliberating on self defeating issues and experiences basically one of our general weaknesses. Regardless of vast areas of problems, belief system and unconstructive lives based on philosophy about adversities and human desires and preferences clearly acknowledged in addition to disturbing themselves, also are innately constructivists because, they found to largely upsetting themselves with their beliefs, emotions and behaviours, they can be helped to, in a multimodal manner, dispute and question these and develop a more workable, more self-helping set of constructs.

The concepts and philosophies of life of unconditional self-acceptance, other-acceptance, and life-acceptance, are effective and philosophical about life in achieving mental wellness and mental health.

That human beings are inherently fallible and imperfect and that they had better accept theirs and other human being's totality and humanity, while at the same time not like some of their behaviours and characteristics that are, better off not measuring their entire self or their 'being' and give up the narrow, grandiose and ultimately destructive notion to give themselves any global rating or report card. This is partly because all humans are continually evolving and are far too complex to accurately rate; all humans do both self- and social-defeating and self- and social-helping deeds, and have both beneficial and un-beneficial attributes and traits at certain times and in certain conditions. Ideas and feelings about self-worth are largely definitional and are not empirically confirmable or falsifiable.

That people had better accept life with its hassles and difficulties not always in accordance with their wants, while trying to change what they can change and live as elegantly as possible with what they cannot change.

Emotions are universal phenomena; however, they are affected by culture. While some emotions are universal and are experienced in similar ways as a reaction to similar events across all cultures, other emotions show considerable cultural differences in their antecedent events, the way they are experienced, the reactions they provoke and the way they are perceived by the surrounding society.

Culture provides structure, guidelines, expectations, and rules to help people understand and interpret behaviours. Several ethnographic studies suggest there are cultural differences in social consequences, particularly when it comes to evaluating emotions. For example, as Jean Briggs described in the Utku Eskimo population, anger was rarely expressed, and in the rare occasion that it did occur, it resulted in social ostracism.

These cultural expectations of emotions are sometimes referred to as display rules. Psychologists (Ekman & Friesen, 1969; Izard, 1980; Sarni, 1999) believe that these rules are learned during a socialization process. Ekman and Friesen (1975) have also suggested that these 'unwritten codes' govern the manner in which emotions may be expressed, and that different rules may be internalized as a function of an individual's culture, gender or family background. Miyamoto & Ryff (2011) used the term cultural scripts to refer to cultural norms that influence how people expect emotions to be regulated.

Cultural scripts dictate how positive and negative emotions should be experienced and combined. Cultural scripts may also guide how people choose to regulate their emotions which ultimately influence an individual's emotional experience. For example, research suggests that in Western cultures, the dominant social script is to maximize positive emotions and minimize negative emotions. In Eastern cultures, the dominant cultural script is grounded in 'dialectical thinking' and seeking to find a middle way by experiencing a balance between positive and negative emotions.

Because normative behaviours in these two cultures vary, it should also be expected that their cultural scripts would also vary. Tsai et al. (2007) argues that not only do cultural factor influence ideal affect (i.e., the affective states that people ideally want to feel) but that that the influence can be detected very early. Their research suggests that preschool aged children are socialized to learn ideal affect through cultural products such as children storybooks. They found that European American preschool children preferred excited (vs. calm) smiles and activities more and perceived an excited (vs. calm) smile as happier than Taiwanese Chinese preschoolers.

Emotions play a critical role in interpersonal relationships and how people relate to each other. Emotional exchanges can have serious social consequences that can result in either maintaining and enhancing positive relationships, or becoming a source of antagonism and discord (Fredrickson, 1998; Gottman & Levenson, 1992).

People may generally 'want to feel better than worse' (Larsen, 2000), how the emotions are regulated may differ across cultures.

Research by Yuri Miyamoto suggests that cultural differences influence emotion regulation strategies. Research also indicates that different cultures socialize their children to regulate their emotions according to their own cultural norms.

For example, ethnographic accounts suggest that American mothers think that it is important to focus on their children's successes while Chinese mothers think it is more important to provide discipline for their children. To further support this theory, a laboratory experiment found that when children succeeded on a test, American mothers were more likely than Chinese mothers to provide positive feedback (e.g. 'You're so smart!'), in comparison to Chinese mothers who provided more neutral or task relevant feedback (e.g. 'Did you understand the questions or did you just guess?'; Ng, Pomerantz, & Lam, 2007). This shows how American mothers are more likely to 'up-regulate' positive emotions by focusing on their children's success whereas Chinese mothers are more likely to 'down-regulate' children's positive emotions by not focusing on their success. Americans see emotions as internal personal reactions; emotions are about the self (Markus & Kityama, 1991).

In America, emotional expression is encouraged by parents and peers while suppression is often disapproved. Keeping emotions inside is viewed as being insincere as well as posing a risk to one's health or well being in Japanese cultures however, emotions reflect relationships in addition to internal states. Some research even suggests that emotions that reflect the inner self cannot be separated from emotions that reflect the larger group. Therefore, unlike American culture, expression of emotions is often discouraged, and suppressing one's individual emotions to better fit in with the emotions of the group is looked at as mature and appropriate.

The role of facial expressions in emotional communication is often debated. While Darwin believed the face was the most preeminent medium of emotion expression, more recent scientific work challenges the theory. Furthermore, research also suggests that cultural contexts behave as cues when people are trying to interpret facial expressions. In everyday life, information from people's environments influences their understanding of what a facial expression means. According to research by Masuda et al. (2008), people can only attend to a small sample of the possible events in their complex and ever- changing environments and increasing evidence suggests that people from different cultural backgrounds allocate their attention very differently.

This means that different cultures may interpret the same social context in very different ways. Since Americans are viewed as individualistic, they should have no trouble inferring people's inner feelings from their facial expressions, whereas Japanese people maybe more likely to look for contextual cues in order to better understand one's emotional state. Evidence of this phenomenon is found in comparisons of Eastern and Western artwork. In Western art there is a preoccupation with the face that does not exist in Eastern art. For example, in Western art the figure occupies a larger part of the frame and is clearly noticeably separated from the ground. In East Asian artwork, the central figure is significantly smaller and also appears to be more embedded in the background.

In a laboratory setting Masuda et al. also tested how sensitive both Americans and Japanese would be to social contexts by showing them pictures of cartoons that included an individual in the context of a group of four other people. They also varied the facial expressions of the central figure and group members. They found that American participants were more narrowly focused with judging the cartoon's emotional states than the Japanese participants were. In their recognition task they also observed that the Japanese participants paid more attention to the emotions of the background figures than Americans did.

One of the biggest challenges in cultural research and human emotions is the lack of diversity in samples. Currently the research literature is dominated by comparisons between Western (usually American) and Eastern Asian (usually Japanese or Chinese) sample groups. This limits our understanding of how emotions vary and future studies should include more countries in their analyses. Another challenge outlined by Matsumoto (1990) is that culture is ever changing and dynamic. Culture is not static. As the cultures continue to evolve it is necessary that research capture these changes. Identifying a culture as 'collectivistic' or 'individualistic' can provide a stable as well as inaccurate picture of what is really taking place.

No one culture is purely collectivistic or individualistic and labelling a culture with these terms does not help account for the cultural differences that exist in emotions. As Matsumoto argues, a more contemporary view of cultural relations reveals that culture is more complex than previously thought. Translation is also a key issue whenever cultures that speak different languages are included in a study. Finding words to describe emotions that have comparable definitions in other languages can be very challenging. For example, happiness, which is considered one of the six basic emotions, in English has a very positive and exuberant meaning. In Hindi, <u>Sukhi</u> is a similar term however it refers to peace and happiness. Although happiness is a part of both definitions, the interpretation of both terms could lead to researchers to making assumptions about happiness that actually do not exist.

Culture affects every aspect of emotions. Identifying which emotions are good or bad, when emotions are appropriate to be expressed, and even how they should be displayed is all influenced by culture. Even more importantly, cultures differentially affect emotions, meaning that exploring cultural contexts is key to understanding emotions. Through incorporating sociological, anthropological and psychological research account it can be concluded exploring emotions in different cultures is very complex and the current literature is equally as complex, reflecting multiple views.

Psychological trauma is a type of damage to the psyche that occurs as a result of a traumatic event. When that trauma leads to posttraumatic stress disorder, damage may involve physical changes inside the brain and to brain chemistry, which changes the person's response to future stress.

A traumatic event involves experience, or enduring or repeating events, which may overwhelm an individual's ability to cope or integrate the ideas and emotions involved with the experience. The sense of being overwhelmed can be delayed by weeks, years or even decades, as the person struggles to cope with the immediate circumstances. Psychological trauma can lead to serious long-term negative consequences that are often overlooked even by mental health professionals: 'If clinicians fail to look through a trauma lens and conceptualize client problems as related possibly to current or past trauma, they may fail to see that trauma victims, young and old, organize much of their lives around repetitive patterns of reliving and warding off traumatic memories, reminders, and affects.'

Trauma can be caused by a wide variety of events, but there are a few common aspects. There is frequently a violation of the person's familiar ideas about the world and of their human rights, putting the person in a state of extreme confusion and insecurity. This is also seen when people or institutions, depended on for survival, violate or betray or disillusion the person in some unforeseen way.

Psychological trauma may accompany physical trauma or exist independently of it. Typical causes and dangers of psychological trauma are sexual abuse, bullying, domestic violence, indoctrination, being the victim of an alcoholic parent, the threat of either, or the witnessing of either, particularly in childhood. Catastrophic events such as earthquakes and volcanic eruptions, war or other mass violence can also cause psychological trauma. Long-term exposure to situations such as extreme poverty or milder forms of abuse, such as verbal abuse, can be traumatic.

However, different people will react differently to similar events. One person may experience an event as traumatic while another person would not suffer trauma as a result of the same event. In other words, not all people who experience a potentially traumatic event will actually become psychologically traumatized.

People who go through these types of extremely traumatic experiences often have certain symptoms and problems afterward such as emotional fatigue. How severe these symptoms are depends on the person, the type of trauma involved, and the emotional support they receive from others. Reactions to and symptoms of trauma can be wide and varied, and differ in severity from person to person. A traumatized individual may experience one or several of them.

After a traumatic experience, a person may re-experience the trauma mentally and physically, hence avoiding trauma reminders, also called triggers, as this can be uncomfortable and even painful. They may turn to psychoactive substances including alcohol to try to escape the feelings. Re-experiencing symptoms are a sign that the body and mind are actively struggling to cope with the traumatic experience.

Triggers and cues act as reminders of the trauma, and can cause anxiety and other associated emotions. Often the person can be completely unaware of what these triggers are. In many cases this may lead a person suffering from traumatic disorders to engage in disruptive or self-destructive coping mechanisms, often without being fully aware of the nature or causes of their own actions. Panic attacks are an example of a psychosomatic response to such emotional triggers.

Consequently, intense feelings of anger may surface frequently, sometimes in very inappropriate or unexpected situations, as danger may always seem to be present, as much as it is actually present and experienced from past events. Upsetting memories such as images, thoughts, or flashbacks may haunt the person, and nightmares may be frequent. Insomnia may occur as lurking fears and insecurity keep the person vigilant and on the lookout for danger, both day and night.

The person may not remember what actually happened while emotions experienced during the trauma may be re-experienced without the person understanding why. This can lead to the traumatic events being constantly experienced as if they were happening in the present, preventing the subject from gaining perspective on the experience. This can produce a pattern of prolonged periods of acute arousal punctuated by periods of physical and mental exhaustion.

In time, emotional exhaustion may set in, leading to distraction, and clear thinking may be difficult or impossible. Emotional detachment, as well as dissociation or 'numbing out', can frequently occur. Dissociating from the painful emotion includes numbing all emotion, and the person may seem emotionally flat, preoccupied, distant, or cold. The person can become confused in ordinary situations and have memory problems.

Some traumatized people may feel permanently damaged when trauma symptoms do not go away and they do not believe their situation will improve. This can lead to feelings of despair, loss of self-esteem, and frequently depression. If important aspects of the person's self and world understanding have been violated, the person may call their own identity into question. Often despite their best efforts, traumatized individuals may have difficulty assisting themselves on how to live their lives on a daily basis due to emotional trauma, unable to self regulate and co-ordinate themselves; feeling of lack of contentment may set in.

My books involves wide range of catharsis is a term in dramatic art that describes 'emotional cleansing' sometimes depicted in a play as occurring for one or more of its characters, as well as the same phenomenon as (an intended) part of the audience's experience. It describes an extreme change in emotion, occurring as of result of experiencing strong feelings (such as sorrow, fear, pity, or even laughter). It has been described as a 'purification' or a 'purging' of such emotions as I have experience over the years in two different parts of the world More recently, such terms as restoration, renewal, and revitalization have been used when referencing the effect on members of the audience.

The Greek philosopher Aristotle was the first to use the term catharsis with reference to the emotions – in his work Poetics. In that context, it refers to a sensation or literary effect that, ideally, would either be experienced by the characters in a play, or be wrought upon the audience at the conclusion of a tragedy; namely, the release of pent-up emotion or energy.

Lessing sidesteps the medical aspect of the issue and focuses more specifically on the role of fecal matter in the development of the human psyche. Also, he translates catharsis as purification, an experience that brings pity and fear into their proper balance: 'in real life,' he explained, 'men are sometimes too much addicted to pity or fear, sometimes too little; tragedy brings them back to a virtuous and happy mean.' Tragedy is then a corrective; through watching tragedy, the audience learns how to feel these emotions at proper levels. Some modern interpreters of the work infer that catharsis is pleasurable, because audience members experience ecstasy (literally: astonishment, meaning: trance) or, in other words, 'relief,' ensuing from an awareness that, compared with what they have just seen portrayed, their own life is less tragic.

Any translator attempting to interpret Aristotle's meaning of the term should take into account that Poetics is largely a response to Plato's claim that poetry encourages people to be hysterical and uncontrolled. Aristotle maintains that, on the contrary, the effect of poetry is to allow people to be less controlled by emotion – not more so – by its providing a healthy outlet for their feelings.

In literary aesthetics, catharsis is developed by the conjunction of stereotyped characters and unique or surprising actions or events over time. Throughout a play, we do not expect the nature of a character to change significantly; rather, pre-existing elements are revealed in a relatively straightforward way, as the character faces these confrontations. This is clearly evident in Oedipus, where King Oedipus is confronted with ever more outrageous actions, until the catharsis/emptying generated by the death of his mother-wife, and by his own act of self-blinding.

In contemporary aesthetics, catharsis may also refer to any purging of emotion experienced by an audience, in relation to drama. The ecstasy perceived in comedy, melodrama and most other dramatic forms. I almost titled this book catharsis or abreaction.

There have been, for political or aesthetic reasons, deliberate attempts made to subvert the effect of catharsis in theatre. For example, Bertolt Brecht viewed catharsis as a pap (pablum) for the bourgeois theatre audience, and designed dramas which left significant emotions unresolved, intending to force social action upon the audience. Brecht reasoned that the absence of a cathartic resolution would require the audience to take political action in the real world, in order to fill the emotional gap they had experienced vicariously. This technique can be seen as early as his agit-prop play The Measures Taken.

In psychology, the term was first employed by Sigmund Freud's colleague Josef Breuer (1842–1925), who developed a 'cathartic' treatment for persons suffering from hysterical symptoms through the use of hypnosis. While under hypnosis, Breuer's patients were able to recall traumatic experiences, and through the process of expressing the original emotions that had been repressed and forgotten, they were relieved of their symptoms. Catharsis was also central to Freud's concept of psychoanalysis, but he replaced hypnosis with free association.

The term catharsis has also been adopted by modern psychotherapy, particularly Freudian psychoanalysis, to describe the act of expressing, or more accurately, experiencing the deep emotions often associated with events in the individual's past which had originally been repressed or ignored, and had never been adequately addressed. Modern psychological opinion is clear on the usefulness of physical non goal-fulfilling cathartic aggression in anger management. 'Blowing off steam'may reduce physiological stress in the short term, but this reduction may act as a reward mechanism, reinforcing the behaviour and promoting future outbursts.

Catharsis is also an emotional release associated with talking about the underlying causes of a problem.

Abreaction is a psychoanalytical term for reliving an experience in order to purge it of its emotional excesses; a type of catharsis. Sometimes it is a method of becoming conscious of repressed traumatic events.

Early in his career, psychoanalyst Carl Jung expressed interest in abreaction, or what he referred to as 'trauma theory', but later decided it had limitations concerning the treatment of neurosis. Jung stated that:

'Though traumata of clearly aetiological significance were occasionally present, the majority of them appeared very improbable. Many traumata were so unimportant, even so normal, that they could be regarded at most as a pretext for the neurosis. But what especially aroused my criticism was the fact that not a few traumata were simply inventions of fantasy that had never happened at all'.

Jung believed that the skill, devotion and self-confidence regarding the way the analyst did his work were much more important to the patient than the rehashing of old traumatic emotions.

Abreaction therapy is a form of psychotherapy in which abreaction is used to assist a patient suffering from post-traumatic stress disorder by re-living the experience in a controlled environment. Hypnosis is often used as a tool for recall in abreaction therapy.

This book makes the statement that thought, action and feeling can occur in any order, it also puts forth ideas life is divided into three groups, emotion, thinking, and feeling. These three groups make humans feel in certain ways; thinking, physical stimulus, and emotion which all contribute to feelings. What are the difference between a thought, emotions, and a feeling? Is there an overlap between the three? Probably, since any emotion can be broken down into the sensations and real events that had caused it, the events lead to all sorts of emotions, feelings and thoughts.

So emotions, feelings and thoughts might all have the same source, they are just expressed differently in the mind. Where do your emotions, feelings and thoughts rate on a scale of clarity about this book? Where do they rate on a scale of focus, attention, growing up, within divers' culture in some cases, unrest, fear, uncertainties are involved, you might even be afraid for your life or those of your parents? How does understanding the psychology of emotions, feelings and thoughts related to children not only a child living in Africa and within the UK from African, Caribbean or Jamaican background coincides in different ways.

Are they shying away from it, showing interest or they do not care or it should all be done away with how does it apply to our consciousness? Moreover powers of juju are customary used for negative purposes. I would prefer a native doctor dose juju for people to become clever or intelligence when this is done their customers might not do things to bring them misfortune through forces of the underworld they have bent to be sublime in carrying out their wish after what they have asked for and not, disruptive to other peoples and not caging the world under such forces amidst such arenas of politics, sociology and social wellbeing can be disturbed.

The whole content of my books are experience and memories of a paranoid schizophrenia how I go through life with these experiences is another expect of my life. The resilient it takes to manage my experience added to my courage and wiliness to have written this book. Read part three of this book as a continuation of this book.

80% of the wrong things and situation parents initiate are not always wrong in the eyes of their children they may consider it wrong, in their consciousness because, they go through their own phase of experiences in life they are pressed to pursue if they consider or take into their heart the wrong done. Even to an extent of murder a child would consider their parents or family member should leave a court with less sentence in due of this situation what could be said to be the right disposition or relationship within parents and their children considering also children under their parent care should do what their parents tell them to do within a family upbringing were their is love and there could be hat.

People with paranoid personality disorder (PPD) have long-term, widespread and unwarranted suspicions that other people are hostile, threatening or demeaning. These beliefs are steadfastly maintained in the absence of any real supporting evidence. The disorder, whose name comes from the Greek word for 'madness,' is one of ten personality disorders described in the 2000 edition of the *Diagnostic and Statistical Manual of Mental Disorders* , (the fourth edition, text revision or *DSM-IVTR*), the standard guidebook used by mental health professionals to diagnose mental disorders. Despite the pervasive suspicions they have of others, patients with PPD are not delusional (except in rare, brief instances brought on by stress). Most of the time, they are in touch with reality, except for their interpretation of others' motives and intentions. PPD patients are not psychotic but their conviction that others are trying to 'get them' or humiliate them in some way often leads to hostility and social isolation.

People with PPD do not trust other people. In fact, the central characteristic of people with PPD is a high degree of mistrustfulness and suspicion when interacting with others. Even friendly gestures are often interpreted as being manipulative or malevolent. Whether the patterns of distrust and suspicion begin in childhood or in early adulthood, they quickly come to dominate the lives of those suffering from PPD. Such people are unable or afraid to form close relationships with others.

They suspect strangers, and even people they know even relatives, of planning to harm or exploit them. As a result of their constant concern about the lack of trustworthiness of others, patients with this disorder often have few intimate friends or close human contacts. Interactions with others are characterized by wariness and not infrequently by hostility.

Despite all the unpleasant aspects of a paranoid lifestyle, however, it is still not sufficient to drive many people with PPD to seek therapy since they would have become socially withdrawn. They do not usually walk into a therapist's office on their own with feeling those who might accompany them would exploit them. Before its advent I wrote to my health centre about taking therapies in art, music to shear me up out of my reveries during certain relapse to my feelings when the time came it was all set up by my mental health centre to undertake such initiatives, I applied and then withdraw why? May be am confused about other people or my community or what other people think of me. They distrust mental health care providers just as they distrust nearly everyone else. If a life crisis, a family member or the judicial system succeeds in getting a patient with PPD to seek help, therapy is often a challenge. Individual counselling seems to work best but it requires a great deal of patience and skill on the patient including resilience partly because sufferers feel people do not trust them. It is not unusual for patients to leave therapy when they perceive some malicious intent on the part of the therapist's or anyone caring for them. If the patient can be persuaded to cooperate something that is not easy to achieve low-dose medications are recommended for treating such specific problems as anxiety, but only for limited periods of time the patent can well explain why, if they are given the right opportunities being given the right opportunity in my terminology is the patient choosing their cares. Having the choice to choose who should care for them removes all strings of stigmas attached to mental illness because within a patents family he or she could be stigmatized by a relative.

Lots of authors on related issues of mental illness imply as if their massage is directed to some particular groups or culture earth is vast lots of people from different countries, race, and ethnic origin dwell in Europe their massage should be clear, open and precise people from all culture and race, go through different emotions and temperaments which are often being overlooked. It's no avoidant people who are viewed with stigmas because of their illness would feel even with a written massage that they are, being told off. It's no different from how people in care homes might feel if they are not being cared for properly, some of them have to sell their properties because of care, go through inheritance emotional state. Yet most of us have no idea what drives people into assisted suicide. Some of them are worried about paying their bills if they have a property.

If a mental health care provider is able to gain the trust of a patient with PPD, it may be possible to help the patient deal with the threats that they perceive. The disorder, however, usually lasts a lifetime. The UK compiles the largest number of people who live in not fear but worried life. You live in Britain and just worry all day long may be because you and I are not egocentric know about the problem we face an egocentric individual does not reflect in the lifestyle of Britain.

No one knows what causes paranoid personality disorder, although there are hints that familial factors may influence the development of the disorder in some cases. There seem to be more cases of PPD in families in which there are no cohesion leading to psychotic disorders as schizophrenia or delusional disorder.

Other possible interpersonal causes have been proposed. For example, some therapists believe that the behaviour that characterizes PPD might be learned. They suggest that such behaviour might be traced but it fluctuates in relation to lots of factors and circumstance. According to this view, children who are exposed to life experience they cannot interpret might not be able to control their emotions, paranoia and gifting in some cases it is predicted outbursts to certain situation are because, there are no way to escape or control their paranoia or delusion or able to make an effort to cope with their stress. PPD would emerge when this type of thinking becomes part of the individual's personality as adulthood approaches.

A core symptom of PPD is a generalized distrust of other people. Comments and actions that healthy people would not notice come across as full of insults and threats to someone with the disorder. Yet, generally, patients with PPD remain in touch with reality; they don't have any of the hallucinations or delusions seen in patients with psychoses. Nevertheless, their suspicions that others are intent on harming or exploiting them are so pervasive and intense that people with PPD often become very isolated. They avoid normal social interactions. And because they feel so insecure in what is a very threatening world for them, patients with PPD are capable of becoming violent. Innocuous comments, harmless jokes and other day-to-day communications are often perceived as insults.

Paranoid suspicions carry over into all realms of life. Those burdened with PPD are frequently convinced that their sexual partners are unfaithful. They may misinterpret compliments offered by employers or co-workers as hidden criticisms or attempts to get them to work harder. Complimenting a person with PPD on their clothing or car, for example, could easily be taken as an attack on their materialism or selfishness.

Because they persistently question the motivations and trustworthiness of others, patients with PPD are not inclined to share intimacies. They fear such information might be used against them. As a result, they become hostile and unfriendly, argumentative or aloof. Their unpleasantness often draws negative responses from those around them. These rebuffs become 'proof' in the patient's mind that others are, indeed, hostile to them. They have little insight into the effects of their attitude and behaviour on their generally unsuccessful interactions with others. Asked if they might be responsible for negative interactions that fill their lives, people with PPD are likely to place all the blame on certain expects of life or what the world has made of them such as making a journey to eternity, destiny is always in a child before, they are born we don't just say goodbye to our existence. They feel most people are less aware of such disposition especially their family members or cares and others. I know of people from my background who would do anything to hypo personalize themselves it's what we do back home in Europe within time of getting familiar with the place of having their stay through immigration, they begin to hypo personalize themselves and with what? While am depressed about certain issues such about upbringing, background and assimilation. Life experiences stays with all realistic humans probably even creatures; we can make changes to assimilate ourselves in life into more appropriate disposition. It is what everybody wants food, shelter; clothing good roads and schools are considerate to have in all parts of the world

What leads to emotional, behavioural and psychiatric disorders that could affect adulthood varies within each community, nation, society and its norms. This can cause stress reaction, which affects the way they thinks, feels and behave.

Individuals react in different ways to events one for example one may find it difficult to sleep and have bad dreams or nightmares. Become preoccupied with thoughts and memories of the event wondering why it had occurred

Sometimes feeling of depression and anxiety goes on for several weeks and may get worse. Flashbacks' of the event, for a few moments, it seems as though you are re-living the experience in your mind, which can be distressing and frightening.

The best approach, immediately after a traumatic event, is to accept that a child will be distressed - this is normal. At this stage, parents can help greatly by letting their child talk about the event if they want to, or helping them to relive it in games and drawings.

Leaving children alone 'to forget things' does not help talking, can help children to adjust. It helps them to make sense of what has happened, to feel less alone with their worries and to regain a sense of control. However, forcing someone to talk about it, when they don't want to, does not seem to be helpful.

Adults commonly tell young people that the teenage years are the 'best years of your life.' The rosy remembrance highlights happy groups of high school students energetically involved at a dance or sporting event, and a bright-eyed couple holding hands or sipping sodas at a local restaurant. This is only part of the picture. Life for many young people is a painful tug of war filled with mixed messages and conflicting demands from parents, teachers, coaches, employers, friends and oneself. Growing up negotiating a path between independence and reliance on others is a tough business. It creates stress; it can create serious depression depending on circumstances.

Young people become stressed for many reasons. Break up with boy/girl friend, increased arguments with parents whilst I was in Africa with my parent there wasn't at anytime I had an augment with any of my parents or thought of doing so. Or with my brothers or sisters in my age of within 9 and 11 years, there where increased arguments between my father and step mothers, thoughts of facing my parents' financial status considering it would bring us happiness.

It is important not to overreact to isolated incidents. Young people will have problems and will learn, at their own rate, to struggle and deal with them. But it is critical for parents and helping adults to be aware of the factors that put a youth at particular risk, especially when stressful events begin to accumulate.

A child's commitment and stress levels are often controlled by a parent or other influential adult. Children typically welcome such events as birthday parties, field trips, and organized activities, and may not recognize overload.

If I grow up under stress without being able to control myself in time, if I react people might begin to think I am misbehaving. The level of approach by parents, teachers, and family members differs across nation in considering such matters depending of the social context.

Some children will express their feelings directly. Others, however, may internalize stress and show it through sadness, depression, or withdrawal. Still others exhibit feelings of stress outwardly and might be said to begin to misbehave.

Stress is a part of growing up, but adults need to keep a watchful eye on children and intervene when they sense something is undermining a child's physical or psychological well-being. The child develops physical symptoms, such as headaches and stomach pains. The child seems restless, tired, and agitated. The child appears depressed and will not communicate how he or she feels. The child seems less interested in an activity that was once very important to him or her. The child's grades begin to fall, and he or she has less interest than usual in attending classes or doing homework. The child exhibits antisocial behaviour, afterwards comes lying or stealing, depending on the type of people they go out with forgets or refuses to do chores, and seems more dependent on themselves than anyone else and it does not necessary have to be a child it could be an adult sometimes, this things starts from childhood and goes on when they are adults. Parents, cares and family members should not fail to notice critical changes in behaviour. Not all backgrounds use some or the same approach in some part of the world, you do not even have a second glance nobody cares to take notice or you may only care not to come out with your feelings because you will have no food in your stomach.

Well-meaning parents and adults can sometimes be the cause of children's being overcommitted at too early an age. If you suspect a child is suffering from stress, evaluate the child's situation or activities, and work with the child to identify solutions. Children are not developmentally able to handle adult-level stress. Because they cannot think or feel the same ways adults do, it is the adult's responsibility to help keep children from becoming stressed and overloaded.

Another major factor that causes stress at adulthood is family problems where a wife or husbands constantly have quibbles. There have only been increases in these domestic problems and they have not only caused stress but they have brought bodily harm and even death. There are many signs that inform me of stress at adulthood the signs inform me when the stress is beginning and if not treated it leads to something else e.g. fatigue. Therefore, as an adult, I need to focus on myself for a while and know what exactly is causing my stress.

Adolescence is a stressful time involving physical, hormonal and intellectual changes. Stresses include identity, sexuality, separation from parents and independence which are risk factor for developing depression. Parents may not recognize depression in adolescents, viewing withdrawal from the family as a 'normal' part of being a teenager. However, parents should watch closely for confusing signs between teenage rebellion and clinical depression.

Greater childhood adversity, higher levels of negative life events and marital stress earlier in adulthood are associated with my depression for which I accustom myself with a prayer from *Psalm 51*.

Biological psychology the study of biological substrates of behaviour and mental processes underlie specific behaviours such as learning and memory and fear responses. Clinical psychology the study and application of psychology for the purpose of understanding, preventing, and relieving psychologically-based distress and promote subjective well-being and personal development. various therapeutic approaches and practices are associated with different theoretical perspectives and employ different procedures intended to form a therapeutic alliance, explore the nature of psychological problems, and encourage new ways of thinking, feeling, or behaving. Four major theoretical perspectives are psychodynamic, cognitive behavioural, existential humanistic, and systems or family therapy.

Cognitive psychology studies cognition, the mental processes underlying mental activity. Perception, attention, reasoning, thinking, problem solving, memory, learning, language and emotion are areas of research.

Comparative psychology refers to the study of the behaviour and mental life of human beings. It is related to disciplines outside of psychology that study animal behaviour such as ethology. Field of psychology is primarily concerned with humans, the behaviour and mental processes of animals is also an important part of psychological research with strong emphasis about evolutionary links, and somewhat more controversially, as a way of gaining an insight into human psychology. This is achieved by means of comparison of emotional and behavioural systems.

Mainly focusing on the development of the human mind through life span, developmental psychology seeks to understand how people come to perceive, understand, and act within the world and how these processes change as they age. This may focus on cognitive, affective, moral, social, or neural development. Researchers who study children use a number of unique research methods to make observations in natural settings or to engage them in experimental tasks. Such tasks often resemble specially designed games and activities that are both enjoyable for the child and scientifically useful. They are constantly devising clever methods to study the mental processes of small infants. In addition to studying children, developmental psychologists also study aging and processes throughout life span, especially at other times of rapid change such as adolescence and old age. Developmental psychologists draw on full range of psychological theories that conform to human experience relating to stress or emotional issues.

Evolutionary psychology examines psychological traits—such as memory, perception, or language—from a modern evolutionary perspective. It seeks to identify which human psychological traits are evolved adaptations, that is, the functional products of natural selection or sexual selection. Evolutionary psychologists suggest that psychological adaptations evolved to solve recurrent problems in human ancestral environments.

Personality psychology is concerned to enduring patterns of behaviour, thought, and emotion in individuals, commonly referred to as personality. Theories of personality vary across different psychological schools and orientations. They carry different assumptions about such issues as the role of the unconscious and the importance of childhood experience.

Social psychology is the study of how humans think about each other and how they relate to each other. Social psychologists study such topics as the influence of others on an individual's behaviour (e.g. conformity, persuasion), and the formation of beliefs, attitudes, and stereotypes about other people. Social cognition fuses elements of social and cognitive psychology in order to understand how people process, remember, reveals information about the nature and potential optimization of leadership, communication, and other phenomena that emerge at least at the <u>micro social</u> level. In recent years, many social psychologists have become increasingly interested in <u>implicit</u> measures, mediation models, and interaction of both person and social variables in accounting for behaviour. The study of human society is therefore a potentially valuable source of information about the causes of psychiatric disorder. Some of the sociological concepts applied to psychiatric disorders are the social role, sick role, social class, life event, culture, social and total institution.

I had this inclination to think whilst watching on television a documentary on tiger poachers while watching the poacher's activities the camera zoomed on one of the tigers beautiful and agile with its eyes blazing it seems as if, the tiger cut an eye towards me and twitched with an exaggerated expression of seriousness directed at me by way of expressing the gravity of the issues at hand. I heard a voice, it was as if it was the voices of the tiger saying to me he had been cut right handed or I have been cut right handed said the tiger I the viewer should not be disturbed and told me that he had been feeding among the heads of creature but he had been cut the tiger complained about the poachers in view, that when they are cut in the wild it is their turn to face the brunt. They are then reaped off of their hides what do the poachers' do with them they are sold to the wealthy in my community. Then I had this chilling feeling and liking for the tiger when he cut an eye towards me again and smiled at me before he moved off all of a sudden the camera captured as it zoomed cut a tiger cub. I was supposed to donate £3.00 a month to adopt a tiger. The use of some animal hides like tigers, leopards and lions are used for jujus, possession, witchcraft they cause hallucination, phobias and paranoia in some mental health case depending on the environment and its culture.

The camera on this documentary Zooming at the cub again I had a chilling feeling the cub looked at me in liking with a coining smile on its face this, is what his happening out here I heard the voice of the cub said and one day, I would be like the other one I had just seen cut on camera I would face the same future and I heard the tiger asked me what is happening out there within civilisation? With a question look and gesture in the way it moved its head sideways steering at me with a look of liking as if, it was giving a shy smile. I looked at the tiger cub in liking in return then it came to my mind in answer as to what was happening not just in my community but around the world it's no different the situation is left, for those who could make a difference.

Things happen in all working environments while walking along the road or street it is customary for people to give you impression or make gestures of what they think or feel about you. It could make one have impressions or make gestures of making one feel something is out of order or in order; to some extent make one do something they should do and certain things, they should not do.

Positive psychology is a discipline that utilizes evidence-based scientific methods to study factors that contribute to human <u>happiness</u> and strength. Positive psychology is concerned with improving the mental well-being of people.

Psychology tends to be <u>eclectic</u>, drawing on knowledge from other fields to help explain and understand psychological phenomena.

Psychology studies developmental trends across life span, in <u>sociology</u> life events throughout lifetimes or generation or as a result of cultural differences across generations.

Because some areas of psychology rely on research methods such as surveys and <u>questionnaires</u>, critics have asserted that psychology is not an objective science. Other phenomena that psychologists are interested in, such as <u>personality</u>, <u>thinking</u>, and <u>emotion</u>, cannot be directly measured some of which lead to mental health and are often inferred from subjective self-reports.

No feeling is permanent. There are constant movement between positive and negative feelings. Emotions are constantly changing, in part because feelings change, and in part due to the constant stream of ideas that flow in the unconscious mind. At the conscious and subconscious levels of mind we can focus on an unconscious idea and use it to pursue trend about something that interests us. In doing so, we can make our emotion last whilst we follow that trend.

The difference between the flow of ideas at the conscious and subconscious levels is mainly related to the issue of change. The conscious flow is easy to change, especially when we are in social company, but the subconscious flow seems to have a life of its own and is highly resistant to conscious attempts to change it. In social company or if we are idealistic we can give preference to our conscious ideas, and hence control our conscious emotional response. But on our own, without the influence of idealism, the subconscious mind usually exerts priority in emotional response. If the conscious mind is not dominant, that is, if we do not value what we are doing at any particular moment, then the subconscious mind is dominant and so we may become subject to uncontrollable moods.

Emotions can be grouped into complementary pairs such as anger and fear and then love and hate or vanity and self-pity. What determines the choice of either emotion in a pair? What governs a person, at a particular moment could be either anger or fear as their response to something. The choice might revolves around dominating influence of value.

We put a value on emotional experience either liking or disliking things, relationships, situations. For example, the way we think may appeal to us, may lead us to choose between love and anger or vanity as our response. Anger allows us to dominate the situation; love enables us to harmonise with other people; vanity lets us feel important. The way that we dislike may focus on fear, hate or self-pity.

At any particular moment we may be focusing on a trend of thought, with a relevant emotion being experienced. Then there is some change in the situation that needs an emotional response from us. Sometimes we can consciously choose our response, particularly if the situation is a pleasant one. But more often than not we act subconsciously. The value we place on situation determines which emotion we display. If we are feeling discontented, we will place little positive value on the experience.

As well as putting value on our situations, we also put value on our thoughts and ideas unconscious idea has two values either good or bad. Good values are supported by pleasant feeling, bad value by the unpleasant feeling. This might lead to choices. We may let our emotions be positive or negative according to whether the feeling is positive or negative.

Otherwise, by placing value on our experience, we can generate positive or negative emotions as we choose. Positive emotion is often difficult if the feeling is negative or if stress is involved.

A personal or cultural value' is an absolute or relative ethical value, basis for which there can be ethical action. Individuals and cultures and are in many ways aligned with belief systems.

Values are preferences concerning appropriate courses of action or outcomes. As such, values reflect a person's sense of right and wrong or what 'ought' to be. 'Equal rights for all', 'Excellence deserves admiration', and 'People should be treated with respect and dignity' are representative of values. Values tend to influence attitudes and behaviour if we value equal rights for all, go to work for an organization that treats its managers much better than it does its workers, we may form attitudes the company is an unfair place to work; we may not produce well or may perhaps leave the company. It is likely if the company has good policies, our attitude and behaviours would be positive.

Personal Values provide an internal reference for what is good, beneficial, important, useful, beautiful, desirable, constructive values generate behaviour and help solve common human problems for survival by comparative rankings of value, the results of which provide answers to questions of why people do what they do and in what order they choose to do them.

Over time the public expression of personal values groups of people find important in their day-to-day lives lay foundations of law, custom and tradition. Personal Values in this way exist in relation to cultural values, either in agreement with or divergent from prevailing norms. A culture is a social system that shares a set of common values, in which such values permit social expectations and collective understandings of the good, beautiful, constructive. Without normative personal values, there would be no cultural reference against which to measure the virtue of individual values and so culture identity would disintegrate.

Values are obtained in a lot of different ways. The most important piece for building values is a person's family. The family is responsible for teaching children what is right and wrong long before there are other influences. There is a theme of saying that, a child is a reflection of their parents. As a child starts school, school helps some to shape the values of children. Then there is religion that the family introduces to a child that plays a role in teaching right and wrong behaviours'.

Values are related to the norms of a culture, but they are more global and abstract than norms. Norms are rules for behaviour in specific situations, while values identify what should be judged as good or evil. Flying the national flag on a holiday is a norm it reflects the value of patriotism. Wearing dark clothing and appearing solemn are normative behaviours at a funeral. In certain cultures they reflect the values of respect and support of friends and family. Different cultures reflect different values.

Do I have choices based on my identity, yet every choice I make determines who I am. Identities I construct yields decisions, attitudes, and actions that are pieces of my life, which fit together intricately to create a beautiful mosaic that is me. What should be my picture reveal I could be proactive or allow others to take me along for the ride? It is easy to figure out who you are, you are who you create yourself to be, who you become. Every decision you make contributes a piece to the art of your existence. Search endlessly to find who you are, and your masterpiece will be filled with longing, existential angst, wandering, and aimlessness. Decide to create a better you, to design yourself around your desires, priorities, beliefs, and gifting and you will see the masterpiece that is meant to be.

By choosing to act in alignment with your core self and follow what path you have chosen, you are already making changes. You may not be who you will become, but you are not who you once were. If you find your identity in others, your self-esteem and sense of worth will be dependent on their choices and leadings. If instead you recognize that you are an original, act like it.

To construct a masterpiece work of art, there are defining lines and shadows. Without the contrast, the beauty and starkness of the image is lost. Contrast allows for the vivid colors to stand out as beautiful as the designer intended. Dark shadows, like hard times, can color a portion of our journey. Will you allow your dark shadows to define you, or will you rise above and make the statement you were intended to contribute to the world.

Why can't we do this in life? Get comfort, take courage, and then try again. Instead, we are often confused on how to handle life? Do you structure your identity around hurts or blows, or do you move on despite your past? You are not defined by what happens to you, but by how you respond to the happenings of life.

If my life were an open book, would people care to read it considering belief system sway with the wind? Am I manipulated by motivational speeches from fast-talkers with empty, shallow promises that do not deliver but often cost money? Do I think my identity depends on my career or other prospects? Do my life's journey correspond to a map, or do I know where I am or where am heading?

Knowing your personality and gifting can help one understand areas for change, and can help us feel proud of who God made us to be. If you have never taken a personality profile test, they can be fun to try, Remember, be honest about it how this identity manifests itself in actions could be based on priorities, interests, hobbies, talents, and gifting, influence and initiative, coping skills and relationships.

You may leave your results in sentence or list form, rewrite it into a poem, create a collage of words (like a tag cloud of your life) or images to represent you, or even create an audio or video recording as a keepsake for loved ones to cherish. Be proud of who you are, and if you are not, then become who you can be proud of.

I am a fighter. I have made it through significant trauma in childhood, I have overcome a life-threatening disorder, and I have changed how I perceive the world and myself to live confident in who, I am and why I am here. My canvas is covered with beautiful vibrant colors, and an emerging pattern that I can only describe as uniquely me. I know God is my guiding compass, and the Bible is my map. In knowing who I am, I also know what I need to change.

People are afraid of themselves, of their own reality; their feelings most of all. People talk about how great love is, not everybody feels the same way, not every one of us has felt love some of us have never been loved therefore cannot describe love. Love has different meaning to every one of us in different ways sometimes we say we love but it's not love. It is a feeling that comes with emotions without emotion it's not love. When love hurts the feeling could be disturbing. People are taught that pain is evil and dangerous. It becomes difficult dealing with love if they're afraid to feel pain. Some people say pain is meant to wake us up that's if a person understands pain some people cannot stand pain how can, when, there is love. People try to hide their pain. But they're wrong hiding pain causes more distress. Pain is not something to carry forward each and every one of us wants to do away with our pain because, we want peace or, we rather want to be loved. You feel your strength in the experience of pain. It's all in how you carry it. That's what matters. Pain is a feeling. Your feelings are a part of you your own reality. If you feel ashamed of them, and hide them, you're letting society destroy your reality. You should stand up for your right to feel and shear your pain.

London Mayor Boris Johnson paid tribute to Prime Minister David Cameron, praising his 'firm leadership' and ability to take 'tough decisions'.

Mr. Johnson began his speech by gazing out into the audience and saying: 'Where is Dave?' Having spotted the prime minister, the London mayor wished him a happy birthday and backed his strategy to 'turn the country round'. Mr. Johnson has had a hero's welcome from Tory activists in Birmingham. But denied, trying to upstage the PM, who gave his big speech that Wednesday. Mr. Johnson, who was riding high after the London Olympics and his re-election, said Britain had a 'chronic tendency to underestimate what they can do'. The London games, he added, showed 'we are a can-do country, a creative, confident can-do country'.

In an upbeat speech - packed with jokes and digressions - he talked up what he sees as his main achievements as mayor, paid tribute to some of the politicians, including Sir John Major and Labour figures such as Tony Blair and Ken Livingstone, who had contributed to making the Olympics a success. He joked that his defeated rival for the mayoralty, Mr. Livingstone, was now well and truly 'finished' after receiving a round of applause at a Tory conference. He joked that Mr. Cameron had called him a 'blond-haired mop' in the Daily Telegraph, adding: 'If I'm a mop then you are a broom, a broom that is cleaning up the mess left by the Labour government and a fantastic job you are doing.

'And I thank you and I congratulate you and your colleagues George Osborne, the dustpan, Michael Gove, the jey cloth, William Hague, the sponge. 'Because it is the historic function of Conservative governments over the last hundred years to be the household implements, so effective on the floor of the house to clear things up after the Labour binge has got out of control.' Mr. Cameron laughed along with Mr. Johnson, the man seen as a potential future leadership rival, even when the mayor, a classical scholar, ribbed him about claiming to not know the meaning of Magna Carta. The mayor ended his speech with a rallying cry to Tory activists, who gave him a standing ovation. He said: 'We fought to keep London from lurching back into the grip of a Marxist cabal of taxpayer-funded chateauneuf du pape-swilling tax minimisers and bendy bus fetishist.

'I will fight to keep this country from lurching back into the grip of the two Eds, Miliband and Balls. Unreformed, unpunished, unrepentant about what they did to the economy and the deficit they racked up.

'We need to go forward now from the age of excess under Labour. 'Through the age of austerity to a new age of enterprise in which we do what we did in the Olympics and build a world-beating platform for Britain for British people and businesses to compete.' Mr. Johnson later told the BBC Radio 4's World At One programme he would welcome the 'spotlight' moving on from talk about his future plans, speculation which he described as 'tired and hackneyed'. Asked about the furore surrounding Mr. Johnson at the conference, Tory donor and strategist Lord Ashcroft said the mayor of London was 'doing a great job' and part of his appeal was that 'he is a comedian'.

But he said talk about Mr. Johnson as a future leader was media-driven and not 'relevant' to the party's primary goal of winning a majority at the next election.

'Those are long-term matters. If he ever had those ambitions, he has to get to Parliament, there has to be a leadership contest... you are talking a long timescale even if it is hypothetically possible.'

Mr. Cameron has insisted he does not envy Mr. Johnson's 'rock star' status, and says he accepts other people will be more popular than him while he is prime minister in difficult times for the country. Asked on BBC Radio 4's Today programme what Mr. Johnson could get him for his birthday, which he is celebrating on Tuesday, Mr. Cameron said: 'He's giving me a relatively light day, which is good of him.

'The point is, we are lucky in the Conservative Party to have some big and popular figures to take the message out across the country as well as having someone who is a first class Mayor of London.'

Asked if Mr. Johnson could be sent abroad to do something following his time as mayor, Mr. Cameron quipped: 'I'm not sure which country deserves him the most, but I will take that one away and think about it.'

An opinion poll for The Observer gave Boris Johnson a net +30 rating among voters, compared with -21 for the prime minister. London mayor Boris Johnson pledged his loyalty to the prime minister, saying no one should 'doubt my admiration for David Cameron'. The London mayor was greeted with a standing ovation as he made his first appearance at the Tory conference.

He hailed the London Olympics and hit back at claims he is out to get the better of the prime minister during the week of the conference.

He later announced that members of the armed forces in uniform will be given free London Underground travel.

The mayor's appearance at the Conservative Home fringe meeting - entitled 'Boris 2012: Re-elected and Olympotastic' - was preceded by a promotional film entitled 'Mission Imborrisible', featuring, among other things, footage of the London mayor trapped on a zip wire at an Olympic event in East London.

In a speech packed with self-deprecating jokes about previous conference appearances, when he was pelted with pork pies by journalists after criticising Jamie Oliver and mocked by 'Austrian cyborg' Arnold Schwarzenegger via a video link, he spoke of his pride at London's successful hosting of the Olympic games.

But he also made a point of praising David Cameron, saying he had been among the handful of Conservative MPs to back Mr. Cameron in 2005 when he was considering a leadership bid.

Banging the table for emphasis, Mr. Johnson said despite his occasional criticism of government policy, such as on Heathrow, 'no one should have cause to doubt his admiration for David Cameron'.

He said Mr. Cameron was doing a good job 'in tough circumstances' and 'doing absolutely what is needed to clear up the mess Labour left'.

In answer to questions from the audience, he voiced his support for 'selective' education and grammar schools and called for more action to help middle income people who could not afford to get on the property ladder.

'Conservative governments get elected when they build enough homes for people to live in,' he told the meeting.

At a second fringe meeting, Mr. Johnson announced that members of the armed forces in uniform will get free Tube travel as a thank you for their role in protecting London during the Olympics.

He was earlier mobbed by the media as he arrived in Birmingham, with onlookers chanting 'Boris! Boris!' as he battled through ranks of photographers to leave New Street station.

Asked if he was out to upstage David Cameron he said: 'I'm here to support the party.'

Rumours that Mr. Johnson will use his week in Birmingham to prepare the ground for a future Tory leadership challenge was dismissed by veteran Cabinet minister Ken Clarke.

A society, or a human society, is a group of people related to each other through persistent relations, or a large social grouping sharing the same geographical or virtual territory, subject to the same political authority and dominant cultural expectations. Human societies are characterized by patterns of relationships (social relations) between individuals who share a distinctive culture and institutions; a given society may be described as the sum total of such relationships among its constituent members. In the social sciences, a larger society often evinces stratification and/or dominance patterns in subgroups.

Insofar as it is collaborative, a society can enable its members to benefit in ways that would not otherwise be possible on an individual basis; both individual and social (common) benefits can thus be distinguished, or in many cases found to overlap.

A society can also consist of like-minded people governed by their own norms and values within a dominant, larger society. This is sometimes referred to as a subculture, a term used extensively within criminology.

More broadly, a society may be described as an economic, social, or industrial infrastructure, made up of a varied collection of individuals. Members of a society may be from different ethnic groups. A society can be a particular ethnic group, such as the Saxons; a nation state, such as Bhutan; or a broader cultural group, such as a Western society. The word *society* may also refer to an organized voluntary association of people for religious, benevolent, cultural, scientific, political, patriotic, or other purposes. A 'society' may even, though more by means of metaphor, refer to a social organism such as an ant colony or any cooperative aggregate such as, for example, in some formulations of artificial intelligence such as a film titled all about Eve.

Aspiring actress Eve Harrington manoeuvres her way into the lives of Broadway star Margo Channing, playwright Lloyd Richards and director Bill Sampson. This classic story of ambition and betrayal has become part of American folklore. Bette Davis claims to have based her character on the persona of film actress Talullah Bankhead. Davis' line 'Fasten your seatbelts, it's going to be a bumpy night' is legendary, but, in fact, the film's entire dialog sparkles with equal brilliance written by Jeanne Baker.

Acting is the work of an actor or actress, which is a person in theatre, television, film, or any other storytelling medium who tells the story by portraying   characters Acting requires a wide range of skills, including vocal projection, clarity of speech, physical expressivity, emotional facility, a well-developed imagination, and the ability to interpret drama. Acting also often demands an ability to employ dialects, accents and body language, improvisation, observation and emulation, I observe some stage combat in this film and a sense of strong emotion is also involved one thing that came to mind on my watching the film was that good thing they do not use juju in Europe or they would have used magic portion against themselves the film was packed filled with expression that were heartfelt. All about Eve and The Shepherd of the Hills were test on self actualisation, perception and reasoning.

All About Eve is simply the perfect film. Fact follows fiction in the casting of Bette Davis, a star who was an incredible actress but fighting the inevitable - the passage of time. First off, Better Davis was always an incredible actress, no matter what part she took and this was the perfect part for her. Anne Baxter is tremendous in the part of Eve - she plays the part well. It's multi-faceted and challenging and she definitely rose to the challenge. Celeste Holm is great, too. She's got a smaller part but does a great job with it. Celeste Holm is an actress who has incredible stature, even in the later years of her career, like when she was in that televisions show 'Promised Land.' But Addison DeWitt - takes the cake. I can see why he won the Oscar. I don't want to say much about the story. The film is one that has to be taken in as a whole to be truly appreciated. I enjoyed it - it's as tasty as honey! One thing - please never let them make a re-make of this film - it's perfect. It's off limits. It would be painting a new version of the Mona Lisa. This one is perfect!

The Shepherd of the Hills is a book written in 1907 by author <u>Harold Bell Wright</u>. It depicts a mostly <u>fictional</u> story of mountain <u>folklore</u> and has been translated into seven languages since its release. It is also a good film I enjoyed it Human nature refers to the distinguishing characteristics, including ways of <u>thinking</u>, <u>feeling</u> and <u>acting</u>, that <u>humans</u> tend to have <u>naturally</u>, i.e. independently of the influence of <u>culture</u>. The questions of what these characteristics are, what causes them, and how fixed human nature is, are amongst the oldest and most important questions in <u>western philosophy</u>. These questions have particularly important implications in <u>ethics</u>, <u>politics</u>, and <u>theology</u>. This is partly because human nature can be regarded as both a source of norms of conduct or ways of life, as well as presenting obstacles or constraints on living a good life. The complex implications of such questions are also dealt with in <u>art</u> and <u>literature</u>, while the multiple branches of the <u>Humanities</u> together form an important domain of inquiry into human nature, and the question of what it means to be human.

One of the defining changes occurring at the end of the Middle Ages is the end of the dominance of Aristotelian philosophy, and its replacement by a new approach to the study of nature, including human nature. In the approach, all attempts at conjecture about formal and <u>final causes</u> were rejected as useless speculation. Also, the term 'law of nature' now applies any regular and predictable pattern in nature, not literally a law made by a divine law-maker, and in the same way 'human nature' becomes not a special metaphysical cause, but simply whatever can be said to be typical tendencies of humans.

For the Socratics, human natures, and all natures, are metaphysical concepts. Aristotle developed the standard presentation of this approach with his theory of four causes. Human nature is an example of a formal cause according to Aristotle. Their teleological concept of nature is associated with humans having a divine component in their psyches, which is most properly exercised in the lifestyle of the philosopher, which is thereby also the happiest and least painful life.

Since human behaviour is so diverse, it can be difficult to find absolutely invariant human behaviours that are of interest to philosophers. A lesser (but still scientifically valid) standard for evidence pertaining to 'human nature' is used by scientists who study behaviour. Biologists look for evidence of genetic predisposition to behavioural patterns. Human behaviour can be influenced by the environment, so penetrance of genetically predisposed behavioural traits is not expected to reach 100%. A type of human behaviour for which there is a strong genetic predisposition can be considered to be part of human nature. In other words, human nature is not seen as something that forces individuals to behave in a certain way, but as something that makes individuals more inclined to act in a certain way than in another.

Common sense is defined by Merriam-Webster as, 'sound and prudent judgment based on a simple perception of the situation or facts.' Thus, 'common sense' (in this view) equates to the knowledge and experience which most people already have, or which the person using the term believes that they do or should have. The Cambridge Dictionary defines it as, 'the basic level of practical knowledge and judgment that we all need to help us live in a reasonable and safe way' According to Aristotle, the common sense (Sensus communis) is an actual power of inner sensation.

Common knowledge is <u>knowledge</u> that is known by everyone or nearly everyone, usually with reference to the <u>community</u> in which the term is used. Common knowledge need not concern one specific subject, e.g., <u>science</u> or <u>history</u>. Rather, common knowledge can be about a broad range of subjects, including science, literature, history, entertainment etc. Often, common knowledge does not need to be <u>cited</u>. Common knowledge is distinct from <u>general knowledge</u>

Consensus reality is that which is generally agreed to be <u>reality</u>, based on a consensus view.

The difficulty with the question stems from the concern that human beings do not in fact fully understand or agree upon the nature of <u>knowledge</u> or knowing, and therefore (it is often argued) it is not possible to be certain beyond doubt what is real. Accordingly, this line of logic concludes, we cannot in fact be sure beyond doubt about the nature of reality. We can, however, seek to obtain some form of consensus, with others, of what is real. We can use this consensus as a pragmatic guide, either on the assumption that it seems to <u>approximate</u> some kind of valid reality, or simply because it is more 'practical' than perceived alternatives. Consensus reality therefore refers to the agreed-upon concepts of reality which people in the world, or a culture or group, believe are real (or treat as real), usually based upon their common experiences as they believe them to be; anyone who does not agree with these is sometimes stated to be 'in effect... living in a different world.

• Other Portrayals

<u>Culture</u> – set of patterns of human activity within a <u>society</u> or social group and the symbolic structures that give such activity significance. Customs, laws, popular styles, social standards, and traditions are all examples of cultural elements. Across the world, millions are tracing their family history and discovering the lives of their ancestors in original records. Who will you discover?

Search records, start our family tree to uncover our ancestors' through regular census Africans would add more to our potentials of discovering our ancestors to add vital branches to our family tree see transcribed details of our ancestors through original census images by finding out where our family lived, who else lived there and what jobs they did and what roles they played within the community they lived in. 'All the great things are simple, and many can be expressed in a single word: freedom, justice, honour, duty, mercy, hope. 'Without true knowledge of our ancestors this we might find difficult to express fully then our family history would not be based on artificial intelligence'.

Genealogy also known as family history is the study of families and the tracing of their lineages and history. Genealogists use oral traditions, historical records, genetic analysis, and other records to obtain information about a family and to demonstrate kinship and pedigrees of its members. The results are often displayed in charts or written as narratives.

The pursuit of family history and origins tends to be shaped by several motivations, including the desire to carve out a place for one's family in the larger historical picture, a sense of responsibility to preserve the past for future generations, and a sense of self-satisfaction in accurate storytelling. In communitarian societies, one's identity is defined as much by one's kin network as by individual achievement, and the question 'Who are you?' would be answered by a description of father, mother, and tribes.

David Cameron: 'People in Europe know I mean what I say. They know I'm capable of saying no' Prime Minister David Cameron said he would veto a new European Union budget 'if necessary'. The EU is beginning negotiations on its next budget for 2014 to 2020. Mr. Cameron also told the BBC in the longer term the EU should have two different budgets - one for countries in the eurozone and one for those outside the single currency. Mr. Cameron vetoed an EU-wide treaty to co-ordinate budget policies and impose penalties on rule-breakers. Speaking on the Andrew Marr show, on the first day of the Conservative Party conference, Mr. Cameron said experience showed that 'people in Europe know he means what he says'. 'He sat round the table of 27 countries, 26 of them signing up to a treaty while he said, it was not in Britain's interests, I don't care how much pressure they put on, I'm not signing, we're not having it.' 'They know I'm capable of saying no and if he doesn't get a good deal he will still say no again.'

He said he would block talks if 'massive increases' in the budget were proposed or if a deal that 'does not have proper control' was put forward. The prime minister said the EU budget was a 'classic example of where we should probably start to draw new lines'. 'There will come a time I believe where you're going to need to have two European budgets - one for the single currency, because they're going to have to support each other much more, and perhaps a wider budget for everybody else.' He added that he did not think this would be achieved this time but it was an indicator of the way Europe is going. Mr. Cameron also said he favoured a referendum on a renegotiated role for Britain in the EU but once again ruled out holding a simple Yes or No vote on Britain's membership. 'The fact is, he thinks most people in our country don't actually want to leave the European Union or just accept how it is at the moment. They want to change it.' David Cameron said he is 'extremely angry and apologetic' for the government's mistakes over its handling of the West Coast rail contract.

The prime minister said No 10 had done 'all it could' to check if decisions had been taken properly but that 'technical errors' had gone undetected. Those responsible for the mistakes would be held to account, he promised. Ahead of the Conservative conference, he also defended government efforts to boost job creation and house building. Mr. Cameron has been on the back foot in the run-up to the autumn conference, with rail franchise row. In addition the concerns over the economy and the direction of the coalition increasing pressure on No 10.

The decision to rerun the franchise process after the Department for Transport admitted it had made mistakes in how it evaluated the bids will cost the taxpayer at least £40m in compensation and experts believe the eventual bill will be far higher. 'I am extremely angry about what has happened, very apologetic that this has happened,' Mr. Cameron told the BBC. I am extremely angry about what happened, extremely apologetic that this had happened' The prime minister said when Virgin Rail launched its legal challenge to the decision to award the franchise to rival First Group, he asked the cabinet secretary to examine how the process had been conducted. 'I think in terms of what No 10 did, we did all we could to check that decisions were being properly made,' he said. 'We didn't pick up on this technical fault in the way that the franchise operation was run.'

Pressed on whether the review would examine what ministers, including former Transport Secretary Justine Greening, knew and what input they had, Mr. Cameron replied: 'Of course it has to include everything, but from all he had seen so far it seems as if there were some technical errors made within the department about how the figures were compiled.' The Department for Transport insisted Ms Greening, who is now international development secretary, did not know about the specific problem which led to the contract being invalidated before she left the job. Sources close to Ms Greening said the permanent secretary at the Department for Transport, its top civil servant, had apologised in person to her for the errors in the process at a meeting with her and her successor Patrick McLoughlin. Ms Greening, the source added, had had continuing and comprehensive reassurances that the process was fair when she was transport secretary.

As Conservative activists prepare to gather for the party's autumn conference in Birmingham, the prime minister also issued an upbeat message about the economy - which has been in recession since the start of the year - and the coalition's growth initiatives. 'Across the country, we have created a million net new jobs in the private sector over the last two years,' he said. 'That is why unemployment has been falling even though; inevitably, there have been some cuts in the public sector.' And he suggested 'radical changes' being made to the housing sector would begin to address some of the bottlenecks in the system. 'The problem in Britain at the moment is not that we are not building enough affordable homes. The problem is we are not building enough homes, period. 'What the government has done is make it easier now for builders to build. We have changed the planning system; they are cutting out on the bureaucracy.' The prime minister also vowed to campaign 'with everything he has got' to keep the UK intact and indicated a deal was 'close' with the Scottish government over a single question referendum that would be put to the Scottish people in 2014.

Mr. Johnson said a new airport was affordable and would create thousands of new jobs Boris Johnson called for the debate over Heathrow's future and alternative airport capacity in southern England to be decided by the end of the following year. The mayor of London said rivals were 'forging ahead' while the UK was deliberating and he described a review due to report in 2015 as 'glacial'. 'There is no reason to go on for three years discussing this,' he said. Some ministers had been 'bewitched' by airlines and others lobbying for a new Heathrow runway, he added. In a speech to business leaders in London, Mr. Johnson restated his call for a new airport to be built in the Thames Estuary which he said could be operational by 2030. He urged ministers to rule out a new runway at Heathrow, saying it would be full up by the time it opened in 2026 at the earliest. The risk of inertia is huge there is a huge prize if we can get on with it now' The intervention comes days before the start of the Conservative Party conference, during which Mr. Johnson will be one of the most closely-watched figures after recent media comment suggesting he might be an alternative to Mr. Cameron as party leader. The mayor and the prime minister met at Mr. Cameron's country residence Chequers over the weekend, holding what were described as 'wide-ranging' talks.

The coalition government ruled out further expansion at Heathrow during the current Parliament while many Conservative MPs want ministers to think again as part of a wider review of the future of UK airports. Prime Minister David Cameron asked economist Sir Howard Davies to examine future capacity options. Although he will report interim findings next year, his full report is not due before the next election due in 2015. The mayor of London said there was 'no easy solution' but the UK was already being left behind by its European competitors and it was imperative the issue was decided much sooner. Boris Johnson didn't hold back in his renewed attack on the government's approach to airport expansion. His message to the airlines and airport operator which have been lobbying for a third runway at Heathrow was blunt: 'Forget about it...it won't happen', he said. His critique of the government was harsh but he resisted - numerous - opportunities to have a dig at the prime minister. In fact, he was supportive and serious when he said the Tories were doing 'remarkably well in the polls' and that David Cameron would win the next election.

The problem is that the assault is now increasingly credible, in that it exposes the delay the coalition has agreed as a coping mechanism because it is split on what to do about the UK' airport capacity. 'The risk of inertia is huge,' he said. 'But there is a huge prize if we can get on with it now.' While praising Sir Howard's appointment, he said he would have preferred ministers to make the decision themselves: 'We are about to embark on a miserable and protracted battle to impose on the people of London an environmental and political disaster that will be obsolete as soon as it is complete.' Mr. Johnson said there was a political consensus among the three largest parties in London against expanding Heathrow. Any attempt to change that, he added, would be tantamount to 'tiptoeing back towards an electrical fence that will electrocute politically anyone who tries to touch it'. He added: 'I have got two messages, it is very simple. My message is, number one, forget about a new runway at Heathrow. Number two, look at the viable alternatives.' The mayor has long argued that building a third runway at Heathrow would be environmentally unsustainable and a 'bolder' long-term solution is required.

Publishing his submission to the government's strategy review he believes there were three potential options: building a brand new airport to the east of London on two potential sites and upgrading Stansted. Mr. Johnson believes a new airport will cost £80bn and can be up and running in 2030 between two and four years later than a new runway at Heathrow would come on stream. He said it could be funded but needed 'political will'. Leading airlines and much of the business community argue the UK is losing out to other destinations and believe a new runway at Heathrow is the only option to maintain the airport's global 'hub status' and boost the economy.

Transport secretary Patrick McLoughlin told the Conservative Party conference the government plans to improve 57 problem points on roads in England. He said the government would spend £170m on the works. But addressing the hall was 'a little daunting', he said. His last appearance was in 1984 when Mr. McLoughlin - a former miner - told delegates he would continue working despite being called a 'Tory scab'. Trying to reclaim the one nation label used by Labour leader Ed Miliband in his conference speech the transport secretary said 'I'm the son of a miner and the grandson of a miner.' 'He wanted to make one point clear. If you want to understand one nation, Mr. Miliband, I'll show you one nation. He is standing at this podium. I am a one nation Tory.'

Announcing funding to fix 'pinchpoints' on England's roads, Mr. McLoughlin said 'Let's face it, we've under-invested as a country for years. 'There's too much congestion, not enough new schemes. Its madness and we are going to sort it out.' He also insisted the government would press ahead with their plans for a high speed rail link between London Birmingham. The proposal was met with opposition from within the Conservative Party. One former cabinet minister has described the planned line as 'terrible'. The transport secretary said 'We can't afford not to build it. Our competitors around the world are investing in the best transport and we must too.' He promised those whose homes and communities were affected by the new line will be properly compensated. And he said the government wants to reduce journey times from London to Scotland to less than three hours. The funding for road improvements is intended to remove bottlenecks and boost the economy by improving access to local enterprise zones. They include work on the M1, M62 and M5 motorways as well as the A1 and A404. Before a tide of Boris mania sweeps through Birmingham, can I commit a small blasphemy?

Can I proffer a modest counter-thesis to check the adoration of the mayor, a pause before we lay down palms as the anointed one enters the conference city? I know others have pointed out that unlike Mr. Cameron, Boris is a winner, he excites his party and wins votes from people who do not normally back the Conservatives. They say his jokes make the Cabinet look dull, and his gravitas makes him look like prime-ministerial. He cheers people up, they cheer him, and he appears authentic, the real deal in an era of insincerity and pre-cooked sound bites. And yet let us consider a few contrary thoughts and questions:

I have yet to speak to a Conservative who thinks David Cameron will stand down or be ousted as leader before the election in 2015. In other words, whatever leadership ambitions Boris may or may not have, they would be for a pretty distant and pretty uncertain future. As one Cabinet minister told me: 'Everyone needs to take a chill pill and relax. The party is not going to get rid of Cameron; it is not even in the foothills of even thinking about it.'

Even if Boris were to break his promise and get back into the Commons through a by-election before his mayoral term is up, he does not have a meaningful powerbase in parliament. There are undoubtedly some London MPs who have held onto his coat-tails but there is no great organisation or fan club ready to grind into action. Many voters may like Boris - the humour, the personality, the character - but do they see him as prime ministerial material? Many Londoners may love him but does his popularity stretch far outside the M25? What do voters in the north think about him? How much would Conservative members across the country still love him when they realise that he shares many, if not more, of Mr. Cameron's modernising instincts such as support for gay marriage? A cheerleader for the capital with few powers is not the same as a national leader with unpopular decisions to make.

Do the media give Boris more welly than he perhaps is worth? Sure, he is always good copy and he is good telly. But it has always been part of the narrative of political journalism that there has to be a great white hope just over the horizon. In more recent years for the Conservatives, it was Michael Portillo and Michael Heseltine. Further back, it was the likes of Rab Butler. Just as with drama, journalism thrives on conflict and competition. In other words, if Boris did not exist, we would invent another like him.

How much is the Boris phenomenon fanned by the somewhat nervous response by Mr. Cameron and his Downing Street machine? The PM often seems to lose his stride in interviews when he is asked about Boris. He summons the mayor to Chequers and Downing Street to encourage harmony before the conference. His staff ring up City Hall to find out what Boris will be saying in his speech.

I am told there was a lot of effort made by Number Ten to make sure that Boris did not give any interviews on Sunday morning when Mr. Cameron was due on the Andrew Marr show. In the Sunday Telegraph, Mr. Cameron said: 'I am relatively, as you can see, relaxed about having the blond-haired mop sounding off from time to time.' Oh how telling is that crucial word 'relatively'! One minister told me it was purely an ego thing. 'It is like you are the boss, but this other guy comes into the room and everyone wants to go and talk to him, and hey, you don't like it.'

The crucial point is that while Boris Johnson may wilfully tweak David Cameron's tail, and while this may wind Mr. Cameron up, the prime minister has actually far more important things to think and worry about. The future of the economy and the state of the government's public sector reforms would justifiably keep him up at night, not another ambitious old Etonian. In other words, Boris may steal the show. But he's not likely to steal the job.

Despite all the above I will be spending much of tomorrow merrily following Boris and the inevitable media scrum all around Birmingham in the hope of illuminating insights or catchy sound bites. With luck you'll be able to see the results on the 10 o'clock news. Britain is considering curbing migration from some European countries in a move that would challenge a core EU principle, David Cameron said. The PM said it was 'right' to include the freedom of movement directive in a review of EU 'competencies'. He also raised prospect of a referendum on Britain's relationship with the EU after the next election but appeared to reject an in/out vote. He threatens to use Britain's veto on a new EU budget 'if necessary'. The comments, on the BBC's Andrew Marr show, come as Conservatives gather in Birmingham for their annual conference. Introducing visa controls on migrants from some European countries would challenge one of the fundamental principles of the EU.

Mr. Cameron said the issue of freedom of movement would be included in a review of the UK's relationship with the EU being carried out by Foreign Secretary William Hague. 'I think it's absolutely right to look at this balance of competencies, to go through every topic and see what is in Britain's interest,' he told Andrew Marr. On the issue of a referendum, he said he wanted Britain to have a free trading agreement with Europe but not 'endless political integration'. Most people in our country don't actually want to leave the

European Union or just accept how it is at the moment. They want to change it' 'I think the opportunity will open up, over time, to get new settlement after the new settlement, after the next election, we should have new consent for the settlement.

'Which can either take place through a referendum or, possibly, it was close to one, at a general election.'

He ruled out an in/out referendum now, as some Conservative MPs are demanding, saying 'I think the trouble with a straight yes or no, as we stand today is, frankly, I'm not happy with the status quo so I don't want to say yes to the status quo but I also don't think it would be right to leave right now.'

And he took a swipe at the UK Independence Party, which some Conservative MPs fear will rob the party of an overall majority at the next election. 'I think UKIP is a complete waste of time, obviously, but I think most people in our country don't actually want to leave the European Union or just accept how it is at the moment. They want to change it.'

Mr. Cameron also threatened to use Britain's veto to block a new EU budget 'if necessary'. He said nations could not go on 'pouring' money into the EU while cutting budgets at home. He said if 'massive increases' in the budget were proposed or a deal that 'does not have proper control' was on the table, he would step in. The EU is beginning negotiations on the budget for 2014 to 2020. Theresa May told The Sunday Times she was concerned about the impact on the British economy of a fresh wave of migration. 'We are looking at this whole area of the abuse of the freedom of movement. But we will go further on this, and the issue of free movement will be part of the review,' she told the newspaper. 'It will be looking at where the decision-making powers are between the EU and the UK, how they are operating and what the impacts of those are.'

Mrs. May did not identify the countries facing possible migration curbs in her Sunday Times interview, but the newspaper says they are understood to include Romania and Bulgaria, which are currently subject to temporary visa restrictions.

David Cameron: 'We need to make sure that every part of plan A is firing on all cylinders' The UK is going through a 'slow and difficult healing process' as it rebalances its economy, Prime Minister David Cameron said. His comments came as the International Monetary Fund said it now expected the UK economy to shrink by 0.4% this year. Mr. Cameron said the government was doing 'everything it can' to encourage growth in difficult economic times. He said they had cut the budget deficit by a quarter in two years and there were 'positive signs' for the future. According to the IMF the prospects for the global economic recovery had weakened as government policies across the world have failed to restore confidence. The fund has downgraded its overall estimate for global growth, with one of the biggest individual country downgrades applied to the UK.

'Progress'

The IMF now expects the British economy to shrink by 0.4% this year 2012, compared with its forecast of 0.2% growth in July. David Cameron defended his government's economic strategy there were 'positive signs' the UK economy was changing. Speaking on BBC Radio 4's Programme, he said: 'What is happening in Britain is a rebalancing of our economy. 'We need more private sector growth, we need a smaller public sector, we need to make more, sell more overseas and manufacture more. 'It's a slow and difficult healing process, it is taking place.' On government prospects for cutting the budget deficit, Mr. Cameron said the government was 'on the right track'. 'People are very understanding of the difficult inheritance we had - a record budget deficit, the biggest of anywhere in the developed world,' he said. 'The deficit is down by one quarter in two years. It was 11% of GDP when we came to power- it's now 8%. That is progress.' He refused to comment on suggestions that figures expected in the chancellor's autumn statement in December will show the deficit has increased this year. 'We don't have those figures yet. We have to wait until the end of the year to see what the deficit is. 'It's wrong to take one month's figures or make a judgement half-way through the year.' In response to the IMF downgrade, the Treasury highlighted the fact that the IMF had 'repeated its advice that the first line of defence against [slowing growth] should be to allow the automatic stabilisers to operate, monetary policy easing and measures to ease the flow of credit - all of which the UK is doing'. Jeremy Hunt: 'Our biggest priority must be... to meet the challenges of an aging population' NHS staff must become the 'best in the world' at looking after the elderly, Health Secretary Jeremy Hunt has told the Conservative Party conference. In his first major speech since taking on the role in the recent reshuffle, he said it was time to change the culture of the organisation. Mr. Hunt attacked Labour, saying no party had a 'monopoly on compassion'.

He also praised doctors and nurses as 'unsung heroes', but added the NHS should be 'honest about failure'. Mr. Hunt, who said his father had worked as an NHS manager and his mother as an A&E nurse and midwife, replaced Andrew Lansley in the cabinet reshuffle. This followed the passing of the Health and Social Care Act, which will give GPs greater power over care budgets via clinical commissioning groups, after abolishing strategic health authorities and primary care trusts. In his speech, Mr. Hunt paid tribute to his predecessor, saying: 'If Andrew is the health secretary who helped gave us the structures for a modern NHS, I want to be the health secretary who helped transform the culture of the system to make it the best in the world at looking after older people.' He added that 'Since it was set up in 1948 the NHS has come to symbolise a deeply held belief about what it means to be British a country fit for heroes where everyone should have a roof over their head, a school for their children and proper treatment for their family when they're sick.

The speech was short. In fact, it was barely 20 minutes long, which was a sharp contrast with the lengthy, policy-heavy speeches made regularly by his predecessor Andrew Lansley. That in itself is telling about what sort of secretary of state Mr. Hunt is likely to be. It is clear Mr. Hunt has been brought in to establish a clear and concise message about the government's position on the NHS. Again and again he talked about improving patient care. His speech was peppered with references to the issue. He mentioned past scandals, such as Mid Staffordshire and Winterbourne View. He talked about making managers accountable for care as well as finances. He also recognised the wider challenge the NHS faces from an ageing population and the need for better solutions to dementia and social care. Beyond that there was little detail about how he plans to proceed. But after a health secretary that went after the structure of the

NHS, Mr. Hunt has his eyes firmly set on its culture. 'That was under the Attlee government. But the NHS does not belong to Labour any more than victory in the Second World War belongs to the Conservatives. No party has a monopoly on compassion and it is an insult to common decency for any party to claim it.' Ministers are looking at introducing a cap on the amount for which people are liable when funding their care in old age.

Mr. Hunt said 'He visited St Thomas', the hospital where he was born. he met a nurse who had been caring for a dying man who had lost touch with his family 20 years earlier. She searched out the family on Google, found them in Ireland, arranged to fly him back there so he was able to spend his last two weeks reunited with his family. 'So much of the NHS is like that unsung heroes who represent the very best of our values.

'But as we celebrate excellence, we must be honest about failure. He was going to name names now because I don't want anything to be swept under the carpet.

Mr. Hunt added 'Last month the Royal College of Physicians published a report about the way older people are looked after in hospitals. 'We have many committed managers in hospitals and care homes. But he need to say this to all managers; you will be held responsible for the care in your establishments. You wouldn't expect to keep your job if you lost control of your finances. Well don't expect to keep it if you lose control of your care.' George Osborne on tax rates 'for the very richest', the 50p tax rate and cap on benefits The government is determined to cut a further £10bn from the benefits budget to fight the deficit, Chancellor George Osborne told the Tory conference. One idea he suggested was limiting the number of children in a family that should be supported on benefits. He said the better-off would pay more in taxes, but the budget could not be balanced 'on the wallets of the rich'. He also unveiled a plan for workers to give up a string of employment rights in return for shares in their employer. The new owner-employee contract allows owners to award shares worth up to £50,000 to their staff, in return for the employee giving up their unfair dismissal, redundancy and training rights and also the right to ask for flexible working. He said there would be no capital gains tax on the profits from the shares, so it would be 'owners, workers and the taxman all in it together'.

The difficult reality for Mr. Osborne is that the coalition has been struggling to deliver on the two goals that were right at the centre of its economic strategy' Mr. Osborne's speech comes with the UK economy in recession, hitting the government's tax takings and its plans to reduce the deficit (the difference between the amount spent by government and the amount it receives from tax etc). In his speech in Birmingham, the chancellor made clear he was not planning to change course and said a further £16bn of savings must be found by 2015/16 to meet his target of balancing the budget within five years. This, he said, would include cutting £10bn more from the welfare bill by 2016-17, on top of the £18bn announced in 2010. Mr. Osborne said: 'Let the message from this conference be clear: we will finish the job we have started.' He told party members 'the economy is healing' but added that 'healing is taking longer than we hoped, because the damage was greater than we feared'. Mr. Osborne spelt out ideas for cutting the welfare bill, such as limiting housing benefit for the under-25s, so that young people without a job have to live at home; possible further curbs on child tax credits; and allowing benefit increases to be lower than the rate of inflation. Deputy Prime Minister Nick Clegg told his own party's conference he would not allow 'wild suggestions' of a £10bn cut in welfare and Chief Secretary to the Treasury Danny Alexander told delegates: 'We simply will not allow the books to be balanced in a way that hits the poorest hardest.'

The Lib Dems advocate a 'mansion tax', under which owners of homes worth more than £2m would pay a 1% annual charge on property values above that level. Mr. Osborne ruled out such a measure, which is unpopular among Conservative MPs, saying: 'It would be sold as a mansion tax, but once the tax inspector has been let in the door, we would soon find most homes in the country incur a mansion tax. 'It's not a mansion tax but a home's tax, and the party of homeowners will have no truck with it.' He said taxes for the most well-off would be increased in some form in the next few years, so that those 'with the broadest shoulders' paid most. However, he said: 'Just as we should never balance the budget on the backs of the poor, it's a delusion to say we can balance it on the wallets of the rich.' BBC political editor Nick Robinson said the comments by Mr. Osborne and senior Lib Dems amounted to 'haggling in public' over the size of tax rises and welfare cuts.

The Liberal Democrats are a social liberal political party in the United Kingdom which supports constitutional and electoral reform, progressive taxation, wealth taxation, environmentalism, human rights laws, cultural liberalism, European integration, banking reform and civil liberties. The party was formed in 1988 by a merger of the Liberal Party and the Social Democratic Party. The two parties had formed the electoral SDP–Liberal Alliance for seven years before then, since the SDP's formation. The Liberals had been in existence for 129 years and in power under leaders such as Gladstone, Asquith and Lloyd George. Nick Clegg was elected Leader in 2007. At the 2010 general election, the Liberal Democrats won 57 seats, making them the third-largest party in the House of Commons behind the Conservatives with 307 and Labour with 258. No party having an overall majority, the Liberal Democrats joined a coalition government with the Conservatives, with Clegg becoming Deputy Prime Minister and other Liberal Democrats taking up ministerial positions. Mr. Osborne presented a united front with Work and Pensions Secretary Iain Duncan Smith, following reports the Treasury wanted to scrap the work and pensions secretary's new Universal Credit over fears costs and complexity were spiralling out of control. Mr. Duncan Smith is understood to have initially resisted the welfare cuts proposal, arguing savings should be found by means-testing benefits such as free bus passes and winter fuel payments for better-off pensioners.

- WELFARE SPENDING
  - The Office for Budget Responsibility forecasts that the government will spend £209.2bn on social security benefits and tax credits during this financial year
  - This figure is predicted to increase to £229bn by 2016/17
  - Total government spending is expected to rise from £683.4bn to £756.3bn during the same period

- In 2010 the government announced welfare cuts of £18bn a year by 2014/15 -
- George Osborne wants to see £10bn welfare cuts over two years 2015-2017

In his speech, Mr. Osborne accused Ed Miliband of lacking an alternative economy strategy, claiming the Labour leader did not mention the budget deficit once in his Labour conference speech. He also announced an extra £200m in government funding for scientific research in English universities and restated his belief in the future possibilities of shale gas. The Research Partnership Investment Fund was launched with £100m of government funding by Mr. Osborne in his Budget. Universities must match any public money with at least double the amount of cash from the private sector or charities, which the government claims could add up to a total investment in research of more than £1bn. The Conservatives began their annual conference with policy announcements aimed at easing the cost of living as they attempt to show they are on the side of hard-pressed families. These include extending the council tax freeze in England for the third year in a succession and capping some rail fare increases to inflation plus 1%. David Cameron also said he would be prepared to veto a new EU budget to prevent 'massive' increases. Global economic recovery weakening, says IMF as the IMF said the ESM was key to tackling the debt crisis and restoring confidence.

The global economic recovery is weakening as government policies failed to restore added that the risk of further deterioration in the economic outlook was 'considerable' and had increased. The IMF downgraded its estimate for global growth in 2013 to 3.6% from the 3.9% in its forecast. One of the biggest downgrades was to the UK economy, which the IMF expects to shrink by 0.4% this year 2012. This compares with its forecast of 0.2% growth in July. Next year 2013, the UK economy should grow by 1.1%, the IMF said, down from its previous forecast of 1.4%. In response to the downgrade, the UK Treasury highlighted the fact that the IMF had 'repeated its advice the first line of defence against slowing growth should be to allow the automatic stabilisers to operate, monetary policy easing and measures to ease the flow of credit - all of which the UK is doing'. The fund's forecast for global growth 2012 has been lowered to 3.3%

from 3.5%. Olivier Blanchard, the IMF's chief economist, said the slowdown was being led by problems within the developed countries: 'Low growth in advanced economies is affecting emerging and developing economies through exports.' David Cameron defended the UK's economic strategy, saying the job would take some time. 'What is happening is a rebalancing of our economy. We have created a million net new jobs and we are now a net exporter of cars,' he told the BBC. 'But has a slow process.'

The shadow treasury minister, Chris Leslie, said the IMF's downward revision of the UK's economic outlook showed the government's economic policies were not working: 'Twelve months ago, the IMF were saying, if the economic situation worsened, we'd need to have an alternative plan, we'd need to have serious action. 'Here we are a year later and, you know, can there be any doubt, can there be any question at all that we've got to have some stimulus to our economy, some action absolutely right now.' The markdown for the UK's prospects comes despite recent data that has pointed to a return to growth. However, Martin Beck, from Capital Economics, said that was mainly due to a recovery from the effects of the Queen's Jubilee celebrations on the economy. 'Recent data had actually been quite promising - industrial output and exports increased quite substantially - but that largely reflected the fact that June was a bad month because of the Jubilee disruption and the extra bank holiday we had then,' he told the BBC. 'We've got a positive growth rate for the third quarter but we expect another contraction in the fourth quarter.' The IMF's report said that overall, '[economic] output is expected to remain sluggish in advanced economies but still relatively solid in many emerging markets and developing economies'.

It highlighted the importance of the European Stability Mechanism (ESM), the eurozone's new permanent fund to bail out struggling economies and banks launched earlier on Monday. The fund added that greater integration of taxation and spending policies across the eurozone was needed, as well as measures to begin the process of banking union. 'The ESM must intervene in banking systems and provide support to sovereigns, while national leaders must work toward true economic and monetary union,' the IMF said. The ESM, hailed on Monday by Jean-Claude Juncker, Prime

Minister of Luxembourg and chair of the fund, as 'an historic milestone in shaping the future of monetary union', will have a lending capacity of 500bn euros (£400bn; $650bn) by 2014. The ESM will be able to lend directly to governments, but it will also be able to buy their sovereign debts, which could help reduce the borrowing costs of highly-indebted countries such as Italy and Spain. In the US, growth depended on a deal to avoid the so-called fiscal cliff, when automatic spending cuts and tax increases will kick in at the beginning of next year, the IMF said.

If policymakers fail to agree to delay these measures and increase America's debt ceiling, 'the US economy could fall back into recession', with serious knock-on effects for the rest of the world, it added. Assuming agreement is reached, the US economy will grow by 2.1% next year, the IMF said, down from its forecast of 2.3% made in July. This year, the economy will actually grow by more than previously forecast - by 2.2% rather than 2%. The IMF also said actions taken by governments already had not gone far enough. Measures to relieve 'chronic household debt burdens' did not address the scale of the problem, it said, while 'efforts to strengthen the regulatory framework for financial institutions and markets have been patchy'. While there had been some success in rebuilding capital bases of banks, not enough had been done to address 'excessive risk taking' in financial markets. The fund also called for further action to address long-term unemployment. 'In advanced economies, growth is now too low to make a substantial dent in unemployment,' it said. Figures released showed that the unemployment rate in the US fell to 7.8%, the lowest rate since January 2009 but still much higher than for most of the past 20 years. Figures also showed unemployment in the eurozone stable at a record high of 11.4%. Spain and Greece, where about one in four of the workforce are out of a job, have the highest rate. Despite relatively strong growth compared with advanced economies, the IMF also downgraded growth prospects for emerging nations.

In Asia, 'the near and medium-term outlooks are less buoyant compared with the region's growth performance in recent years', the fund said. It highlighted weaker exports as a result of lower demand for goods in the West. China, the world's second-largest economy, would grow by 7.8% this year, down from its previous forecast of 8%, and by 8.2% next year, down from 8.5%. It also revised dramatically its growth forecasts for India, which would grow by 4.9% this year and 6.1% next, the IMF said. Weaker demand for exports would also impact on Latin American economies, as would lower domestic demand due to government policy tightening, the fund said. As a result, Brazil's economy would grow by 1.5% this year, down from the previous forecast of 2.5%. Greece relies on tourism for 20% of its income, but visitor numbers are dwindling Tourism is the lifeblood of the Greek economy. It makes up almost 20% of the country's economic output - the largest share - and an estimated one in five Greeks works in the industry.

Iain Duncan Smith attacked what he called Labour's 'bitter legacy' of welfare dependency The government will bring about a 'complete cultural shift' in its efforts to end reliance on benefits, Iain Duncan Smith has promised. The work and pensions secretary told the Conservative conference the country was on 'a journey back from dependence to independence'. Planned housing benefit cuts would lead more people to look for work, he added. Mr. Duncan Smith's speech followed Chancellor George Osborne promising an extra £10bn of welfare spending cuts. The savings, to come in by 2016-17, would come on top of £18bn in savings announced in 2010.

Mr. Duncan Smith is understood to have initially resisted the latest proposal, arguing money should be found by means-testing benefits such as free bus passes and winter fuel payments for better-off pensioners.

But, in his speech, he backed the chancellor and instead attacked Labour for leaving a 'bitter legacy' of excessive spending on benefits, adding: 'You won't solve an economic problem by denying it.' The government is altering the system by introducing a cap on welfare payments of £26,000 per household from next April and bringing in a 'universal benefit', replacing the current range of out-of-work benefits. Mr. Duncan Smith said: 'Now we are toughening up the penalty for failure to seek work. Where claimants fail to meet their clear responsibilities, benefit will be withdrawn for three months for the first offence, six months for the second and three years for the third. 'Despite all of the progress we've made in the last two years, there is still much to do.' He added: 'We will have reduced welfare bills by £18bn at the time of the next election and reformed welfare so it will be more effective.

'Early action to cut spending has helped reduce the deficit by a quarter but, with the rest of Europe and the USA in trouble, it's small wonder the UK economy isn't growing as we had hoped. 'George Osborne and I recognise this means we will have to make further savings in the welfare budget, but as we save we are agreed we must relentlessly focus what we do on transforming lives. 'Gone must be the days when governments spent money to buy their way out of a problem.' Mr. Duncan Smith cited Department for Work and Pensions research that suggests the cap on housing benefit - due to come in next year - meant a third of people in receipt of payments would look for work. He said: 'Even before we bring it in, capping benefits is having an effect.' Concluding his speech, Mr. Duncan Smith told delegates in Birmingham: '[It] must be our mission, plain and simple - a mission, not to change people but to restore them. Through fair government, give them the same hope and aspiration that we would all want for our children. 'To deliver this mission is to govern as Conservatives. That and only that is the way to win the next election.'

Tory conference: Activist anger over gay marriage Mr. Cameron angered a swathe of his party with his commitment to legalising gay marriage. And a significant number of them - about 1,000 in total - ran the gauntlet of protesters outside the venue to voice their anger, dismay and, in many cases, sheer incomprehension at his stance. The fringe event - normally sedate affairs, with bored activists picking over sandwiches - felt more like a revivalist meeting. They shouted, they cheered. They cried out 'Amen'. It fell to Ann Widdecombe to put into words what they were feeling - in particular their anger at being labelled 'bigots' by those campaigning for the legalisation of gay marriage. 'Is it bigoted to recognise that the complementarity of a man and a woman in a union open to procreation is unique and cannot be replicated by other unions?' she asked, to cheers. 'The real bigots, those who really deserve to be described as such, the real extremists, the real nasties, are those who believe that those who dissent from their views have no right to do so and that the state itself should silence them.' She poured scorn on the idea that the words 'husband' and 'wife' could be replaced in official documents by terms such as 'partner' or 'progenitor'. The proposal will throw up so many complications and lead to so much prejudice against teachers and foster parents who oppose gay marriage that it would be a disaster for Britain, she argued, not to mention the Conservative Party.

Former Archbishop of Canterbury Lord Carey spoke about the special place marriage between a man and a woman had in Christian teaching, adding: 'The matter is so serious... that we cannot allow politicians to plunder something as sacred as this institution.'

When it comes to social housing, people will no longer be able to live in houses with more bedrooms than they need. For example, if a single person is living in a two-bedroom flat, they will no longer receive the same amount of housing benefit. So to stay in the same property they would have to make up the shortfall in rent from their benefits.

This has a particular impact in Northern Ireland because of our housing stock. Researchers at Magee in Londonderry have said we simply do not have enough one-bedroomed properties in Northern Ireland to offer alternative accommodation for those affected by this reform.

There is the further problem of demographics. There may be enough one-bedroomed houses in a Protestant area but not in a Catholic area - or vice versa. That could create problems for people being forced to move home.

- *The Prime Minister warns Britain faces an 'hour of reckoning' but calls on the public to keep faith with the austerity drive. 10 October 2012 David Cameron has warned that Britain faces its 'hour of reckoning', but insisted the coalition has put the country back on the road to recovery. The Prime Minister, in a sombre party conference speech, said the UK was back 'on the right track' - but warned the challenges ahead were still 'daunting'. Speaking just 24 hours after the International Monetary Fund slashed its forecast for UK growth; he declared the choice for Britain was 'sink or swim, do or decline'. 'Unless we act, unless we take difficult, painful decisions, unless we show determination and imagination, Britain may not be in the future what it has been in the past,' he said.*

- *'Because the truth is this: we are in a global race today and that means an hour of reckoning for countries like ours. Sink or swim. Do or decline. 'To take office at such a moment is a duty and an honour and we will rise to the challenge.' He added: 'I know you are asking whether the plan is working and here's the truth: the damage was worse than we thought and it's taking longer than we hoped.' But Mr. Cameron insisted: 'We are making progress.' He added: 'Nothing matters more. Every battle we fight, every plan we make, every decision we take is to achieve that end - Britain on the rise.'*

- *I kind of appreciate the uniqueness of British and the American politics the manner in which they conduct themselves and the way the people they govern conduct themselves it's what I would like to see in my own native background. The United Kingdom is unique among nations with long uninterrupted democracy in modern history, the UK has a strong tradition of gradual political change, History has seemed to sweep the UK along a sufficiently progressive,, common sense, prosperous, and sensible path while much of it is owed to not only the politician but the sensible ways people try to live their lives the government making its self accountable gives them strength and courage working towards the progress of their country yet, they have their disagreements the efforts and charisma in which they are conducted and settles when it comes to problem and conflicts are quite unique by using common sense or being reasoning and they are very tolerant to other ethic race, culture and diversity. How we see, perceive, how we see ourselves determines how we relate to each other It would also determine how we conduct ourselves.*

- *The Europeans and Americans express deeper level of love, we Africans, Jamaicans, Caribbean's Barbados,*

Asians, and Trinidadians should follow how to show affection, believe in ourselves, freedom and liberty, they have drawn us to themselves and also given us the chance to confront them as individuals I wonder why we are not able to shear such feelings within ourselves. They have also drawn the Middle East to themselves for a bid for democracy for world leaders to have consideration for their action and to make the world a better place. I need not wonder why to some extent, affection runs dry within us. It comes each time the time is right with each apocalypse if we do the right things, with concern, and in perspective through initiatives, how wonderful our lives and existence would be. If we show more of affection, the concept of self actualization is achieved while our worries, hopes and problems are always inevitable easily comes a zeal to deal with them amicably. Within the modern years, we have come to affiliating ourselves with love songs half of our other music are of tears and cries. When you love someone and you have done all, you have to do, it would all come back to you with no regrets.

- *We have translated written text such as the holy bible into our own languages; we have adopted some of their constitutional values and morals into our own culture and ways of life. Technology, engineering and science have also become our ways of living infarct they have over centuries brought new ways of life to all third world nations it is time to tidy up, redress and conceptualize ourselves to conformity though process of holding our future in our hands and care. No more conflict, let us embrace one another in understanding its one reason why Barack Obama might have become the president of the united state of America. It has everything to do with our past, beliefs, religion, culture and concept on which we hold each other and it has everything to do with the entire occupants of planet earth this, is not a time to be prejudice against one another or in disunity world leaders need to come out and openly shear their views and those among them who, are not living up to expectation should be cautioned to harder to reason should be made to comply the world at this stage needs mutual understanding. Blessed are those who show such mutual understanding. For some countries and its people because of ethnic diversity or corrupt leaders, there needs to be concept of perception towards a mutual understanding.*

* *The Europeans brought modern civilization to us they thought us how to read and write, they have also counted their blessings on us God bless them it is time for us to use our own initiatives to better ourselves than we have been doing over the years though we see ourselves as a reflection of pain we went through it for a reason to create an affair that would last for all season, it must have been for reasons that we should be lovers, to mend the cracks in our hearts. We should seek to help each other its good when there is someone to lean on I wait for the day humans would not hurt each other anymore. Existence is a journey take the fair chances nothing stays the same.*

Suffering, or pain in a broad sense, is an experience of unpleasantness and aversion associated with the perception of harm or threat of harm in an individual. Suffering is the basic element that makes up the negative valence of affective phenomena.

Suffering may be qualified as physical or mental. It may come in all degrees of intensity, from mild to intolerable. Factors of duration and frequency of occurrence usually compound that of intensity. Attitudes toward suffering may vary widely, in a sufferer or other people, according to how much it is regarded as avoidable or unavoidable, useful or useless, deserved or undeserved.

Suffering occurs in the lives of sentient beings in numerous manners, and often dramatically. As a result, many fields of human activity are concerned, from their own points of view, with some aspects of suffering. These aspects may include the nature of suffering, its processes, its origin and causes, its meaning and significance, its related personal, social, and cultural behaviours, its remedies, management, and uses.

The word suffering is sometimes used in the narrow sense of physical pain, but more often it refers to mental or emotional pain, or more often yet to pain in the broad sense, i.e. to any unpleasant feeling, emotion or sensation. The word pain usually refers to physical pain, but it is also a common synonym of suffering. The words pain and suffering are often used both together in different ways. For instance, they may be used as interchangeable synonyms. Or they may be used in 'contradistinction' to one another, as in 'pain is physical, suffering is mental', or 'pain is inevitable, suffering is optional'. Or they may be used to define each other, as in 'pain is physical suffering', or 'suffering is severe physical or mental pain'.

Qualifiers, such as mental, emotional, psychological, and spiritual, are often used for referring to certain types of pain or suffering. In particular, mental pain (or suffering) may be used in relationship with physical pain (or suffering) for distinguishing between two wide categories of pain or suffering. A first caveat concerning such a distinction is that it uses physical pain in a sense that normally includes not only the 'typical sensory experience of physical pain' but also other unpleasant bodily experiences such as itching or nausea. A second caveat is that the terms physical or mental should not be taken too literally: physical pain or suffering, as a matter of fact, happens through conscious minds and involves emotional aspects, while mental pain or suffering happens through physical brains and, being an emotion, involves important physiological aspects.

Unpleasantness, another synonym of suffering or pain in the broad sense, is used in physical pain science to refer to the basic affective dimension of pain (its suffering aspect), usually in contrast with the sensory dimension, as for instance in this sentence from Professor Donald Price: 'Pain-unpleasantness is often, though not always, closely linked to both the intensity and unique qualities of the painful sensation.' Words that are roughly synonymous with suffering, in addition to pain and unpleasantness, include distress, sorrow, unhappiness, misery, affliction, woe, ill, discomfort, displeasure, disagreeableness

Mr. Dotun Sobowale had been the one helping me since when I became unwell in 2007 and had to be out of work. He is from Ogun state from Ijebu. My mother is also from Ogun state from Abeokuta there are wild arrays of conflict in Western Nigeria within the Ijabu's and the Abeokuta's but I took Mr. Dotun as a friend he is also known as Mr. Dax Sobowale. This world we live in now is becoming a small place Mr. Dotun Sobowale has two twin daughters Taye and Kehinde Sobowale who are at University.

My lat father Chief Dr Frank Megbele died at Ibadan he died there because he went there while receiving treatment for diabetic. He has slight resemblance to Nigerian leader Olusegun Obasanjo who as more than once a Nigerian leader who plays huge part within Friends and relatives in the Reformed Ogboni Fraternity cult.

Oluṣẹgun Mathew Okikiọla Arẹmu Ọbasanjọ, Yoruba born circa 5 March 1937) is a former Nigerian Army general and former President of Nigeria. A Nigerian of Yoruba descent, Obasanjo was a career soldier before serving twice as his nation's head of state, as a military ruler between 13 February 1976 to 1 October 1979; and as elected President from 29 May 1999 to 29 May 2007.

His current home is Abeokuta, the Capital City of Ogun State, where he is a nobleman as the holder of the titles of the Balogun of the Owu Lineage and the Ekerin Balogun of the Egba clan of Yorubala

Brillian.

Salsa compilation this is one of the best Salsa compilations you can buy. Best record for Salsa is 'La Receta' and best for Merengue is 'El Tiburon' which always gets me out of my seat to dance. This is real up-to-date Latin music with a regular beat. Excellent, if you're teaching or learning Salsa dance and are bored with old classics or newer commercial records...

Salsa for beginners although I really enjoyed the music, I did find a lot of the tracks very fast to keep up with being a complete beginner. You either have to go ultra slow or extremely fast. I found there were only a few tracks that went at the right speed to comfortably practice as a novice. Will keep it for when I'm an expert! If anyone out there knows of a CD with a more suitable for..., it was one I had bought from my local Woolwich Sainsbury's food chain store in Woolwich, it's a compilation of essential dance classic hits I love Salsa. I enjoy plying the CD whenever I remember Africa as I dwell in the UK I am thrilled with Salsa music sometime I even dance in my flat of Salsa songs but it was not the same as I had song and danced in traditional clothing's of Itsekiri and Yoruba during the making of a king of Ogiame Atuwatse the second and when my late father become a chief. Warri South is a <u>Local Government Area</u> of <u>Delta State</u>, <u>Nigeria</u>. Its headquarters are in the city of <u>Warri</u>. As I got in doors into my flat I played my CD of I love Salsa though I did not understand the language it was festinating listening to it. The young psychiatrist young man is known within my neighbourhood he lives close to my flat he had tried to get acquainted with me several times while I always decline his advance of friendship but this time I could not he really pulled me in. Some of our cares show signs of aloof towards their patients if only they are aware patients who show signs of managing schizophrenia or bipolar show signs of withdrawal to mental health patients who do not show such signs of trying to manage the illness. I have grown up realising I have become very withdrawn if other people do not pull me in to gain my attention nevertheless am a sort of an outgoing individual when I get to know other people. Africans come into the UK through immigration each year we should be trying to find lasting relationship within ourselves as we are allowed to dwell in the UK. East and South Africans from Negro decent have gone Salsa music so, I have to express our African culture and politics in the UK Salsa music is exotic. It's the music European dance to at home and abroad a friend of mine Mr. Harry Gordon Slade has a wide collection of Salsa Music he lives at Lewisham.

Salsa music is a general term referring to what is essentially Cuban popular <u>dance music</u> which was internationalized outside Cuba. The term 'Salsa' was initially recorded, promoted and marketed in <u>New York City</u> during the 1970s. The various musical genres comprising salsa include the Cuban <u>son montuno</u>, <u>guaracha</u>, <u>chachachá</u>, <u>mambo</u>, <u>bolero</u> and, to a lesser degree, non-Cuban genres such as the Puerto Rican <u>bomba</u> and <u>plena</u>, the Dominican <u>merengue</u>, and the Colombian <u>cumbia</u>. <u>Latin jazz</u>, which name was also developed in New York City, has had a significant influence on salsa arrangers, piano <u>guajeos</u>, and instrumental soloists. Salsa occasionally incorporates elements from North American <u>rock</u>, <u>R&B</u>, and <u>funk</u>. All of these non-Cuban elements are included into of the commercial term salsa, or Cuban son montuno template when performed within the context of salsa. For example, Mauleón's merengue chart includes clave, which is essential to Cuban popular music, but is not a component of the traditional Dominican rhythm. The first salsa bands were predominantly 'Nuyorican'(New Yorkers of Puerto Rican descent). The music eventually spread throughout the Western Hemisphere.Ultimately, salsa's popularity spread globally. Some of the founding salsa artists include Johnny Pacheco (the creator of the Fania All-Stars), Ray Barretto, Willie Colón, Larry Harlow, Roberto Roena, Bobby Valentín, and Eddie Palmieri

Calypso is a style of Afro-Caribbean music that originated in Trinidad and Tobago from African and European roots. The roots of the genre lay in the arrival of enslaved Africans, who, not being allowed to speak to each other, communicated through song. This forged a sense of community among the Africans, who saw their colonial master's change rapidly, bringing French, Spanish, and British music styles to the island of Trinidad. The French brought Carnival to Trinidad, and calypso competitions at Carnival grew in popularity, especially after the abolition of slavery in 1834. While most authorities stress the African roots of calypso, in his 1986 book, Calypso from France to Trinidad: 800 Years of History, that veteran calypsonian, The Roaring Lion (Rafael de Leon) asserted that calypso descends from the music of the medieval French troubadours.

The Itsekiri (also called the, Isekiri, Itsekri or Ishekiri or Itsekhiri) are an ethnic group of Nigeria's Niger Delta area, Delta State. The Itsekiri presently number between 600,000–800,000 people and live mainly in the Warri South, Warri North and Warri South West local government districts of Delta State on the Atlantic Coast of Nigeria. Significant communities of Itsekiris can be found in parts of Edo and Ondo states and in various other Nigerian cities including Lagos, Sapele, Benin City, Port Harcourt and Abuja. Many people of Itsekiri descent also reside in the United Kingdom, the USA and Canada. The Itsekiris traditionally refer to their land as the Kingdom of Warri or 'Iwerre' as its proper name – which is geographically contiguous to the area covered by the three Warri local government districts. The area is a key centre of Nigeria's crude oil and natural gas production and petroleum refining and the main town Warri (a multi-ethnic metropolis) forms the industrial and commercial nucleus of the Delta State region.

The Itsekiri monarch is known by the title 'Olu of Warri'. The Itsekiris speak a language very closely akin to Yoruba but which has also been significantly influenced by other languages particularly Portuguese, Edo (Benin), English. Although linguistically related to the Yoruba ethnic group, however, through centuries of intermingling modern day Itsekiris are of very mixed ethnic origins (primarily of Yoruba (Ijebu, Ilaje,Ondo and Owo), Edo, Urhobo, Ijo, Anglo-Scottish and Portuguese descent) and are today mainly Christian (Protestant and Roman Catholic) by religion. Thus having had 6 centuries of direct cultural exposure to Western Christianity and other African influences, contemporary Itsekiri language and culture has successfully evolved into a hybrid of the many cultures that have influenced its development. Similarly owing to the complex genetic mix of most Itsekiris over the centuries, many individuals self-identifying as Itsekiri would usually be a complex mix of any of the aforementioned ethnic and racial groups.

In the fifteenth century, the early Itsekiris (a Yoruba group) adopted a prince (Ginuwa) from the Kingdom of Benin as a monarch, and quickly coalesced into a kingdom under his rule. Traditionally fishermen and traders, the Itsekiri were among the first in the region to make contact with Portuguese traders. These interactions in the 16th Century led the Itsekiri to become primarily Roman Catholic. The Itsekiri monarchy has continued to the present day, with the coronation of Ogiame Atuwatse II in 1987. The Itsekiri's historical capital is Ode-Itsekiri, though the monarch maintains a palace in Warri town the largest city in the area and home to diverse other communities including the Urhobos, Yorubas, Isoko and many other Nigerian and expatriate groups working in the oil and gas industry.

The Itsekiri, though a minority group within Nigeria, are considered to be a highly educated and affluent ethnic group with a very high rate of literacy and a rich cultural heritage. The Itsekiris have one of the oldest histories of western education in West Africa, and are noted for producing one of its earliest university graduates – the Itsekiri king Olu Antonio Dom Domingo a 17th century graduate of Coimbra University in Portugal. Today, many Itsekiris can be found working in the professions particularly medicine, law and the academic professions and in business, trade and industry and were among the pioneers that led the development of the professions in Nigeria during the early-to-mid 20th century.

The Itsekiris traditionally lived in a society that was governed by a monarchy (the Olu) and council of chiefs who form the nobility or aristocracy. Itsekiri society itself was organised along the lines of an upper class made up of the royal family and the aristocracy – the 'Oloyes and Olareajas' these were mainly drawn from noble houses including the Royal Houses and the Houses of Olgbotsere (Prime Minister or king maker) and Iyatsere (defence minister). The middle class or Omajaja were free-born Itsekiris or burghers. As a result of the institution of slavery and the slave trade there was a third class 'Oton-Eru' or those descended from the slave class whose ancestors had come from elsewhere and settled in Itsekiriland as indentured or slave labourers. In modern day Itsekiri society the slave class no longer exists as all are considered free-born.

Traditionally, Itsekiri men wear a long sleeved shirt called a Kemeje, tie a George wrapper around their waist and wear a cap with a feather stuck to it. The women wear a blouse and also tie a George wrapper around their waist. They wear colourful head gears known as Nes (scarf) or coral beads. Itsekiris are also famed for their traditional fishing skills, melodious songs, gracefully fluid traditional dances and colourful masquerades and boat regattas.

Before the introduction of Christianity in the 16th Century, like many other African groups, the Itsekiris largely followed a traditional form of religion known as Ebura-tsitse (based on ancestral worship) which has become embedded in modern day traditional Itsekiri culture. Once the dominant form of western Christianity in Itsekiriland for centuries, only a minority of Itsekiris are Roman Catholics today whilst the majorities are Protestants notably Baptist and Anglican.

Whilst genetically, the Itsekiris are a complex mixture of the many different ethnicities and races that have settled in their area, however, the Itsekiri language is very closely related to the south-eastern and Ilaje Yoruba dialects and to the Igala. It has also been influenced significantly by the Bini, Portuguese and English languages due to centuries of interaction with people from those nations. However, it remains a key branch of the Yoruboid family of languages even retaining archaic or lost elements of the proto Yoruba language due to its relative isolation in the Niger-Delta where it developed away from the main cluster of Yoruba language dialects. Unlike nearly all key Nigerian Languages, the Itsekiri language does not have dialects and is uniformly spoken with little or no variance in pronunciation apart from the use of 'ch' for the regular 'ts' (sh) in the pronunciation of some individual Itsekiris, e.g. Chekiri instead of the standard Shekiri but these are individual pronunciation traits rather than dialectal differences. This may be a relic of past dialectal differences. The English language continues to exert a strong influence on the Itsekiri language both in influencing its development and in its widespread usage as a first language amongst the younger generation. Modern standard Yoruba (the variety spoken in Lagos) also appears to be influencing the Itsekiri language partly due to the similarity between both languages and the ease of absorbing colloquial Yoruba terms by the large Itsekiri population living in Western Nigerian cities. Itsekiri is now taught in local schools up to university degree level in Nigeria.

There are a number of semi-autonomous Itsekiri communities such as Ugborodo whose history predates the 15th century establishment of the Warri Kingdom. The Ugborodo community claims direct descent from the Ijebu a major Yoruba sub-ethnic group.

Is witchcraft real? Like in the movies the craft can they really happen? And if they can are they all that bad, like against Gods will? And if you practice it, can you, like change things about yourself or other people. We have had such a hard time how did we get by I have you and you have me witchcraft have existed with us since time began lots of what we watch on TV are revealing itself as witchcraft that took place and over the years still arrays itself in our livelihood we all spend life time looking for that special meaning. We do not see much of magician acts on our televisions these days rather it's more based on revealing secrets of magic. Why and how do you relate jujus to voodoo are there any way of implying magic is involved if so, what would be its repercussions? I enjoy watching Western Cowboy DVDs what I do most is pay attention to the stories, characters and watch the horses carefully to understand its history more in-depth, how it relates to lives to the 21st centuries history never dies it continues from generation to generation regardless if we change this, is why it is always good to change for the better.

How can real magic be about meditation? When you meditate you go into a trance, this is the same type of trance you subconsciously go into when you sleep at night so that you can access your own energy for the purpose of resting it against magic or spells. The right side of the brain is the 'Occult' side of the brain, when a trance is accessed our brainwaves slowdown so we can focus more and we allow ourselves to access the right side of our brain. The more the right side of the brain is used the stronger it becomes, like lifting weights that are medications....if you go into a trance for the first time don't expect to be able to lift your neighbor's car or it would be attributed to emotional psychosis. While emotional feeling for love is now attributed to emotional psychosis a man would do anything for a woman give her money buy her cloths give her is love, heart and time to keep her happy and satisfied at the end of the day I wonder why she should treat him so bad. This calls for emotional state of mind leading to mind and body problem and a man can do juju, voodoo, witchcraft and talisman to obtain rich, love and success vice versa a woman could do the same thing.

When one is advanced in power of meditation and understands and has a good feel for energy of outliving mental illness, then that's when the fun begins and at this time do not fornicate with anything unnatural not even smoking, taking drugs buying things, you do not necessary need in real aspects it could be witchcraft being imposed on you or your being derailed from your true self or meditation. In time it could outlive you of your mind and sanity. Such as change your hair color, use too much cosmetics juju, witchcraft and voodoo and the use of talisman is more on empowering once self we are living in time of what men of power wants, in a time when everyone wants power at every social level poor or rich. You are not diagnosed with mental illness the thoughts comes to you all of a sudden or because someone asked you the other day 'are you all right', three days later you met with the same person who, told you, you are looking good the next thing you look at yourself in the mirror you suddenly have this strange feeling that changing your hair color would be the best thing ever. This are times to control our emotional self because with simple words this days, gestures like parties, receiving gifts you can be bewitched. Is witchcraft real this would depend on who you are to believe it exists or that you can be part of it or that you could have the power of witchcraft, juju or voodoo.

Cares are now applying they also can hear voices after long times of doubts within cares and patients, The voice could sometimes make one feel bad or cry out loud within once self how now that they accept we hear these voices what if I say, I hear voices of creature and feeling all creature in my neighborhood are very clever and civilized in their own way and want to form attachment with me another doubts sets in within a care and patient.

I hear voices of almost all my family, I have come to realize those whose voices am about to hear I had not been hearing before I start hearing their voice as I hear voices of my other relatives at first I experience flashes images of them they are trying to apply something in my life such as reason for having said or done something in the past or present. It come with my own feeling and what relationship we have had as relatives that apply if they are good or bad voices some level are paranoiac or paranormal because of past experience but in time I could resolute with the voices or hallucinate to either accept or reject it. Why, or how do such forces, feeling comes to me? . I come from a very ritualistic background if the voices, hallucination, and past memories where right love is a memory. Whether or not I believe it's all out of juju or witchcraft which has gone into the wrong hands from my experience, if I succumb to feeling the voices or hallucination are right, if I am happy with hearing their voices and hallucinating about them and whatever feeling it involves, if ever there love there was if ever a dream was lost and the feeling is right it was theirs and mine. And what if it's not a happy one, it leaves scares. Infarct if my own voice goes out to some of my relatives as well about the things I do or my true feeling either positive or negative, what could sip out of me that could make them hear my voice or know about what am going through? What do I call it while I do not drink or smoke out of implying am enjoying life in the UK there are English and African foods at my disposal I cannot cook or eat well at times what could it relate to my upbringing. Living in the UK and in relation to my illness, I cannot eat out. It has come to a level of not eating with the rest of my families at their homes or at parties.

I do not know if astronomers observe this recently that the stars at night seems to be lifting themselves higher some of them seem to be pulling itself further up the skies while I feel am being lifted up with the stars.

Why are music full of cries music is a good thing it's an emotional up-liftment for me it makes me recuperate from my illness, my disturbed emotion, uncertainty if I have done anything wrong in life I would not have such feelings about music.

What types of witches are out there? Many kinds belonging to many different ethnic groups, believing many different things and conceptions having many different intentions both good and bad I know my psychiatrist would admit this to paranoia as a result of my illness witchcraft inter relates itself in science and medicine if witches can be all over the world they can be found in any organization. infarct this is where you find most witches, juju and voodoo in their administration because they want to understand or believe if juju, witchcraft, voodoo and the use of talisman are real but in closed doors. Food is being declared in airports very soon across European nations why should my father, have come to my private lodging a one bedroom council flat in his traditional regalia when it's not for an occasion I have neighbors with different opinions when it comes to race relation while concord airplanes flying high in sky was about to be grounded.

Schizophrenia is a challenging disorder that makes it difficult to distinguish between what is real and unreal, think clearly, manage emotions, relate to others, and function normally is this really true? But that doesn't mean there isn't hope. Schizophrenia can be successfully managed. The first step is to identify the signs and symptoms. The second step is to seek help without delay and the third is to stick with the treatment. With the right treatment and support, a person with schizophrenia can lead a happy, fulfilling life we are told. Are witchcraft, juju, voodoo, magic, and possession in exorcism anything like what the movies projects? Except you have had an experience, have been used in its practice or you have knowledge of such issues it can even through birth be born in any human.

In our past most witches, and juju can make anything happen to others or for themselves at this age its implementation is likely creating mind and body problem even with technology this can occur for some people. It shuns into the human brain, mind and soul. You can feel it and know it is being inflicted on you.

Witchcraft has been practiced all over the World, in one form or another, for thousands of years, but is witchcraft real? Deciding if something is real or not requires evidence and facts, but as Witchcraft can only be explain through perceptions it's something one can feel, such as holding a stone and feeling it is possessed is not what everyone can understand because not everybody feels the same way but the spirit or individual of the possession can feel it and they would not let other people know so, how do one explain it when some people could not relate it to mental illness, it could also be argued that belief itself is enough to make it real. I will outline the more common points of view and present some facts if it exist in my family but would my family members or those involve come out openly to say what I implied are true witchcraft, juju and voodoo are an ongoing thing till this day they exist, within our family, homes, work and social life while but not all of them are bad.

People talk about magic spells and where you can buy them from. There are a wide variety of spells we would love to be able to cast ourselves, from making someone love us to making obscene amounts of money, and anything in between but not when you are down with an illness you feel it has something to do with it.

Traditional Witchcraft reveres Nature and I shall use that as its core belief to uncover some history. Archaeologists' have discovered many paintings in ancient caves which clearly depict early man worshiping nature, more specifically the Sun, Moon or Earth. Some of their paintings date back centuries ago, I believe in reincarnation some of their relics from Africa into the 21st century have drifted through reincarnation into the UK, France and Germany in particular working for the NHS, social security, law and they are only concern in paper work, medication and social care and it's a sure way of welding their authority within their ethnic groups. Does this mean that our ancestors were practicing witches? To us possibly, but to our ancestors they were merely following their own way of life and quite probably had no actual term for it. Caribbean's Jamaican have interpreted juju as Voodoo and phased it in to Europe where they do not believe in such things. If only they can come out openly to say how it involves their lives. Philosophically it could be why they allow such fantasy with all their scientific wisdom I guess; they have always wanted to fraternize juju from the onset.

If we understand sin, hat, lasciviousness, lies, greed, jealousy etc or you understand its prose and cones we would accept that juju, witchcraft, voodoo and the use of talismans exist and would be with us all our existence and it comprise all the seven deadly sins no matter what it yields for our earthly gain. The effects are drastic one of it is mental illness, emotional problems and headache because the cup in which it is placed is now full to the brim infarct it is likely it is overflowing. Since God no longer delight in sacrifice since then humans then tend to serve nature in the things they do, the way they live their lives or create in many ways it has been programmed by God then we would realise what it means having a pure and contrite heart meaning of sacrifice is an act of slaughtering an animal or person or surrendering a possession as an offering to a deity.

Jumping forwards in time to the Roman period there is plenty of evidence that a large part of northern Europe worshiped nature. The followers of this time were Pagans, as were the early Romans, and they followed a whole host of differing practices. This is one thing that sets paganism and Witchcraft apart from most other religious belief systems. Even if two adjacent villages or clans worshiped the same thing that did not mean that their practices were the same, or even close, but there would be some fundamental common ground.

The middle Ages are where the term Witchcraft became much more widely used and known. Naturally the practitioners of Witchcraft were not the ones that decided to draw so much attention to themselves as they were more than happy to carry on using their various arts out of the main public eye. The average healer would have quite happily remained anonymous and continued to practice herbalist to help his or her village. Sadly outside forces would forever change the practice of Witchcraft. Comprehensive course on Traditional Witchcraft in the British Isles, including a chapter on the various festivals and practices associated with it, as well as the concepts and beliefs of Traditional Witchcraft and much more are always in discussion in various universities. The Catholic Church had grown into the major faith of the time and a variety of Popes had begun to target heresy from as early as the 12th century. The Inquisition was the primary way to dispense the will of the Catholic Church and it was initially not barbaric. By the time Pope John XXII formalized the persecution of witches in 1320 things were beginning to change. Witches became routinely burnt at the stake with a minimum of proof but this practice altered towards hanging after a few years. Estimates of the death toll range from 40,000 to 100,000 with 12,000 executions confirmed from witch trials in Europe alone. Needless to say the majority of people killed were not witches. Witchcraft by necessity became an underground practice during these years and would remain so for centuries. In the late 1940's to early 1950's a new and more modern variation of Witchcraft came into force. This combined many aspects of pagan Witchcraft cultism that came before it and was a more open form of practice. Wicca was popularized by Gerald Gardner in 1954 in the British Isles.

Naturally Witches believe in Witchcraft and always have which makes them a little biased, but there are plenty of other people that believe it to be real. The Catholic Church clearly is a believer or it would not have persecuted Witches during the Middle Ages as heretics. Judaism and Muslim faiths also believe in Witchcraft as there are several passages in their scriptures that prohibit its practices. The majority of more modern religions have at one time or another targeted heresy or unbelievers and chose Sorcery as one part of their displeasure. Sorcery and Spirit worship are often linked to Witchcraft as are satanic practices. This has led to Witchcraft receiving a very bad press at various times during its evolution. Witches say that Satan does not exist to them which would rule out Satanism if that is true. Spirits do play a part in some forms of Witchcraft which some would say is evidence enough of bad practices but Witches would contend otherwise. Ever been to a séance? Spirits are summoned during these rituals but these are accepted practices. Other religions are the main believers in Witchcraft, outside of Witches themselves, and these religions have many tens of millions of followers. They believe Witchcraft is real, therefore it must be! Then again do we really want to believe another faith based belief system when it comes to what is real or not? Who is to say that their own religion is actually real, but if we are to believe in one then we must, by default, believe in them all.

Magic is the common term used for the casting of spells. Magic is drawn from nature which is all around us. Practitioners of magic know that we all have some form of magic power and with practice it can flourish and grow.

Most Witches will say that spells are not to be used to harm another person's physical or psychological state, know your own state. Witchcraft is, therefore, not used to harm others as is a common misconception in many parts of the world. You could argue that just because a Witch says that they don't use spells to harm others does not make it true they do. There is a spell for just about anything you could imagine and if you believe in magic and spells, a fundamental cornerstone of Witchcraft, then they will work. Not all witches practice magic and spells but all Traditional witches do. More modern varieties of Witchcraft may or may not be practitioners of the magic arts. Some of the newer religious forms of Witchcraft make their spell books available but you will be very hard pressed to find anything written by a Traditional witch.

There are a few reasons why you will not find books of spells, known as Grimoires, on Traditional Witchcraft. The first is the fact that it is an old type of practice and until fairly recently in its history very few people could actually read or write. The practice of Witchcraft was forced underground during the middle ages which meant that most people who practiced Witchcraft did not write anything down as it could be used as evidence against them. Finally it is by nature a secretive order unlike the more modern Neopagan religion based practices. Traditional Witchcraft is taught more by word and action although some witches will write things down to aid in their own practice.

The book continues...
TITLED PARADIGM OF MY SCHIZOPHRENIA

www.ingramcontent.com/pod-product-compliance
Lightning Source LLC
Chambersburg PA
CBHW020653270326
41928CB00005B/102